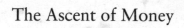

The Ascent of Money

NIALL FERGUSON

The Ascent of Money

A Financial History of the World

ALLEN LANE
an imprint of
PENGUIN BOOKS

In Memoriam
Gerald D. Feldman
(1937–2007)

ALLEN LANE

Published by the Penguin Group
Penguin Books Ltd, 80 Strand, London WC2R ORL, England
Penguin Group (USA) Inc., 375 Hudson Street, New York, New York 10014, USA
Penguin Group (Canada), 90 Eglinton Avenue East, Suite 700, Toronto, Ontario, Canada M4P 2Y3
(a division of Pearson Penguin Canada Inc.)
Penguin Ireland, 25 St Stephen's Green, Dublin 2, Ireland
(a division of Penguin Books Ltd)
Penguin Group (Australia), 250 Camberwell Road, Camberwell, Victoria 3124, Australia
(a division of Pearson Australia Group Pty Ltd)
Penguin Books India Pvt Ltd, 11 Community Centre, Panchsheel Park, New Delhi – 110 017, India
Penguin Group (NZ), 67 Apollo Drive, Rosedale, North Shore 0632, New Zealand
(a division of Pearson New Zealand Ltd)
Penguin Books (South Africa) (Pty) Ltd, 24 Sturdee Avenue, Rosebank, Johannesburg 2196, South Africa

Penguin Books Ltd, Registered Offices: 80 Strand, London WC2R ORL, England

www.penguin.com

First published 2008
4

Copyright © Niall Ferguson, 2008

The moral right of the author has been asserted

Set in 11.25/16 pt PostScript Linotype Sabon
Typeset by Rowland Phototypesetting Ltd, Bury St Edmunds, Suffolk
Printed in England by Clays Ltd, St Ives plc

A CIP catalogue record for this book is available from the British Library

HARDBACK ISBN: 978-1-846-14106-5
PAPERBACK ISBN: 978-1-846-14192-8

www.greenpenguin.co.uk

Penguin Books is committed to a sustainable future
for our business, our readers and our planet.
The book in your hands is made from paper
certified by the Forest Stewardship Council.

Contents

Introduction

Bread, cash, dosh, dough, loot, lucre, moolah, readies, the where-withal: call it what you like, money matters. To Christians, the love of it is the root of all evil. To generals, it is the sinews of war; to revolutionaries, the shackles of labour. But what exactly is money? Is it a mountain of silver, as the Spanish conquistadors thought? Or will mere clay tablets and printed paper suffice? How did we come to live in a world where most money is invisible, little more than numbers on a computer screen? Where did money come from? And where did it all go?

Last year (2007) the income of the average American (just under $34,000) went up by at most 5 per cent.[1] But the cost of living rose by 4.1 per cent. So in real terms Mr Average actually became just 0.9 per cent better off. Allowing for inflation, the income of the median household in the United States has in fact scarcely changed since 1990, increasing by just 7 per cent in eighteen years.[2] Now compare Mr Average's situation with that of Lloyd Blankfein, chief executive officer at Goldman Sachs, the investment bank. In 2007 he received $68.5 million in salary, bonus and stock awards, an increase of 25 per cent on the previous year, and roughly two thousand times more than Joe Public earned. That same year, Goldman Sachs's net revenues of $46 billion exceeded the entire gross domestic product (GDP) of more than a hundred countries, including Croatia, Serbia and Slovenia; Bolivia, Ecuador and Guatemala; Angola, Syria and Tunisia. The bank's total assets for the first time passed the $1 trillion mark.[3] Yet Lloyd Blankfein is far from being the financial world's highest earner. The veteran hedge fund manager George Soros made $2.9 billion. Ken Griffin of Citadel, like the founders of two other leading hedge funds, took home more than $2 billion. Meanwhile nearly a billion people around the world struggle to get by on just $1 a day.[4]

Angry that the world is so unfair? Infuriated by fat-cat capitalists and billion-bonus bankers? Baffled by the yawning chasm between the Haves, the Have-nots – and the Have-yachts? You are not alone. Throughout the history of Western civilization, there has been a recurrent hostility to finance and financiers, rooted in the idea that those who make their living from lending money are somehow parasitical on the 'real' economic activities of agriculture and manufacturing. This hostility has three causes. It is partly because debtors have tended to outnumber creditors and the former have seldom felt very well disposed towards the latter. It is partly because financial crises and scandals occur frequently enough to make finance appear to be a cause of poverty rather than prosperity, volatility rather than stability. And it is partly because, for centuries, financial services in countries all over the world were disproportionately provided by members of ethnic or religious minorities, who had been excluded from land ownership or public office but enjoyed success in finance because of their own tight-knit networks of kinship and trust.

Despite our deeply rooted prejudices against 'filthy lucre', however, money is the root of most progress. To adapt a phrase from Jacob Bronowski (whose marvellous television history of scientific progress I watched avidly as a schoolboy), the ascent of money has been essential to the ascent of man. Far from being the work of mere leeches intent on sucking the life's blood out of indebted families or gambling with the savings of widows and orphans, financial innovation has been an indispensable factor in man's advance from wretched subsistence to the giddy heights of material prosperity that so many people know today. The evolution of credit and debt was as important as any technological innovation in the rise of civilization, from ancient Babylon to present-day Hong Kong. Banks and the bond market provided the material basis for the splendours of the Italian Renaissance. Corporate finance was the indispensable foundation of both the Dutch and British empires, just as the triumph of the United States in the twentieth century was inseparable from advances in insurance, mortgage finance and consumer credit. Perhaps, too, it will be a financial crisis that signals the twilight of American global primacy.

Behind each great historical phenomenon there lies a financial secret, and this book sets out to illuminate the most important of these. For example, the Renaissance created such a boom in the market for art and architecture because Italian bankers like the Medici made fortunes by applying Oriental mathematics to money. The Dutch Republic prevailed over the Habsburg Empire because having the world's first modern stock market was financially preferable to having the world's biggest silver mine. The problems of the French monarchy could not be resolved without a revolution because a convicted Scots murderer had wrecked the French financial system by unleashing the first stock market bubble and bust. It was Nathan Rothschild as much as the Duke of Wellington who defeated Napoleon at Waterloo. It was financial folly, a self-destructive cycle of defaults and devaluations, that turned Argentina from the world's sixth-richest country in the 1880s into the inflation-ridden basket case of the 1980s.

Read this book and you will understand why, paradoxically,

the people who live in the world's safest country are also the world's most insured. You will discover when and why the English-speaking peoples developed their peculiar obsession with buying and selling houses. Perhaps most importantly, you will see how the globalization of finance has, among many other things, blurred the old distinction between developed and emerging markets, turning China into America's banker – the Communist creditor to the capitalist debtor, a change of epochal significance.

At times, the ascent of money has seemed inexorable. In 2006 the measured economic output of the entire world was around $47 trillion. The total market capitalization of the world's stock markets was $51 trillion, 10 per cent larger. The total value of domestic and international bonds was $68 trillion, 50 per cent larger. The amount of derivatives outstanding was $473 trillion, more than ten times larger. Planet Finance is beginning to dwarf Planet Earth. And Planet Finance seems to spin faster too. Every day two trillion dollars change hands on foreign exchange markets. Every month seven trillion dollars change hands on global stock markets. Every minute of every hour of every day of every week, someone, somewhere, is trading. And all the time new financial life forms are evolving. In 2006, for example, the volume of leveraged buyouts (takeovers of firms financed by borrowing) surged to $753 billion. An explosion of 'securitization', whereby individual debts like mortgages are 'tranched' then bundled together and repackaged for sale, pushed the total annual issuance of mortgage backed securities, asset-backed securities and collateralized debt obligations above $3 trillion. The volume of derivatives – contracts derived from securities, such as interest rate swaps or credit default swaps (CDS) – has grown even faster, so that by the end of 2007 the notional value of all 'over-the-counter' derivatives (excluding those traded on public exchanges) was just under $600 trillion. Before the 1980s, such things were virtually unknown. New institutions, too, have proliferated. The first hedge fund was set up in the 1940s and, as recently as 1990, there were just 610 of them, with $38 billion under management. There are now over seven thousand, with $1.9 trillion under management. Private equity partnerships have also multiplied, as well as a veritable shadow banking system of 'conduits' and 'structured investment vehicles' (SIVs), designed to keep risky assets off bank balance sheets. If the last four millennia witnessed the ascent of man the thinker, we now seem to be living through the ascent of man the banker.

In 1947 the total value added by the financial sector to US gross domestic product was 2.3 per cent; by 2005 its contribution had risen to 7.7 per cent of GDP. In other words, approximately $1 of every $13 paid to employees in the United States now goes to people working in finance.[5] Finance is even more important in Britain, where it accounted for 9.4 per cent of GDP in 2006. The financial sector has also become the most powerful magnet in the world for academic talent. Back in 1970 only around 5 per cent of the men graduating from Harvard, where I teach, went into finance. By 1990 that figure had risen to 15 per cent.* Last year the proportion was even higher. According to the *Harvard Crimson*, more than 20 per cent of the men in the Class of 2007, and 10 per cent of the women, expected their first jobs to be at banks. And who could blame them? In recent years, the pay packages in finance have been nearly three times the salaries earned by Ivy League graduates in other sectors of the economy.

At the time the Class of 2007 graduated, it certainly seemed as if nothing could halt the rise and rise of global finance. Not

---

* Revealingly, the increase for female graduates was from 2.3 to 3.4 per cent. The masters of the universe still outnumber the mistresses.

terrorist attacks on New York and London. Not raging war in the Middle East. Certainly not global climate change. Despite the destruction of the World Trade Center, the invasions of Afghanistan and Iraq, and a spike in extreme meteorological events, the period from late 2001 until mid 2007 was characterized by sustained financial expansion. True, in the immediate aftermath of 9/11, the Dow Jones Industrial Average declined by as much as 14 per cent. Within just over two months, however, it had regained its pre-9/11 level. Moreover, although 2002 was a disappointing year for US equity investors, the market surged ahead thereafter, exceeding its previous peak (at the height of the 'dot com' mania) in the autumn of 2006. By early October 2007 the Dow stood at nearly double the level it had reached in the trough of five years before. Nor was the US stock market's performance exceptional. In the five years to 31 July 2007, all but two of the world's equity markets delivered double-digit returns on an annualized basis. Emerging market bonds also rose strongly and real estate markets, especially in the English-speaking world, saw remarkable capital appreciation. Whether they put their money into commodities, works of art, vintage wine or exotic asset-backed securities, investors made money.

How were these wonders to be explained? According to one school of thought, the latest financial innovations had brought about a fundamental improvement in the efficiency of the global capital market, allowing risk to be allocated to those best able to bear it. Enthusiasts spoke of the death of volatility. Self-satisfied bankers held conferences with titles like 'The Evolution of Excellence'. In November 2006 I found myself at one such conference in the characteristically luxurious venue of Lyford Cay in the Bahamas. The theme of my speech was that it would not take much to cause a drastic decline in the liquidity that was then cascading through the global financial system and that we should be cautious about expecting the good times to last indefinitely. My audience was distinctly unimpressed. I was dismissed as an alarmist. One of the most experienced investors there went so far as to suggest to the organizers that they 'dispense altogether with an outside speaker next year, and instead offer a screening of Mary Poppins'.[6] Yet the mention of Mary Poppins stirred a childhood memory in me. Julie Andrews fans may recall that the plot of the evergreen musical revolves around a financial event which, when the film was made in the 1960s, already seemed quaint: a bank run – that is, a rush by depositors to withdraw their money – something not seen in London since 1866.

The family that employs Mary Poppins is, not accidentally, named Banks. Mr Banks is indeed a banker, a senior employee of the Dawes, Tomes Mousley, Grubbs, Fidelity Fiduciary Bank. At his insistence, the Banks children are one day taken by their new nanny to visit his bank, where Mr Dawes Sr. recommends that Mr Banks's son Michael deposit his pocket-money (tuppence). Unfortunately, young Michael prefers to spend the money on feeding the pigeons outside the bank, and demands that Mr Dawes 'Give it back! Gimme back my money!' Even more unfortunately, some of the bank's other clients overhear Michael's request. The result is that they begin to withdraw their money. Soon a horde of account holders are doing the same, forcing the bank to suspend payments. Mr Banks is duly sacked, prompting the tragic lament that he has been 'brought to wrack and ruin in his prime'. These words might legitimately have been echoed by Adam Applegarth, the former chief executive of the English bank Northern Rock, who suffered a similar fate in September 2007 as customers queued outside his bank's branches to withdraw their cash. This followed the announcement that Northern Rock had requested a 'liquidity support facility' from the Bank of England.

The financial crisis that struck the Western world in the summer of 2007 provided a timely reminder of one of the perennial truths of financial history. Sooner or later every bubble bursts. Sooner or later the bearish sellers outnumber the bullish buyers. Sooner or later greed turns to fear. As I completed my research for this book in the early months of 2008, it was already a distinct possibility that the US economy might suffer a recession. Was this because American companies had got worse at designing new products? Had the pace of technological innovation suddenly slackened? No. The proximate cause of the economic uncertainty of 2008 was financial: to be precise, a spasm in the credit markets caused by mounting defaults on a species of debt known euphemistically as subprime mortgages. So intricate has our global financial system become, that relatively poor families in states from Alabama to Wisconsin had been able to buy or remortgage their homes with often complex loans that (unbeknown to them) were then bundled together with other, similar loans, repackaged as collateralized debt obligations (CDOs) and sold by banks in New York and London to (among others) German regional banks and Norwegian municipal authorities, who thereby became the effective mortgage lenders. These CDOs had been so sliced and diced that it was possible to claim that a tier of the interest payments from the original borrowers was as dependable a stream of income as the interest on a ten-year US Treasury bond, and therefore worthy of a coveted triple-A rating. This took financial alchemy to a new level of sophistication, apparently turning lead into gold.

However, when the original mortgages reset at higher interest rates after their one- or two-year 'teaser' periods expired, the borrowers began to default on their payments. This in turn signalled that the bubble in US real estate was bursting, triggering the sharpest fall in house prices since the 1930s. What followed resembled a slow but ultimately devastating chain reaction. All kinds of asset-backed securities, including many instruments not in fact backed with subprime mortgages, slumped in value. Institutions like conduits and structured investment vehicles, which had been set up by banks to hold these securities off the banks' balance sheets, found themselves in severe difficulties. As the banks took over the securities, the ratios between their capital and their assets lurched down towards their regulatory minima. Central banks in the United States and Europe sought to alleviate the pressure on the banks with interest rate cuts and offers of funds through special 'term auction facilities'. Yet, at the time of writing (May 2008), the rates at which banks could borrow money, whether by issuing commercial paper, selling bonds or borrowing from each other, remained substantially above the official Federal funds target rate, the minimum lending rate in the US economy. Loans that were originally intended to finance purchases of corporations by private equity partnerships were also only saleable at significant discounts. Having suffered enormous losses, many of the best-known American and European banks had to turn not only to Western central banks for short-term assistance to rebuild their reserves but also to Asian and Middle Eastern sovereign wealth funds for equity injections in order to rebuild their capital bases.

All of this may seem arcane to some readers. Yet the ratio of a bank's capital to its assets, technical though it may sound, is of more than merely academic interest. After all, a 'great contraction' in the US banking system has convincingly been blamed for the outbreak and course of the Great Depression between 1929 and 1933, the worst economic disaster of modern history.[7] If US banks have lost significantly more than the $255 billion to which they have so far admitted as a result of the subprime mortgage crisis and credit crunch, there is a real danger that a much larger

– perhaps tenfold larger – contraction in credit may be necessary to shrink the banks' balance sheets in proportion to the decline in their capital. If the shadow banking system of securitized debt and off-balance-sheet institutions is to be swept away completely by this crisis, the contraction could be still more severe.

This has implications not just for the United States but for the world as a whole, since American output presently accounts for more than a quarter of total world production, while many European and Asian economies in particular are still heavily reliant on the United States as a market for their exports. Europe already seems destined to experience a slowdown comparable with that of the United States, particularly in those countries (such as Britain and Spain) that have gone through similar housing bubbles. The extent to which Asia can ride out an American recession, in the way that America rode out the Asian crisis of 1997–8, remains uncertain. What is certain is that the efforts of the Federal Reserve to mitigate the credit crunch by cutting interest rates and targeting liquidity at the US banking system have put severe downward pressure on the external value of the dollar. The coincidence of a dollar slide and continuing Asian industrial growth has caused a spike in commodity prices comparable not merely with the 1970s but with the 1940s. It is not too much to say that in mid-2008 we witnessed the inflationary symptoms of a world war without the war itself.

Anyone who can read a paragraph like the preceding one without feeling anxious does not know enough financial history. One purpose of this book, then, is to educate. It is a well-established fact, after all, that a substantial proportion of the general public in the English-speaking world is ignorant of finance. According to one 2007 survey, four in ten American credit card holders do not pay the full amount due every month on the card they use most often, despite the punitively high interest rates charged by credit card companies. Nearly a third (29 per cent) said they had no idea what the interest rate on their card was. Another 30 per cent claimed that it was below 10 per cent, when in reality the overwhelming majority of card companies charge substantially in excess of 10 per cent. More than half of the respondents said they had learned 'not too much' or 'nothing at all' about financial issues at school.[8] A 2008 survey revealed that two thirds of Americans did not understand how compound interest worked.[9] In one survey conducted by researchers at the University of Buffalo's School of Management, a typical group of high school seniors scored just 52 per cent in response to a set of questions about personal finance and economics.[10] Only 14 per cent understood that stocks would tend to generate a higher return over eighteen years than a US government bond. Less than 23 per cent knew that income tax is charged on the interest earned from a savings account if the account holder's income is high enough. Fully 59 per cent did not know the difference between a company pension, Social Security and a 401(k) plan.* Nor is this a uniquely American phenomenon. In 2006, the British Financial Services Authority carried out a survey of public financial literacy which revealed that one person in five had no idea what the effect would be on the purchasing power of their savings of an inflation rate of 5 per cent and an interest rate of 3 per cent. One in ten did not know which was the better discount for a television originally priced at £250: £30 or 10 per cent. As that example makes clear, the questions posed in these surveys were of the most basic nature.

---

* 401(k) plans were introduced in 1980 as a form of defined contribution retirement plan. Employees can elect to have a portion of their wages or salaries paid or 'deferred' into a 401(k) account. They are then offered choices as to how the money should be invested. With a few exceptions, no tax is paid on the money until it is withdrawn.

It seems reasonable to assume that only a handful of those polled would have been able to explain the difference between a 'put' and a 'call' option, for example, much less the difference between a CDO and a CDS.

Politicians, central bankers and businessmen regularly lament the extent of public ignorance about money, and with good reason. A society that expects most individuals to take responsibility for the management of their own expenditure and income after tax, that expects most adults to own their own homes and that leaves it to the individual to determine how much to save for retirement and whether or not to take out health insurance, is surely storing up trouble for the future by leaving its citizens so ill-equipped to make wise financial decisions.

The first step towards understanding the complexities of modern financial institutions and terminology is to find out where they came from. Only understand the origins of an institution or instrument and you will find its present-day role much easier to grasp. Accordingly, the key components of the modern financial system are introduced sequentially. The first chapter of this book traces the rise of money and credit; the second the bond market; the third the stock market. Chapter 4 tells the story of insurance; Chapter 5 the real estate market; and Chapter 6 the rise, fall and rise of international finance. Each chapter addresses a key historical question. When did money stop being metal and mutate into paper, before vanishing altogether? Is it true that, by setting long-term interest rates, the bond market rules the world? What is the role played by central banks in stock market bubbles and busts? Why is insurance not necessarily the best way to protect yourself from risk? Do people exaggerate the benefits of investing in real estate? And is the economic inter-dependence of China and America the key to global financial stability, or a mere chimera?

In trying to cover the history of finance from ancient Mesopotamia to modern microfinance, I have set myself an impossible task, no doubt. Much must be omitted in the interests of brevity and simplicity. Yet the attempt seems worth making if it can bring the modern financial system into sharper focus in the mind's eye of the general reader.

I myself have learned a great deal in writing this book, but three insights in particular stand out. The first is that poverty is not the result of rapacious financiers exploiting the poor. It has much more to do with the *lack* of financial institutions, with the absence of banks, not their presence. Only when borrowers have access to efficient credit networks can they escape from the clutches of loan sharks, and only when savers can deposit their money in reliable banks can it be channelled from the idle rich to the industrious poor. This point applies not just to the poor countries of the world. It can also be said of the poorest neighbourhoods in supposedly developed countries – the 'Africas within' – like the housing estates of my birthplace, Glasgow, where some people are scraping by on just £6 a day, for everything from toothpaste to transport, but where the interest rates charged by local loan sharks can be over eleven million per cent a year.

My second great realization has to do with equality and its absence. If the financial system has a defect, it is that it reflects and magnifies what we human beings are like. As we are learning from a growing volume of research in the field of behavioural finance, money amplifies our tendency to overreact, to swing from exuberance when things are going well to deep depression when they go wrong. Booms and busts are products, at root, of our emotional volatility. But finance also exaggerates the differences between us, enriching the lucky and the smart, impoverishing the unlucky and not-so-smart. Financial globalization means that, after more than three hundred years of divergence,

THE ASCENT OF MONEY

the world can no longer be divided neatly into rich developed countries and poor less-developed countries. The more integrated the world's financial markets become, the greater the opportunities for financially knowledgeable people wherever they live – and the bigger the risk of downward mobility for the financially illiterate. It emphatically is not a flat world in terms of overall income distribution, simply because the returns on capital have soared relative to the returns on unskilled and semi-skilled labour. The rewards for 'getting it' have never been so immense. And the penalties for financial ignorance have never been so stiff.

Finally, I have come to understand that few things are harder to predict accurately than the timing and magnitude of financial crises, because the financial system is so genuinely complex and so many of the relationships within it are non-linear, even chaotic. The ascent of money has never been smooth, and each new challenge elicits a new response from the bankers and their ilk. Like an Andean horizon, the history of finance is not a smooth upward curve but a series of jagged and irregular peaks and valleys. Or, to vary the metaphor, financial history looks like a classic case of evolution in action, albeit in a much tighter time-frame than evolution in the natural world. 'Just as some species become extinct in nature,' remarked US Assistant Secretary of the Treasury Anthony W. Ryan before Congress in September 2007, 'some new financing techniques may prove to be less successful than others.' Such Darwinian language seems remarkably apposite as I write.

Are we on the brink of a 'great dying' in the financial world – one of those mass extinctions of species that have occurred periodically, like the end-Cambrian extinction that killed off 90 per cent of Earth's species, or the Cretaceous-Tertiary catastrophe that wiped out the dinosaurs? It is a scenario that many biologists have reason to fear, as man-made climate change wreaks havoc with natural habitats around the globe. But a great dying of financial institutions is also a scenario that we should worry about, as another man-made disaster works its way slowly and painfully through the global financial system.

For all these reasons, then – whether you are struggling to make ends meet or striving to be a master of the universe – it has never been more necessary to understand the ascent of money than it is today. If this book helps to break down that dangerous barrier which has arisen between financial knowledge and other kinds of knowledge, then I shall not have toiled in vain.

I

Dreams of Avarice

Imagine a world with no money. For over a hundred years, Communists and anarchists – not to mention some extreme reactionaries, religious fundamentalists and hippies – have dreamt of just that. According to Friedrich Engels and Karl Marx, money was merely an instrument of capitalist exploitation, replacing all human relationships, even those within the family, with the callous 'cash nexus'. As Marx later sought to demonstrate in *Capital*, money was commoditized labour, the surplus generated by honest toil, appropriated and then 'reified' in order to satisfy the capitalist class's insatiable lust for accumulation. Such notions die hard. As recently as the 1970s, some European Communists were still yearning for a moneyless world, as in this Utopian effusion from the *Socialist Standard*:

Money will disappear . . . Gold can be reserved in accordance with Lenin's wish, for the construction of public lavatories . . . In communist societies goods will be freely available and free of charge. The organisation of society to its very foundations will be without money . . . The frantic and neurotic desire to consume and hoard will disappear. It will be absurd to want to accumulate things: there will no longer be money to be pocketed nor wage-earners to be hired . . . The new people will resemble their hunting and gathering ancestors who trusted in a nature which supplied them freely and often abundantly with what they needed to live, and who had no worry for the morrow . . .[1]

Yet no Communist state – not even North Korea – has found it practical to dispense with money.[2] And even a passing acquaintance with real hunter-gatherer societies suggests there are considerable disadvantages to the cash-free life.

Five years ago, members of the Nukak-Makú unexpectedly wandered out of the Amazonian rainforest at San José del Guaviare in Colombia. The Nukak were a tribe that time forgot, cut off from the rest of humanity until this sudden emergence. Subsisting solely on the monkeys they could hunt and the fruit they could gather, they had no concept of money. Revealingly, they had no concept of the future either. These days they live in a clearing near the city, reliant for their subsistence on state handouts. Asked if they miss the jungle, they laugh. After lifetimes of trudging all day in search of food, they are amazed that perfect strangers now give them all they need and ask nothing from them in return.[3]

The life of a hunter-gatherer is indeed, as Thomas Hobbes said of the state of nature, 'solitary, poor, nasty, brutish, and short'. In some respects, to be sure, wandering through the jungle bagging monkeys may be preferable to the hard slog of subsistence agriculture. But anthropologists have shown that many of the hunter-gatherer tribes who survived into modern times were less placid than the Nukak. Among the Jivaro of Ecuador, for example, nearly 60 per cent of male deaths were due to violence. The figure for the Brazilian Yanomamo was nearly 40 per cent. When two groups of such primitive peoples chanced upon each other, it seems, they were more likely to fight over scarce resources (food and fertile women) than to engage in commercial exchange.

Hunter-gatherers do not trade. They raid. Nor do they save, consuming their food as and when they find it. They therefore have no need of money.

The Money Mountain

More sophisticated societies than the Nukak have functioned without money, it is true. Five hundred years ago, the most sophisticated society in South America, the Inca Empire, was also moneyless. The Incas appreciated the aesthetic qualities of rare metals. Gold was the 'sweat of the sun', silver the 'tears of the moon'. Labour was the unit of value in the Inca Empire, just as it was later supposed to be in a Communist society. And, as under Communism, the economy depended on often harsh central planning and forced labour. In 1532, however, the Inca Empire was brought low by a man who, like Christopher Columbus, had come to the New World expressly to search for and monetize precious metal.*

The illegitimate son of a Spanish colonel, Francisco Pizarro had crossed the Atlantic to seek his fortune in 1502.[4] One of the first Europeans to traverse the isthmus of Panama to the Pacific, he led the first of three expeditions into Peru in 1524. The terrain was harsh, food scarce and the first indigenous peoples they encountered hostile. However, the welcome their second expedition received in the Tumbes region, where the inhabitants hailed them as the 'children of the sun', convinced Pizarro and

---

* The conquistadors came looking for both gold and silver. Columbus's first settlement, La Isabela in Hispaniola (now the Dominican Republic), was established to exploit local deposits of gold. He also believed he had found silver, but the only traces have subsequently been shown to have been in the sample ores Columbus and his men had brought from Spain.

his confederates to persist. Having returned to Spain to obtain royal approval for his plan 'to extend the empire of Castile'* as 'Governor of Peru', Pizarro raised a force of three ships, twenty-seven horses and one hundred and eighty men, equipped with the latest European weaponry: guns and mechanical crossbows.[5] This third expedition set sail from Panama on 27 December 1530. It took the would-be conquerors just under two years to achieve their objective: a confrontation with Atahuallpa, one of the two feuding sons of the recently deceased Incan emperor Huayna Capac. Having declined Friar Vincente Valverd's proposal that he submit to Christian rule, contemptuously throwing his Bible to the ground, Atahuallpa could only watch as the Spaniards, relying mainly on the terror inspired by their horses (animals unknown to the Incas), annihilated his army. Given how out-numbered they were, it was a truly astonishing coup.[6] Atahuallpa soon came to understand what Pizarro was after, and sought to buy his freedom by offering to fill the room where he was being held with gold (once) and silver (twice). In all, in the subsequent months the Incas collected 13,420 pounds of 22 carat gold and 26,000 pounds of pure silver.[7] Pizarro nevertheless determined to execute his prisoner, who was publicly garrotted in August 1533.[8] With the fall of the city of Cuzco, the Inca Empire was torn apart in an orgy of Spanish plundering. Despite a revolt led by the supposedly puppet Inca Manco Capac in 1536, Spanish rule was unshakeably established and symbolized by the construction of a new capital, Lima. The Empire was formally dissolved in 1572.

Pizarro himself died as violently as he had lived, stabbed to death in Lima in 1541 after a quarrel with one of his fellow

---

* From the marriage of Ferdinand and Isabella in 1474 until the eighteenth century, the country we call Spain was technically the union of two kingdoms: Aragon and Castile.

conquistadors. But his legacy to the Spanish crown ultimately exceeded even his own dreams. The conquistadors had been inspired by the legend of El Dorado, an Indian king who was believed to cover his body with gold dust at festival times. In what Pizarro's men called Upper Peru, a stark land of mountains and mists where those unaccustomed to high altitudes have to fight for breath, they found something just as valuable. With a peak that towers 4,824 metres (15,827 feet) above sea level, the uncannily symmetrical Cerro Rico – literally the 'rich hill' – was the supreme embodiment of the most potent of all ideas about money: a mountain of solid silver ore. When an Indian named Diego Gualpa discovered its five great seams of silver in 1545, he changed the economic history of the world.[9]

The Incas could not understand the insatiable lust for gold and silver that seemed to grip Europeans. 'Even if all the snow in the Andes turned to gold, still they would not be satisfied,' complained Manco Capac.[10] The Incas could not appreciate that, for Pizarro and his men, silver was more than shiny, decorative metal. It could be made into money: a unit of account, a store of value – portable power.

To work the mines, the Spaniards at first relied on paying wages to the inhabitants of nearby villages. But conditions were so harsh that from the late sixteenth century a system of forced labour (la mita) had to be introduced, whereby men aged between 18 and 50 from the sixteen highland provinces were conscripted for seventeen weeks a year.[11] Mortality among the miners was horrendous, not least because of constant exposure to the mercury fumes generated by the patio process of refinement, whereby ground-up silver ore was trampled into an amalgam with mercury, washed and then heated to burn off the mercury.[12] The air down the mineshafts was (and remains) noxious and miners had to descend seven-hundred-foot shafts on the most primitive of

The Cerro Rico at Potosí: the Spanish Empire's mountain of money

steps, clambering back up after long hours of digging with sacks of ore tied to their backs. Rock falls killed and maimed hundreds. The new silver-rush city of Potosí was, declared Domingo de Santo Tomás, 'a mouth of hell, into which a great mass of people enter every year and are sacrificed by the greed of the Spaniards to their "god".' Rodrigo de Loaisa called the mines 'infernal pits', noting that 'if twenty healthy Indians enter on Monday, half may emerge crippled on Saturday'.[13] In the words of the Augustinian monk Fray Antonio de la Calancha, writing in 1638: 'Every peso coin minted in Potosí has cost the life of ten Indians who have died in the depths of the mines.' As the indigenous workforce was depleted, thousands of African slaves were imported to take their places as 'human mules'. Even today there is still something hellish about the stifling shafts and tunnels of the Cerro Rico.

A place of death for those compelled to work there, Potosí was where Spain struck it rich. Between 1556 and 1783, the 'rich hill' yielded 45,000 tons of pure silver to be transformed into bars and coins in the Casa de Moneda (mint), and shipped to Seville. Despite its thin air and harsh climate, Potosí rapidly became one of the principal cities of the Spanish Empire, with a population at its zenith of between 160,000 and 200,000 people, larger than most European cities at that time. *Valer un potosí*, 'to be worth a potosí', is still a Spanish expression meaning to be worth a fortune. Pizarro's conquest, it seemed, had made the Spanish crown rich beyond the dreams of avarice.

Money, it is conventional to argue, is a medium of exchange, which has the advantage of eliminating inefficiencies of barter; a unit of account, which facilitates valuation and calculation; and a store of value, which allows economic transactions to be conducted over long periods as well as geographical distances. To perform all these functions optimally, money has to be available, affordable, durable, fungible, portable and reliable. Because they fulfil most of these criteria, metals such as gold, silver and bronze were for millennia regarded as the ideal monetary raw material. The earliest known coins date back as long ago as 600 BC and were found by archaeologists in the Temple of Artemis at Ephesus (near Izmir in modern-day Turkey). These ovular Lydian coins, which were made of the gold-silver alloy known as electrum and bore the image of a lion's head, were the forerunners of the Athenian tetradrachm, a standardized silver coin with the head of the goddess Athena on one side and an owl (associated with her for its supposed wisdom) on the obverse. By Roman times, coins were produced in three different metals: the aureus (gold), the denarius (silver) and the sestertius (bronze), ranked in that order according to the relative scarcity of the metals in question, but all bearing the head of the reigning emperor on one side, and the legendary figures of Romulus and Remus on the other. Coins were not unique to the ancient Mediterranean, but they clearly arose there first. It was not until 221 BC that a standardized bronze coin was introduced to China by the 'first Emperor', Qin Shihuangdi. In each case, coins made of precious metal were associated with powerful sovereigns who monopolized the minting of money partly to exploit it as a source of revenue.

The Roman system of coinage outlived the Roman Empire itself. Prices were still being quoted in terms of silver denarii in the time of Charlemagne, king of the Franks from 768 to 814. The difficulty was that by the time Charlemagne was crowned *Imperator Augustus* in 800, there was a chronic shortage of silver in Western Europe. Demand for money was greater in the much more developed commercial centres of the Islamic Empire that dominated the southern Mediterranean and the Near East, so that precious metal tended to drain away from backward Europe. So rare was the denarius in Charlemagne's time that twenty-four of them sufficed to buy a Carolingian cow. In some parts of Europe, peppers and squirrel skins served as substitutes for currency; in others *pecunia* came to mean land rather than money. This was a problem that Europeans sought to overcome in one of two ways. They could export labour and goods, exchanging slaves and timber for silver in Baghdad or for African gold in Cordoba and Cairo. Or they could plunder precious metal by making war on the Muslim world. The Crusades, like the conquests that followed, were as much about overcoming Europe's monetary shortage as about converting heathens to Christianity.[14]

Crusading was an expensive affair and the net returns were modest. To compound their monetary difficulties, medieval and early modern governments failed to find a solution to what economists have called the big problem of small change: the difficulty of establishing stable relationships between coins made of different kinds of metal, which meant that smaller denomination coins were subject to recurrent shortages, yet also to depreciations and debasements.[15] At Potosí, and the other places in the New World where they found plentiful silver (notably Zacatecas in Mexico), the Spanish conquistadors therefore appeared to have broken a centuries-old constraint. The initial beneficiary was, of course, the Castilian monarchy that had sponsored the conquests. The convoys of ships – up to a hundred at a time – which transported 170 tons of silver a year across the Atlantic, docked at Seville. A fifth of all that was produced was reserved to the crown, accounting for 44 per cent of total royal expenditure at the peak in the late sixteenth century.[16] But the way the money was spent ensured that Spain's newfound wealth provided the entire continent with a monetary stimulus. The Spanish 'piece of eight', which was based on the German *thaler* (hence, later, the 'dollar'), became the world's first truly global currency, financing not only the protracted wars Spain fought in Europe, but also the rapidly expanding trade of Europe with Asia.

And yet all the silver of the New World could not bring the rebellious Dutch Republic to heel; could not secure England for the Spanish crown; could not save Spain from an inexorable economic and imperial decline. Like King Midas, the Spanish monarchs of the sixteenth century, Charles V and Philip II, found that an abundance of precious metal could be as much a curse as a blessing. The reason? They dug up so much silver to pay for their wars of conquest that the metal itself dramatically declined in value – that is to say, in its purchasing power with respect to other goods. During the so-called 'price revolution', which affected all of Europe from the 1540s until the 1640s, the cost of food – which had shown no sustained upward trend for three hundred years – rose markedly. In England (the country for which we have the best price data) the cost of living increased by a factor of seven in the same period; not a high rate of inflation these days (on average around 2 per cent per year), but a revolutionary increase in the price of bread by medieval standards. Within Spain, the abundance of silver also acted as a 'resource curse', like the abundant oil of Arabia, Nigeria, Persia, Russia and Venezuela in our own time, removing the incentives for more productive economic activity, while at the same time strengthening rent-seeking autocrats at the expense of representative assemblies (in Spain's case the Cortes).[17]

What the Spaniards had failed to understand is that the value of precious metal is not absolute. Money is worth only what someone else is willing to give you for it. An increase in its supply will not make a society richer, though it may enrich the government that monopolizes the production of money. Other things being equal, monetary expansion will merely make prices higher.

*

There was in fact no reason other than historical happenstance that money was for so long equated in the Western mind with metal. In ancient Mesopotamia, beginning around five thousand years ago, people used clay tokens to record transactions involving agricultural produce like barley or wool, or metals such as silver. Rings, blocks or sheets made of silver certainly served as ready money (as did grain), but the clay tablets were just as important, and probably more so. A great many have survived, reminders that when human beings first began to produce written records of their activities they did so not to write history, poetry or philosophy, but to do business.[18] It is impossible to pick up such ancient financial instruments without a feeling of awe. Though made of base earth, they have endured much longer than the silver dollars in the Potosí mint. One especially well-preserved token, from the town of Sippar (modern-day Tell Abu Habbah in Iraq), dates from the reign of King Ammi-ditana (1683–1647 BC) and states that its bearer should receive a specific amount of barley at harvest time. Another token, inscribed during the reign of his successor, King Ammi-saduqa, orders that the bearer should be given a quantity of silver at the end of a journey.[19]

If the basic concept seems familiar to us, it is partly because a modern banknote does similar things. Just take a look at the magic words on any Bank of England note: 'I promise to pay the bearer on demand the sum of . . .'. Banknotes (which originated in seventh-century China) are pieces of paper which have next to no intrinsic worth. They are simply promises to pay (hence their original Western designation as 'promissory notes'), just like the clay tablets of ancient Babylon four millennia ago. 'In God We Trust' it says on the back of the ten-dollar bill, but the person you are really trusting when you accept one of these in payment is the successor to the man on the front (Alexander Hamilton, the first Secretary of the US Treasury), who at the time of writing

A clay tablet from second millennium BC
Mesopotamia, front (above) and rear (opposite). The inscription
states that Amil-mirra will pay 330 measures of barley to the
bearer of the tablet at harvest time.

happens to be Lloyd Blankfein's predecessor as chief executive
of Goldman Sachs, Henry M. Paulson, Jr. When an American
exchanges his goods or his labour for a fistful of dollars, he
is essentially trusting 'Hank' Paulson (and by implication the
Chairman of the Federal Reserve System, Ben Bernanke) not to
repeat Spain's error and manufacture so many of these things
that they end up being worth no more than the paper they are
printed on.

Today, despite the fact that the purchasing power of the dollar

has declined appreciably over the past fifty years, we remain
more or less content with paper money – not to mention coins
that are literally made from junk. Stores of value these are not.
Even more amazingly, we are happy with money we cannot even
see. Today's electronic money can be moved from our employer,
to our bank account, to our favourite retail outlets without ever
physically materializing. It is this 'virtual' money that now
dominates what economists call the money supply. Cash in the
hands of ordinary Americans accounts for just 11 per cent of the
monetary measure known as M2. The intangible character of
most money today is perhaps the best evidence of its true nature.
What the conquistadors failed to understand is that money is a
matter of belief, even faith: belief in the person paying us; belief

in the person issuing the money he uses or the institution that honours his cheques or transfers. Money is not metal. It is trust inscribed. And it does not seem to matter much where it is inscribed: on silver, on clay, on paper, on a liquid crystal display. Anything can serve as money, from the cowrie shells of the Maldives to the huge stone discs used on the Pacific islands of Yap.[20] And now, it seems, in this electronic age nothing can serve as money too.

The central relationship that money crystallizes is between lender and borrower. Look again at those Mesopotamian clay tablets. In each case, the transactions recorded on them were repayments of commodities that had been loaned; the tablets were evidently drawn up and retained by the lender (often in a sealed clay container) to record the amount due and the date of repayment. The lending system of ancient Babylon was evidently quite sophisticated. Debts were transferable, hence 'pay the bearer' rather than a named creditor. Clay receipts or drafts were issued to those who deposited grain or other commodities at royal palaces or temples. Borrowers were expected to pay interest (a concept which was probably derived from the natural increase of a herd of livestock), at rates that were often as high as 20 per cent. Mathematical exercises from the reign of Hammurabi (1792–1750 BC) suggest that something like compound interest could be charged on long-term loans. But the foundation on which all of this rested was the underlying credibility of a borrower's promise to repay. (It is no coincidence that in English the root of 'credit' is *credo*, the Latin for 'I believe'.) Debtors might periodically be relieved – indeed the Laws of Hammurabi prescribed debt forgiveness every three years – but this does not appear to have deterred private as well as public lenders from doing business in the reasonable expectation of getting their money back.[21] On the contrary, the long-term trend in ancient

Mesopotamia was for private finance to expand. By the sixth century BC, families like the Babylonian Egibi had emerged as powerful landowners and lenders, with commercial interests as far afield as Uruk over a hundred miles to the south and Persia to the east. The thousands of clay tablets that survive from that period testify to the number of people who at one time or another were in debt to the Egibi. The fact that the family thrived for five generations suggests that they generally collected their debts.

It would not be quite correct to say that credit was invented in ancient Mesopotamia. Most Babylonian loans were simple advances from royal or religious storehouses. Credit was not being created in the modern sense discussed later in this chapter. Nevertheless, this was an important beginning. Without the foundation of borrowing and lending, the economic history of our world would scarcely have got off the ground. And without the ever-growing network of relationships between creditors and debtors, today's global economy would grind to a halt. Contrary to the famous song in the musical *Cabaret*, money does not literally make the world go round. But it does make staggering quantities of people, goods and services go around the world.

The remarkable thing is how belatedly and hesitantly the idea of credit took root in the very part of the world where it has flourished most spectacularly.

Loan Sharks

Northern Italy in the early thirteenth century was a land subdivided into multiple feuding city-states. Among the many remnants of the defunct Roman Empire was a numerical system (i, ii, iii, iv . . .) singularly ill-suited to complex mathematical calculation, let alone the needs of commerce. Nowhere was this more of a problem than in Pisa, where merchants also had to contend with seven different forms of coinage in circulation. By comparison, economic life in the Eastern world – in the Abassid caliphate or in Sung China – was far more advanced, just as it had been in the time of Charlemagne. To discover modern finance, Europe needed to import it. In this, a crucial role was played by a young mathematician called Leonardo of Pisa, or Fibonacci.

The son of a Pisan customs official based in what is now Bejaia in Algeria, the young Fibonacci had immersed himself in what he called the 'Indian method' of mathematics, a combination of Indian and Arab insights. His introduction of these ideas was to revolutionize the way Europeans counted. Nowadays he is best remembered for the Fibonacci sequence of numbers (0, 1, 1, 2, 3, 5, 8, 13, 21 . . .), in which each successive number is the sum of the previous two, and the ratio between a number and its immediate antecedent tends towards a 'golden mean' (around 1.618). It is a pattern that mirrors some of the repeating properties to be found in the natural world (for example in the fractal geometry of ferns and sea shells).* But the Fibonacci sequence was only one of many Eastern mathematical ideas introduced to Europe in his path-breaking book *Liber Abaci*, 'The Book of Calculation', which he published in 1202. In it, readers could find fractions explained, as well as the concept of present value (the discounted value today of a future revenue stream).[22] Most important of all was Fibonacci's introduction of Hindu-Arabic numerals. He not only gave Europe the decimal system, which makes all kinds of calculation far easier than with Roman numerals; he also showed how it could be applied to commercial

* The Fibonacci sequence appears in *The Da Vinci Code*, which is probably why most people have heard of it. However, the sequence first appeared, under the name *mātrāmeru* (mountain of cadence), in the work of the Sanskrit scholar Pingala.

bookkeeping, to currency conversions and, crucially, to the calculation of interest. Significantly, many of the examples in the *Liber Abaci* are made more vivid by being expressed in terms of commodities like hides, peppers, cheese, oil and spices. This was to be the application of mathematics to making money and, in particular, to lending money. One characteristic example begins:

A man placed 100 pounds at a certain [merchant's] house for 4 denarii per pound per month interest and he took back each year a payment of 30 pounds. One must compute in each year the 30 pounds reduction of capital and the profit on the said 30 pounds. It is sought how many years, months, days and hours he will hold money in the house . . .

Italian commercial centres like Fibonacci's home town of Pisa or nearby Florence proved to be fertile soil for such financial seeds. But it was above all Venice, more exposed than the others to Oriental influences, that became Europe's great lending laboratory. It is not coincidental that the most famous moneylender in Western literature was based in Venice. His story brilliantly illuminates the obstacles that for centuries impeded the translation of Fibonacci's theories into effective financial practice. These obstacles were not economic, or political. They were cultural.

Shakespeare's play *The Merchant of Venice* is based on a story in a fourteenth-century Italian book called *Il Pecorone* ('The Dunce'), a collection of tales and anecdotes written in 1378 by Giovanni Fiorentino. One story tells of a wealthy woman who marries an upstanding young gentleman. Her husband needs money and his friend, eager to help, goes to a moneylender to borrow the cash on his friend's behalf. The moneylender, like Shylock a Jew, demands a pound of flesh as security, to be handed over if the money is not paid back. As Shakespeare rewrote it, the Jewish moneylender Shylock agrees to lend the lovelorn suitor Bassanio three thousand ducats, but on the security of Bassanio's friend, the merchant Antonio. As Shylock says, Antonio is a 'good' man – meaning not that he is especially virtuous, but that his credit is 'sufficient'. However, Shylock also points out that lending money to merchants (or their friends) is risky. Antonio's ships are scattered all over the world, one going to North Africa, another to India, a third to Mexico, a fourth to England:

... his means are in supposition: he hath an argosy bound to Tripolis, another to the Indies; I understand moreover, upon the Rialto, he hath a third at Mexico, a fourth for England, and other ventures he hath, squandered abroad. But ships are but boards, sailors but men: there be land-rats and water-rats, water-thieves and land-thieves, I mean pirates, and then there is the peril of waters, winds and rocks.

That is precisely why anyone who lends money to a merchant, if only for the duration of an ocean voyage, needs to be compensated. We usually call the compensation interest: the amount paid to the lender over and above the sum lent, or the principal. Overseas trade of the sort that Venice depended on could not have happened if its financiers had not been rewarded in some way for risking their money on mere boards and men.

But why does Shylock turn out to be such a villain, demanding literally a pound of flesh – in effect Antonio's death – if he cannot fulfil his obligations? The answer is of course that Shylock is one of the many moneylenders in history to have belonged to an ethnic minority. By Shakespeare's time, Jews had been providing commercial credit in Venice for nearly a century. They did their business in front of the building once known as the Banco Rosso, sitting behind their tables – their *tavule* – and on their benches, their *banci*. But the Banco Rosso was located in a cramped ghetto some distance away from the centre of the city.

There was a good reason why Venetian merchants had to come to the Jewish ghetto if they wanted to borrow money. For Christians, lending money at interest was a sin. Usurers, people who lent money at interest, had been excommunicated by the Third Lateran Council in 1179. Even arguing that usury was not a sin had been condemned as heresy by the Council of Vienna in 1311–12. Christian usurers had to make restitution to the Church before they could be buried on hallowed ground. They were especially detested by the Franciscan and Dominican orders, founded in 1206 and 1216 (just after the publication of Fibonacci's *Liber Abaci*). The power of this taboo should not be underestimated, though it had certainly weakened by Shakespeare's time.[23]

In Florence's Duomo (cathedral) there is a fresco by Domenico di Michelino that shows the great Florentine poet Dante Alighieri holding his book the *Divine Comedy*. As Dante imagined it in Canto XVII of his masterpiece, there was a special part of the seventh circle of Hell reserved for usurers:

Sorrow . . . gushed from their eyes and made their sad tears flow;
While this way and that they flapped their hands, for ease
From the hot soil now, and now from the burning snow,

Behaving, in fact, exactly as one sees
Dogs in the summer, scuffing with snout and paw
When they're eaten up with gnats and flies and fleas.

I looked at many thus scorched by the fiery flaw,
And though I scanned their faces with the utmost heed,
There was no one there I recognized; but I saw

How, stamped with charge and tincture plain to read,
About the neck of each a great purse hung,
Whereon their eyes seemed still to fix and feed.

Jews, too, were not supposed to lend at interest. But there was a convenient get-out clause in the Old Testament book of Deuteronomy: 'Unto a stranger thou mayest lend upon usury; but unto thy brother thou shalt not lend upon usury.' In other words, a Jew might legitimately lend to a Christian, though not to another Jew. The price of doing so was social exclusion.

Jews had been expelled from Spain in 1492. Along with many Portuguese *conversos*, Jews who were forced to adopt Christianity by a decree of 1497, they sought refuge in the Ottoman Empire. From Constantinople and other Ottoman ports they then established trading relationships with Venice. The Jewish presence in Venice dates from 1509, when Jews living in Mestre sought refuge from the War of the League of Cambrai. At first the city's government was reluctant to accept the refugees, but it soon became apparent that they might prove a useful source of money and financial services, since they could be taxed as well as borrowed from.[24] In 1516 the Venetian authorities designated a special area of the city for Jews on the site of an old iron foundry which became known as the *ghetto nuovo* (*getto* literally means casting). There they were to be confined every night and on Christian holidays. Those who stayed in Venice for more than two weeks were supposed to wear a yellow O on their backs or a yellow (later scarlet) hat or turban.[25] Residence was limited to a stipulated period on the basis of *condotte* (charters) renewed every five years.[26] A similar arrangement was reached in 1541 with some Jews from Romania, who were accorded the right to live in another enclave, the *ghetto vecchio*. By 1590 there were around 2,500 Jews in Venice. Buildings in the ghetto grew seven storeys high to accommodate the newcomers.

Throughout the sixteenth century, the position of the Venetian Jews remained conditional and vulnerable. In 1537, when war broke out between Venice and the Ottoman Empire, the Venetian

Senate ordered the sequestration of the property of 'Turks, Jews and other Turkish subjects'. Another war from 1570 to 1573 led to the arrest of all Jews and the seizure of their property, though they were freed and had their assets returned after peace had been restored.[27] To avoid a repetition of this experience, the Jews petitioned the Venetian government to be allowed to remain free during any future war. They were fortunate to be represented by Daniel Rodriga, a Jewish merchant of Spanish origin who proved to be a highly effective negotiator. The charter he succeeded in obtaining in 1589 granted all Jews the status of Venetian subjects, permitted them to engage in the Levant trade – a valuable privilege – and allowed them to practise their religion openly. Nevertheless, important restrictions remained. They were not allowed to join guilds or to engage in retail trade, hence restricting them to financial services, and their privileges were subject to revocation at eighteen months' notice. As citizens, Jews now stood more chance of success than Shylock in the Venetian law courts. In 1623, for example, Leon Voltera sued Antonio dalla Donna, who had stood security for a knight who had borrowed certain items from Voltera and then vanished. In 1636–7, however, a scandal involving the bribery of judges, in which some Jews were implicated, seems once again to have raised the threat of expulsion.[28]

Though fictional, the story of Shylock is therefore not entirely removed from Venetian reality. Indeed, Shakespeare's play quite accurately illustrates three important points about early modern money-lending: the power of lenders to charge extortionate interest rates when credit markets are in their infancy; the importance of law courts in resolving financial disputes without recourse to violence; but above all the vulnerability of minority creditors to a backlash by hostile debtors who belong to the ethnic majority. For in the end, of course, Shylock is thwarted. Although the court recognizes his right to insist on his bond – to claim his pound of flesh – the law also prohibits him from shedding Antonio's blood. And, because he is an alien, the law requires the loss of his goods and life for plotting the death of a Christian. He escapes only by submitting to baptism. Everyone lives happily ever after – except Shylock.

The Merchant of Venice raises profound questions about economics as well as anti-Semitism. Why don't debtors always default on their creditors – especially when the creditors belong to unpopular ethnic minorities? Why don't the Shylocks always lose out?

Loan sharks, like the poor on whom they prey, are always with us. They thrive in East Africa, for example. But there is no need to travel to the developing world to understand the workings of primitive money-lending. According to a 2007 report by the Department of Trade and Industry, approximately 165,000 households in the UK use illegal moneylenders, borrowing in aggregate up to £40 million a year, but repaying three times that amount. To see just why one-man moneylenders are nearly always unpopular, regardless of their ethnicity, all you need do is pay a visit to my home town, Glasgow. The deprived housing estates of the city's East End have long been fertile breeding grounds for loan sharks. In districts like Shettleston, where my grandparents lived, there are steel shutters over the windows of derelict tenements and sectarian graffiti on the bus shelters. Once, Shettleston's economic life revolved around the pay packets of the workers employed at Boyd's ironworks. Now it revolves around the benefit payments made into the Post Office accounts of the unemployed. Male life expectancy in Shettleston is around 64, thirteen years less than the UK average and the same as in Pakistan, which means that a newborn boy there typically will not live long enough to collect his state pension.

Such deprived areas of Glasgow are perfect hunting grounds for loan sharks. In the district of Hillington, Gerard Law was for twenty years the number one loan shark. He used the Argosy pub on Paisley Road West as his office, spending most working days there, despite himself being a teetotaller. Law's system was simple. Borrowers would hand over their benefit books or Post Office cashcards to him in return for a loan, the terms of which he recorded in his loan book. When a benefit cheque was due, Law would give the borrower back his card and wait to collect his interest. The loan book itself was strikingly crude: a haphazard compilation of transactions in which the same twenty or thirty names and nicknames feature again and again alongside sums of varying sizes: 'Beardy Al 15', 'Jibber 100', 'Bernadett 150', 'Wee Caffy 1210'. The standard rate of interest Law charged his clients was a staggering 25 per cent a week. Typically, the likes of Beardy Al borrowed ten pounds and paid back £12.50 (principal plus interest) a week later. Often, however, Law's clients could not afford to make their scheduled repayments; hardly surprising when some people in the area have to live on as little as £5.90 a day. So they borrowed some more. Soon some clients owed him hundreds, even thousands, of pounds. The speed with which they became entirely trapped by their debts is scarcely surprising. Twenty-five per cent a week works out at over 11 million per cent compound interest a year.

Over the very long run, interest rates in Europe have tended to decline. So why do some people in Britain today pay eight-digit interest rates on trivial loans? These, surely, are loans you would be mad *not* to default on. Some of Law's clients were in fact mentally subnormal. Yet there were evidently reasons why his sane clients felt it would be inadvisable to renege on their commitments to him, no matter how extortionate. As the *Scotsman* newspaper put it: 'many of his victims were terrified to

The arrest of a loan shark: Gerard Law is led away by police
officers of Glasgow's Illegal Money-Lending Unit

risk missing a payment due to his reputation' – though it is not
clear that Law ever actually resorted to violence.[29] Behind every
loan shark, as the case of Shylock also shows, there lurks an
implicit threat.

It is easy to condemn loan sharks as immoral and, indeed,
criminal. Gerard Law was sentenced to ten months in prison for
his behaviour. Yet we need to try to understand the economic
rationale for what he did. First, he was able to take advantage of
the fact that no mainstream financial institution would extend
credit to the Shettleston unemployed. Second, Law had to be
rapacious and ruthless precisely because the members of his small
clientele were in fact very likely to default on their loans. The
fundamental difficulty with being a loan shark is that the business
is too small-scale and risky to allow low interest rates. But the

high rates make defaults so much more likely that only intimidation ensures that people keep paying. So how did moneylenders learn to overcome the fundamental conflict: if they were too generous, they made no money; if they were too hard-nosed, like Gerard Law, people eventually called in the police?

The answer is by growing big – and growing powerful.

The Birth of Banking

Shylock was far from the only moneylender to discover the inherent weakness of the creditor, especially when the creditor is a foreigner. In the early fourteenth century, finance in Italy had been dominated by the three Florentine houses of Bardi, Peruzzi and Acciaiuoli. All three were wiped out in the 1340s as a result of defaults by two of their principal clients, King Edward III of England and King Robert of Naples. But if that illustrates the potential weakness of moneylenders, the rise of the Medici illustrates the very opposite: their potential power.

Perhaps no other family left such an imprint on an age as the Medici left on the Renaissance. Two Medici became popes (Leo X and Clement VII); two became queens of France (Catherine and Marie); three became dukes (of Florence, Nemours and Tuscany). Appropriately, it was that supreme theorist of political power, Niccolò Machiavelli, who wrote their history. Their patronage of the arts and sciences ran the gamut of genius from Michelangelo to Galileo. And their dazzling architectural legacy still surrounds the modern-day visitor to Florence. Only look at the villa of Cafaggiolo, the monastery of San Marco, the basilica of San Lorenzo and the spectacular palaces occupied by Duke Cosimo de' Medici in the mid sixteenth century: the former Pitti Palace, the redecorated Palazzo Vecchio and the new city offices

(Uffizi) with their courtyard running down to the River Arno.[30] But what were the origins of all this splendour? Where did the money come from that paid for masterpieces like Sandro Botticelli's radiant *Birth of Venus*? The simple answer is that the Medici were foreign exchange dealers: members of the *Arte de Cambio* (the Moneychangers' Guild). They came to be known as bankers (*banchieri*) because, like the Jews of Venice, they did their business literally seated at benches behind tables in the street. The original Medici bank (stall would be a better description) was located near the Cavalcanti palace, at the corner of the present-day via dia Porta Rossa and the Via dell' Arte della Lana, a short walk from the main Florentine wool market.

Prior to the 1390s, it might legitimately be suggested, the Medici were more gangsters than bankers: a small-time clan, notable more for low violence than for high finance. Between 1343 and 1360 no fewer than five Medici were sentenced to death for capital crimes.[31] Then came Giovanni di Bicci de' Medici. It was his aim to make the Medici legitimate. And through hard work, sober living and careful calculation, he succeeded.

In 1385 Giovanni became manager of the Roman branch of the bank run by his relation Vieri di Cambio de' Medici, a moneylender in Florence. In Rome, Giovanni built up his reputation as a currency trader. The papacy was in many ways the ideal client, given the number of different currencies flowing in and out of the Vatican's coffers. As we have seen, this was an age of multiple systems of coinage, some gold, some silver, some base metal, so that any long-distance trade or tax payment was complicated by the need to convert from one currency to another. But Giovanni clearly saw even greater opportunities in his native Florence, whence he returned in 1397. By the time he passed on the business to his eldest son Cosimo in 1420, he had established a branch of the bank in Venice as well as Rome; branches were

A banker on his bench: Quentin Massys, *The Banker* (1514)

later added in Geneva, Pisa, London and Avignon. Giovanni had also acquired interests in two Florence wool factories.

Of particular importance in the Medici's early business were the bills of exchange (*cambium per literas*) that had developed in the course of the Middle Ages as a way of financing trade.[32] If one merchant owed another a sum that could not be paid in cash until the conclusion of a transaction some months hence, the creditor could draw a bill on the debtor and either use the bill as a means of payment in its own right or obtain cash for it at a discount from a banker willing to act as broker. Whereas the charging of interest was condemned as usury by the Church, there was nothing to prevent a shrewd trader making profits on such transactions. That was the essence of the Medici business. There were no cheques; instructions were given orally and written in the bank's books. There was no interest; depositors were given *discrezione* (in proportion to the annual profits of the firm) to compensate them for risking their money.[33]

The *libro segreto* – literally the secret book* – of Giovanni di Bicci de' Medici sheds fascinating light on the family's rise.[34] In part, this was simply a story of meticulous bookkeeping. By modern standards, to be sure, there were imperfections. The Medici did not systematically use the double-entry method, though it was known in Genoa as early as the 1340s.[35] Still, the modern researcher cannot fail to be impressed by the neatness and orderliness of the Medici accounts. The archives also contain a number of early Medici balance sheets, with reserves and deposits correctly arranged on one side (as liabilities or *vostro*) and loans to clients or commercial bills on the other side (as assets or *nostro*). The Medici did not invent these techniques, but they applied them on a larger scale than had hitherto been seen in Florence. The real key to the Medicis' success, however, was not so much size as diversification. Whereas earlier Italian banks had been monolithic structures, easily brought down by one defaulting debtor, the Medici bank was in fact multiple related partnerships, each based on a special, regularly renegotiated contract. Branch managers were not employees but junior partners who were remunerated with a share of the profits. It was this

* The term was used for books which recorded income and profits as well as specific agreements or contracts of importance. The other books kept by the Medici were the *libro di entrata e uscita* (book of income and expenditures) and the *libro dei debitori e creditori* (book of debtors and creditors).

Detail from a ledger of the Medici bank

decentralization that helped make the Medici bank so profitable. With a capital of around 20,000 florins in 1402 and a payroll of at most seventeen people, it made profits of 151,820 florins between 1397 and 1420 – around 6,326 florins a year, a rate of return of 32 per cent. The Rome branch alone was soon posting returns of over 30 per cent.[36] The proof that the model worked can be seen in the Florentine tax records, which list page after page of Giovanni di Bicci's assets, totalling some 91,000 florins.[37]

When Giovanni died in 1429 his last words were an exhortation to his heirs to maintain his standards of financial acumen. His funeral was attended by twenty-six men of the name Medici, all paying homage to the self-made *capo della casa*. By the time Pius II became pope in 1458, Giovanni's son Cosimo de' Medici effectively was the Florentine state. As the Pope himself put it: 'Political questions are settled at his house. The man he chooses holds office . . . He it is who decides peace and war and controls the laws ... He is King in everything but name.' Foreign rulers were advised to communicate with him personally and not to waste their time by approaching anyone else in Florence. The Florentine historian Francesco Guicciardini observed: 'He had a reputation such as probably no private citizen has ever enjoyed from the fall of Rome to our own day.' One of Botticelli's most popular portraits – of a strikingly handsome young man – was actually intended as a tribute to a dead banker. The face on the medal is that of Cosimo de' Medici, and alongside it is the inscription *pater patriae*: 'father of his country'. By the time Lorenzo the Magnificent, Cosimo's grandson, took over the bank in 1469, the erstwhile Sopranos had become the Corleones – and more. And it was all based on banking.

More than anything else, it is Botticelli's *Adoration of the Magi* that captures the transfiguration of finance that the Medici had achieved. On close inspection, the three wise men are all Medici: the older man washing the feet of the baby Jesus is Cosimo the Elder; below him, slightly to the right, are his two sons Piero (in red) and Giovanni (in white). Also in the picture are Lorenzo (in a pale blue robe) and, clasping his sword, Giuliano. The painting was commissioned by the head of the Bankers' Guild as a tribute to the family. It should perhaps have been called *The Adoration of the Medici*. Having once been damned, bankers were now close to divinity.

The subjugation of the Florentine republic to the power of one super-rich banking family inevitably aroused opposition. Between October 1433 and September 1434 Cosimo and many of his supporters were exiled from Florence to Venice. In 1478 Lorenzo's brother Giuliano was murdered in the Pazzi family's brutal attempt to end Medici rule. The bank itself suffered as a result of Lorenzo's neglect of business in favour of politics. Branch managers like Francesco Sassetti of Avignon or Tommaso

Portinari of Bruges became more powerful and less closely super-vised. Increasingly, the bank depended on attracting deposits; its earnings from trade and foreign exchange grew more volatile. Expensive mistakes began to be made, like the loans made by the Bruges branch to Charles the Bold, the Duke of Burgundy, or by the London branch to King Edward IV, which were never wholly repaid. To keep the firm afloat, Lorenzo was driven to raid the municipal Monte delle Dote (a kind of mutual fund for the pay-ment of daughters' dowries).[38] Finally, in 1494, amid the chaos of a French invasion, the family was expelled and all its property confiscated and liquidated. Blaming the Medici for the town's misfortunes, the Dominican preacher Girolamo Savonarola called for a purgative 'Bonfire of the Vanities', a call answered when a mob invaded the Medici palace and burned most of the bank's records. (Black scorch marks are still visible on the papers that survived.) As Lorenzo himself had put it in a song he composed in the 1470s: 'If you would be happy, be so. / There is no certainty about tomorrow.'

Yet when the wealthy elite of Florence contemplated the fire-brand Savonarola and the plebeian mob as alternatives to Medici rule they soon began to feel nostalgic for the magnificent family. In 1537, at the age of 17, Cosimo de' Medici (the Younger) was summoned back to Florence and in 1569 was created Grand Duke of Tuscany. The ducal line endured for more than two hundred years, until 1743. The coin-like *palle* (pills) on the Medici coat of arms served as an enduring reminder of the family's origins.

Though others had tried before them, the Medici were the first bankers to make the transition from financial success to heredi-tary status and power. They achieved this by learning a crucial lesson: in finance small is seldom beautiful. By making their bank bigger and more diversified than any previous financial institution, they found a way of spreading their risks. And by engaging in currency trading as well as lending, they reduced their vulnerability to defaults.

The Italian banking system became the model for those North European nations that would achieve the greatest commercial success in the coming centuries, notably the Dutch and the English, but also the Swedes. It was in Amsterdam, London and Stockholm that the next decisive wave of financial innovation occurred, as the forerunners of modern central banks made their first appearance. The seventeenth century saw the foundation of three distinctly novel institutions that, in their different ways, were intended to serve a public as well as a private financial function. The Amsterdam Exchange Bank (*Wisselbank*) was set up in 1609 to resolve the practical problems created for merchants by the circulation of multiple currencies in the United Provinces, where there were no fewer than fourteen different mints and copious quantities of foreign coins. By allowing merchants to set up accounts denominated in a standardized currency, the Exchange Bank pioneered the system of cheques and direct debits or transfers that we take for granted today. This allowed more and more commercial transactions to take place without the need for the sums involved to materialize in actual coins. One merchant could make a payment to another simply by arranging for his account at the bank to be debited and the counterparty's account to be credited.[39] The limitation on this system was simply that the Exchange Bank maintained something close to a 100 per cent ratio between its deposits and its reserves of precious metal and coin. As late as 1760, when its deposits stood at just under 19 million florins, its metallic reserve was over 16 million. A run on the bank was therefore a virtual impossibility, since it had enough cash on hand to satisfy nearly all of its depositors if, for some reason, they all wanted to liquidate their deposits at once. This made the bank secure, no doubt, but it prevented it performing what would now be seen as the defining characteristic of a bank, credit creation.

It was in Stockholm nearly half a century later, with the foundation of the Swedish Riksbank in 1656, that this barrier was broken through. Although it performed the same functions as the Dutch *Wisselbank*, the Riksbank was also designed to be a *Lanebank*, meaning that it engaged in lending as well as facilitating commercial payments. By lending amounts in excess of its metallic reserve, it may be said to have pioneered the practice of what would later be known as fractional reserve banking, exploiting the fact that money left on deposit could profitably be lent out to borrowers. Since depositors were highly unlikely to ask *en masse* for their money, only a fraction of their money needed to be kept in the Riksbank's reserve at any given time. The liabilities of the bank thus became its deposits (on which it paid interest) plus its reserve (on which it could collect no interest); its assets became its loans (on which it could collect interest).

The third great innovation of the seventeenth century occurred in London with the creation of the Bank of England in 1694. Designed primarily to assist the government with war finance (by converting a portion of the government's debt into shares in the bank), the Bank was endowed with distinctive privileges. From 1709 it was the only bank allowed to operate on a joint-stock basis (see Chapter 3); and from 1742 it established a partial monopoly on the issue of banknotes, a distinctive form of promissory note that did not bear interest, designed to facilitate payments without the need for both parties in a transaction to have current accounts.

To understand the power of these three innovations, first-year MBA students at Harvard Business School play a simplified money game. It begins with a notional central bank paying the professor $100 on behalf of the government, for which he has done some not very lucrative consulting. The professor takes the banknotes to a bank notionally operated by one of his students and deposits them there, receiving a deposit slip. Assuming, for the sake of simplicity, that this bank operates a 10 per cent reserve ratio (that is, it wishes to maintain the ratio of its reserves to its total liabilities at 10 per cent), it deposits $10 with the central bank and lends the other $90 to one of its clients. While the client decides what to do with his loan, he deposits the money in another bank. This bank also has a 10 per cent reserve rule, so it deposits $9 at the central bank and lends out the remaining $81 to another of its clients. After several more rounds, the professor asks the class to compute the increase in the supply of money. This allows him to introduce two of the core definitions of modern monetary theory: M0 (also known as the monetary base or high-powered money), which is equal to the total liabilities of the central bank, that is, cash plus the reserves of private sector banks on deposit at the central bank; and M1 (also known as narrow money), which is equal to cash in circulation plus demand or 'sight' deposits. By the time money has been deposited at three different student banks, M0 is equal to $100 but M1 is equal to $271 ($100 + $90 + $81), neatly illustrating, albeit in a highly simplified way, how modern fractional reserve banking allows the creation of credit and hence of money.

The professor then springs a surprise on the first student by asking for his $100 back. The student has to draw on his reserves and call in his loan to the second student, setting off a domino effect that causes M1 to contract as swiftly as it expanded. This illustrates the danger of a bank run. Since the first bank had only one depositor, his attempted withdrawal constituted a call ten times larger than its reserves. The survival of the first banker clearly depended on his being able to call in the loan he had made to his client, who in turn had to withdraw all of his deposit from the second bank, and so on. When making their loans, the bankers should have thought more carefully about how easily they could call back the money – essentially a question about the liquidity of the loan.

Definitions of the money supply have, it must be acknowledged, a somewhat arbitrary quality. Some measures of M1 included travellers' cheques in the total. M2 adds savings accounts, money market deposit accounts and certificates of deposit. M3 is broader still, including eurodollar deposits held in offshore markets, and repurchase agreements between banks and other financial intermediaries. The technicalities need not detain us here. The important point to grasp is that with the spread throughout the Western world of a) cashless intra-bank and inter-bank transactions b) fractional reserve banking and c) central bank monopolies on note issue, the very nature of money evolved in a profoundly important way. No longer was money to be understood, as the Spaniards had understood it in the sixteenth century, as precious metal that had been dug up, melted down and minted into coins. Now money represented the sum total of specific liabilities (deposits and reserves) incurred by banks. Credit was, quite simply, the total of banks' assets (loans). Some of this money might indeed still consist of precious metal, though a rising proportion of that would be held in the central bank's vault. But most of it would be made up of those banknotes and token coins recognized as legal tender along with the invisible money that existed only in deposit account statements. Financial innovation had taken the inert silver of Potosí and turned it into the basis for a modern monetary system, with relationships between debtors and creditors brokered or 'intermediated' by increasingly numerous institutions called banks. The core function of these institutions was now information gathering and risk management. Their source of profits lay in maximizing the difference between the costs of their liabilities and the earnings on their assets, without reducing reserves to such an extent that the bank became vulnerable to a run – a crisis of confidence in a bank's ability to satisfy depositors, which leads to escalating withdrawals and ultimately bankruptcy: literally the breaking of the bank.

Significantly, even as Italian banking techniques were being improved in the financial centres of Northern Europe, one country lagged unexpectedly far behind. Cursed with an abundance of precious metal, mighty Spain failed to develop a sophisticated banking system, relying instead on the merchants of Antwerp for short-term cash advances against future silver deliveries. The idea that money was really about credit, not metal, never quite caught on in Madrid. Indeed, the Spanish crown ended up defaulting on all or part of its debt no fewer than fourteen times between 1557 and 1696. With a track record like that, all the silver in Potosí could not make Spain a secure credit risk. In the modern world, power would go to the bankers, not the bankrupts.

The Evolution of Banking

Financial historians disagree as to how far the growth of banking after the seventeenth century can be credited with the acceleration of economic growth that began in Britain in the late eighteenth century and then spread to Western Europe and Europe's off-shoots of large-scale settlement in North America and Austral-asia.[40] There is no question, certainly, that the financial revolution preceded the industrial revolution. True, the decisive breakthroughs in textile manufacturing and iron production, which were the spearheads of the industrial revolution, did not rely very heavily on banks for their financing.[41] But banks played a more important role in continental European industrialization than they did in England's. It may in fact be futile to seek a simplistic causal relationship (more sophisticated financial institutions caused growth or growth spurred on financial development). It seems perfectly plausible that the two processes were interdependent and self-reinforcing. Both processes also exhibited a distinctly evolutionary character, with recurrent mutation (technical innovation), speciation (the creation of new kinds of firm) and punctuated equilibrium (crises that would determine which firms would survive and which would die out).

In the words of Adam Smith, 'The judicious operation of banking, by substituting paper in the room of a great part of . . . gold and silver . . . provides . . . a sort of waggon-way through the air.' In the century after he published *The Wealth of Nations* (1776), there was an explosion of financial innovation which saw a wide variety of different types of bank proliferate in Europe and North America. The longest-established were bill-discounting banks, which helped finance domestic and international trade by discounting the bills of exchange drawn by one merchant on another. Already in Smith's day London was home to a number of highly successful firms like Barings, who specialized in transatlantic merchant banking (as this line of business came to be known). For regulatory reasons, English banks in this period were nearly all private partnerships, some specializing in the business of the City, that square mile of London which for centuries had been the focus for mercantile finance, while others specialized in the business of the landowning elite. These latter were the so-called 'country banks', whose rise and fall closely followed the rise and fall of British agriculture.

A decisive difference between natural evolution and financial evolution is the role of what might be called 'intelligent design' – though in this case the regulators are invariably human, rather than divine. Gradually, by a protracted process of trial and error, the Bank of England developed public functions, in return for the reaffirmation of its monopoly on note issue in 1826, establishing branches in the provinces and gradually taking over the country banks' note-issuing business.* Increasingly, the Bank also came to play a pivotal role in inter-bank transactions. More and more of the clearing of sums owed by one bank to another went through the Bank of England's offices in Threadneedle Street. With the final scrapping in 1833 of the usury laws that limited its discount rate on commercial bills, the Bank was able fully to exploit its scale advantage as the biggest bank in the City. Increasingly, its discount rate was seen as the minimum short-term interest rate in the so-called money market (for short-term credit, mostly through the discounting of commercial bills).

The question that remained unresolved for a further forty years was what the relationship ought to be between the Bank's reserves and its banknote circulation. In the 1840s the position of the Governor, J. Horsley Palmer, was that the reserve should essentially be regulated by the volume of discounting business, so long as one third of it consisted of gold coin or bullion. The Prime Minister, Sir Robert Peel, was suspicious of this arrangement, believing that it ran the risk of excessive banknote creation and inflation. Peel's 1844 Bank Charter Act divided the Bank in two: a banking department, which would carry on the Bank's own commercial business, and an issue department, endowed with £14 million of securities and an unspecified amount of coin and bullion which would fluctuate according to the balance of trade

* Technically, the monopoly applied only within a 65-mile radius of London and, as in the eighteenth century, private banks were not prohibited from issuing notes.

between Britain and the rest of the world. The so-called fiduciary note issue was not to exceed the sum of the securities and the gold. Repeated crises (in 1847, 1857 and 1866) made it clear that this was an excessively rigid straitjacket, however; in each case the Act had to be temporarily suspended to avoid a complete collapse of liquidity.* It was only after the last of these crises, which saw the spectacular run that wrecked the bank of Overend Gurney, that the editor of *The Economist*, Walter Bagehot, reformulated the Bank's proper role in a crisis as the 'lender of last resort', to lend freely, albeit at a penalty rate, to combat liquidity crises.[42]

The Victorian monetary problem was not wholly solved by Bagehot, it should be emphasized. He was no more able than the other pre-eminent economic theorists of the nineteenth century to challenge the sacred principle, established in Sir Isaac Newton's time as Master of the Mint, that a pound sterling should be convertible into a fixed and immutable quantity of gold according to the rate of £3 17s 10½d per ounce of gold. To read contemporary discussion of the gold standard is to appreciate that, in many ways, the Victorians were as much in thrall to precious metal as the conquistadors three centuries before. 'Precious Metals alone are money,' declared one City grandee, Baron Overstone. 'Paper notes are money because they are representations of Metallic Money. Unless so, they are false and spurious pretenders. One depositor can get metal, but all cannot, therefore deposits are not money.'[43] Had that principle been adhered to, and had the money supply of the British economy genuinely hinged on the quantity

---

* Illiquidity is when a firm cannot sell sufficient assets to meet its liabilities. It has the right amount of assets, but they are not marketable because there are too few potential buyers. Insolvency is when the value of the liabilities clearly exceeds the value of the assets. The distinction is harder to draw than is sometimes assumed. A firm in a liquidity crisis might be able to sell its assets, but only at prices so low as to imply insolvency.

of gold coin and bullion in the Bank of England's reserve, the growth of the UK economy would have been altogether choked off, even allowing for the expansionary effects of new gold discoveries in the nineteenth century. So restrictive was Bank of England note issuance that its bullion reserve actually exceeded the value of notes in circulation from the mid 1890s until the First World War. It was only the proliferation of new kinds of bank, and particularly those taking deposits, that made monetary expansion possible. After 1858, the restrictions on joint-stock banking were lifted, paving the way for the emergence of a few big commercial banks: the London & Westminster (founded in 1833), the National Provincial (1834), the Birmingham & Midland (1836), Lloyds (1884) and Barclays (1896). Industrial investment banks of the sort that took off in Belgium (Société Générale), France (the Crédit Mobilier) and Germany (the Darmstädter Bank) fared less well in Britain after the failure of Overend Gurney. The critical need was not in fact for banks to buy large blocks of shares in industrial companies; it was for institutions that would attract savers to hand over their deposits, creating an ever expanding basis for new bank lending on the other side of the balance sheet.

In this process an especially important role was played by the new savings banks that proliferated at the turn of the century. By 1913 British savings bank deposits amounted to £256 million, roughly a quarter of all UK deposits. The assets of German savings banks were more than two and a half times greater than those of the better known 'great banks' like Darmstädter, Deutsche, Dresdner and the Disconto-Gesellschaft. All told, by the eve of the First World War, residents' deposits in British banks totalled nearly £1.2 billion, compared with a total bank-note circulation of just £45.5 million. Money was now primarily inside banks, out of sight, even if never out of mind.

Although there was variation, most advanced economies essentially followed the British lead when it came to regulation through a monopolistic central bank operating the gold standard, and concentration of deposit-taking in a relatively few large institutions. The Banque de France was established in 1800, the German Reichsbank in 1875, the Bank of Japan in 1882 and the Swiss National Bank in 1907. In Britain, as on the Continent, there were marked tendencies towards concentration, exemplified by the decline in the number of country banks from a peak of 755 in 1809 to just seventeen in 1913.

The evolution of finance was quite different in the United States. There the aversion of legislators to the idea of over-mighty financiers twice aborted an embryonic central bank (the first and second Banks of the United States), so that legislation was not passed to create the Federal Reserve System until 1913. Up until that point, the US was essentially engaged in a natural experiment with wholly free banking. The 1864 National Bank Act had significantly reduced the barriers to setting up a privately owned bank, and capital requirements were low by European standards. At the same time, there were obstacles to setting up banks across state lines. The combined effect of these rules was a surge in the number of national and state-chartered banks during the late nineteenth and early twentieth centuries, from fewer than 12,000 in 1899 to more than 30,000 at the peak in 1922. Large numbers of under-capitalized banks were a recipe for financial instability, and panics were a regular feature of American economic life – most spectacularly in the Great Depression, when a major banking crisis was exacerbated rather than mitigated by a monetary authority that had been operational for little more than fifteen years. The introduction of deposit insurance in 1933 did much to reduce the vulnerability of American banks to runs. However, the banking sector remained highly fragmented until 1976, when

Maine became the first state to legalize interstate banking. It was not until 1993, after the Savings and Loans crisis (see Chapter 5), that the number of national banks fell below 3,600 for the first time in nearly a century.

In 1924 John Maynard Keynes famously dismissed the gold standard as a 'barbarous relic'. But the liberation of bank-created money from a precious metal anchor happened slowly. The gold standard had its advantages, no doubt. Exchange rate stability made for predictable pricing in trade and reduced transaction costs, while the long-run stability of prices acted as an anchor for inflation expectations. Being on gold may also have reduced the costs of borrowing by committing governments to pursue prudent fiscal and monetary policies. The difficulty of pegging currencies to a single commodity based standard, or indeed to one another, is that policymakers are then forced to choose between free capital movements and an independent national monetary policy. They cannot have both. A currency peg can mean higher volatility in short-term interest rates, as the central bank seeks to keep the price of its money steady in terms of the peg. It can mean deflation, if the supply of the peg is constrained (as the supply of gold was relative to the demand for it in the 1870s and 1880s). And it can transmit financial crises (as happened throughout the restored gold standard after 1929). By contrast, a system of money based primarily on bank deposits and floating exchange rates is freed from these constraints. The gold standard was a long time dying, but there were few mourners when the last meaningful vestige of it was removed on 15 August 1971, the day that President Richard Nixon closed the so-called gold 'window' through which, under certain restricted circumstances, dollars could still be exchanged for gold. From that day onward, the centuries-old link between money and precious metal was broken.

Bankrupt Nation

Memphis, Tennessee, is famous for blue suede shoes, barbecues and bankruptcies. If you want to understand how today's bankers – the successors to the Medici – deal with the problem of credit risk created by unreliable borrowers, Memphis surely is the place to be.

On average, there are between one and two million bankruptcy cases every year in the United States, nearly all of them involving individuals who elect to go bust rather than meet unmanageable obligations. A strikingly large proportion of them happen in Tennessee. The remarkable thing is how relatively painless this process seems to be – compared, that is, with what went on in sixteenth-century Venice or, for that matter, some parts of present-day Glasgow. Most borrowers who run into difficulties in Memphis can escape or at least reduce their debts, stigma-free and physically unharmed. One of the great puzzles is that the world's most successful capitalist economy seems to be built on a foundation of easy economic failure.

When I visited Memphis for the first time in the early summer of 2007 I was fascinated by the ubiquity and proximity of both easy credit and easy bankruptcy. All I had to do was to take a walk down a typical street near the city centre. First there were the shopping malls and fast food joints, which is where Tennesseans do much of their spending. Right next door was a 'tax advisor' ready to help those short of cash to claim their low-earners' tax credits. I saw a shop offering loans against cars and, next door to it, a second-mortgage company, as well as a cheque-cashing shop offering advances on pay packets (at 200 per cent interest), not to mention a pawnshop the size of a department store. Conveniently located for those who had already pawned all their possessions was a Rent–A–Center offering cheap furniture and televisions for hire. And next door to that? The Plasma Center, offering $55 a go for blood donations. Modern Memphis gives a whole new meaning to the expression 'bled dry'. A pint of blood may not be quite as hard to give up as a pound of flesh, but the general idea seems disconcertingly similar.

Yet the consequences of default in Memphis are far less grave than the risk of death Antonio ran in Venice. After the Plasma Center, my next stop was the office of George Stevenson, one of the lawyers who make a living by advising bankrupts at the United States Bankruptcy Court Western District of Tennessee. At the time of my trip to Tennessee, the annual number of bankruptcy filings in the Memphis area alone was around 10,000, so I wasn't surprised to find the Bankruptcy Court crowded with people. The system certainly appears to work very smoothly. One by one, the individuals and couples who have fallen into insolvency sit down with a lawyer who negotiates on their behalf with their creditors. There is even a fast-track lane for speedy bankruptcies – though on average only three out of five bankrupts are discharged (meaning that an agreement is reached with their creditors).

The ability to walk away from unsustainable debts and start all over again is one of the distinctive quirks of American capitalism. There were no debtors' prisons in the United States in the early 1800s, at a time when English debtors could end up languishing in jail for years. Since 1898, it has been every American's right to file for Chapter VII (liquidation) or XIII (voluntary personal reorganization). Rich and poor alike, people in the United States appear to regard bankruptcy as an 'unalienable right' almost on a par with 'life, liberty and the pursuit of happiness'. The theory is that American law exists to encourage entrepreneurship – to facilitate the creation of new businesses. And that means giving people a break when their plans go wrong, even for the second time, thereby allowing the natural-born risk-takers to learn through trial and error until they finally figure out how to make that million. After all, today's bankrupt might well be tomorrow's successful entrepreneur.

At first sight, the theory certainly seems to work. Many of America's most successful businessmen failed in their early endeavours, including the ketchup king John Henry Heinz, the circus supremo Phineas Barnum and the automobile magnate Henry Ford. All of these men eventually became immensely rich, not least because they were given a chance to try, to fail and to start over. Yet on closer inspection what happens in Tennessee is rather different. The people in the Memphis Bankruptcy Court are not businessmen going bust. They are just ordinary individuals who cannot pay their bills – often the large medical bills that Americans can suddenly face if they are not covered by private health insurance. Bankruptcy may have been designed to help entrepreneurs and their businesses, but nowadays 98 per cent of filings are classified as non-business. The principal driver of bankruptcy turns out to be not entrepreneurship but indebtedness. In 2007 US consumer debt hit a record $2.5 trillion. Back in 1959, consumer debt was equivalent to 16 per cent of disposable personal income. Now it is 24 per cent.* One of the challenges for any financial historian today is to understand the causes of this explosion of household indebtedness and to estimate what the likely consequences will be if, as seems inevitable, there is an increase in the bankruptcy rate in states like Tennessee.

Before we can answer these questions properly, we need to introduce the other key components of the financial system: the

* In the same period mortgage debt has risen from 54 per cent of disposable personal income to 140 per cent.

bond market, the stock market, the insurance market, the real estate market and the extraordinary globalization of all these markets that has taken place over the past twenty years. The root cause, however, must lie in the evolution of money and the banks whose liabilities are its key component. The inescapable reality seems to be that breaking the link between money creation and a metallic anchor has led to an unprecedented monetary expansion – and with it a credit boom the like of which the world has never seen. Measuring liquidity as the ratio of broad money to output* over the past hundred years, it is very clear that the trend since the 1970s has been for that ratio to rise – in the case of broad money in the major developed economies from around 70 per cent before the closing of the gold window to more than 100 per cent by 2005.[44] In the eurozone, the increase has been especially steep, from just over 60 per cent as recently as 1990 to just under 90 per cent today. At the same time, the capital adequacy of banks in the developed world has been slowly but steadily declining. In Europe bank capital is now equivalent to less than 10 per cent of assets, compared with around 25 per cent at the beginning of the twentieth century.[45] In other words, banks are not only taking in more deposits; they are lending out a greater proportion of them, and minimizing their capital base. Today, banking assets (that is, loans) in the world's major economies are equivalent to around 150 per cent of those countries' combined GDP.[46] According to the Bank for International Settlements, total international banking assets in December 2006 were equivalent to around $29 trillion, roughly 63 per cent of world GDP.[47]

Is it any wonder, then, that money has ceased to hold its value

* A ratio known to economists as Marshallian k after the economist Alfred Marshall. Strictly speaking, k is the ratio of the monetary base to nominal GDP.

The New York closing price of gold ($ per oz., log scale), 1908–2008

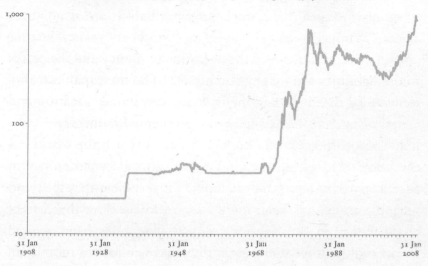

in the way that it did in the era of the gold standard? The modern-day dollar bill acquired its current design in 1957. Since then its purchasing power, relative to the consumer price index, has declined by a staggering 87 per cent. Average annual inflation in that period has been over 4 per cent, twice the rate Europe experienced during the so-called price revolution unleashed by the silver of Potosí. A man who had exchanged his $1,000 of savings for gold in 1970, while the gold window was still ajar, would have received just over 26.6 ounces of the precious metal. At the time of writing, with gold trading at close to $1,000 an ounce, he could have sold his gold for $26,596.

A world without money would be worse, much worse, than our present world. It is wrong to think (as Shakespeare's Antonio did) of all lenders of money as mere leeches, sucking the life's blood out of unfortunate debtors. Loan sharks may behave that way, but banks have evolved since the days of the Medici precisely in order (as the 3rd Lord Rothschild succinctly put it), to 'facilitate the movement of money from point A, where it is, to point B, where it is needed'.[48] Credit and debt, in short, are among the essential building blocks of economic development, as vital to creating the wealth of nations as mining, manufacturing or mobile telephony. Poverty, by contrast, is seldom directly attributable to the antics of rapacious financiers. It often has more to do with the lack of financial institutions, with the absence of banks, not their presence. It is only when borrowers in places like the East End of Glasgow have access to efficient credit networks that they can escape from the clutches of the loan sharks; only when savers can put their money in reliable banks that it can be channelled from the idle to the industrious.

The evolution of banking was thus the essential first step in the ascent of money. The financial crisis that began in August 2007 had relatively little to do with traditional bank lending or, indeed, with bankruptcies, which (because of a legal change) actually declined in 2007. Its prime cause was the rise and fall of 'securitized lending', which allowed banks to originate loans but then repackage and sell them on. And that was only possible because the rise of banks was followed by the ascent of the second great pillar of the modern financial system: the bond market.

2

Of Human Bondage

Early in Bill Clinton's first hundred days as president, his campaign manager James Carville made a remark that has since become famous. 'I used to think if there was reincarnation, I wanted to come back as the president or the pope or a .400 baseball hitter,' he told the *Wall Street Journal*. 'But now I want to come back as the bond market. You can intimidate everybody.' Rather to his surprise, bond prices had risen in the wake of the previous November's election, a movement that had actually preceded a speech by the president in which he pledged to reduce the federal deficit. 'That investment market, they're a tough crowd,' observed Treasury Secretary Lloyd Bentsen. 'Is this a credible effort [by the president]? Is the administration going to hang in there pushing it? They have so judged it.' If bond prices continued to rally, said Federal Reserve Chairman Alan Greenspan, it would be 'by far the most potent [economic] stimulus that I can imagine.'[1] What could make public officials talk with such reverence, even awe, about a mere market for the buying and selling of government IOUs?

After the creation of credit by banks, the birth of the bond was the second great revolution in the ascent of money. Governments (and large corporations) issue bonds as a way of borrowing money from a broader range of people and institutions than just

Japanese government ten-year bonds, complete with coupons

banks. Take the example of a Japanese government ten-year bond with a face value of 100,000 yen and a fixed interest rate or 'coupon' of 1.5 per cent – a tiny part of the vast 838 trillion yen mountain of public debt that Japan has accumulated, mostly since the 1980s. The bond embodies a promise by the Japanese government to pay 1.5 per cent of 100,000 yen every year for the next ten years to whoever owns the bond. The initial purchaser of the bond has the right to sell it whenever he likes at whatever price the market sets. At the time of writing, that price is around 102,333 yen. Why? Because the mighty bond market says so.

From modest beginnings in the city-states of northern Italy some eight hundred years ago, the market for bonds has grown to a vast size. The total value of internationally traded bonds today is around $18 trillion. The value of bonds traded domestically (such as Japanese bonds owned by Japanese investors) is a staggering $50 trillion. All of us, whether we like it or not (and most of us do not even know it), are affected by the bond market in two important ways. First, a large part of the money we put aside for our old age ends up being invested in the bond market. Secondly, because of its huge size, and because big governments are regarded as the most reliable of borrowers, it is the bond market that sets long-term interest rates for the economy as a whole. When bond prices fall, interest rates soar, with painful consequences for all borrowers. The way it works is this. Someone has 100,000 yen they wish to save. Buying a 100,000 yen bond keeps the capital sum safe while also providing regular payments to the saver. To be precise, the bond pays a fixed rate or 'coupon' of 1.5 per cent: 1,500 yen a year in the case of a 100,000 yen bond. But the *market* interest rate or current yield is calculated by dividing the coupon by the market price, which is currently 102,333 yen: 1,500 ÷ 102,333 = 1.47 per cent.* Now imagine a scenario in which the bond market took fright at the huge size of the Japanese government's debt. Suppose investors began to worry that Japan might be unable to meet the annual payments to which it had committed itself. Or suppose they began to worry about the health of the Japanese currency, the yen, in which bonds are denominated and in which the interest is paid. In such circumstances, the price of the bond would drop as nervous investors sold off their holdings. Buyers would only be found at a price low enough to compensate them for the increased risk of a Japanese default or currency depreciation. Let us imagine the

* This should not be confused with the yield to maturity, which takes account of the amount of time before the bond is redeemed at par by the issuing government.

price of our bond fell to 80,000. Then the yield would be 1,500 ÷ 80,000 = 1.88 per cent. At a stroke, long-term interest rates for the Japanese economy as a whole would have jumped by just over two fifths of one per cent, from 1.47 per cent to 1.88. People who had invested in bonds for their retirement before the market move would be 22 per cent worse off, since their capital would have declined by as much as the bond price. And people who wanted to take out a mortgage after the market move would find themselves paying at least 0.41 per cent a year (in market parlance, 41 basis points) more. In the words of Bill Gross, who runs the world's largest bond fund at the Pacific Investment Management Company (PIMCO), 'bond markets have power because they're the fundamental base for all markets. The cost of credit, the interest rate [on a benchmark bond], ultimately determines the value of stocks, homes, all asset classes.'

From a politician's point of view, the bond market is powerful partly because it passes a daily judgement on the credibility of every government's fiscal and monetary policies. But its real power lies in its ability to punish a government with higher borrowing costs. Even an upward move of half a percentage point can hurt a government that is running a deficit, adding higher debt service to its already high expenditures. As in so many financial relationships, there is a feedback loop. The higher interest payments make the deficit even larger. The bond market raises its eyebrows even higher. The bonds sell off again. The interest rates go up again. And so on. Sooner or later the government faces three stark alternatives. Does it default on a part of its debt, fulfilling the bond market's worst fears? Or, to reassure the bond market, does it cut expenditures in some other area, upsetting voters or vested interests? Or does it try to reduce the deficit by raising taxes? The bond market began by facilitating government borrowing. In a crisis, however, it can end up dictating government policy.

So how did this 'Mr Bond' become so much more powerful than the Mr Bond created by Ian Fleming? Why, indeed, do both kinds of bond have a licence to kill?

Mountains of Debt

'War', declared the ancient Greek philosopher Heraclitus, 'is the father of all things.' It was certainly the father of the bond market. In Pieter van der Heyden's extraordinary engraving, *The Battle about Money*, piggy banks, money bags, barrels of coins, and treasure chests – most of them heavily armed with swords, knives and lances – attack each other in a chaotic free-for-all. The Dutch verses below the engraving say: 'It's all for money and goods, this fighting and quarrelling.' But what the inscription could equally well have said is: 'This fighting is possible only if you can raise the money to pay for it.' The ability to finance war through a market for government debt was, like so much else in financial history, an invention of the Italian Renaissance.

For much of the fourteenth and fifteenth centuries, the medieval city-states of Tuscany – Florence, Pisa and Siena – were at war with each other or with other Italian towns. This was war waged as much by money as by men. Rather than require their own citizens to do the dirty work of fighting, each city hired military contractors (*condottieri*) who raised armies to annex land and loot treasure from its rivals. Among the *condottieri* of the 1360s and 1370s one stood head and shoulders above the others. His commanding figure can still be seen on the walls of Florence's Duomo – a painting originally commissioned by a grateful Florentine public as a tribute to his 'incomparable leadership'. Unlikely though it may seem, this master mercenary was an Essex boy born and raised in Sible Hedingham. So skilfully did Sir John

Pieter van der Heyden after Pieter Bruegel the Elder, *The Battle about Money*, after 1570. The Dutch inscription reads: 'It's all for money and goods, this fighting and quarrelling.'

Hawkwood wage war on their behalf that the Italians called him *Giovanni Acuto*, John the Acute. The Castello di Montecchio outside Florence was one of many pieces of real estate the Florentines gave him as a reward for his services. Yet Hawkwood was a mercenary, who was willing to fight for anyone who would pay him, including Milan, Padua, Pisa or the pope. Dazzling frescos in Florence's Palazzo Vecchio show the armies of Pisa and Florence clashing in 1364, at a time when Hawkwood was fighting for Pisa. Fifteen years later, however, he had switched to serve Florence, and spent the rest of his military career in that city's employ. Why? Because Florence was where the money was.

The cost of incessant war had plunged Italy's city-states into crisis. Expenditures even in years of peace were running at double tax revenues. To pay the likes of Hawkwood, Florence was drowning in deficits. You can still see in the records of the Tuscan State Archives how the city's debt burden increased a hundred-fold from 50,000 florins at the beginning of the fourteenth century to 5 million by 1427.[2] It was literally a mountain of debt – hence its name: the *monte commune* or communal debt mountain.[3] By the early fifteenth century, borrowed money accounted for nearly 70 per cent of the city's revenue. The 'mountain' was equivalent to more than half the Florentine economy's annual output.

From whom could the Florentines possibly have borrowed such a huge sum? The answer is from themselves. Instead of paying a property tax, wealthier citizens were effectively obliged to lend money to their own city government. In return for these forced loans (*prestanze*), they received interest. Technically, this was not usury (which, as we have seen, was banned by the Church) since the loans were obligatory; interest payments could therefore be reconciled with canon law as compensation (*damnum emergens*) for the real or putative costs arising from a compulsory investment. As Hostiensis (or Henry) of Susa put it in around 1270:

If some merchant, who is accustomed to pursue trade and the commerce of fairs, and there profit from, has, out of charity to me, who needs it badly, lent money with which he would have done business, I remain obliged to his *interesse* [note this early use of the term 'interest'] . . .[4]

A crucial feature of the Florentine system was that such loans could be sold to other citizens if an investor needed ready money; in other words, they were relatively liquid assets, even though the bonds at this time were no more than a few lines in a leather-bound ledger.

In effect, then, Florence turned its citizens into its biggest investors. By the early fourteenth century, two thirds of households had contributed in this way to financing the public debt, though the bulk of subscriptions were accounted for by a few thousand wealthy individuals.[5] The Medici entries in the 'Ruolo delle prestanze' testify not only to the scale of their wealth at this time, but also to the extent of their contributions to the city-state's coffers. One reason that this system worked so well was that they and a few other wealthy families also controlled the city's government and hence its finances. This oligarchical power structure gave the bond market a firm political foundation. Unlike an unaccountable hereditary monarch, who might arbitrarily renege on his promises to pay his creditors, the people who issued the bonds in Florence were in large measure the same people who bought them. Not surprisingly, they therefore had a strong interest in seeing that their interest was paid.

Nevertheless, there was a limit to how many more or less unproductive wars could be waged in this way. The larger the debts of the Italian cities became, the more bonds they had to issue; and the more bonds they issued, the greater the risk that they might default on their commitments. Venice had in fact developed a system of public debt even earlier than Florence, in the late twelfth century. The *monte vecchio* (Old Mountain) as the consolidated debt was known, played a key role in funding Venice's fourteenth-century wars with Genoa and other rivals. A new mountain of debt arose after the protracted war with the Turks that raged between 1463 and 1479: the *monte nuovo*.[6] Investors received annual interest of 5 per cent, paid twice yearly from the city's various excise taxes (which were levied on articles of consumption like salt). Like the Florentine *prestanze*, the Venetian *prestiti* were forced loans, but with a secondary market which allowed investors to sell their bonds to other investors for cash.[7] In the late fifteenth century, however, a series of Venetian military reverses greatly weakened the market for *prestiti*. Having stood at 80 (20 per cent below their face value) in 1497, the bonds of the Venetian *monte nuovo* were worth just 52 by 1500, recovering to 75 by the end of 1502 and then collapsing from 102 to 40 in 1509. At their low points in the years 1509 to 1529, *monte vecchio* sold at just 3 and *monte nuovo* at 10.[8]

Now, if you buy a government bond while war is raging you are obviously taking a risk, the risk that the state in question may not pay your interest. On the other hand, remember that the interest is paid on the *face value* of the bond, so if you can buy a 5 per cent bond at just 10 per cent of its face value you can earn a handsome yield of 50 per cent. In essence, you expect a return proportional to the risk you are prepared to take. At the same time, as we have seen, it is the bond market that sets interest rates for the economy as a whole. If the state has to pay 50 per cent, then even reliable commercial borrowers are likely to pay some kind of war premium. It is no coincidence that the year 1499, when Venice was fighting both on land in Lombardy and at sea against the Ottoman Empire, saw a severe financial crisis as bonds crashed in value and interest rates soared.[9] Likewise, the bond market rout of 1509 was a direct result of the defeat of the Venetian armies at Agnadello. The result in each case was the same: business ground to a halt.

It was not only the Italian city-states that contributed to the rise of the bond market. In Northern Europe, too, urban polities grappled with the problem of financing their deficits without falling foul of the Church. Here a somewhat different solution was arrived at. Though they prohibited the charging of interest on a loan (*mutuum*), the usury laws did not apply to the medieval contract known as the *census*, which allowed one party to buy a stream of annual payments from another. In the thirteenth century, such annuities started to be issued by northern French towns like Douai and Calais and Flemish towns like Ghent. They took one of two forms: *rentes heritables* or *erfelijkrenten*, perpetual revenue streams which the purchaser could bequeath to his heirs, or *rentes viagères* or *lijfrenten*, which ended with the purchaser's death. The seller, but not the buyer, had the right to redeem the *rente* by repaying the principal. By the mid sixteenth century, the sale of annuities was raising roughly 7 per cent of the revenues of the province of Holland.[10]

Both the French and Spanish crowns sought to raise money in the same way, but they had to use towns as intermediaries. In the French case, funds were raised on behalf of the monarch by the Paris *hôtel de ville*; in the Spanish case, royal *juros* had to be marketed through Genoa's Casa di San Giorgio (a private syndicate that purchased the right to collect the city's taxes) and Antwerp's *beurs*, a forerunner of the modern stock market. Yet investors in royal debt had to be wary. Whereas towns, with their oligarchical forms of rule and locally held debts, had incentives not to default, the same was not true of absolute rulers. As we saw in Chapter 1, the Spanish crown became a serial defaulter in the late sixteenth and seventeenth centuries, wholly or partially suspending payments to creditors in 1557, 1560, 1575, 1596, 1607, 1627, 1647, 1652 and 1662.[11]

Part of the reason for Spain's financial difficulties was the extreme costliness of trying and failing to bring to heel the rebellious provinces of the northern Netherlands, whose revolt against Spanish rule was a watershed in financial as well as political history. With their republican institutions, the United Provinces combined the advantages of the city-state with the scale of a nation-state. They were able to finance their wars by developing Amsterdam as the market for a whole range of new securities: not only life and perpetual annuities, but also lottery loans (whereby investors bought a small probability of a large return). By 1650 there were more than 65,000 Dutch *rentiers*, men who had invested their capital in one or other of these debt instruments and thereby helped finance the long Dutch struggle to preserve their independence. As the Dutch progressed from self-defence to imperial expansion, their debt mountain grew high indeed, from 50 million guilders in 1632 to 250 million in 1752. Yet the yield on Dutch bonds declined steadily, to a low of just 2.5 per cent in 1747 – a sign not only that capital was abundant in the United Provinces, but also that investors had little fear of an outright Dutch default.[12]

With the Glorious Revolution of 1688, which ousted the Catholic James II from the English throne in favour of the Dutch Protestant Prince of Orange, these and other innovations crossed the English Channel from Amsterdam to London. The English fiscal system was already significantly different from that of the continental monarchies. The lands owned by the crown had been sold off earlier than elsewhere, increasing the power of parliaments to control royal expenditure at a time when their powers were waning in Spain, France and the German lands. There was already an observable move in the direction of a professional civil service, reliant on salaries rather than peculation. The Glorious Revolution accentuated this divergence. From now on there would be no more regular defaulting (the 'Stop of Exchequer' of 1672, when, with the crown deep in debt, Charles II had suspended payment of his bills, was still fresh in the memories of London investors). There would be no more debasement of the coinage, particularly after the adoption of the gold standard in 1717. There would be parliamentary scrutiny of royal finances. And there would be a sustained effort to consolidate the various debts that the Stuart dynasty had incurred over the years, a process that culminated in 1749 with the creation by Sir Henry Pelham of the Consolidated Fund*.[13] This was the very opposite of the financial direction taken in France,

* Hence the name 'consols' for the new standardized British government bonds.

where defaults continued to happen regularly; offices were sold to raise money rather than to staff the civil service; tax collection was privatized or farmed out; budgets were rare and scarcely intelligible; the Estates General (the nearest thing to a French parliament) had ceased to meet; and successive controllers-general struggled to raise money by issuing *rentes* and *tontines* (annuities sold on the lives of groups of people) on terms that were excessively generous to investors.[14] In London by the mid eighteenth century there was a thriving bond market, in which government consols were the dominant securities traded, bonds that were highly liquid – in other words easy to sell – and attractive to foreign (especially Dutch) investors.[15] In Paris, by contrast, there was no such thing. It was a financial divergence that would prove to have profound political consequences.

Since it was arguably the most successful bond ever issued, it is worth pausing to look more closely at the famed British consol. By the late eighteenth century it was possible to invest in two types: those bearing a 3 per cent coupon, and those bearing a 5 per cent coupon. They were otherwise identical, in that they were perpetual bonds, without a fixed maturity date, which could be bought back (redeemed) by the government only if their market price equalled or exceeded their face value (par). The illustration opposite shows a typical consol, a partially printed, partially handwritten receipt, stating the amount invested, the face value of the security, the investor's name and the date:

Received this 22 Day of January 1796 of Mrs. Anna Hawes the Sum of One hundred and one pounds being the Consideration for One hundred pounds Interest or Share in the Capital or Joint Stock of Five per Cent Annuities, consolidated July 6th, 1785 ... transferable at the Bank of England ...

A 5 per cent consol purchased by Anna Hawes in January 1796

Given that she paid £101 for a £100 consol, Mrs Hawes was securing an annual yield on her investment of 4.95 per cent. This was not an especially well-timed investment. April that year saw the first victory at Montenotte of a French army led by a young Corsican commander named Napoleon Bonaparte. He won again at Lodi in May. For the next two decades, this man would pose a greater threat to the security and financial stability of the British Empire, not to mention the peace of Europe, than all the Habsburgs and Bourbons put together. Defeating him would lead to the rise of yet another mountain of debt. And as the mountain rose, so the price of individual consols declined – by as much as 30 per cent at the lowest point in Britain's fortunes.

The meteoric rise of a diminutive Corsican to be Emperor of France and master of the European continent was an event few could have predicted in 1796, least of all Mrs Anna Hawes. Yet an even more remarkable (and more enduring) feat of social mobility was to happen in almost exactly the same timeframe. Within just a few years of Napoleon's final defeat at Waterloo, a man who had grown up amid the gloom of the Frankfurt ghetto had emerged as a financial Bonaparte: the master of the bond market and, some ventured to suggest, the master of European politics as well. That man's name was Nathan Rothschild.

The Bonaparte of Finance

Master of unbounded wealth, he boasts that he is the arbiter of peace and war, and that the credit of nations depends upon his nod; his correspondents are innumerable; his couriers outrun those of sovereign princes, and absolute sovereigns; ministers of state are in his pay. Paramount in the cabinets of continental Europe, he aspires to the domination of our own.[16]

Those words were spoken in 1828 by the Radical MP Thomas Dunscombe. The man he was referring to was Nathan Mayer Rothschild, founder of the London branch of what was, for most of the nineteenth century, the biggest bank in the world.[17] It was the bond market that made the Rothschild family rich – rich enough to build forty-one stately homes all over Europe, among them Waddesdon Manor in Buckinghamshire, which has been restored in all its gilded glory by the 4th Lord Rothschild, Nathan's great-great-great-grandson. His illustrious forebear, according to Lord Rothschild, was 'short, fat, obsessive, extremely clever, wholly focused . . . I can't imagine he would have been a very pleasant person to have dealings with.' His cousin Evelyn de Rothschild takes a similar view. 'I think he was very ambitious,' he says, contemplating Nathan Rothschild's portrait in the boardroom at the offices of N. M. Rothschild in London's

St Swithin's Lane, 'and I think he was very determined. I don't think he suffered fools lightly.'

Though the Rothschilds were compulsive correspondents, relatively few of Nathan's letters to his brothers have survived. There is one page, however, that clearly conveys the kind of man he was. Written, like all their letters, in almost indecipherable *Judendeutsch* (German transliterated into Hebrew characters), it epitomizes what might be called his Jewish work ethic and his impatience with his less mercurial brothers:

I am writing to you giving my opinion, as it is my damned duty to write to you . . . I am reading through your letters not just once but maybe a hundred times. You can well imagine that yourself. After dinner I usually have nothing to do. I do not read books, I do not play cards, I do not go to the theatre, my only pleasure is my business and in this way I read Amschel's, Salomon's, James's and Carl's letters . . . As far as Carl's letter [about buying a bigger house in Frankfurt] is concerned . . . all this is a lot of nonsense because as long as we have good business and are rich everybody will flatter us and those who have no interest in obtaining revenues through us begrudge us for it all. Our Salomon is too good and agreeable to anything and anybody and if a parasite whispers something into his ear he thinks that all human beings are noble minded[;] the truth is that all they are after is their own interest.[18]

Small wonder his brothers called Nathan 'the general in chief'. 'All you ever write', complained Salomon wearily in 1815, 'is pay this, pay that, send this, send that.'[19] It was this phenomenal drive, allied to innate financial genius, that propelled Nathan from the obscurity of the Frankfurt *Judengasse* to mastery of the London bond market. Once again, however, the opportunity for financial innovation was provided by war.

*

On the morning of 18 June 1815, 67,000 British, Dutch and German troops under the Duke of Wellington's command looked out across the fields of Waterloo, not far from Brussels, towards an almost equal number of French troops commanded by the French Emperor, Napoleon Bonaparte. The Battle of Waterloo was the culmination of more than two decades of intermittent conflict between Britain and France. But it was more than a battle between two armies. It was also a contest between rival financial systems: one, the French, which under Napoleon had come to be based on plunder (the taxation of the conquered); the other, the British, based on debt.

Never had so many bonds been issued to finance a military conflict. Between 1793 and 1815 the British national debt increased by a factor of three, to £745 million, more than double the annual output of the UK economy. But this increase in the supply of bonds had weighed heavily on the London market. Since February 1792, the price of a typical £100 3 per cent consol had fallen from £96 to below £60 on the eve of Waterloo, at one time (in 1797) sinking below £50. These were trying times for the likes of Mrs Anna Hawes.

According to a long-standing legend, the Rothschild family owed the first millions of their fortune to Nathan's successful speculation about the effect of the outcome of the battle on the price of British bonds. In some versions of the story, Nathan witnessed the battle himself, risked a Channel storm to reach London ahead of the official news of Wellington's victory and, by buying bonds ahead of a huge surge in prices, pocketed between £20 and £135 million. It was a legend the Nazis later did their best to embroider. In 1940 Joseph Goebbels approved the release of *Die Rothschilds*, which depicts an oleaginous Nathan bribing a French general to ensure the Duke of Wellington's victory, and then deliberately misreporting the outcome in

London in order to precipitate panic selling of British bonds, which he then snaps up at bargain-basement prices. Yet the reality was altogether different.[20] Far from making money from Wellington's victory, the Rothschilds were very nearly ruined by it. Their fortune was made not because of Waterloo, but despite it.

After a series of miscued interventions, British troops had been fighting against Napoleon on the Continent since August 1808, when the future Duke of Wellington, then Lieutenant-General Sir Arthur Wellesley, led an expeditionary force to Portugal, invaded by the French the previous year. For the better part of the next six years, there would be a recurrent need to get men and *matériel* to the Iberian Peninsula. Selling bonds to the public had certainly raised plenty of cash for the British government, but banknotes were of little use on distant battlefields. To provision the troops and pay Britain's allies against France, Wellington needed a currency that was universally acceptable. The challenge was to transform the money raised on the bond market into gold coins, and to get them to where they were needed. Sending gold guineas from London to Lisbon was expensive and hazardous in time of war. But when the Portuguese merchants declined to accept the bills of exchange that Wellington proffered, there seemed little alternative but to ship cash.

The son of a moderately successful Frankfurt antique dealer and bill broker, Nathan Rothschild had arrived in England only in 1799 and had spent most of the next ten years in the newly industrializing North of England, purchasing textiles and shipping them back to Germany. He did not go into the banking business in London until 1811. Why, then, did the British government turn to him in its hour of financial need? The answer is that Nathan had acquired valuable experience as a smuggler of gold to the Continent, in breach of the blockade that Napoleon had imposed on trade between England and Europe. (Admittedly, it was a breach the French authorities tended to wink at, in the simplistic mercantilist belief that outflows of gold from England must tend to weaken the British war effort.) In January 1814, the Chancellor of the Exchequer authorized the Commissary-in-Chief, John Charles Herries, to 'employ that gentleman [Nathan] in the most secret and confidential manner to collect in Germany, France and Holland the largest quantity of French gold and silver coins, not exceeding in value £600,000, which he may be able to procure within two months from the present time.' These were then to be delivered to British vessels at the Dutch port of Helvoetsluys and sent on to Wellington, who had by now crossed the Pyrenees into France. It was an immense operation, which depended on the brothers' ability to tap their cross-Channel credit network and to manage large-scale bullion transfers. They executed their commission so well that Wellington was soon writing to express his gratitude for the 'ample . . . supplies of money'. As Herries put it: 'Rothschild of this place has executed the various services entrusted to him in this line admirably well, and though a Jew [sic], we place a good deal of confidence in him.' By May 1814 Nathan had advanced nearly £1.2 million to the government, double the amount envisaged in his original instructions.

Mobilizing such vast amounts of gold even at the tail end of a war was risky, no doubt. Yet from the Rothschilds' point of view, the hefty commissions they were able to charge more than justified the risks. What made them so well suited to the task was that the brothers had a ready-made banking network within the family – Nathan in London, Amschel in Frankfurt, James (the youngest) in Paris, Carl in Amsterdam and Salomon roving wherever Nathan saw fit. Spread out around Europe, the five Rothschilds were uniquely positioned to exploit price and exchange rate differences between markets, the process known as arbitrage. If the price of gold was higher in, say, Paris than in London, James in Paris would sell gold for bills of exchange, then send these to London, where Nathan would use them to buy a larger quantity of gold. The fact that their own transactions on Herries's behalf were big enough to affect such price differentials only added to the profitability of the business. In addition, the Rothschilds also handled some of the large subsidies paid to Britain's continental allies. By June 1814, Herries calculated that they had effected payments of this sort to a value of 12.6 million francs. 'Mr Rothschild', remarked the Prime Minister, Lord Liverpool, had become 'a very useful friend'. As he told the Foreign Secretary Lord Castlereagh, 'I do not know what we should have done without him . . .'. By now his brothers had taken to calling Nathan the master of the Stock Exchange.

After his abdication in April 1814, Napoleon had been exiled to the small Italian island of Elba, which he proceeded to rule as an empire in miniature. It was too small to hold him. On 1 March 1815, to the consternation of the monarchs and ministers gathered to restore the old European order at the Congress of Vienna, he returned to France, determined to revive his Empire. Veterans of the *grande armée* rallied to his standard. Nathan Rothschild responded to this 'unpleasant news' by immediately resuming gold purchases, buying up all the bullion and coins he and his brothers could lay their hands on, and making it available to Herries for shipment to Wellington. In all, the Rothschilds provided gold coins worth more than £2 million – enough to fill 884 boxes and fifty-five casks. At the same time, Nathan offered to take care of a fresh round of subsidies to Britain's continental allies, bringing the total of his transactions with Herries in 1815 to just under £9.8 million. With commissions on all this business ranging from 2 to 6 per cent, Napoleon's return promised to make the Rothschilds rich men. Yet there was a risk that Nathan had underestimated. In furiously buying up such a huge quantity of gold, he had assumed that, as with all Napoleon's wars, this would be a long one. It was a near fatal miscalculation.

Wellington famously called the Battle of Waterloo 'the nearest run thing you ever saw in your life'. After a day of brutal charges, countercharges and heroic defence, the belated arrival of the Prussian army finally proved decisive. For Wellington, it was a glorious victory. Not so for the Rothschilds. No doubt it was gratifying for Nathan Rothschild to receive the news of Napoleon's defeat first, thanks to the speed of his couriers, nearly forty-eight hours before Major Henry Percy delivered Wellington's official despatch to the Cabinet. No matter how early it reached him, however, the news was anything but good from Nathan's point of view. He had expected nothing as decisive so soon. Now he and his brothers were sitting on top of a pile of cash that nobody needed – to pay for a war that was over. With the coming of peace, the great armies that had fought Napoleon could be disbanded, the coalition of allies dissolved. That meant no more soldiers' wages and no more subsidies to Britain's wartime allies. The price of gold, which had soared during the war, would be bound to fall. Nathan was faced not with the immense profits of legend but with heavy and growing losses.

But there was one possible way out: the Rothschilds could use their gold to make a massive and hugely risky bet on the bond market. On 20 July 1815 the evening edition of the London *Courier* reported that Nathan had made 'great purchases of stock', meaning British government bonds. Nathan's gamble was that the British victory at Waterloo, and the prospect of a reduction in government borrowing, would send the price of British bonds soaring upwards. Nathan bought more and, as the price of consols duly began to rise, he kept on buying. Despite

The price of consols (UK perpetual bonds), 1812–1822

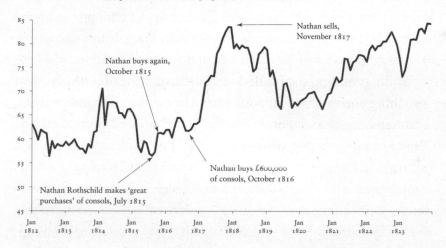

his brothers' desperate entreaties to realize profits, Nathan held his nerve for another year. Eventually, in late 1817, with bond prices up more than 40 per cent, he sold. Allowing for the effects on the purchasing power of sterling of inflation and economic growth, his profits were worth around £600 million today. It was one of the most audacious trades in financial history, one which snatched financial victory from the jaws of Napoleon's military defeat. The resemblance between victor and vanquished was not lost on contemporaries. In the words of one of the partners at Barings, the Rothschilds' great rivals, 'I must candidly confess that I have not the nerve for his operations. They are generally well planned, with great cleverness and adroitness in execution – but he is in money and funds what Bonaparte was in war.'[21] To the Austrian Chancellor Prince Metternich's secretary, the Rothschilds were simply *die Finanzbonaparten*.[22] Others went still further, though not without a hint of irony. 'Money is the god of our time,' declared the German poet Heinrich Heine in March 1841, 'and Rothschild is his prophet.'[23]

*

To an extent that even today remains astonishing, the Rothschilds went on to dominate international finance in the half century after Waterloo. So extraordinary did this achievement seem to contemporaries that they often sought to explain it in mystical terms. According to one account dating from the 1830s, the Rothschilds owed their fortune to the possession of a mysterious 'Hebrew talisman' that enabled Nathan Rothschild, the founder of the London house, to become 'the leviathan of the money markets of Europe'.[24] Similar stories were being told in the Pale of Settlement, to which Russian Jews were confined, as late as the 1890s.[25] As we have seen, the Nazis preferred to attribute the rise of the Rothschilds to the manipulation of stock market news and other sharp practice. Such myths are current even today. According to Song Hongbing's best-selling book *Currency Wars*, published in China in 2007, the Rothschilds continue to control the global monetary system through their alleged influence over the Federal Reserve System.[26]

The more prosaic reality was that the Rothschilds were able to build on their successes during the final phase of the Napoleonic Wars to establish themselves as the dominant players in an increasingly international London bond market. They did this by establishing a capital base and an information network that were soon far superior to those of their nearest rivals, the Barings. Between 1815 and 1859, it has been estimated that the London house issued fourteen different sovereign bonds with a face value of nearly £43 million, more than half the total issued by all banks in London.[27] Although British government bonds were the principal security they marketed to investors, they also sold French, Prussian, Russian, Austrian, Neapolitan and Brazilian bonds.[28] In addition, they all but monopolized bond issuance by the Belgian government after 1830. Typically, the Rothschilds would buy a tranche of new bonds outright from a government, charging a commission for distributing these to their network of brokers and investors throughout Europe, and remitting funds to the government only when all the instalments had been received from buyers. There would usually be a generous spread between the price the Rothschilds paid the sovereign borrower and the price they asked of investors (with room for an additional price 'run up' after the initial public offering). Of course, as we have seen, there had been large-scale international lending before, not-ably in Genoa, Antwerp and Amsterdam.[29] But a distinguishing feature of the London bond market after 1815 was the Roths-childs' insistence that most new borrowers issue bonds denomi-nated in sterling, rather than their own currency, and make interest payments in London or one of the other markets where the Rothschilds had branches. A new standard was set by their 1818 initial public offering of Prussian 5 per cent bonds, which – after protracted and often fraught negotiations* – were issued not only in London, but also in Frankfurt, Berlin, Hamburg and Amsterdam.[30] In his book *On the Traffic in State Bonds* (1825), the German legal expert Johann Heinrich Bender singled out this as one of the Rothschilds' most important financial innovations :

* At one point, when the Director of the Prussian Treasury, Christian Rother, attempted to modify the terms after the loan contract had been signed, Nathan exploded: 'Dearest friend, I have now done my duty by God, your king and the Finance Minister von Rother, my money has all gone to you in Berlin . . . now it is your turn and duty to yours, to keep your word and not to come up with new things, and everything must remain as it was agreed between men like us, and that is what I expected, as you can see from my deliveries of money. The cabal there can do nothing against N. M. Rothschild, he has the money, the strength and the power, the cabal has only impotence and the King of Prussia, my Prince Hardenberg and Minister Rother should be well pleased and thank Rothschild, who is sending you so much money [and] raising Prussia's credit.' That a Jew born in the Frankfurt ghetto could write in these terms to a Prussian official speaks volumes about the social revolution Nathan Rothschild and his brothers personified.

'Any owner of government bonds . . . can collect the interest at his convenience in several different places without any effort.'[31] Bond issuance was by no means the only business the Rothschilds did, to be sure: they were also bond traders, currency arbitrageurs, bullion dealers and private bankers, as well as investors in insurance, mines and railways. Yet the bond market remained their core competence. Unlike their lesser competitors, the Rothschilds took pride in dealing only in what would now be called investment grade securities. No bond they issued in the 1820s was in default by 1829, despite a Latin American debt crisis in the middle of the decade (the first of many).

With success came ever greater wealth. When Nathan died in 1836, his personal fortune was equivalent to 0.62 per cent of British national income. Between 1818 and 1852, the combined capital of the five Rothschild 'houses' (Frankfurt, London, Naples, Paris and Vienna) rose from £1.8 million to £9.5 million. As early as 1825 their combined capital was nine times greater than that of Baring Brothers and the Banque de France. By 1899, at £41 million, it exceeded the capital of the five biggest German joint-stock banks put together. Increasingly the firm became a multinational asset manager for the wealth of the managers' extended family. As their numbers grew from generation to generation, familial unity was maintained by a combination of periodically revised contracts between the five houses and a high level of intermarriage between cousins or between uncles and nieces. Of twenty-one marriages involving descendants of Nathan's father Mayer Amschel Rothschild that were solemnized between 1824 and 1877, no fewer than fifteen were between his direct descendants. In addition, the family's collective fidelity to the Jewish faith, at a time when some other Jewish families were slipping into apostasy or mixed marriage, strengthened their sense of common identity and purpose as 'the Caucasian [Jewish] royal family'.

Old Mayer Amschel had repeatedly admonished his five sons: 'If you can't make yourself loved, make yourself feared.' As they bestrode the mid-nineteenth-century financial world as masters of the bond market, the Rothschilds were already more feared than loved. Reactionaries on the Right lamented the rise of a new form of wealth, higher-yielding and more liquid than the landed estates of Europe's aristocratic elites. As Heinrich Heine discerned, there was something profoundly revolutionary about the financial system the Rothschilds were creating:

The system of paper securities frees . . . men to choose whatever place of residence they like; they can live anywhere, without working, from the interest on their bonds, their portable property, and so they gather together and constitute the true power of our capital cities. And we have long known what it portends when the most diverse energies can live side by side, when there is such centralization of the intellectual and of social authority.

In Heine's eyes, Rothschild could now be mentioned in the same breath as Richelieu and Robespierre as one of the 'three terroristic names that spell the gradual annihilation of the old aristocracy'. Richelieu had destroyed its power; Robespierre had decapitated its decadent remnant; now Rothschild was providing Europe with a new social elite by

raising up the system of government bonds to supreme power . . . [and] endowing money with the former privileges of land. To be sure, he has thereby created a new aristocracy, but this is based on the most unreliable of elements, on money . . . [which] is more fluid than water and less steady than the air . . .[32]

Meanwhile, Radicals on the Left bemoaned the rise of a new power in the realm of politics, which wielded a veto power over government finance and hence over most policy. Following the success of Rothschild bond issues for Austria, Prussia and Russia, Nathan was caricatured as the insurance broker to the 'Hollow Alliance', helping to protect Europe against liberal political fires.[33] In 1821 he even received a death threat because of 'his connexion with foreign powers, and particularly the assistance rendered to Austria, on account of the designs of that government against the liberties of Europe'.[34] The liberal historian Jules Michelet noted in his journal in 1842: 'M. Rothschild knows Europe prince by prince, and the bourse courtier by courtier. He has all their accounts in his head, that of the courtiers and that of the kings; he talks to them without even consulting his books. To one such he says: "Your account will go into the red if you appoint such a minister."'[35] Predictably, the fact that the Rothschilds were Jewish gave a new impetus to deep-rooted anti-Semitic prejudices. No sooner had the Rothschilds appeared on the American scene in the 1830s than the governor of Mississippi was denouncing 'Baron Rothschild' for having 'the blood of Judas and Shylock flow[ing] in his veins, and . . . unit[ing] the qualities of both his countrymen.' Later in the century, the Populist writer 'Coin' Harvey would depict the Rothschild bank as a vast, black octopus stretching its tentacles around the world.[36]

Yet it was the Rothschilds' seeming ability to permit or prohibit wars at will that seemed to arouse the most indignation. As early as 1828, Prince Pückler-Muskau referred to 'Rothschild . . . without whom no power in Europe today seems able to make war'.[37] One early-twentieth-century commentator* pointedly posed the question:

* This was J. A. Hobson, author of *Imperialism: A Study* (1902). Though still renowned as one of the earliest liberal critics of imperialism, Hobson articulated a classically anti-Semitic hostility towards finance: 'In handling large masses of stocks and shares, in floating companies, in manipulating fluctuations of values, the magnates of the Bourse find their gain. These

Does anyone seriously suppose that a great war could be undertaken by any European State, or any great State loan subscribed, if the house of Rothschild and its connexions set their face against it?[38]

It might, indeed, be assumed that the Rothschilds needed war. It was war, after all, that had generated Nathan Rothschild's biggest deal. Without wars, nineteenth-century states would have had little need to issue bonds. As we have seen, however, wars tended to hit the price of existing bonds by increasing the risk that (like sixteenth-century Venice) a debtor state would fail to meet its interest payments in the event of defeat and losses of territory. By the middle of the nineteenth century, the Rothschilds had evolved from traders into fund managers, carefully tending to their own vast portfolio of government bonds. Now, having made their money, they stood to lose more than they gained from conflict. It was for this reason that they were consistently hostile to strivings for national unity in both Italy and Germany. And it was for this reason that they viewed with unease the descent of the United States into internecine warfare. The Rothschilds had decided the outcome of the Napoleonic Wars by putting their financial weight behind Britain. Now they would help decide the outcome of the American Civil War – by choosing to sit on the sidelines.

---

great businesses – banking, broking, bill discounting, loan floating, company promoting – form the central ganglion of international capitalism. United by the strongest bonds of organisation, always in closest and quickest touch with one another, situated in the very heart of the business capital of every State, controlled, so far as Europe is concerned, chiefly by men of a single and peculiar race, who have behind them many centuries of financial experience, they are in a unique position to control the policy of nations.'

Driving Dixie Down

In May 1863, two years into the American Civil War, Major-General Ulysses S. Grant captured Jackson, the Mississippi state capital, and forced the Confederate army under Lieutenant-General John C. Pemberton to retreat westward to Vicksburg on the banks of the Mississippi River. Surrounded, with Union gunboats bombarding their positions from behind, Pemberton's army repulsed two Union assaults but they were finally starved into submission by a grinding siege. On 4 July, Independence Day, Pemberton surrendered. From now on, the Mississippi was firmly in the hands of the North. The South was literally split in two.

The fall of Vicksburg is always seen as one of the great turning points in the war. And yet, from a financial point of view, it was really not the decisive one. The key event had happened more than a year before, two hundred miles downstream from Vicksburg, where the Mississippi joins the Gulf of Mexico. On 29 April 1862 Flag Officer David Farragut had run the guns of Fort Jackson and Fort St Philip to seize control of New Orleans. This was a far less bloody and protracted clash than the siege of Vicksburg, but equally disastrous for the Southern cause.

The finances of the Confederacy are one of the great might-have-beens of American history.[39] For, in the final analysis, it was as much a lack of hard cash as a lack of industrial capacity or manpower that undercut what was, in military terms, an impressive effort by the Southern states. At the beginning of the war, in the absence of a pre-existing system of central taxation, the fledgling Confederate Treasury had paid for its army by selling bonds to its own citizens, in the form of two large loans for $15 million and $100 million. But there was a finite amount of liquid capital available in the South, with its many self-contained farms and relatively small towns. To survive, it was later alleged, the Confederacy turned to the Rothschilds, in the hope that the world's greatest financial dynasty might help them beat the North as they had helped Wellington beat Napoleon at Waterloo.

The suggestion was not altogether fanciful. In New York, the Rothschild agent August Belmont had watched with horror as the United States slid into Civil War. As the Democratic Party's national chairman, he had been a leading supporter of Stephen A. Douglas, Abraham Lincoln's opponent in the presidential election of 1860. Belmont remained a vocal critic of what he called Lincoln's 'fatal policy of confiscation and forcible emancipation'.[40] Salomon de Rothschild, James's third son, had also expressed pro-Southern sympathies in his letters home before the war began.[41] Some Northern commentators drew the obvious inference: the Rothschilds were backing the South. 'Belmont, the Rothschilds, and the whole tribe of Jews ... have been buying up Confederate bonds,' thundered the *Chicago Tribune* in 1864. One Lincoln supporter accused the 'Jews, Jeff Davis [the Confederate president] and the devil' of being an unholy trinity directed against the Union.[42] When he visited London in 1863, Belmont himself told Lionel de Rothschild that 'soon the North would be conquered'. (It merely stoked the fires of suspicion that the man charged with recruiting Britain to the South's cause, the Confederate Secretary of State Judah Benjamin, was himself a Jew.)

In reality, however, the Rothschilds opted not to back the South. Why? Perhaps it was because they felt a genuine distaste for the institution of slavery. But of at least equal importance was a sense that the Confederacy was not a good credit risk (after all, the Confederate president Jefferson Davis had openly advocated the repudiation of state debts when he was a US senator). That mistrust seemed to be widely shared in Europe. When the Confederacy tried to sell conventional bonds in

European markets, investors showed little enthusiasm. But the Southerners had an ingenious trick up their sleeves. The trick (like the sleeves themselves) was made of cotton, the key to the Confederate economy and by far the South's largest export. The idea was to use the South's cotton crop not just as a source of export earnings, but as collateral for a new kind of cotton-backed bond. When the obscure French firm of Emile Erlanger and Co. started issuing cotton-backed bonds on the South's behalf, the response in London and Amsterdam was more positive. The most appealing thing about these sterling bonds, which had a 7 per cent coupon and a maturity of twenty years, was that they could be converted into cotton at the pre-war price of six pence a pound. Despite the South's military setbacks, they retained their value for most of the war for the simple reason that the price of the underlying security, cotton, was rising as a consequence of increased wartime demand. Indeed, the price of the bonds actually doubled between December 1863 and September 1864, despite the Confederate defeats at Gettysburg and Vicksburg, because the price of cotton was soaring.[43] Moreover, the South was in the happy position of being able to raise that price still further – by restricting the cotton supply.

In 1860 the port of Liverpool was the main artery for the supply of imported cotton to the British textile industry, then the mainstay of the Victorian industrial economy. More than 80 per cent of these imports came from the southern United States. The Confederate leaders believed this gave them the leverage to bring Britain into the war on their side. To ratchet up the pressure, they decided to impose an embargo on all cotton exports to Liverpool. The effects were devastating. Cotton prices soared from 6¼d per pound to 27¼d. Imports from the South slumped from 2.6 million bales in 1860 to less than 72,000 in 1862. A typical English cotton mill like the one that has been preserved at Styal, south of

Confederate cotton bond with coupons, only the first four of
which have been clipped

Manchester, employed around 400 workers, but that was just a
fraction of the 300,000 people employed by King Cotton across
Lancashire as a whole. Without cotton there was literally nothing
for those workers to do. By late 1862 half the workforce had
been laid off; around a quarter of the entire population of Lancashire was on poor relief.[44] They called it the cotton famine. This,
however, was a man-made famine. And the men who made it
seemed to be achieving their goal. Not only did the embargo
cause unemployment, hunger and riots in the north of England;
the shortage of cotton also drove up the price and hence the value
of the South's cotton-backed bonds, making them an irresistibly
attractive investment for key members of the British political
elite. The future Prime Minister, William Ewart Gladstone,
bought some, as did the editor of *The Times*, John Delane.[45]

Yet the South's ability to manipulate the bond market depended on one overriding condition: that investors should be able to take physical possession of the cotton which underpinned the bonds if the South failed to make its interest payments. Collateral is, after all, only good if a creditor can get his hands on it. And that is why the fall of New Orleans in April 1862 was the real turning point in the American Civil War. With the South's main port in Union hands, any investor who wanted to get hold of Southern cotton had to run the Union's naval blockade not once but twice, in and out. Given the North's growing naval power in and around the Mississippi, that was not an enticing prospect.

If the South had managed to hold on to New Orleans until the cotton harvest had been offloaded to Europe, they might have managed to sell more than £3 million of cotton bonds in London. Maybe even the risk-averse Rothschilds might have come off the financial fence. As it was, they dismissed the Erlanger loan as being 'of so speculative a nature that it was very likely to attract all wild speculators . . . we do not hear of any respectable people having anything to do with it'.[46] The Confederacy had overplayed its hand. They had turned off the cotton tap, but then lost the ability to turn it back on. By 1863 the mills of Lancashire had found new sources of cotton in China, Egypt and India. And now investors were rapidly losing faith in the South's cotton-backed bonds. The consequences for the Confederate economy were disastrous.

With its domestic bond market exhausted and only two paltry foreign loans, the Confederate government was forced to print unbacked paper dollars to pay for the war and its other expenses, 1.7 billion dollars' worth in all. Both sides in the Civil War had to print money, it is true. But by the end of the war the Union's 'greenback' dollars were still worth about 50 cents in gold,

A Confederate 'greyback' State of Louisiana five-dollar bill

whereas the Confederacy's 'greybacks' were worth just one cent, despite a vain attempt at currency reform in 1864.[47] The situation was worsened by the ability of Southern states and municipalities to print paper money of their own; and by rampant forgery, since Confederate notes were crudely made and easy to copy. With ever more paper money chasing ever fewer goods, inflation exploded. Prices in the South rose by around 4,000 per cent during the Civil War.[48] By contrast, prices in the North rose by just 60 per cent. Even before the surrender of the principal Confederate armies in April 1865, the economy of the South was collapsing, with hyperinflation as the sure harbinger of defeat.

The Rothschilds had been right. Those who had invested in Confederate bonds ended up losing everything, since the victorious North pledged not to honour the debts of the South. In the end, there had been no option but to finance the Southern war effort by printing money. It would not be the last time in history that an attempt to buck the bond market would end in ruinous inflation and military humiliation.

The Euthanasia of the Rentier

The fate of those who lost their shirts on Confederate bonds was not especially unusual in the nineteenth century. The Confederacy was far from the only state in the Americas to end up disappointing its bondholders; it was merely the northernmost delinquent. South of the Rio Grande, debt defaults and currency depreciations verged on the commonplace. The experience of Latin America in the nineteenth century in many ways foreshadowed problems that would become almost universal in the middle of the twentieth century. Partly this was because the social class that was most likely to invest in bonds – and therefore to have an interest in prompt interest payment in a sound currency – was weaker there than elsewhere. Partly it was because Latin American republics were among the first to discover that it was relatively painless to default when a substantial proportion of bondholders were foreign. It was no mere accident that the first great Latin American debt crisis happened as early as 1826–9, when Peru, Colombia, Chile, Mexico, Guatemala and Argentina all defaulted on loans issued in London just a few years before.[49]

In many ways, it was true that the bond market was powerful. By the later nineteenth century, countries that defaulted on their debts risked economic sanctions, the imposition of foreign control over their finances and even, in at least five cases, military intervention.[50] It is hard to believe that Gladstone would have ordered the invasion of Egypt in 1882 if the Egyptian government had not threatened to renege on its obligations to European bondholders, himself among them. Bringing an 'emerging market' under the aegis of the British Empire was the surest way to remove political risk from investors' concerns.[51] Even those outside the Empire risked a visit from a gunboat if they defaulted, as

Venezuela discovered in 1902, when a joint naval expedition by Britain, Germany and Italy temporarily blockaded the country's ports. The United States was especially energetic (and effective) in protecting bondholders' interests in Central America and the Caribbean.[52]

But in one crucial respect the bond market was potentially vulnerable. Investors in the City of London, the biggest international financial market in the world throughout the nineteenth century, were wealthy but not numerous. In the early nineteenth century the number of British bondholders may have been fewer than 250,000, barely 2 per cent of the population. Yet their wealth was more than double the entire national income of the United Kingdom; their income in the region of 7 per cent of national income. In 1822 this income – the interest on the national debt – amounted to roughly half of total public spending, yet more than two thirds of tax revenue was indirect and hence fell on consumption. Even as late as 1870 these proportions were still, respectively, a third and more than half. It would be quite hard to devise a more regressive fiscal system, with taxes imposed on the necessities of the many being used to finance interest payments to the very few. Small wonder Radicals like William Cobbett were incensed. 'A national debt, and all the taxation and gambling belonging to it,' Cobbett declared in his *Rural Rides* (1830), 'have a natural tendency to *draw wealth into great masses . . . for the gain of a few*.'[53] In the absence of political reform, he warned, the entire country would end up in the hands of 'those who have had borrowed from them the money to uphold this monster of a system . . . the loan-jobbers, stock-jobbers . . . Jews and the whole tribe of tax-eaters'.[54]

Such tirades did little to weaken the position of the class known in France as the *rentiers* – the recipients of interest on government bonds like the French *rente*. On the contrary, the decades after

1830 were a golden age for the *rentier* in Europe. Defaults became less and less frequent. Money, thanks to the gold standard, became more and more dependable.[55] This triumph of the *rentier*, despite the generalized widening of electoral franchises, was remarkable. True, the rise of savings banks (which were often mandated to hold government bonds as their principal assets) gave new segments of society indirect exposure to, and therefore stakes in, the bond market. But fundamentally the *rentiers* remained an elite of Rothschilds, Barings and Gladstones – socially, politically, but above all economically intertwined. What ended their dominance was not the rise of democracy or socialism, but a fiscal and monetary catastrophe for which the European elites were themselves responsible. That catastrophe was the First World War.

'Inflation', wrote Milton Friedman in a famous definition, 'is always and everywhere a monetary phenomenon, in the sense that it cannot occur without a more rapid increase in the quantity of money than in output.' What happened in all the combatant states during and after the First World War illustrates this pretty well. There were essentially five steps to high inflation:

1. War led not only to shortages of goods but also to
2. short-term government borrowing from the central bank,
3. which effectively turned debt into cash, thereby expanding the money supply,
4. causing public expectations of inflation to shift and the demand for cash balances to fall
5. and prices of goods to rise.*

* In the language of economics the relationships can be simplified as $MV = PQ$ where M is the quantity of money in circulation, V is the velocity of money (frequency of transactions), P is the price level and Q is the real value of total transactions.

Pure monetary theory, however, cannot explain why in one country the inflationary process proceeds so much further or faster than in another. Nor can it explain why the consequences of inflation vary so much from case to case. If one adds together the total public expenditures of the major combatant powers between 1914 and 1918, Britain spent rather more than Germany and France much more than Russia. Expressed in terms of dollars, the public debts of Britain, France and the United States increased much more between April 1914 and March 1918 than that of Germany.[56] True, the volume of banknotes in circulation rose by more in Germany between 1913 and 1918 (1,040 per cent) than in Britain (708 per cent) or France (386 per cent), but for Bulgaria the figure was 1,116 per cent and for Romania 961 per cent.[57] Relative to 1913, wholesale prices had risen further by 1918 in Italy, France and Britain than in Germany. The cost-of-living index for Berlin in 1918 was 2.3 times higher than its pre-war level; for London it was little different (2.1 times higher).[58] Why, then, was it Germany that plunged into hyperinflation after the First World War? Why was it the mark that collapsed into worthlessness? The key lies in the role of the bond market in war and post-war finance.

All the warring countries went on war bonds sales-drives during the war, persuading thousands of small savers who had never previously purchased government bonds that it was their patriotic duty to do so. Unlike Britain, France, Italy and Russia, however, Germany did not have access to the international bond market during the war (having initially spurned the New York market and then been shut out of it). While the Entente powers could sell bonds in the United States or throughout the capital-rich British Empire, the Central powers (Germany, Austria-Hungary and Turkey) were thrown back on their own resources. Berlin and Vienna were important financial centres, but they lacked the depth of London, Paris and New York. As a result, the sale of war bonds grew gradually more difficult for the Germans and their allies, as the appetite of domestic investors became sated. Much sooner, and to a much greater extent than in Britain, the German and Austrian authorities had to turn to their central banks for short-term funding. The growth of the volume of Treasury bills in the central bank's hands was a harbinger of inflation because, unlike the sale of bonds to the public, exchanging these bills for banknotes increased the money supply. By the end of the war, roughly a third of the Reich debt was 'floating' or unfunded, and a substantial monetary overhang had been created, which only wartime price controls prevented from manifesting itself in higher inflation.

Defeat itself had a high price. All sides had reassured taxpayers and bondholders that the enemy would pay for the war. Now the bills fell due in Berlin. One way of understanding the post-war hyperinflation is therefore as a form of state bankruptcy. Those who had bought war bonds had invested in a promise of victory; defeat and revolution represented a national insolvency, the brunt of which necessarily had to be borne by the Reich's creditors. Quite apart from defeat, the revolutionary events between November 1918 and January 1919 were scarcely calculated to reassure investors. Nor was the peace conference at Versailles, which imposed an unspecified reparations liability on the fledgling Weimar Republic. When the total indemnity was finally fixed in 1921, the Germans found themselves saddled with a huge new external debt with a nominal capital value of 132 billion 'gold marks' (pre-war marks), equivalent to more than three times national income. Although not all this new debt was immediately interest-bearing, the scheduled reparations payments accounted for more than a third of all Reich expenditure in 1921 and 1922. No investor who contemplated

Germany's position in the summer of 1921 could have felt optimistic, and such foreign capital as did flow into the country after the war was speculative or 'hot' money, which soon departed when the going got tough.

Yet it would be wrong to see the hyperinflation of 1923 as a simple consequence of the Versailles Treaty. That was how the Germans liked to see it, of course. Their claim throughout the post-war period was that the reparations burden created an unsustainable current account deficit; that there was no alternative but to print yet more paper marks in order to finance it; that the inflation was a direct consequence of the resulting depreciation of the mark. All of this was to overlook the domestic political roots of the monetary crisis. The Weimar tax system was feeble, not least because the new regime lacked legitimacy among higher income groups who declined to pay the taxes imposed on them. At the same time, public money was spent recklessly, particularly on generous wage settlements for public sector unions. The combination of insufficient taxation and excessive spending created enormous deficits in 1919 and 1920 (in excess of 10 per cent of net national product), before the victors had even presented their reparations bill. The deficit in 1923, when Germany had suspended reparations payments, was even larger. Moreover, those in charge of Weimar economic policy in the early 1920s felt they had little incentive to stabilize German fiscal and monetary policy, even when an opportunity presented itself in the middle of 1920.[59] A common calculation among Germany's financial elites was that runaway currency depreciation would force the Allied powers into revising the reparations settlement, since the effect would be to cheapen German exports relative to American, British and French manufactures. It was true, as far as it went, that the downward slide of the mark boosted German exports. What the Germans overlooked was that the inflation-induced boom of 1920–22, at a time when the US and UK economies were in the depths of a post-war recession, caused an even bigger surge in imports, thus negating the economic pressure they had hoped to exert. At the heart of the German hyperinflation was a miscalculation. When the French cottoned on to the insincerity of official German pledges to fulfil their reparations commitments, they drew the conclusion that reparations would have to be collected by force and invaded the industrial Ruhr region. The Germans reacted by proclaiming a general strike ('passive resistance'), which they financed with yet more paper money. The hyperinflationary endgame had now arrived.

Inflation is a monetary phenomenon, as Milton Friedman said. But hyperinflation is always and everywhere a *political* phenomenon, in the sense that it cannot occur without a fundamental malfunction of a country's political economy. There surely were less catastrophic ways to settle the conflicting claims of domestic and foreign creditors on the diminished national income of post-war Germany. But a combination of internal gridlock and external defiance – rooted in the refusal of many Germans to accept that their empire had been fairly beaten – led to the worst of all possible outcomes: a complete collapse of the currency and of the economy itself. By the end of 1923 there were approximately 4.97×10^{20} marks in circulation. Twenty-billion mark notes were in everyday use. The annual inflation rate reached a peak of 182 billion per cent. Prices were on average 1.26 *trillion* times higher than they had been in 1913. True, there had been some short-term benefits. By discouraging saving and encouraging consumption, accelerating inflation had stimulated output and employment until the last quarter of 1922. The depreciating mark, as we have seen, had boosted German exports. Yet the collapse of 1923 was all the more severe for having been postponed. Industrial production dropped to half its 1913 level.

The price of hyperinflation: a German billion mark note from
November 1923

Unemployment soared to, at its peak, a quarter of trade union members, with another quarter working short time. Worst of all was the social and psychological trauma caused by the crisis. 'Inflation is a crowd phenomenon in the strictest and most concrete sense of the word,' Elias Canetti later wrote of his experiences as a young man in inflation-stricken Frankfurt. '[It is] a witches' sabbath of devaluation where men and the units of their money have the strongest effects on each other. The one stands for the other, men feeling themselves as "bad" as their money; and this becomes worse and worse. Together they are all at its mercy and all feel equally worthless.'[60]

Worthlessness was the hyperinflation's principal product. Not only was money rendered worthless; so too were all the forms of wealth and income fixed in terms of that money. That included bonds. The hyperinflation could not wipe out Germany's external debt, which had been fixed in pre-war currency. But it could and did wipe out all the internal debt that had been accumulated during and after the war, levelling the debt mountain like some devastating economic earthquake. The effect was akin to a tax: a tax not only on bondholders but also on anyone living on a fixed cash income. This amounted to a great levelling, since it affected primarily the upper middle classes: *rentiers*, senior civil servants, professionals. Only entrepreneurs were in a position to insulate themselves by adjusting prices upwards, hoarding dollars, investing in 'real assets' (such as houses or factories) and paying off debts in depreciating banknotes. The enduring economic legacy of the hyperinflation was bad enough: weakened banks and chronically high interest rates, which now incorporated a substantial inflation risk premium. But it was the social and political consequences of the German hyperinflation that were the most grievous. The English economist John Maynard Keynes had theorized in 1923 that the 'euthanasia of the *rentier*' through inflation was preferable to mass unemployment through deflation – 'because it is worse in an impoverished world to provoke unemployment than to disappoint the rentier'.[61] Yet four years earlier, he himself had given a vivid account of the negative consequences of inflation:

By a continuing process of inflation, governments can confiscate, secretly and unobserved, an important part of the wealth of their citizens. By this method, they not only confiscate, but they confiscate *arbitrarily*; and, while the process impoverishes many, it actually enriches some. The sight of this arbitrary rearrangement of riches strikes not only at security, but at confidence in the equity of the existing distribution of wealth. Those to whom the system brings windfalls . . . become 'profiteers', who are the object of the hatred of the bourgeoisie, whom the inflationism has impoverished not less than of the proletariat. As the inflation proceeds . . . all permanent relations between debtors and creditors, which form the ultimate foundation of capitalism, become so utterly disordered as to be almost meaningless . . .[62]

It was to Lenin that Keynes attributed the insight that 'There is no subtler, no surer means of overturning the existing basis of society than to debauch the currency.' No record survives of Lenin saying any such thing, but his fellow Bolshevik Yevgeni Preobrazhensky* did describe the banknote-printing press as 'that machine-gun of the Commissariat of Finance which poured fire into the rear of the bourgeois system'.[63]

The Russian example is a reminder that Germany was not the only vanquished country to suffer hyperinflation after the First World War. Austria – as well as the newly independent Hungary and Poland – also suffered comparably bad currency collapses between 1917 and 1924. In the Russian case, hyperinflation came after the Bolsheviks had defaulted outright on the entire Tsarist debt. Bondholders would suffer similar fates in the aftermath of the Second World War, when Germany, Hungary and Greece all saw their currencies and bond markets collapse.†

If hyperinflation were exclusively associated with the costs of losing world wars, it would be relatively easy to understand. Yet there is a puzzle. In more recent times, a number of countries have been driven to default on their debts – either directly by suspending interest payments, or indirectly by debasing the currency in which the debts are denominated – as a result of far less serious disasters. Why is it that the spectre of hyperinflation has not been banished along with the spectre of global conflict?

PIMCO boss Bill Gross began his money-making career as a blackjack player in Las Vegas. To his eyes, there is always an

---

* Murder rather than euthanasia was Preobrazhensky's forte; he was of all the Bolshevik leaders the one most directly implicated in the execution of Nicholas II and his family.

† The highest recorded inflation rate in history was in Hungary in July 1946, when prices increased by 4.19 quintillion per cent (419 followed by sixteen zeros).

element of gambling involved when an investor buys a bond. Part of that gamble is that an upsurge in inflation will not consume the value of the bond's annual interest payments. As Gross explains it, 'If inflation goes up to ten per cent and the value of a fixed rate interest is only five, then that basically means that the bond holder is falling behind inflation by five per cent.' As we have seen, the danger that rising inflation poses is that it erodes the purchasing power of both the capital sum invested and the interest payments due. And that is why, at the first whiff of higher inflation, bond prices tend to fall. Even as recently as the 1970s, as inflation soared around the world, the bond market made a Nevada casino look like a pretty safe place to invest your money. Gross vividly recalls the time when US inflation was surging into double digits, peaking at just under 15 per cent in April 1980. As he puts it, 'that was very bond-unfriendly, and it produced . . . perhaps the worst bond bear market not just in memory but in history.' To be precise, real annual returns on US government bonds in the 1970s were minus 3 per cent, almost as bad as during the inflationary years of the world wars. Today, only a handful of countries have inflation rates above 10 per cent and only one, Zimbabwe, is afflicted with hyperinflation.* But back in 1979 at least seven countries had an annual inflation rate above 50 per cent and more than sixty countries, including Britain and the United States, had inflation in double digits. Among the countries worst affected, none suffered more severe long-term damage than Argentina.

Once, Argentina was a byword for prosperity. The country's very name means the land of silver. The river on whose banks the capital Buenos Aires stands is the Rio de la Plata – in English

---

* At the time of writing (March 2008), a funeral in Zimbabwe costs 1 billion Zimbabwean dollars. The annual inflation rate is 100,000 per cent.

the Silver River – a reference not to its colour, which is muddy brown, but to the silver deposits supposed to lie upstream. In 1913, according to recent estimates, Argentina was one of the ten richest countries in the world. Outside the English-speaking world, per capita gross domestic product was higher in only Switzerland, Belgium, the Netherlands and Denmark. Between 1870 and 1913, Argentina's economy had grown faster than those of both the United States and Germany. There was almost as much foreign capital invested there as in Canada. It is no coincidence that there were once two Harrods stores in the world: one in Knightsbridge, in London, the other on the Avenida Florida, in the heart of Buenos Aires. Argentina could credibly aspire to be the United Kingdom, if not the United States, of the southern hemisphere. In February 1946, when the newly elected president General Juan Domingo Perón visited the central bank in Buenos Aires, he was astonished at what he saw. 'There is so much gold,' he marvelled, 'you can hardly walk through the corridors.'

The economic history of Argentina in the twentieth century is an object lesson that all the resources in the world can be set at nought by financial mismanagement. Particularly after the Second World War the country consistently underperformed its neigh- bours and most of the rest of the world. So miserably did it fare in the 1960s and 1970s, for example, that its per capita GDP was the same in 1988 as it had been in 1959. By 1998 it had sunk to 34 per cent of the US level, compared with 72 per cent in 1913. It had been overtaken by, among others, Singapore, Japan, Taiwan and South Korea – not forgetting, most painful of all, the country next door, Chile. What went wrong? One possible answer is inflation, which was in double digits between 1945 and 1952, between 1956 and 1968 and between 1970 and 1974; and in treble (or quadruple) digits between 1975 and 1990, peaking at an annual rate of 5,000 per cent in 1989. Another answer is debt default: Argentina let down foreign creditors in 1982, 1989, 2002 and 2004. Yet these answers will not quite suffice. Argentina had suffered double-digit inflation in at least eight years between 1870 and 1914. It had defaulted on its debts at least twice in the same period. To understand Argentina's economic decline, it is once again necessary to see that inflation was a political as much as a monetary phenomenon.

An oligarchy of landowners had sought to base the country's economy on agricultural exports to the English-speaking world, a model that failed comprehensively in the Depression. Large-scale immigration without (as in North America) the freeing of agricultural land for settlement had created a disproportionately large urban working class that was highly susceptible to populist mobilization. Repeated military interventions in politics, beginning with the coup that installed José F. Uriburu in 1930, paved the way for a new kind of quasi-fascistic politics under Perón, who seemed to offer something for everyone: better wages and conditions for workers and protective tariffs for industrialists. The anti-labour alternative to Péron, which was attempted between 1955 (when he was deposed) and 1966, relied on currency devaluation to try to reconcile the interests of agriculture and industry. Another military coup in 1966 promised technological modernization but instead delivered more devaluation, and higher inflation. Perón's return in 1973 was a fiasco, coinciding as it did with the onset of a global upsurge in inflation. Annual inflation surged to 444 per cent. Yet another military coup plunged Argentina into violence as the *Proceso de Reorganización Nacional* (National Reorganization Process) condemned thousands to arbitrary detention and 'disappearance'. In economic terms, the junta achieved precisely nothing other than to saddle Argentina with a rapidly growing external debt, which by 1984 exceeded 60 per cent of GDP (though this was less than half the peak level of indebtedness attained in the early 1900s). As so often in inflationary crises, war played a part: internally against supposed subversives, externally against Britain over the Falkland Islands. Yet it would be wrong to see this as yet another case of a defeated regime liquidating its debts through inflation. What made Argentina's inflation so unmanageable was not war, but the constellation of social forces: the oligarchs, the *caudillos*, the producers' interest groups and the trade unions – not forgetting the impoverished underclass or *descamizados* (literally the shirtless). To put it simply, there was no significant group with an interest in price stability. Owners of capital were attracted to deficits and devaluation; sellers of labour grew accustomed to a wage–price spiral. The gradual shift from financing government deficits domestically to financing them externally meant that bondholding was outsourced.[64] It is against this background that the failure of successive plans for Argentine currency stabilization must be understood.

In his short story 'The Garden of Forking Paths', Argentina's greatest writer Jorge Luis Borges imagined the writing of a Chinese sage, Ts'ui Pên:

In all fictional works, each time a man is confronted with several alternatives, he chooses one and eliminates the others; in the fiction of Ts'ui Pên, he chooses – simultaneously – all of them. *He creates*, in this way, diverse futures; diverse times which themselves also proliferate and fork . . . In the work of Ts'ui Pên, all possible outcomes occur; each one is the point of departure for other forkings . . . [Ts'ui Pên] did not believe in a uniform, absolute time. He believed in an infinite series of times, in a growing, dizzying net of divergent, convergent and parallel times.[65]

This is not a bad metaphor for Argentine financial history in the past thirty years. Where Bernardo Grinspun attempted debt rescheduling and Keynesian demand management, Juan Sourrou-ille tried currency reform (the Austral Plan) along with wage and price controls. Neither was able to lead the critical interest groups down his own forking path. Public expenditure continued to exceed tax revenue; arguments for a premature end to wage and price controls prevailed; inflation resumed after only the most fleeting of stabilizations. The forking paths finally and calami-tously reconverged in 1989: the *annus mirabilis* in Eastern Europe; the *annus horribilis* in Argentina.

In February 1989 Argentina was suffering one of the hottest summers on record. The electricity system in Buenos Aires struggled to cope. People grew accustomed to five-hour power cuts. Banks and foreign exchange houses were ordered to close as the government tried to prevent the currency's exchange rate from collapsing. It failed: in the space of just a month the austral fell 140 per cent against the dollar. At the same time, the World Bank froze lending to Argentina, saying that the government had failed to tackle its bloated public sector deficit. Private sector lenders were no more enthusiastic. Investors were hardly likely to buy bonds with the prospect that inflation would wipe out their real value within days. As fears grew that the central bank's reserves were running out, bond prices plunged. There was only one option left for a desperate government: the printing press. But even that failed. On Friday 28 April Argentina literally ran out of money. 'It's a physical problem,' Central Bank Vice-President Roberto Eilbaum told a news conference. The mint had literally run out of paper and the printers had gone on strike. 'I don't know how we're going to do it, but the money has got to be there on Monday,' he confessed.

By June, with the *monthly* inflation rate rising above 100 per cent, popular frustration was close to boiling point. Already in April customers in one Buenos Aires supermarket had overturned trolleys full of goods after the management announced over a loudspeaker that all prices would immediately be raised by 30 per cent. For two days in June crowds in Argentina's second largest city, Rosario, ran amok in an eruption of rioting and looting that left at least fourteen people dead. As in the Weimar Republic, however, the principal losers of Argentina's hyperinflation were not ordinary workers, who stood a better chance of matching price hikes with pay rises, but those reliant on incomes fixed in cash terms, like civil servants or academics on inflexible salaries, or pensioners living off the interest on their savings. And, as in 1920s Germany, the principal beneficiaries were those with large debts, which were effectively wiped out by inflation. Among those beneficiaries was the government itself, in so far as the money it owed was denominated in australes.

Yet not all Argentina's debts could be got rid of so easily. By 1983 the country's external debt, which was denominated in US dollars, stood at $46 billion, equivalent to around 40 per cent of national output. No matter what happened to the Argentine currency, this dollar-denominated debt stayed the same. Indeed, it tended to grow as desperate governments borrowed yet more dollars. By 1989 the country's external debt was over $65 billion. Over the next decade it would continue to grow until it reached $155 billion. Domestic creditors had already been mulcted by inflation. But only default could rid Argentina of its foreign debt burden. As we have seen, Argentina had gone down this road more than once before. In 1890 Baring Brothers had been brought to the brink of bankruptcy by its investments in Argentine securities (notably a failed issue of bonds for the Buenos Aires Water Supply and Drainage Company) when the Argentine government defaulted on its external debt. It was the Barings' old rivals the Rothschilds who persuaded the British government to contribute £1 million towards what became a £17 million bailout fund, on the principle that the collapse of Barings would be 'a terrific calamity for English commerce all over the world'.[66] And it was also the first Lord Rothschild who chaired a committee of bankers set up to impose reform on the wayward Argentines. Future loans would be conditional on a currency reform that pegged the peso to gold by means of an independent and inflexible currency board.[67] A century later, however, the Rothschilds were more interested in Argentine vineyards than in Argentine debt. It was the International Monetary Fund that had to perform the thankless task of trying to avert (or at least mitigate the effects of) an Argentine default. Once again the remedy was a currency board, this time pegging the currency to the dollar.

When the new *peso convertible* was introduced by Finance Minister Domingo Cavallo in 1991, it was the sixth Argentine currency in the space of a century. Yet this remedy, too, ended in failure. True, by 1996 inflation had been brought down to zero; indeed, it turned negative in 1999. But unemployment stood at 15 per cent and income inequality was only marginally better than in Nigeria. Moreover, monetary stricture was never accompanied by fiscal stricture; public debt rose from 35 per cent of GDP at the end of 1994 to 64 per cent at the end of 2001 as central and provincial governments alike tapped the international bond market rather than balance their budgets. In short, despite pegging the currency and even slashing inflation, Cavallo had failed to change the underlying social and institutional drivers that had caused so many monetary crises in the past. The stage was set for yet another Argentine default, and yet another currency. After two bailouts in January ($15 billion) and May ($8 billion), the IMF declined to throw a third lifeline. On 23 December 2001, at the end of a year in which per capita GDP had declined by an agonizing 12 per cent, the government announced a moratorium on the entirety of its foreign debt, including bonds worth $81 billion: in nominal terms the biggest debt default in history.

The history of Argentina illustrates that the bond market is less powerful than it might first appear. The average 295 basis point spread between Argentine and British bonds in the 1880s scarcely compensated investors like the Barings for the risks they were running by investing in Argentina. In the same way, the average 664 basis point spread between Argentine and US bonds from 1998 to 2000 significantly underpriced the risk of default as the Cavallo currency peg began to crumble. When the default was announced, the spread rose to 5,500; by March 2002 it exceeded 7,000 basis points. After painfully protracted negotiations (there were 152 varieties of paper involved, denominated in six different currencies and governed by eight jurisdictions) the majority of approximately 500,000 creditors agreed to accept new bonds worth roughly 35 cents on the dollar, one of the most drastic 'haircuts' in the history of the bond market.[68] So successful did Argentina's default prove (economic growth has since surged while bond spreads are back in the 300–500 basis point range) that many economists were left to ponder why any sovereign debtor ever honours its commitments to foreign bondholders.[69]

The Resurrection of the Rentier

In the 1920s, as we have seen, Keynes had predicted the 'euthanasia of the *rentier*', anticipating that inflation would eventually eat up all the paper wealth of those who had put their money in government bonds. In our time, however, we have seen a miraculous resurrection of the bondholder. After the Great Inflation of the 1970s, the past thirty years have seen one country after another reduce inflation to single digits.[70] (Even in Argentina, the official inflation rate is below 10 per cent, though unofficial estimates compiled by the provinces of Mendoza and San Luis put it above 20 per cent.) And, as inflation has fallen, so bonds have rallied in what has been one of the great bond bull markets of modern history. Even more remarkably, despite the spectacular Argentine default – not to mention Russia's in 1998 – the spreads on emerging market bonds have trended steadily downwards, reaching lows in early 2007 that had not been seen since before the First World War, implying an almost unshakeable confidence in the economic future. Rumours of the death of Mr Bond have clearly proved to be exaggerated.

Inflation has come down partly because many of the items we buy, from clothes to computers, have got cheaper as a result of technological innovation and the relocation of production to low-wage economies in Asia. It has also been reduced because of a worldwide transformation in monetary policy, which began with the monetarist-inspired increases in short-term rates imple-mented by the Bank of England and the Federal Reserve in the late 1970s and early 1980s, and continued with the spread of central bank independence and explicit targets in the 1990s. Just as importantly, as the Argentine case shows, some of the struc-tural drivers of inflation have also weakened. Trade unions have become less powerful. Loss-making state industries have been privatized. But, perhaps most importantly of all, the social con-stituency with an interest in positive real returns on bonds has grown. In the developed world a rising share of wealth is held in the form of private pension funds and other savings institutions that are required, or at least expected, to hold a high proportion of their assets in the form of government bonds and other fixed income securities. In 2007 a survey of pension funds in eleven major economies revealed that bonds accounted for more than a quarter of their assets, substantially lower than in past decades, but still a substantial share.[71] With every passing year, the proportion of the population living off the income from such funds goes up, as the share of retirees increases.

Which brings us back to Italy, the land where the bond market was born. In 1965, on the eve of the Great Inflation, just 10 per cent of Italians were aged 65 or over. Today the proportion is twice that: around a fifth. And by 2050 it is projected by the United Nations to be just under a third. In such a greying society, there is a huge and growing need for fixed income securities, and for low inflation to ensure that the interest they pay retains its purchasing power. As more and more people leave the workforce, recurrent public sector deficits ensure that the bond market will never be short of new bonds to sell. And the fact that Italy has surrendered its monetary sovereignty to the European Central Bank means that there should never be another opportunity for Italian politicians to print money and set off the inflationary spiral.

That does not mean, however, that the bond market rules the world in the sense that James Carville meant. Indeed, the kind of discipline he associated with the bond market in the 1990s has been conspicuous by its absence under President Clinton's successor, George W. Bush. Just months before President Bush's election, on 7 September 2000, the National Debt Clock in New York's Times Square was shut down. On that day it read as follows: 'Our national debt: $5,676,989,904,887. Your family share: $73,733.' After three years of budget surpluses, both candidates for the presidency were talking as if paying off the national debt was a viable project. According to CNN

Democratic presidential nominee Al Gore has outlined a plan that he says would eliminate the debt by 2012. Senior economic advisers to Texas Governor and Republican presidential candidate George W.

Bush agree with the principle of paying down the debt but have not committed to a specific date for eliminating it.[72]

That lack of commitment on the latter candidate's part was by way of being a hint. Since Bush entered the White House, his administration has run a budget deficit in seven out of eight years. The federal debt has increased from $5 trillion to more than $9 trillion. The Congressional Budget Office forecasts a continued rise to more than $12 trillion by 2017. Yet, far from punishing this profligacy, the bond market has positively rewarded it. Between December 2000 and June 2003, the yield on ten-year Treasury bonds *declined* from 5.24 per cent to 3.33 per cent, and remains just above 4 per cent at the time of writing.

It is, however, impossible to make sense of this 'conundrum' – as Alan Greenspan called this failure of bond yields to respond to short-term interest rate rises[73] – by studying the bond market in isolation. We therefore turn now from the market for government debt to its younger and in many ways more dynamic sibling: the market for shares in corporate equity, known colloquially as the stock market.

3

Blowing Bubbles

The Andes stretch for more than four thousand miles like a jagged, crooked spine down the western side of the South American continent. Formed roughly a hundred million years ago, as the Nazca tectonic plate began its slow but tumultuous slide beneath the South American plate, their highest peak, Mount Aconcagua in Argentina, rises more than 22,000 feet above sea level. Aconcagua's smaller Chilean brethren stand like gleaming white sentinels around Santiago. But it is only when you are up in the Bolivian highlands that you really grasp the sheer scale of the Andes. When the rain clouds lift on the road from La Paz to Lake Titicaca, the mountains dominate the skyline, tracing a dazzling, irregular saw-tooth right across the horizon.

Looking at the Andes, it is hard to imagine that any kind of human organization could overcome such a vast natural barrier. But for one American company, their jagged peaks were no more daunting than the dense Amazonian rainforests that lie to the east of them. That company set out to construct a gas pipeline from Bolivia across the continent to the Atlantic coast of Brazil, and another – the longest in the world – from the tip of Patagonia to the Argentine capital Buenos Aires.

Such grand schemes, exemplifying the vaulting ambition of modern capitalism, were made possible by the invention of one of the most fundamental institutions of the modern world: the company. It is the company that enables thousands of individuals to pool their resources for risky, long-term projects that require the investment of vast sums of capital before profits can be realized. After the advent of banking and the birth of the bond market, the next step in the story of the ascent of money was therefore the rise of the joint-stock, limited-liability corporation: joint-stock because the company's capital was jointly owned by multiple investors; limited-liability because the separate existence of the company as a legal 'person' protected the investors from losing all their wealth if the venture failed. Their liability was limited to the money they had used to buy a stake in the company. Smaller enterprises might operate just as well as partnerships. But those who aspired to span continents needed the company.[1]

However, the ability of companies to transform the global economy depended on another, related innovation. In theory, the managers of joint-stock companies are supposed to be disciplined by vigilant shareholders, who attend annual meetings, and seek to exert influence directly or indirectly through non-executive directors. In practice, the primary discipline on companies is exerted by stock markets, where an almost infinite number of small slices of companies (call them stocks, shares or equities, whichever you prefer) are bought and sold every day. In essence, the price people are prepared to pay for a piece of a company tells you how much money they think that company will make in the future. In effect, stock markets hold hourly referendums on the companies whose shares are traded there: on the quality of their management, on the appeal of their products, on the prospects of their principal markets.

Yet stock markets also have a life of their own. The future is in large measure uncertain, so our assessments of companies' future profitability are bound to vary. If we were all calculating machines we would simultaneously process all the available information and come to the same conclusion. But we are human beings, and as such are prone to myopia and to mood swings. When stock market prices surge upwards in sync, as they often do, it is as if investors are gripped by a kind of collective euphoria: what the former chairman of the Federal Reserve Alan Greenspan memorably called irrational exuberance.[2] Conversely, when investors' 'animal spirits' flip from greed to fear, the bubble of their earlier euphoria can burst with amazing suddenness. Zoological imagery is of course an integral part of stock market culture. Optimistic buyers of stocks are bulls, pessimistic sellers are bears. Investors these days are said to be an electronic herd, happily grazing on positive returns one moment, then stampeding for the farmyard gate the next. The real point, however, is that stock markets are mirrors of the *human* psyche. Like *homo sapiens*, they can become depressed. They can even suffer complete breakdowns. Yet hope – or is it amnesia? – always seems able to triumph over such bad experiences.

In the four hundred years since shares were first bought and sold, there has been a succession of financial bubbles. Time and again, share prices have soared to unsustainable heights only to crash downwards again. Time and again, this process has been accompanied by skulduggery, as unscrupulous insiders have sought to profit at the expense of naive neophytes. So familiar is this pattern that it is possible to distil it into five stages:

1. *Displacement*: Some change in economic circumstances creates new and profitable opportunities for certain companies.
2. *Euphoria* or overtrading: A feedback process sets in whereby rising expected profits lead to rapid growth in share prices.
3. *Mania* or bubble: The prospect of easy capital gains attracts

first-time investors and swindlers eager to mulct them of their money.

4. *Distress*: The insiders discern that expected profits cannot possibly justify the now exorbitant price of the shares and begin to take profits by selling.

5. *Revulsion* or discredit: As share prices fall, the outsiders all stampede for the exits, causing the bubble to burst altogether.[3]

Stock market bubbles have three other recurrent features. The first is the role of what is sometimes referred to as asymmetric information. Insiders – those concerned with the management of bubble companies – know much more than the outsiders, whom the insiders want to part from their money. Such asymmetries always exist in business, of course, but in a bubble the insiders exploit them fraudulently.[4] The second theme is the role of cross-border capital flows. Bubbles are more likely to occur when capital flows freely from country to country. The seasoned speculator, based in a major financial centre, may lack the inside knowledge of the true insider. But he is much more likely to get his timing right – buying early and selling before the bubble bursts – than the naive first-time investor. In a bubble, in other words, not everyone is irrational; or, at least, some of the exuberant are less irrational than others. Finally, and most importantly, without easy credit creation a true bubble cannot occur. That is why so many bubbles have their origins in the sins of omission or commission of central banks.

Nothing illustrates more clearly how hard human beings find it to learn from history than the repetitive history of stock market bubbles. Consider how readers of the magazine *Business Week* saw the world at two moments in time, separated by just twenty years. On 13 August 1979, the front cover featured a crumpled share certificate in the shape of a crashed paper dart under the headline: 'The Death of Equities: How inflation is destroying the stock market'. Readers were left in no doubt about the magnitude of the crisis:

The masses long ago switched from stocks to investments having higher yields and more protection from inflation. Now the pension funds – the market's last hope – have won permission to quit stocks and bonds for real estate, futures, gold, and even diamonds. The death of equities looks like an almost permanent condition.[5]

On that day, the Dow Jones Industrial Average, the longest-running American stock market index, closed at 875, barely changed from its level ten years before, and nearly 17 per cent below its peak of 1052 in January 1973. Pessimism after a decade and half of disappointment was understandable. Yet, far from expiring, US equities were just a few years away from one of the great bull runs of modern times. Having touched bottom in August 1982 (777), the Dow proceeded to more than treble in the space of just five years, reaching a record high of 2,700 in the summer of 1987. After a short, sharp sell-off in October 1987, the index resumed its upward rise. After 1995, the pace of its ascent even quickened. On 27 September 1999, it closed at just under 10,395, meaning that the average price of a major US corporation had risen nearly twelve-fold in just twenty years. On that day, readers of *Business Week* read with excitement that:

Conditions don't have to get a lot better to justify Dow 36,000, say James K. Glassman and Kevin A. Hassett in *Dow 36,000: The New Strategy for Profiting From the Coming Rise in the Stock Market*. They argue that the market already merits 36K, and that stock prices will advance toward that target over the next 3 to 5 years as investors come to that conclusion, too ... The market – even at a price-to-earnings ratio of 30* – is a steal. By their estimates, a 'perfectly reasonable price' for the market . . . is 100 times earnings.[6]

This article was published less than four months before the collapse of the dot-com bubble, which had been based on exaggerated expectations about the future earnings of technology companies. By October 2002 the Dow was down to 7,286, a level not seen since late 1997. At the time of writing (April 2008), it is still trading at one third of the level Glassman and Hassett predicted.

The performance of the American stock market is perhaps best measured by comparing the total returns on stocks, assuming the reinvestment of all dividends, with the total returns on other financial assets such as government bonds and commercial or Treasury bills, the last of which can be taken as a proxy for any short-term instrument like a money market fund or a demand deposit at a bank. The start date, 1964, is the year of the author's birth. It will immediately be apparent that if my parents had been able to invest even a modest sum in the US stock market at that date, and to continue reinvesting the dividends they earned each year, they would have been able to increase their initial investment by a factor of nearly seventy by 2007. For example, $10,000 would have become $700,000. The alternatives of bonds or bills would have done less well. A US bond fund would have gone up by a factor of under 23; a portfolio of bills by a factor of just 12. Needless to say, such figures must be adjusted downwards to take account of the cost of living, which has risen by a factor of nearly

---

* A ratio of stock prices divided by earnings including dividends. The long-run average (since 1871) of the price–earnings ratio in the United States is 15.5. Its maximum was reached in 1999: 32.6. It currently stands at 18.6 (figures for the Standard and Poor's 500 index, as extended back in time by Global Financial Data).

seven in my lifetime. In real terms, stocks increased by a factor of 10.3; bonds by a factor of 3.4; bills by a factor of 1.8. Had my parents made the mistake of simply buying $10,000 in dollar bills in 1964, the real value of their son's nest egg would have declined in real terms by 85 per cent.

No stock market has out-performed the American over the long run. One estimate of long-term real stock market returns showed an average return for the US market of 4.73 per cent per year between the 1920s and the 1990s. Sweden came next (3.71), followed by Switzerland (3.03), with Britain barely in the top ten on 2.28 per cent. Six out of the twenty-seven markets studied suffered at least one major interruption, usually as a result of war or revolution. Ten markets suffered negative long-term real returns, of which the worst were Venezuela, Peru, Colombia and, at the very bottom, Argentina (–5.36 per cent).[7] 'Stocks for the long run' is very far from being a universally applicable nostrum.[8] It nevertheless remains true that, in most countries for which long-run data are available, stocks have out-performed bonds – by a factor of roughly five over the twentieth century.[9] This can scarcely surprise us. Bonds, as we saw in Chapter 2, are no more than promises by governments to pay interest and ultimately repay principal over a specified period of time. Either through default or through currency depreciation, many governments have failed to honour those promises. By contrast, a share is a portion of the capital of a profit-making corporation. If the company succeeds in its undertakings, there will not only be dividends, but also a significant probability of capital appreciation. There are of course risks, too. The returns on stocks are less predictable and more volatile than the returns on bonds and bills. There is a significantly higher probability that the average corporation will go bankrupt and cease to exist than that the average sovereign state will disappear. In the event of a corporate bankruptcy, the holders of bonds and other forms of debt will be satisfied first; the equity holders may end up with nothing. For these reasons, economists see the superior returns on stocks as capturing an 'equity risk premium' – though clearly in some cases this has been a risk well worth taking.

The Company You Keep

Behind the ornate baroque façade of Venice's San Moise church, literally under the feet of the tens of thousands of tourists who visit the church each year, there is a remarkable but seldom noticed inscription:

HONORI ET MEMORIAL JOANNIS LAW EDINBURGENSES REGII
GALLIARUM AERARII PREFECTI CLARISSIMA

'To the honour and memory of John Law of Edinburgh. Most distinguished controller of the treasury of the kings of the French.' It is a rather unlikely resting place for the man who invented the stock market bubble.

An ambitious Scot, a convicted murderer, a compulsive gambler and a flawed financial genius, John Law was not only responsible for the first true boom and bust in asset prices. He also may be said to have caused, indirectly, the French Revolution by comprehensively blowing the best chance that the *ancien régime* monarchy had to reform its finances. His story is one of the most astonishing yet least well understood tales of adventure in all financial history. It is also very much a story for our times.

Born in Edinburgh in 1671, Law was the son of a successful goldsmith and the heir to Lauriston Castle, overlooking the Firth of Forth. He went to London in 1692, but quickly began to fritter away his patrimony in a variety of business ventures and gambling escapades. Two years later he fought a duel with his neighbour, who objected to sharing the same building as the dissolute Law and his mistress, and killed him. He was tried for duelling and sentenced to death, but escaped from prison and fled to Amsterdam.

Law could not have picked a better town in which to lie low. By the 1690s Amsterdam was the world capital of financial innovation. To finance their fight for independence against Spain in the late sixteenth century, as we saw in the previous chapter, the Dutch had improved on the Italian system of public debt (introducing, among other things, lottery loans which allowed people to gamble as they invested their savings in government debt). They had also reformed their currency by creating what was arguably the world's first central bank, the Amsterdam Exchange Bank (*Wisselbank*), which solved the problem of debased coinage by creating a reliable form of bank money (see Chapter 1). But perhaps the single greatest Dutch invention of all was the joint-stock company.

The story of the company had begun a century before Law's arrival and had its origins in the efforts of Dutch merchants to wrest control of the lucrative Asian spice trade from Portugal and Spain. Europeans craved spices like cinnamon, cloves, mace, nutmeg and pepper not merely to flavour their food but also to preserve it. For centuries, these commodities had come overland from Asia to Europe along the Spice Road. But with the Portuguese discovery of the sea route to the East Indies via the Cape of Good Hope, new and irresistibly attractive business opportunities opened up. The Amsterdam Historical Museum is full of paintings that depict Dutch ships en route to and from the East Indies. One early example of the genre bears the inscription: 'Four ships sailed to go and get the spices towards Bantam and also established trading posts. And came back richly laden to . . . Amsterdam.

Departed May 1, 1598. Returned July 19, 1599.' As that suggests, however, the round trip was a very long one (fourteen months was in fact well below the average). It was also hazardous: of twenty-two ships that set sail in 1598, only a dozen returned safely. For these reasons, it made sense for merchants to pool their resources. By 1600 there were around six fledgling East India companies operating out of the major Dutch ports. However, in each case the entities had a limited term that was specified in advance – usually the expected duration of a voyage – after which the capital was repaid to investors.[10] This business model could not suffice to build the permanent bases and fortifications that were clearly necessary if the Portuguese and their Spanish allies* were to be supplanted. Actuated as much by strategic calculations as by the profit motive, the Dutch States-General, the parliament of the United Provinces, therefore proposed to merge the existing companies into a single entity. The result was the United East India Company – the *Vereenigde Nederlandsche Geoctroyeerde Oostindische Compagnie* (United Dutch Chartered East India Company, or VOC for short), formally chartered in 1602 to enjoy a monopoly on all Dutch trade east of the Cape of Good Hope and west of the Straits of Magellan.[11]

The structure of the VOC was novel in a number of respects. True, like its predecessors, it was supposed to last for a fixed period, in this case twenty-one years; indeed, Article 7 of its charter stated that investors would be entitled to withdraw their money at the end of just ten years, when the first general balance was drawn up. But the scale of the enterprise was unprecedented. Subscription to the Company's capital was open to all residents of the United Provinces and the charter set no upper limit on how much might be raised. Merchants, artisans and even servants

* Between 1580 and 1640 the crowns of Spain and Portugal were united.

rushed to acquire shares; in Amsterdam alone there were 1,143 subscribers, only eighty of whom invested more than 10,000 guilders, and 445 of whom invested less than 1,000. The amount raised, 6.45 million guilders, made the VOC much the biggest corporation of the era. The capital of its English rival, the East India Company, founded two years earlier, was just £68,373 – around 820,000 guilders – shared between a mere 219 subscribers.[12] Because the VOC was a government-sponsored enterprise, every effort was made to overcome the rivalry between the different provinces (and particularly between Holland, the richest province, and Zeeland). The capital of the Company was divided (albeit unequally) between six regional chambers (Amsterdam, Zeeland, Enkhuizen, Delft, Hoorn and Rotterdam). The seventy directors (*bewindhebbers*), who were each substantial investors, were also distributed between these chambers. One of their roles was to appoint seventeen people to act as the *Heeren XVII* – the Seventeen Lords – as a kind of company board. Although Amsterdam accounted for 57.4 per cent of the VOC's total capital, it nominated only eight out of the Seventeen Lords. Among the founding directors was Dirck Bas, a profit-oriented *paterfamilias* who (to judge by his portrait) was far from embarrassed by his riches.[13]

Ownership of the Company was thus divided into multiple *partijen* or *actien*, literally actions (as in 'a piece of the action'). Payment for the shares was in instalments, due in 1603, 1605, 1606 and 1607. The certificates issued were not quite share certificates in the modern sense, but more like receipts; the key document in law was the VOC stock ledger, where all stockholders' names were entered at the time of purchase.[14] The principle of limited liability was implied: shareholders stood to lose only their investment in the company and no other assets in the event that it failed.[15] There was, on the other hand, no guarantee

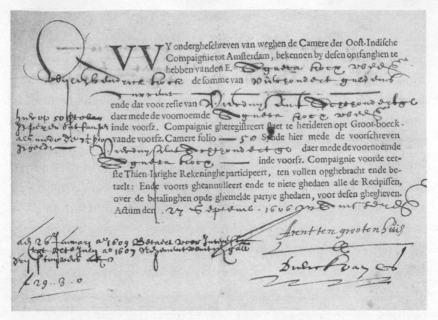

The oldest share: share no. 6 of the Dutch East India Company
(not strictly speaking a share certificate but a receipt for part
payment of share, issued by the Camere Amsterdam on 27 September
1606, and signed by Arent ten Grotenhuys and Dirck van Os)

of returns; Article 17 of the VOC charter merely stated that a
payment would be made to shareholders as soon as profits equivalent to 5 per cent of the initial capital had been made.

The VOC was not in fact an immediate commercial success.
Trade networks had to be set up, the mode of operation established and secure bases established. Between 1603 and 1607, a
total of twenty-two ships were fitted out and sent to Asia, at a
cost of just under 3.7 million guilders. The initial aim was to
establish a number of factories (saltpetre refineries, textile facilities and warehouses), the produce of which would then be
exchanged for spices. Early successes against the Portuguese saw
footholds established at Masulipatnam in the Bay of Bengal and
Amboyna (today Ambon) in the Moluccas (Malukus), but in

1606 Admiral Matelief failed to capture Malacca (Melaka) on the Malay Peninsula and an attack on Makian (another Moluccan island) was successfully repulsed by a Spanish fleet. An attempt to build a fort on Banda Neira, the biggest of the nutmeg-producing Banda islands, also failed.[16] By the time a twelve-year truce was signed with Spain in 1608, the VOC had made more money from capturing enemy vessels than from trade.[17] One major investor, the Mennonite Pieter Lijntjens, was so dismayed by the Company's warlike conduct that he withdrew from the Company in 1605. Another early director, Isaac le Maire, resigned in protest at what he regarded as the mismanagement of the Company's affairs.[18]

But how much power did even large shareholders have? Little. When the Company's directors petitioned the government to be released from their obligation to publish ten-year accounts in 1612 – the date when investors were supposed to be able to withdraw their capital if they chose to – permission was granted and publication of the accounts and the repayment of investors' capital were both postponed. The only sop to shareholders was that in 1610 the Seventeen Lords agreed to make a dividend payment the following year, though at this stage the Company was so strapped for cash that the dividend had to be paid in spices. In 1612 it was announced that the VOC would not be liquidated, as originally planned. This meant that any shareholders who wanted their cash back had no alternative but to sell their shares to another investor.[19]

The joint-stock company and the stock market were thus born within just a few years of each other. No sooner had the first publicly owned corporation come into existence with the first-ever initial public offering of shares, than a secondary market sprang up to allow these shares to be bought and sold. It proved to be a remarkably liquid market. Turnover in VOC shares was high: by 1607 fully one third of the Company's stock had been transferred from the original owners.[20] Moreover, because the Company's books were opened rather infrequently – purchases were formally registered monthly or quarterly – a lively forward market in VOC shares soon developed, which allowed sales for future delivery. To begin with, such transactions were done in informal open-air markets, on the Warmoesstraat or next to the Oude Kerk. But so lively was the market for VOC stock that in 1608 it was decided to build a covered *Beurs* on the Rokin, not far from the town hall. With its quadrangle, its colonnades and its clock tower, this first stock exchange in the world looked for all the world like a medieval Oxford college. But what went on there between noon and two o'clock each workday was recognizably revolutionary. One contemporary captured the atmosphere on the trading floor as a typical session drew to a close: 'Handshakes are followed by shouting, insults, impudence, pushing and shoving.' Bulls (*liefhebbers*) did battle with bears (*contremines*). The anxious speculator 'chews his nails, pulls his fingers, closes his eyes, takes four paces and four times talks to himself, raises his hand to his cheek as if he has a toothache and all this accompanied by a mysterious coughing'.[21]

Nor was it coincidental that this same period saw the foundation (in 1609) of the Amsterdam Exchange Bank, since a stock market cannot readily function without an effective monetary system. Once Dutch bankers started to accept VOC shares as collateral for loans, the link between the stock market and the supply of credit began to be forged. The next step was for banks to lend money so that shares might be purchased with credit. Company, bourse and bank provided the triangular foundation for a new kind of economy.

For a time it seemed as if the VOC's critics, led by the disgruntled ex-director le Maire, might exploit this new market to put pressure on the Company's directors. A concerted effort to drive down the price of VOC shares by short selling on the nascent futures market was checked by the 1611 dividend payment, ruining le Maire and his associates.[22] Further cash dividends were paid in 1612, 1613 and 1618.[23] The Company's critics (the 'dissenting investors' or *Doleanten*) remained dissatisfied, however. In a tract entitled *The Necessary Discourse* (*Nootwendich Discours*), published in 1622, an anonymous author lamented the lack of transparency which characterized the 'self-serving governance of certain of the directors', who were ensuring that 'all remained darkness': 'The account book, we can only surmise, must have been rubbed with bacon and fed to the dogs.'[24] Directorships should be for fixed terms, the dissenters argued, and all major shareholders should have the right to appoint a director.

The campaign for a reform of what would now be called the VOC's corporate governance duly bore fruit. In December 1622, when the Company's charter was renewed, it was substantially modified. Directors would no longer be appointed for life but could serve for only three years at a time. The 'chief participants' (shareholders with as much equity as directors) were henceforth entitled to nominate 'Nine Men' from among themselves, whom the Seventeen Lords were obliged to consult on 'great and important matters', and who would be entitled to oversee the annual accounting of the six chambers and to nominate, jointly with the Seventeen Lords, future candidates for directorships. In addition, in March 1623, it was agreed that the Nine Men would be entitled to attend (but not to vote at) the meetings of the Seventeen Lords and to scrutinize the annual purchasing accounts. The chief participants were also empowered to appoint auditors (*rekeningopnemers*) to check the accounts submitted to the States-General.[25] Shareholders were further mollified by the decision, in 1632, to set a standard 12.5 per cent dividend, twice the rate at which the Company was able to borrow money.* The result of this policy was that virtually all of the Company's net profits thereafter were distributed to the shareholders.[26] Shareholders were also effectively guaranteed against dilution of their equity. Amazingly, the capital base remained essentially unchanged throughout the VOC's existence.[27] When capital expenditures were called for, the VOC raised money not by issuing new shares but by issuing debt in the form of bonds. Indeed, so good was the Company's credit by the 1670s that it was able to act as an intermediary for a two-million-guilder loan by the States of Holland and Zeeland.

None of these arrangements would have been sustainable, of course, if the VOC had not become profitable in the mid seventeenth century. This was in substantial measure the achievement of Jan Pieterszoon Coen, a bellicose young man who had no illusions about the relationship between commerce and coercion. As Coen himself put it: 'We cannot make war without trade, nor trade without war.'[28] He was ruthless in his treatment of competitors, executing British East India Company officials at Amboyna and effectively wiping out the indigenous Bandanese. A natural-born empire builder, Coen seized control of the small Javanese port of Jakarta in May 1619, renamed it Batavia and, aged just 30, duly became the first governor-general of the Dutch East Indies. He and his successor, Antonie van Diemen, systematically expanded Dutch power in the region, driving the British from the Banda Islands, the Spaniards from Ternate and Tidore, and the Portuguese from Malacca. By 1657 the Dutch controlled most of Ceylon (Sri Lanka); the following decade saw further expansion along the Malabar coast on the subcontinent

---

* Technically, the removal of uncertainty about future dividends gave the shares the character of preference shares or even bonds.

and into the island of Celebes (Sulawesi). There were also thriving Dutch bases on the Coromandel coast.[29] Fire-power and foreign trade sailed side by side on ships like the *Batavia* – a splendid replica of which can be seen today at Lelystad on the coast of Holland.

The commercial payoffs of this aggressive strategy were substantial. By the 1650s, the VOC had established an effective and highly lucrative monopoly on the export of cloves, mace and nutmeg (the production of pepper was too widely dispersed for it to be monopolized) and was becoming a major conduit for Indian textile exports from Coromandel.[30] It was also acting as a hub for intra-Asian trade, exchanging Japanese silver and copper for Indian textiles and Chinese gold and silk. In turn, Indian textiles could be traded for pepper and spices from the Pacific islands, which could be used to purchase precious metals from the Middle East.[31] Later, the Company provided financial services to other Europeans in Asia, not least Robert Clive, who transferred a large part of the fortune he had made from conquering Bengal back to London via Batavia and Amsterdam.[32] As the world's first big corporation, the VOC was able to combine economies of scale with reduced transaction costs and what economists call network externalities, the benefit of pooling information between multiple employees and agents.[33] As was true of the English East India Company, the VOC's biggest challenge was the principal–agent problem: the tendency of its men on the spot to trade on their own account, bungle transactions or simply defraud the company. This, however, was partially countered by an unusual compensation system, which linked remuneration to investments and sales, putting a priority on turnover rather than net profits.[34] Business boomed. In the 1620s, fifty VOC ships had returned from Asia laden with goods; by the 1690s the number was 156.[35] Between 1700 and 1750 the tonnage of Dutch shipping sailing back around the Cape doubled. As late as 1760 it was still roughly three times the amount of British shipping.[36]

The economic and political ascent of the VOC can be traced in its share price. The Amsterdam stock market was certainly volatile, as investors reacted to rumours of war, peace and shipwrecks in a way vividly described by the Sephardic Jew Joseph Penso de la Vega in his aptly named book *Confusión de Confusiones* (1688). Yet the long-term trend was clearly upward for more than a century after the Company's foundation. Between 1602 and 1733, VOC stock rose from par (100) to an all-time peak of 786, this despite the fact that from 1652 until the Glorious Revolution of 1688 the Company was being challenged by bellicose British competition.[37] Such sustained capital appreciation, combined with the regular dividends and stable consumer prices,* ensured that major shareholders like Dirck Bas became very wealthy indeed. As early as 1650, total dividend payments were already eight times the original investment, implying an annual rate of return of 27 per cent.[38] The striking point, however, is that there was never such a thing as a Dutch East India Company *bubble*. Unlike the Dutch tulip futures bubble of 1636–7, the ascent of the VOC stock price was gradual, spread over more than a century, and, though its descent was more rapid, it still took more than sixty years to fall back down to 120 in December 1794. This rise and fall closely tracked the rise and fall of the Dutch Empire. The prices of shares in other monopoly trading companies, outwardly similar to the VOC, would behave very

* A measure of the success of the Bank of Amsterdam was that consumer price inflation fell from 2 per cent per annum between 1550 and 1608 to 0.9 per cent p.a. between 1609 and 1658 and just 0.1 per cent p.a. between 1659 and 1779. The nearly eight-fold appreciation in the VOC stock price therefore compares reasonably well with the inflation-adjusted performance of modern stock markets.

differently, soaring and slumping in the space of just a few months. To understand why, we must rejoin John Law.

To the renegade Scotsman, Dutch finance came as a revelation. Law was fascinated by the relationships between the East India Company, the Exchange Bank and the stock exchange. Always attracted by gambling, Law found the Amsterdam *Beurs* more exciting than any casino. He marvelled at the antics of short-sellers, who spread negative rumours to try to drive down VOC share prices, or the specialists in *windhandel*, who traded speculatively in shares they did not themselves even own. Financial innovation was all around. Law himself floated an ingenious scheme to insure holders of Dutch national lottery tickets against drawing blanks.

Yet the Dutch financial system struck Law as not quite complete. For one thing, it seemed wrong-headed to restrict the number of East India Company shares when the market was so enamoured of them. Law was also puzzled by the conservatism of the Amsterdam Exchange Bank. Its own 'bank money' had proved a success, but it largely took the form of columns of figures in the bank's ledgers. Apart from receipts issued to merchants who deposited coin with the bank, the money had no physical existence. The idea was already taking shape in Law's mind of a breathtaking modification of these institutions, which would combine the properties of a monopoly trading company with a public bank that issued notes in the manner of the Bank of England. Law was soon itching to try out a whole new system of finance on an unsuspecting nation. But which one?

He first tried his luck in Genoa, trading foreign currency and securities. He spent some time in Venice, trading by day, gambling by night. In partnership with the Earl of Islay, he also built up a substantial portfolio on the London stock market. (As this suggests, Law was well connected. But there remained a disreputable quality to his conduct. Lady Catherine Knowles, daughter of the Earl of Banbury, passed as his wife and was the mother of his two children, despite the fact that she was married to another man. In 1705 he submitted to the Scottish parliament a proposal for a new bank, later published as *Money and Trade Considered*. His central idea was that the new bank should issue interest-bearing notes that would supplant coins as currency. It was rejected by the parliament shortly before the Act of Union with England.[39] Disappointed by his homeland, Law travelled to Turin and in 1711 secured an audience with Victor Amadeus II, Duke of Savoy. In *The Piedmont Memorials*, he again made the case for a paper currency. According to Law, confidence alone was the basis for public credit; with confidence, banknotes would serve just as well as coins. 'I have discovered the secret of the philosopher's stone, he told a friend, 'it is to make gold out of paper.'[40] The Duke demurred, saying 'I am not rich enough to ruin myself.'

The First Bubble

Why was it in France that Law was given the chance to try out his financial alchemy? The French knew him for what he was, after all: in 1708 the Marquis of Torcy, Louis XIV's Foreign Minister, had identified him as a professional *joueur* (gambler) and possible spy. The answer is that France's fiscal problems were especially desperate. Saddled with enormous public debt as a result of the wars of Louis XIV, the government was on the brink of its third bankruptcy in less than a century. A review (*Visa*) of the crown's existing debts was thought necessary, which led to the cancellation and reduction of many of them, in effect a partial default. Even so, 250 million new interest-bearing notes called *billets d'état* still had to be issued to fund the current deficit. Matters were only made worse by an attempt to reduce the quantity of gold and silver coinage, which plunged the economy into recession.[41] To all these problems Law claimed to have the solution.

In October 1715 Law's first proposal for a public note-issuing bank was submitted to the royal council, but it was rejected because of the opposition of the Duke of Noailles to Law's bold suggestion that the bank should also act as the crown's cashier, receiving all tax payments. A second proposal for a purely private bank was more successful. The Banque Générale was established under Law's direction in May 1716. It was licensed to issue notes payable in specie (gold or silver) for a twenty-year period. The capital was set at 6,000,000 livres (1,200 shares of 5,000 livres each), three quarters to be paid in now somewhat depreciated *billets d'état* (so the effective capital was closer to 2,850,000 livres).[42] It seemed at first quite a modest enterprise, but Law always had a grander design in mind, which he was determined to sell to the Duke of Orleans, the Regent during the minority of Louis XV. In 1717 he took another step forward when it was decreed that Banque Générale notes should be used in payment for all taxes, a measure initially resisted in some places but effectively enforced by the government.

Law's ambition was to revive economic confidence in France by establishing a public bank, on the Dutch model, but with the difference that this bank would issue paper money. As money was invested in the bank, the government's huge debt would be consolidated. At the same time, paper money would revive French trade – and with it French economic power. 'The bank is not the only, nor the grandest of my ideas,' he told the Regent. 'I will produce a work which will surprise Europe by the changes which it will effect in favour of France – changes more powerful than were produced by the discovery of the Indies . . .'[43]

Law had studied finance in republican Holland, but from the outset he saw absolutist France as a better setting for what became known as his System. 'I maintain', he wrote, 'that an absolute prince who knows how to govern can extend his credit further and find needed funds at a lower interest rate than a prince who is limited in his authority.' This was an absolutist theory of finance, based on the assertion that 'in credit as in military and legislative authorities, supreme power must reside in only one person'.[44] The key was to make royal credit work more pro- ductively than in the past, when the crown had borrowed money in a hand-to-mouth way to finance its wars. In Law's scheme, the monarch would effectively delegate his credit 'to a trading company, into which all the materials of trade in the kingdom fall successively, and are amassed into one'. The whole nation would, as he put it, 'become a body of traders, who have for cash the royal bank, in which by consequence all the commerce, money, and merchandise re-unite'.[45]

As in the Dutch case, empire played a key role in Law's vision. In his view, too little was being done to develop France's overseas possessions. He therefore proposed to take over France's trade with the Louisiana territory, a vast but wholly undeveloped tract of land stretching from the Mississippi delta across the Midwest – equivalent to nearly a quarter of what is now the United States. In 1717 a new 'Company of the West' (*Compagnie d'Occident*) was granted the monopoly of the commerce of Louisiana (as well as the control of the colony's internal affairs) for a period of twenty-five years. The Company's capital was fixed at 100 million livres, an unprecedented sum in France. Shares in the Company were priced at 500 livres each, and Frenchmen, regardless of rank, as well as foreigners were encouraged to buy them (in instalments) with the *billets d'état*, which were to be retired and converted into 4 per cent *rentes* (perpetual bonds). Law's name headed the list of directors.

There was some initial resistance to Law's System, it is true. The Duke of Saint-Simon observed wisely that:

An establishment of this sort may be good in itself; but it is only so in a republic or in a monarchy like England, whose finances are controlled by those alone who furnish them, and who only furnish as much as they please. But in a state which is weak, changeable, and absolute, like France, stability must necessarily be wanting to it; since the King ... may overthrow the Bank – the temptation to which would be too great, and at the same time too easy.[46]

As if to put this to the test, in early 1718 the Parlement of Paris launched fierce attacks on the new Finance Minister René D'Argenson (and on Law's bank) following a 40 per cent debasement of the coinage ordered by the former, which had caused, the Parlement complained, 'a chaos so great and so obscure that nothing about it can be known'.[47] A rival company, set up by the Pâris brothers, was meanwhile proving more successful in attracting investors than Law's Company of the West. In true absolutist fashion, however, the Regent forcefully reasserted the prerogatives of the crown, much to Law's delight – and benefit. ('How great is the benefit of a despotic power', he observed, 'in the beginnings of an institution subject to so much opposition on the part of a nation that has not yet become accustomed to it!')[48] Moreover, from late 1718 onwards the government granted privileges to the Company of the West that were calculated to increase the appeal of its shares. In August it was awarded the right to collect all the revenue from tobacco. In December it acquired the privileges of the Senegal Company. In a further attempt to bolster Law's position, the Banque Générale was given the royal seal of approval: it became the Banque Royale in December 1718, in effect the first French central bank. To increase the appeal of its notes, these could henceforth be exchanged for either *écus de banque* (representing fixed amounts of silver) or the more commonly used *livres tournois* (a unit of account whose relationship to gold and silver could vary). In July, however, the *écu* notes were discontinued and withdrawn,[49] while a decree of 22 April 1719 stipulated that banknotes should not share in the periodic 'diminutions' (in price) to which silver was subject.[50] France's transition from coinage to paper money had begun.

Meanwhile, the Company of the West continued to expand. In May 1719 it took over the East India and China companies, to form the Company of the Indies (*Compagnie des Indes*), better known as the Mississippi Company. In July Law secured the profits of the royal mint for a nine-year term. In August he wrested the lease of the indirect tax farms from a rival financier, who had been granted it a year before. In September the Company agreed to lend 1.2 billion livres to the crown to pay off the entire royal debt. A month later Law took control of the collection ('farm') of direct taxes.

Law was proud of his System. What had existed before, he wrote, was not much more than 'a method of receipts and disbursements'. Here, by contrast, 'you have a chain of ideas which support one another, and display more and more the principle they flow from.'[51] In modern terms, what Law was attempting could be described as reflation. The French economy had been in recession in 1716 and Law's expansion of the money supply with banknotes clearly did provide a much-needed stimulus.[52] At the same time, he was (not unreasonably) trying to convert a badly managed and burdensome public debt into the equity of an enormous, privatized tax-gathering and monopoly trading company.[53] If he were successful, the financial difficulties of the French monarchy would be at an end.

But Law had no clear idea where to stop. On the contrary, as the majority shareholder in what was now a vast corporation, he had a strong personal interest in allowing monetary expansion, which his own bank could generate, to fuel an asset bubble from which he more than anyone would profit. It was as if one man was simultaneously running all five hundred of the top US corporations, the US Treasury and the Federal Reserve System. Would such a person be likely to raise corporation taxes or interest rates at the risk of reducing the value of his massive share portfolio? Moreover, Law's System had to create a bubble or it would fail. The acquisition of the various other companies and tax farms was financed, not out of company profits, but simply by issuing new shares. On 17 June 1719 the Mississippi Company issued 50,000 of these at a price of 550 livres apiece (though each share had a face value of 500 livres, as with the earlier Company of the West shares). To ensure the success of the issue, Law personally underwrote it, a characteristic gamble that even he admitted cost him a sleepless night. And to avoid the imputation that he alone would profit if the shares rose in price, he gave existing Company of the West shareholders the exclusive right to acquire these new shares (which hence became known as 'daughters'; the earlier shares were 'mothers').[54] In July 1719 Law issued a third tranche of 50,000 shares (the 'granddaughters') – now priced at 1,000 livres each – to raise the 50 million livres he needed to pay for the royal mint. Logically, this dilution of the existing shareholders ought to have caused the price of an individual share to decline. How could Law justify a doubling of the issue price?

Ostensibly, the 'displacement' that justified higher share prices was the promise of future profits from Louisiana. That was why

No 84   Compagnie des Indes.
DIVIDENDE D'UN DIXIÈME D'ACTION; SIX
DERNIERS MOIS mil sept cent cinquante-six.

No 84   Compagnie des Indes.
DIVIDENDE D'UN DIXIÈME D'ACTION; SIX
PREMIERS MOIS mil sept cent cinquante-sept.

No 84   Compagnie des Indes.
DIVIDENDE D'UN DIXIÈME D'ACTION; SIX
DERNIERS MOIS mil sept cent cinquante-sept.

DIXIÈME D'ACTION de la Compagnie des Indes.
No 84
LE Porteur a intérêt dans la Compagnie des Indes, pour
UN DIXIÈME D'ACTION. A Paris, le 2 Janvier 1755.

CONTROLLÉ EN VERTU DE LA   Signé pour la COMPAGNIE DES INDES, en vertu
MÊME DÉLIBÉRATION.   de la Délibération du 3 Juillet 1754.

The object of speculation: A one-tenth share
in the *Compagnie des Indes* (otherwise
known as the Mississippi Company)

Law devoted so much effort to conjuring up rosy visions of
the colony as a veritable Garden of Eden, inhabited by friendly
savages, eager to furnish a cornucopia of exotic goods for shipment to France. To conduct this trade, a grand new city was
established at the mouth of the Mississippi: New Orleans, named
to flatter the always susceptible Regent. Such visions, as we know,
were not wholly without foundation, but their realization lay far
in the future. To be sure, a few thousand impoverished Germans
from the Rhineland, Switzerland and Alsace were recruited to act
as colonists. But what the unfortunate immigrants encountered
when they reached Louisiana was a sweltering, insect-infested

swamp. Within a year 80 per cent of them had died of starvation or tropical diseases like yellow fever.*

In the short term, then, a different kind of displacement was needed to justify the 40 per cent dividends Law was now paying. It was provided by paper money. From the summer of 1719 investors who wished to acquire the 'daughters' and 'granddaughters' were generously assisted by the Banque Royale, which allowed share-holders to borrow money, using their shares as collateral; money they could then invest in more shares. Predictably, the share price soared. The original 'mothers' stood at 2,750 livres on 1 August, 4,100 on 30 August and 5,000 on 4 September. This prompted Law to issue 100,000 more shares at this new market price. Two further issues of the same amount followed on 28 September and 2 October, followed by a smaller block of 24,000 shares two days later (though these were never offered to the public). In the autumn of 1719 the share price passed 9,000 livres, reaching a new high (10,025) on 2 December. The informal futures market saw them trading at 12,500 livres for delivery in March 1720. The mood was now shifting rapidly from euphoria to mania.[55]

A few people smelt a rat. 'Have you all gone crazy in Paris?' wrote Voltaire to M. de Génonville in 1719. 'It is a chaos I cannot fathom . . .'[56] The Irish banker and economist Richard Cantillon was so sure that Law's System would implode that he sold up and left Paris in early August 1719.[57] From London Daniel Defoe was dismissive: the French had merely 'run up a piece of re-fined air'. Law's career, he sneered, illustrated a new strategy for success in life:

You must put on a sword, kill a beau or two, get into Newgate [prison], be condemned to be hanged, break prison if you can –

---

* Traces of the survivors can still be found in the Acadiana parishes of St Charles, St James and St John the Baptist.

remember that by the way – get over to some strange country, turn stock-jobber, set up a Mississippi stock, bubble a nation, and you will soon be a great man; if you have but great good luck . . .[58]

But a substantial number of better-off Parisians were seduced by Law. Flush with cash of his own making, he offered to pay pension arrears and indeed to pay pensions in advance – a sure way to build support among the privileged classes. By September 1719 there were hundreds of people thronging the rue Quincampoix, a narrow thoroughfare between the rue St Martin and the rue St Denis where the Company had its share-issuing office. A clerk at the British embassy described it as 'crowded from early in the morning to late at night with princes and princesses, dukes and peers and duchesses etc., in a word all that is great in France. They sell estates and pawn jewels to purchase Mississippi.'[59] Lady Mary Wortley Montagu, who visited Paris in 1719, was 'delighted . . . to see an Englishman (at least a Briton) absolute in Paris, I mean Mr. Law, who treats their dukes and peers extremely *de haut en bas* and is treated by them with the utmost submission and respect – Poor souls!'[60] It was in these heady times that the word *millionaire* was first coined. (Like entrepreneurs, millionaires were invented in France.)

Small wonder John Law was seen at Mass for the first time on 10 December, having converted to Catholicism in order to be eligible for public office. He had much to thank his Maker for. When he was duly appointed Controller General of Finances the following month, his triumph was complete. He was now in charge of:

> the collection of all France's indirect taxes;
> the entire French national debt;
> the twenty-six French mints that produced the country's gold and silver coins;

The end of the show in the rue Quincampoix, 1719, from *The Great Scene of Folly*, published in Amsterdam a year later

the colony of Louisiana;

the Mississippi Company, which had a monopoly on the import and sale of tobacco;

the French fur trade with Canada; and

all France's trade with Africa, Asia and the East Indies.

Further, in his own right, Law owned:

the Hôtel de Nevers in the rue de Richelieu (now the Bibliothèque Nationale);

the Mazarin Palace, where the Company had its offices;

more than a third of the buildings at the place Vendôme (then place Louis le Grand);

more than twelve country estates;
several plantations in Louisiana; and
100 million livres of shares in the Mississippi Company.[61]

Louis XIV of France had said '*L'état, c'est moi*': I am the state. John Law could legitimately say '*L'économie, c'est moi*': I am the economy.

In truth, John Law preferred gambling to praying. In March 1719, for example, he had bet the Duke of Bourbon a thousand new louis d'or that there would be no more ice that winter or spring. (He lost.) On another occasion he wagered 10,000 to 1 that a friend could not throw a designated number with six dice at one throw. (He probably won on that occasion, since the odds against doing so are 6^6 to 1, or 46,656 to 1.) But his biggest bet was on his own System. Law's 'daily discourse', reported an uneasy British diplomat in August 1719, was that he would 'set France higher than ever she was before, and put her in a condition to give the law to all Europe; that he can ruin the trade and credit of England and Holland, whenever he pleases; that he can break our bank, whenever he has a mind; and our East India Company.'[62] Putting his money where his mouth was, Law had made a bet with Thomas Pitt, Earl of Londonderry (and uncle of the Prime Minister William Pitt), that British shares would fall in price in the year ahead. He sold £100,000 of East India stock short for £180,000 (that is at a price of £180 per share, or 80 per cent above face value) for delivery on 25 August 1720.[63] (The price of the shares at the end of August 1719 was £194, indicating Law's expectation of a £14 price decline.)

Yet the con at the heart of Law's confidence could not be sustained indefinitely. Even before his appointment as Controller General, the first signs of phase 4 of the five-stage bubble cycle –

distress – had begun to manifest themselves. When the Mississippi share price began to decline in December 1719, touching 7,930 livres on 14 December, Law resorted to the first of many artificial expedients to prop it up, opening a bureau at the Banque Royale that guaranteed to buy (and sell) the shares at a floor price of 9,000 livres. As if to simplify matters, on 22 February 1720 it was announced that the Company was taking over the Banque Royale. Law also created options (*primes*) costing 1,000 livres which entitled the owner to buy a share for 10,000 livres over the following six months (that is an effective price of 11,000 livres – 900 livres above the actual peak price of 10,100 reached on 8 January). These measures sufficed to keep the share price above 9,000 livres until mid-January (though the effect of the floor price was to render the options worthless; generously Law allowed holders to convert them into shares at the rate of ten *primes* per share).

Inflation, however, was now accelerating alarmingly outside the stock market. At their peak in September 1720, prices in Paris were roughly double what they had been two years before, with most of the increase coming in the previous eleven months. This was a reflection of the extraordinary increase in note circulation Law had caused. In the space of little more than a year he had more than doubled the volume of paper currency. By May 1720 the total money supply (banknotes and shares held by the public, since the latter could be turned into cash at will) was roughly four times larger in livre terms than the gold and silver coinage France had previously used.[64] Not surprisingly, some people began to anticipate a depreciation of the banknotes, and began to revert to payment in gold and silver. Ever the absolutist, Law's initial response was to resort to compulsion. Banknotes were made legal tender. The export of gold and silver was banned as was the production and sale of gold and silver objects. By the

The Mississippi Bubble: Money and share prices (livres)

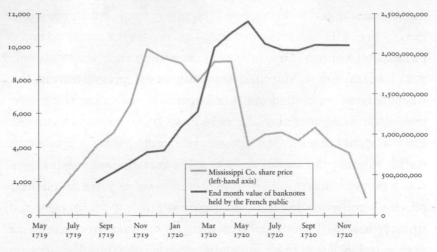

arrêt of 27 February 1720, it became illegal for a private citizen to possess more than 500 livres of metal coin. The authorities were empowered to enforce this measure by searching people's houses. Voltaire called this 'the most unjust edict ever rendered' and 'the final limit of a tyrannical absurdity'.[65]

At the same time, Law obsessively tinkered with the exchange rate of the banknotes in terms of gold and silver, altering the official price of gold twenty-eight times and the price of silver no fewer than thirty-five times between September 1719 and December 1720 – all in an effort to make banknotes more attractive than coins to the public. But the flow of sometimes contradictory regulations served only to bewilder people and to illustrate the propensity of an absolutist regime to make up the economic rules to suit itself. 'By an all new secret magic,' one observer later recalled, 'words assembled and formed Edicts that no one comprehended, and the air was filled with obscure ideas and chimeras.'[66] One day gold and silver could be freely exported; the next day not. One day notes were being printed as fast as the printing presses could operate; the next Law was aiming to cap the banknote supply at 1.2 million livres. One day there was a floor price of 9,000 livres for Mississippi shares; the next day not. When this floor was removed on 22 February the shares predictably slumped. By the end of the month they were down to 7,825 livres. On 5 March, apparently under pressure from the Regent, Law performed another U-turn, reinstituting the 9,000 livre floor and reopening the bureau to buy them at this price. But this meant that the lid was once again removed from the money supply – despite the assertion in the same decree that 'the banknote was a money which could not be altered in value', and despite the previous commitment to a 1.2 million livre cap.[67] By now the smarter investors were more than happy to have 9,000 livres in cash for their each of their shares. Between February and May 1720 there was a 94 per cent increase in the public's holdings of banknotes. Meanwhile their holdings of shares slumped to less than a third of the total number issued. It seemed inevitable that before long all the shares would be unloaded on the Company, unleashing a further flood of banknotes and a surge in inflation.

On 21 May, in a desperate bid to avert meltdown, Law induced the Regent to issue a deflationary decree, reducing the official price of Company shares in monthly steps from 9,000 livres to 5,000 and at the same time halving the number of banknotes in circulation. He also devalued the banknotes, having revoked the previous order guaranteeing that this would not happen. This was when the limits of royal absolutism, the foundation of Law's System, suddenly became apparent. Violent public outcry forced the government to revoke these measures just six days after their announcement, but the damage to confidence in the System was, by this time, irrevocable. After an initial lull, the share price slid from 9,005 livres (16 May) to 4,200 (31 May). Angry crowds gathered outside the Bank, which had difficulty meeting the demand for notes. Stones were thrown, windows broken. 'The heaviest loss', wrote one British observer, 'falls on the people of this country and affects all ranks and conditions among them. It is not possible to express how great and general their consternation and despair have appeared to be on this occasion; the Princes of the blood and all the great men exclaim very warmly against it.'[68] Law was roundly denounced at an extraordinary meeting of the Parlement. The Regent retreated, revoking the 21 May decree. Law offered his resignation, but was dismissed outright on 29 May. He was placed under house arrest; his enemies wanted to see him in the Bastille. For the second time in his life, Law faced jail, conceivably even death. (An investigative commission quickly found evidence that Law's issues of banknotes had breached the authorized limit, so grounds existed for a prosecution.) The Banque Royale closed its doors.

John Law was an escape artist as well as a con artist. It quickly became apparent that no one but him stood any chance of averting a complete collapse of the financial system – which was, after all, his System. His recall to power (in the less exalted post of Intendant General of Commerce) caused a rally on the stock market, with Mississippi Company shares rising back to 6,350 livres on 6 June. It was, however, only a temporary reprieve. On 10 October the government was forced to reintroduce the use of gold and silver in domestic transactions. The Mississippi share price resumed its downward slide not long after, hitting 2,000 livres in September and 1,000 in December. Full-blown panic could no longer be postponed. It was at this moment that Law, vilified by the people, and lampooned by the press, finally fled the country. He had a 'touching farewell' with the Duke of Orleans before he went. 'Sire,' said Law, 'I acknowledge that I have made great mistakes. I made them because I am only human, and all men are liable to err. But I declare that none of these acts proceeded from malice or dishonesty, and that nothing of that character will be discovered in the whole course of my conduct.'[69] Nevertheless, his wife and daughter were not allowed to leave France so long as he was under investigation.

As if pricked by a sword, the Mississippi Bubble had now burst, and the noise of escaping air resounded throughout Europe. So incensed was one Dutch investor that he had a series of satirical plates specially commissioned in China. The inscription on one reads: 'By God, all my stock's worthless!' Another is even more direct: 'Shit shares and wind trade.' As far as investors in Amsterdam were concerned, Law's company had been trading in nothing more substantial than wind – in marked contrast to the Dutch East India Company, which had literally delivered the goods in the form of spices and cloth. As the verses on one satirical Dutch cartoon flysheet put it:

> This is the wondrous Mississippi land,
> Made famous by its share dealings,
> Which through deceit and devious conduct,
> Has squandered countless treasures.
> However men regard the shares,
> It is wind and smoke and nothing more.

A series of humorously allegorical engravings were produced and published as *The Great Scene of Folly*, which depicted bare-arsed stockbrokers eating coin and excreting Mississippi stock; demented investors running amok in the rue Quincampoix, before being hauled off to the madhouse; and Law himself, blithely passing by castles in the air in a carriage pulled by two bedraggled Gallic cockerels.[70]

Law himself did not walk away financially unscathed. He left France with next to nothing, thanks to his bet with Londonderry that English East India stock would fall to £180. By April 1720 the price had risen to £235 and it continued to rise as investors

Brokers turning coin into Mississippi stock and wind: engraving
from *The Great Scene of Folly* (1720)

exited the Paris market for what seemed the safer haven of
London (then in the grip of its own less spectacular South Sea
Bubble). By June the price was at £420, declining only slightly to
£345 in August, when Law's bet fell due. Law's London banker,
George Middleton, was also ruined in his effort to honour his
client's obligation. The losses to France, however, were more
than just financial. Law's bubble and bust fatally set back France's
financial development, putting Frenchmen off paper money and
stock markets for generations. The French monarchy's fiscal crisis
went unresolved and for the remainder of the reigns of Louis XV
and his successor Louis XVI the crown essentially lived from
hand to mouth, lurching from one abortive reform to another
until royal bankruptcy finally precipitated revolution. The magnitude of the catastrophe was perhaps best captured by Bernard

A page from Fibonacci's *Liber Abaci* ('The Book of Calculation'), published in 1202, which applied Hindu and Arabic numerals and mathematics to financial problems like the calculation of interest.

(*above*) Botticelli's *Adoration of the Magi*: the nativity of the respectable banker, with members of the Medici family striking biblical poses.

(*left*) Nathan Mayer Rothschild: 'the financial Bonaparte' and master of the early nineteenth-century bond market.

N° 180. 4° année. 16 Avril 1898.　　　　　　　　　　　　　　15 centimes.

Le Rire

JOURNAL HUMORISTIQUE PARAISSANT LE SAMEDI

Un an : Paris, 8 fr.
Départements, 9 fr. Étranger, 11 fr.

Six mois : France, 5 fr. Étranger, 6 fr.

M. Félix JUVEN, Directeur. — Partie artistique : M. Arsène ALEXANDRE

La reproduction des dessins du RIRE est absolument interdite aux publications, françaises ou étrangères, sans autorisation.

10, rue Saint-Joseph, 10
PARIS

Les manuscrits et dessins non
insérés ne sont pas rendus.

LE GOTHA DU « RIRE » — N° IX　　　　　　　　　　ROTHSCHILD

Dessin de C. LÉANDRE

'Rothschild': anti-Semitic cartoon from the French satirical magazine
Le Rire, 1898.

The sinews of Civil War: Union gunships in action on the Mississippi at the Battle of Vicksburg.

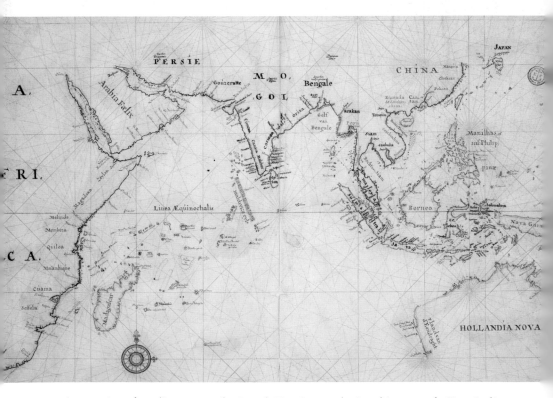

An empire of trading posts: the Dutch Empire, as depicted in an early East India Company map.

Emanuel de Witte, *Beurs van Amsterdam* (*The Amsterdam Bourse*), 1653: the first true stock exchange, where shares in the East India Company could be bought and sold.

Portrait of John Law, convicted murderer, monetary theorist
and architect of the first great stock market bubble.

(*top*) Map of Louisiana, the land of plenty from which the Mississippi
Company was supposed to make its money.

(*below*) Image of Louisiana for the consumption of Mississippi Company investors.

Two Dutch plates inspired by the Mississippi Crash: the first reads, 'By God, all my stock's worthless!'; the caption on the second is 'shit shares and wind trade'.

Bernard Picart, *Monument Consecrated to Posterity* (1721)

Picart in his elaborate engraving *Monument Consecrated to Posterity* (1721). On the left, penniless Dutch investors troop morosely into the sickhouse, the madhouse and the poorhouse. But the Parisian scene to the right is more apocalyptic. A naked Fortuna rains down Mississippi stock and options on a mob emanating from the rue Quincampoix, while a juggernaut drawn by Indians crushes an accountant under a huge wheel of fortune and two men brawl in the foreground.[71]

In Britain, by contrast, the contemporaneous South Sea Bubble was significantly smaller and ruined fewer people – not least because the South Sea Company never gained control of the Bank of England the way Law had controlled the Banque Royale. In essence, his English counterpart John Blunt's South Sea scheme was to convert government debt of various kinds, most of it

155

created to fund the War of the Spanish Succession, into the equity of a company that had been chartered to monopolize trade with the Spanish Empire in South America. Having agreed on conversion prices for the annuities and other debt instruments, the directors of the South Sea Company stood to profit if they could get the existing holders of government annuities to accept South Sea shares at a high market price, since this would leave the directors with surplus shares to sell to the public.[72] In this they succeeded, using tricks similar to those employed by Law in Paris. Shares were offered to the public in four tranches, with the price rising from £300 per share in April 1720 to £1,000 in June. Instalment payment was permitted. Loans were offered against shares. Generous dividends were paid. Euphoria duly gave way to mania; as the poet Alexander Pope observed, it was 'ignominious (in this Age of Hope and Golden Mountains) not to Venture'.[73]

Unlike Law, however, Blunt and his associates had to contend with competition from the Bank of England, which drove up the terms they had to offer the annuitants. Unlike Law, they also had to contend with political opposition in the form of the Whigs in Parliament, which drove up the bribes they had to pay to secure favourable legislation (the Secretary to the Treasury alone made £249,000 from his share options). And, unlike Law, they were unable to establish monopolistic positions on the stock market and the credit market. On the contrary, there was such a rush of new companies – 190 in all – seeking to raise capital in 1720 that the South Sea directors had to get their allies in Parliament to pass what came to be known as the Bubble Act, designed to restrict new company flotations.* At the same time, when the demand for cash created by the South Sea's third subscription

* The Bubble Act made it illegal to establish new companies without statutory authority and prevented existing companies from conducting activities not specified in their charters.

exceeded the money market's resources, there was nothing the directors could do to inject additional liquidity; indeed, the South Sea Company's bank, the Sword Blade Company, ended up failing on 24 September. (Unlike the Bank of England, and unlike the Banque Royale, its notes were not legal tender.) The mania of May and June was followed, after a hiatus of distress in July (when the insiders and foreign speculators took their profits), by panic in August. 'Most people thought it wou'd come,' lamented the hapless and now poorer Swift, 'but no man prepar'd for it; no man consider'd it would come *like a Thief in the night*, exactly as it happens in the case of death.'[74]

Yet the damage caused by the bursting of the bubble was much less fatal than on the other side of the Channel. From par to peak, prices rose by a factor of 9.5 in the case of South Sea stock, compared with 19.6 in the case of Mississippi stock. Other stocks (Bank of England and East India Company) rose by substantially smaller multiples. When stock prices came back down to earth in London, there was no lasting systemic damage to the financial system, aside from the constraint on future joint-stock company formation represented by the Bubble Act. The South Sea Company itself continued to exist; the government debt conversion was not reversed; foreign investors did not turn away from English securities.[75] Whereas all France was affected by the inflationary crisis Law had unleashed, provincial England seems to have been little affected by the South Sea crash.[76] In this tale of two bubbles, it was the French that had the worst of times.

Bulls and Bears

On 16 October 1929 Yale University economics professor Irving Fisher declared that US stock prices had 'reached what looks like a permanently high plateau'.[77] Eight days later, on 'Black Thursday', the Dow Jones Industrial Average declined by 2 per cent. This is when the Wall Street crash is conventionally said to have begun, though in fact the market had been slipping since early September and had already suffered a sharp 6 per cent drop on 23 October. On 'Black Monday' (28 October) it plunged by 13 per cent; the next day by a further 12 per cent. In the course of the next three years the US stock market declined a staggering 89 per cent, reaching its nadir in July 1932. The index did not regain its 1929 peak until November 1954. What was worse, this asset price deflation coincided with, if it did not actually cause, the worst depression in all history. In the United States, output collapsed by a third. Unemployment reached a quarter of the civilian labour force, closer to a third if a modern definition is used. It was a global catastrophe that saw prices and output decline in nearly every economy in the world, though only the German slump was as severe as the American. World trade shrank by two thirds as countries sought vainly to hide behind tariff barriers and import quotas. The international financial system fell to pieces in a welter of debt defaults, capital controls and currency depreciations. Only the Soviet Union, with its autarkic, planned economy, was unaffected. Why did it happen?

Some financial disasters have obvious causes. Arguably a much worse stock market crash had occurred at the end of July 1914, when the outbreak of the First World War precipitated such a total meltdown that the world's principal stock markets – including New York's – simply had to close their doors. And closed they remained from August until the end of 1914.[78] But that was the effect of a world war that struck financial markets like a bolt from the blue.[79] The crash of October 1929 is much harder to explain. Page 1 of the *New York Times* on the day before Black Thursday featured articles about the fall of the French premier

Aristide Briand and a vote in the US Senate about duties on imported chemicals. Historians sometimes see the deadlock over Germany's post-First World War reparations and the increase of American protectionism as triggers of the Depression. But page 1 also features at least four reports on the atrocious gales that had battered the Eastern seaboard the previous day.[80] Maybe historians should blame bad weather for the Wall Street crash. (That might not be such a far-fetched proposition. Many veterans of the City of London still remember that Black Monday – 19 October 1987 – came after the hurricane-force winds that had unexpectedly swept the south-east of England the previous Friday.)

Contemporaries sensed that there was a psychological dimension to the crisis. In his inaugural address, President Franklin Roosevelt argued that all that Americans had to fear was 'fear itself'. John Maynard Keynes spoke of a 'failure in the immaterial devices of the mind'. Yet both men also intimated that the crisis was partly due to financial misconduct. Roosevelt took a swipe at 'the unscrupulous money changers' of Wall Street; in his *General Theory*, Keynes likened the stock market to a casino.

In some measure, it can be argued, the Great Depression had its roots in the global economic dislocations arising from the earlier crisis of 1914. During the First World War, non-European agricultural and industrial production had expanded. When European production came back on stream after the return of peace, there was chronic over-capacity, which had driven down prices of primary products long before 1929. This had made it even harder for countries with large external war debts (including Germany, saddled with reparations) to earn the hard currency they needed to make interest payments to their foreign creditors. The war had also increased the power of organized labour in most combatant countries, making it harder for employers to cut wages in response to price falls. As profit margins were squeezed by rising real wages, firms were forced to lay off workers or risk going bust. Nevertheless, the fact remains that the United States, which was the epicentre of the crisis, was in many respects in fine economic fettle when the Depression struck. There was no shortage of productivity-enhancing technological innovation in the inter-war period by companies like DuPont (nylon), Procter & Gamble (soap powder), Revlon (cosmetics), RCA (radio) and IBM (accounting machines). 'A prime reason for expecting future earnings to be greater,' argued Yale's Irving Fisher, 'was that we in America were applying science and invention to industry as we had never applied them before.'[81] Management practices were also being revolutionized by men like Alfred Sloan at General Motors.

Yet precisely these strengths may have provided the initial displacement that set in motion a classic stock market bubble. To observers like Fisher, it really did seem as if the sky was the limit, as more and more American households aspired to equip themselves with automobiles and consumer durables – products which instalment credit put within their reach. RCA, the tech stock of the 1920s, rose by a dizzying 939 per cent between 1925 and 1929; its price-earnings ratio at the peak of the market was 73.[82] Euphoria encouraged a rush of new initial public offerings (IPOs); stock worth $6 billion was issued in 1929, one sixth of it during September. There was a proliferation of new financial institutions known as investment trusts, designed to capitalize on the stock market boom. (Goldman Sachs chose 8 August 1929 to announce its own expansion plan, in the form of the Goldman Sachs Trading Corporation; had this not been a free-standing entity, its subsequent collapse might well have taken down Goldman Sachs itself.) At the same time, many small investors (like Irving Fisher himself) relied on leverage to increase their stock market exposure, using brokers' loans (which were often supplied by corporations rather than banks) to buy stocks on margin, thus paying only a fraction of the purchase price with their own money. As in 1719, so in 1929, there were unscrupulous insiders, like Charles E. Mitchell of National City Bank or William Crapo Durant of GM, and ingenuous outsiders, like Groucho Marx.[83] As in 1719, flows of hot money between financial markets served to magnify and transmit shocks. And, as in 1719, it was the action of the monetary authorities that determined the magnitude of the bubble and of the consequences when it burst.

In perhaps the most important work of American economic history ever published, Milton Friedman and Anna Schwartz argued that it was the Federal Reserve System that bore the primary responsibility for turning the crisis of 1929 into a Great Depression.[84] They did not blame the Fed for the bubble itself, arguing that with Benjamin Strong at the Federal Reserve Bank of New York a reasonable balance had been struck between the international obligation of the United States to maintain the restored gold standard and its domestic obligation to maintain price stability. By sterilizing the large gold inflows to the United States (preventing them for generating monetary expansion), the Fed may indeed have prevented the bubble from growing even larger. The New York Fed also responded effectively to the October 1929 panic by conducting large-scale (and unauthorized) open market operations (buying bonds from the financial sector) to inject liquidity into the market. However, after Strong's death from tuberculosis in October 1928, the Federal Reserve Board in Washington came to dominate monetary policy, with disastrous results. First, too little was done to counteract the credit contraction caused by banking failures. This problem had already surfaced several months before the stock market crash, when commercial banks with deposits of more than $80 million suspended payments. However, it reached critical mass in November and December 1930, when 608 banks failed, with deposits totalling $550 million, among them the Bank of United States, which accounted for more than a third of the total deposits lost. The failure of merger talks that might have saved the Bank was a critical moment in the history of the Depression.[85] Secondly, under the pre-1913 system, before the Fed had been created, a crisis of this sort would have triggered a restriction of convertibility of bank deposits into gold. However, the Fed made matters worse by reducing the amount of credit outstanding (December 1930–April 1931). This forced more and more banks to sell assets in a frantic dash for liquidity, driving down bond prices and worsening the general position. The next wave of bank failures, between February and August 1931, saw commercial bank deposits fall by $2.7 billion, 9 per cent of the total.[86] Thirdly, when Britain abandoned the gold standard in September 1931, precipitating a rush by foreign banks to convert dollar holdings into gold, the Fed raised its discount rate in two steps to 3.5 per cent. This halted the external drain, but drove yet more US banks over the edge: the period August 1931 to January 1932 saw 1,860 banks fail with deposits of $1.45 billion.[87] Yet the Fed was in no danger of running out of gold. On the eve of the pound's departure the US gold stock was at an all-time high of $4.7 billion – 40 per cent of the world's total. Even at its lowest point that October, the Fed's gold reserves exceeded its legal requirements for cover by more than $1 billion.[88] Fourthly, only in April 1932, as a result of massive political pressure, did the Fed attempt large-scale open market operations, the first serious step it had taken to counter the liquidity crisis. Even this did not suffice to avert a final wave of bank failures in the last quarter of 1932, which precipitated the first state-wide 'bank holidays', temporary closures of all banks.[89] Fifthly, when rumours that the new Roosevelt administration would devalue the dollar led to a renewed domestic and foreign flight from dollars into gold, the Fed once again raised the discount rate, setting the scene for the nationwide bank holiday proclaimed by Roosevelt on 6 March 1933, two days after his inauguration – a holiday from which 2,000 banks never returned.[90]

The Fed's inability to avert a total of around 10,000 bank failures was crucial not just because of the shock to consumers whose deposits were lost or to shareholders whose equity was lost, but because of the broader effect on the money supply and the volume of credit. Between 1929 and 1933, the public succeeded in increasing its cash holdings by 31 per cent; commercial bank reserves were scarcely altered (indeed, surviving banks built up excess reserves); but commercial bank deposits decreased by 37 per cent and loans by 47 per cent. The absolute numbers reveal the lethal dynamic of the 'great contraction'. An increase of cash in public hands of $1.2 billion was achieved at the cost of a decline in bank deposits of $15.6 billion and a decline in bank loans of $19.6 billion, equivalent to 19 per cent of 1929 GDP.[91]

There was a time when academic historians felt squeamish about claiming that lessons could be learned from history. This is a feeling unknown to economists, two generations of whom have struggled to explain the Great Depression precisely in order to avoid its recurrence. Of all the lessons to have emerged from this collective effort, this remains the most important: that inept or inflexible monetary policy in the wake of a sharp decline in asset prices can turn a correction into a recession and a recession into a depression. According to Friedman and Schwartz, the Fed should have aggressively sought to inject liquidity into the banking system from 1929 onwards, using open market operations on a large scale, and expanding rather than contracting lending through the discount window. They also suggest that less attention should have been paid to gold outflows. More recently, it has been argued that the inter-war gold standard itself was the problem, in that it transmitted crises (like the 1931 European bank and currency crises) around the world.[92] A second lesson of history would therefore seem to be that the benefits of a stable exchange rate are not so great as to exceed the costs of domestic deflation. Anyone who today doubts that there are lessons to be learned from history needs do no more than compare the academic writings and recent actions of the current chairman of the Federal Reserve System.[93]

A Tale of Fat Tails

Sometimes the most important historical events are the non-events: the things that did not occur. The economist Hyman Minsky put it well when he observed: 'The most significant economic event of the era since World War II is something that has not happened: there has not been a deep and long-lasting depression'.[94] This is indeed surprising, since the world has not been short of 'Black Days'.

If movements in stock market indices were statistically distributed like human heights there would hardly be any such days. Most would be clustered around the average, with only a tiny number of extreme ups or downs. After all, not many of us are below four feet in height or above eight feet. If I drew a histogram of the heights of the male students in my financial history class according to their frequency, the result would be a classic bell-shaped curve, with nearly everyone clustered within around five inches of the US average of around 5' 10''. But in financial markets, it doesn't look like this. If you plot all the monthly movements of the Dow Jones index on a chart, there is much less clustering around the average, and there are many more big rises and falls out at the extremes, which the statisticians call 'fat tails'. If stock market movements followed the 'normal distribution' or bell curve, like human heights, an annual drop of 10 per cent or more would happen only once every 500 years, whereas on the Dow Jones it has happened about once every five years.[95] And stock market plunges of 20 per cent or more would be unheard of – rather like people just a foot tall – whereas in fact there have been nine such crashes in the past century.

On 'Black Monday', 19 October 1987, the Dow fell by a terrifying 23 per cent, one of just four days when the index has fallen by more than 10 per cent in a single trading session. The *New York Times*'s front page the next morning said it all when it asked 'Does 1987 Equal 1929?' From peak to trough, the fall was of nearly one third, a loss in the value of American stocks of close to a trillion dollars. The causes of the crash were much debated at the time. True, the Fed had raised rates the previous month from 5.5 to 6 per cent. But the official task force chaired by Nicholas Brady laid much of the blame for the crash on 'mechanical, price-insensitive selling by a [small] number of institutions employing portfolio insurance strategies and a small number of mutual fund groups reacting to redemptions', as well as 'a number of aggressive trading-oriented institutions [which tried] to sell in anticipation of further market declines'. Matters were made worse by a breakdown in the New York Stock Exchange's automated transaction system, and by the lack of 'circuit breakers' which might have interrupted the sell-off on the futures and options markets.[96] The remarkable thing, however, was what happened next – or rather, what didn't happen. There was no Great Depression of the 1990s, despite the forebodings of Lord Rees-Mogg and others.[97] There wasn't even a recession in 1988 (only a modest one in 1990–91). Within little more than a year of Black Monday, the Dow was back to where it had been before the crash. For this, some credit must unquestionably be given to the central bankers, and particularly the then novice Federal Reserve Chairman Alan Greenspan, who had taken over from Paul Volcker just two months before. Greenspan's response to the Black Monday crash was swift and effective. His terse statement on 20 October, affirming the Fed's 'readiness to serve as a source of liquidity to support the economic and financial system', sent a signal to the markets, and particularly the New York banks, that if things got really bad he stood ready to bail them out.[98] Aggressively buying government bonds in the open market, the Fed injected badly needed cash into the system, pushing down the cost of borrowing from the Fed by nearly 2 per cent in the space of sixteen days. Wall Street breathed again. What Minsky called 'It' had not happened.

Having contained a panic once, the dilemma that lurked in the back of Greenspan's mind thereafter was whether or not to act pre-emptively the next time – to prevent the panic altogether. This dilemma came to the fore as a classic stock market bubble took shape in the mid 1990s. The displacement in this case was the explosion of innovation by the technology and software industry as personal computers met the Internet. But, as in all history's bubbles, an accommodative monetary policy also played a role. From a peak of 6 per cent in June 1995, the Federal funds target rate* had been reduced to 5.25 per cent (January

* This is the interest rate at which banks lend balances held at the Federal Reserve to one another, usually overnight. The Federal Open Market Committee, which is made up of the seven Federal Reserve Board governors and the presidents of the twelve regional Federal Reserve banks, sets a target rate at its regular meetings. The Federal Reserve Bank of New York has the job

1996–February 1997). It had been raised to 5.5 per cent in March 1997, but then cut in steps between September and November 1998 down to 4.75 per cent; and it remained at that level until May 1999, by which time the Dow had passed the 10,000 mark. Rates were not raised until June 1999.

Why did the Fed allow euphoria to run loose in the 1990s? Greenspan himself had felt constrained to warn about 'irrational exuberance' on the stock market as early as 5 December 1996, shortly after the Dow had risen above 6,000.* Yet the quarter point rate increase of March 1997 was scarcely sufficient to dispel that exuberance. Partly, Greenspan and his colleagues seem to have underestimated the momentum of the technology bubble. As early as December 1995, with the Dow just past the 5,000 mark, members of the Fed's Open Market Committee speculated that the market might be approaching its peak.[99] Partly, it was because Greenspan felt it was not for the Fed to worry about asset price inflation, only consumer price inflation; and this, he believed, was being reduced by a major improvement in productivity due precisely to the tech boom.[100] Partly, as so often happens in stock market bubbles, it was because international pressures – in this case, the crisis precipitated by the Russian debt default of August 1998 – required contrary action.[101] Partly, it was because Greenspan and his colleagues no longer believed it was the role of the Fed to remove the punchbowl from the party,

---

of making this rate effective through open market operations (buying or selling bonds in the New York market).

* His wording was characteristically opaque: 'Clearly, sustained low inflation implies less uncertainty about the future, and lower risk premiums imply higher prices of stocks . . . But how do we know when irrational exuberance has unduly escalated asset values . . . ? We as central bankers need not be concerned if a collapsing financial asset bubble does not threaten to impair the real economy . . . But we should not underestimate, or become complacent about, the complexity of the interactions of asset markets and the economy'.

in the phrase of his precursor but three, William McChesney Martin, Jr.[102] To give Greenspan his due, his 'just-in-time monetary policy' certainly averted a stock market crash. Not only were the 1930s averted; so too was a repeat of the Japanese experience, when a conscious effort by the central bank to prick an asset bubble ended up triggering an 80 per cent stock market sell-off and a decade of economic stagnation. But there was a price to pay for this strategy. Not for the first time in stock market history, an asset-price bubble created the perfect conditions for malfeasance as well as exuberance.

The nineties seemed to some nervous observers uncannily like a re-run of the Roaring Twenties; and indeed the trajectory of the stock market in the 1990s was almost identical to that of the 1920s. Yet in some ways it was more like a rerun of the 1720s. What John Law's Mississippi Company had been to the bubble that launched the eighteenth century, so another company would be to the bubble that ended the twentieth. It was a company that promised its investors wealth beyond their wildest imaginings. It was a company that claimed to have reinvented the entire financial system. And it was a company that took full advantage of its impeccable political connections to ride all the way to the top of the bull market. Named by *Fortune* magazine as America's Most Innovative Company for six consecutive years (1996–2001), that company was Enron.

In November 2001, Alan Greenspan received a prestigious award, adding his name to a roll of honour that included Mikhail Gorbachev, Colin Powell and Nelson Mandela. The award was the Enron Prize for Distinguished Public Service. Greenspan had certainly earned his accolade. From February 1995 until June 1999 he had raised US interest rates only once. Traders had begun to speak of the 'Greenspan put' because having him at the Fed was

like having a 'put' option on the stock market (an option but not
an obligation to sell stocks at a good price in the future). Since
the middle of January 2000, however, the US stock market had
been plummeting, belatedly vindicating Greenspan's earlier warn-
ings about irrational exuberance. There was no one Black Day,
as in 1987. Indeed, as the Fed slashed rates, from 6.5 per cent
down in steps to 3.5 per cent by August 2001, the economy
looked like having a soft landing; at worst a very short recession.
And then, quite without warning, a Black Day did dawn in New
York – in the form not of a financial crash but of two deliberate
plane crashes. Amid talk of war and fears of a 1914-style market
shutdown, Greenspan slashed rates again, from 3.5 per cent to
3 per cent and then on down – and down – to an all-time low of
1 per cent in June 2003. More liquidity was pumped out by the
Fed after 9/11 than by all the fire engines in Manhattan. But it
could not save Enron. On 2 December 2001, just two weeks
after Greenspan collected his Enron award, the company filed for
bankruptcy.

The resemblances between the careers of John Law, perpetrator
of the Mississippi bubble, and Kenneth Lay, chief executive of
Enron, are striking, to say the least. John Law's philosopher's
stone had allowed him 'to make gold out of paper'. Ken Lay's
equivalent was 'to make gold out of gas'. Law's plan had been to
revolutionize French government finance. Lay's was to revolutionize the global energy business. For years the industry had
been dominated by huge utility companies that both physically
provided the energy – pumped the gas and generated the electricity – and sold it on to consumers. Lay's big idea, supplied by
McKinsey consultant Jeffrey K. Skilling, was to create a kind
of Energy Bank, which would act as the intermediary between
suppliers and consumers.[103] Like Law, Lay, the son of a poor
Missouri preacher, had provincial beginnings – as did Enron,

Alan Greenspan and Kenneth Lay

originally a small gas company in Omaha, Nebraska. It was Lay who renamed the company* and relocated its headquarters to Houston, Texas. Like Law, too, Lay had friends in high places. Himself a long-time ally of the Texan energy industry, President George H. W. Bush supported legislation in 1992 that deregulated the industry and removed government price controls. Around three quarters of Enron's $6.6 million in political contributions went to the Republican Party, including $355,000 from Lay and his wife in the 2000 election. Senator Phil Gramm was Enron's second-largest recipient of campaign contributions in 1996, and a strong proponent of Californian energy deregulation.

By the end of 2000, Enron was America's fourth-largest

* The company was originally going to be called Enteron until the *Wall Street Journal* pointed out that 'enteron' is a Greek-derived word for the intestines.

company, employing around 21,000 people. It controlled a quarter of the US natural gas business. Riding a global wave of energy sector privatization, the company snapped up assets all over the world. In Latin America alone the company had interests in Colombia, Ecuador, Peru and Bolivia, from where Enron laid its pipeline across the continent to Brazil. In Argentina, following the intervention of Lay's personal friend George W. Bush, Enron bought a controlling stake in the largest natural gas pipeline network in the world. Above all, however, Enron traded, not only in energy but in virtually all the ancient elements of earth, water, fire and air. It even claimed that it could trade in Internet bandwidth. In a scene straight out of *The Sting*, bank analysts were escorted through fake trading floors where employees sat in front of computers pretending to do broadband deals. It was the Mississippi Company all over again. And, just as in 1719, the rewards to investors seemed irresistible. In the three years after 1997, Enron's stock price increased by a factor of nearly five, from less than $20 a share to more than $90. For Enron executives, who were generously 'incentivized' with share options, the rewards were greater still. In the final year of its existence Enron paid its top 140 executives an average of $5.3 million each. Luxury car sales went through the roof. So did properties in River Oaks, Houston's most exclusive neighbourhood. 'I've thought about this a lot,' remarked Skilling, who became Enron chief operating officer in 1997, 'and all that matters is money . . . You buy loyalty with money. This touchy-feely stuff isn't as important as cash. That's what drives performance.'[104] 'You got multiples of your annual base pay at Enron,' Sherron Watkins recalled when I met her outside the now defunct Enron headquarters in Houston. 'You were really less thought of if you got a percentage, even if it was 75 per cent of your annual base pay. Oh, you were getting a percentage. You wanted multiples. You wanted two times your annual base pay, three times, four times your annual base pay, as a bonus.'[105] In the euphoria of April 1999, the Houston Astros even renamed their ballpark Enron Field.

The only problem was that, like John Law's System, the Enron 'System' was an elaborate fraud, based on market manipulation and cooked books. In tapes that became public in 2004, Enron traders can be heard asking the El Paso Electric Company to shut down production in order to maintain prices. Another exchange concerns 'all the money you guys stole from those poor grand-mothers of California'. The results of such machinations were not only the higher prices Enron wanted, but also blackouts for consumers. In the space of just six months after the deregulation law came into effect, California experienced no fewer than thirty-eight rolling blackouts. (In another tape, traders watching tele-vision reports of Californian forest fires shout 'Burn, baby, burn!' as electricity pylons buckle and fall.) Even with such market-rigging, the company's stated assets and profits were vastly inflated, while its debts and losses were concealed in so-called special-purpose entities (SPEs) which were not included in the company's consolidated statements. Each quarter the company's executives had to use more smoke and more mirrors to make actual losses look like bumper profits. Skilling had risen to the top by exploiting new financial techniques like mark-to-market accounting and debt securitization. But not even chief finance officer Andrew Fastow could massage losses into profits indefi-nitely, especially as he was now using SPEs like the aptly named Chewco Investments to line his and other executives' pockets. Enron's international business, in particular, was haemorrhaging money by the mid 1990s, most spectacularly after the cancellation of a major power generation project in the Indian state of Mahar-ashtra. EnronOnline, the first web-based commodity-trading system, had a high turnover; but did it make any money? In

Houston, the euphoria was fading; the insiders were feeling the first symptoms of distress. Fastow's SPEs were being given increasingly ominous names: Raptor I, Talon. He and others surreptitiously unloaded $924 million of Enron shares while the going was good.

Investors had been assured that Enron's stock price would soon hit $100. When (for 'personal reasons') Skilling unexpectedly announced his resignation on 14 August 2001, however, the price tumbled to below $40. That same month, Sherron Watkins wrote to Lay to express her fear that Enron would 'implode in a wave of accounting scandals'. This was precisely what happened. On 16 October Enron reported a $618 million third-quarter loss and a $1.2 billion reduction in shareholder equity. Eight days later, with a Securities and Exchange Commission inquiry pending, Fastow stepped down as CFO. On 8 November the company was obliged to revise its profits for the preceding five years; the overstatement was revealed to be $567 million. When Enron filed for bankruptcy on 2 December, it was revealed that the audited balance sheet had understated the company's long-term debt by $25 billion: it was in fact not $13 billion but $38 billion. By now, distress had turned to revulsion; and panic was hard on its heels. By the end of 2001 Enron shares were worth just 30 cents.

In May 2006 Lay was found guilty of all ten of the charges against him, including conspiracy, false statements, securities fraud and bank fraud. Skilling was found guilty on 18 out of 27 counts. Lay died before sentencing while on holiday in Aspen, Colorado. Skilling was sentenced to 24 years and 4 months in prison and ordered to repay $26 million to the Enron pension fund; an appeal is pending. All told, sixteen people pled guilty to Enron-related charges and five others (so far) have been found guilty at trial. The firm's auditors, Arthur Andersen, were destroyed by the scandal. The principal losers, however, were the ordinary employees and small shareholders whose savings went up in smoke, turned into mere 'wind', just like the millions of livres lost in the Mississippi crash.

Invented almost exactly four hundred years ago, the joint-stock, limited-liability company is indeed a miraculous institution, as is the stock market where its ownership can be bought and sold. And yet throughout financial history there have been crooked companies, just as there have been irrational markets. Indeed the two go hand in hand – for it is when the bulls are stampeding most enthusiastically that people are most likely to get taken for the proverbial ride. A crucial role, however, is nearly always played by central bankers, who are supposed to be the cowboys in control of the herd. Clearly, without his Banque Royale, Law could never have achieved what he did. Equally clearly, without the loose money policy of the Federal Reserve in the 1990s, Ken Lay and Jeff Skilling would have struggled to crank up the price of Enron stock to $90. By contrast, the Great Depression offers a searing lesson in the dangers of excessively restrictive monetary policy during a stock market crash. Avoiding a repeat of the Great Depression is sometimes seen as an end that justifies any means. Yet the history of the Dutch East India Company, the original joint-stock company, shows that, with sound money of the sort provided by the Amsterdam Exchange Bank, stock market bubbles and busts can be avoided.

In the end, the path of financial markets can never be as smooth as we might like. So long as human expectations of the future veer from the over-optimistic to the over-pessimistic – from greed to fear – stock prices will tend to trace an erratic path; indeed, a line not unlike the jagged peaks of the Andes. As an investor you just have to hope that, when you have to come down from the summit of euphoria, it will be on a smooth ski-slope and not over a sheer cliff.

But is there nothing we can do to protect ourselves from real and metaphorical falls? As we shall see in Chapter 4, the evolution of insurance, from humble eighteenth-century beginnings, has created a range of answers to that question, each of which offers at least some protection from the sheer cliffs and fat tails of financial history.

4

The Return of Risk

The most basic financial impulse of all is to save for the future, because the future is so unpredictable. The world is a dangerous place. Not many of us get through life without having a little bad luck. Some of us end up having a lot. Often, it's just a matter of being in the wrong place at the wrong time: like the Mississippi delta in the last week of August 2005, when Hurricane Katrina struck not once but twice. First there was the howling 140-mile-an-hour wind that blew many of the area's wooden houses clean off their concrete foundations. Then, two hours later, came the thirty-foot storm surge that breached three of the levees that protect New Orleans from Lake Pontchartrain and the Mississippi, pouring millions of gallons of water into the city. Wrong place, wrong time. Like the World Trade Center on 11 September 2001. Or Baghdad on pretty much any day since the US invasion of 2003. Or San Francisco when – as it one day will – a really big earthquake occurs along the San Andreas fault.

Stuff happens, as the former Secretary of Defense Donald Rumsfeld insouciantly observed after the overthrow of Saddam Hussein unleashed an orgy of looting in the Iraqi capital. Some people argue that such stuff is more likely to happen than in the past, whether because of climate change, the rise of terrorism or the blowback from American foreign policy blunders. The question is, how do we deal with the risks and uncertainties of the future? Does the onus fall on the individual to insure against misfortune? Should we rely on the voluntary charity of our fellow human beings when things go horribly wrong? Or should we be able to count on the state – in other words on the compulsory contributions of our fellow taxpayers – to bail us out when the flood comes?

The history of risk management is one long struggle between our vain desire to be financially secure – as secure as, say, a Scottish widow – and the hard reality that there really is no such thing as 'the future', singular. There are only multiple, unforeseeable futures, which will never lose their capacity to take us by surprise.

The Big Uneasy

In the Westerns I watched as a boy I was fascinated by ghost towns, short-lived settlements that had been left behind by the fast pace of change on the American frontier. It was not until I went to New Orleans in the wake of Hurricane Katrina that I encountered what could very well become America's first ghost city.

I had happy if hazy memories of the 'Big Easy'. As a teenager between school and university, savouring my first taste of freedom, I discovered it was about the only place in the United States where I could get served beer despite being underage, which certainly made the geriatric jazz musicians in Preservation Hall sound good. Twenty-five years on, and nearly two years after the great storm struck, the city is a forlorn shadow of its former self. Saint Bernard Parish was one of the districts that was worst affected by the storm. Only five homes out of around 26,000 were not flooded. In all, 1,836 Americans lost their lives as a result of Katrina, of whom the overwhelming majority were from Louisiana. In Saint Bernard alone, the death toll was forty-seven. You can still the see the symbols on the doors of abandoned houses, indicating whether or not a corpse was found inside. It invites comparison with medieval England at the time of the Black Death.

When I revisited New Orleans in June 2007, Councilman Joey DiFatta and the rest of Saint Bernard's municipal government were still working in trailers behind their old office building, which the flood gutted. DiFatta stayed at his desk during the storm, eventually retreating to the roof as the waters kept rising. From there, he and his colleagues could only watch helplessly as their beloved neighbourhood vanished under filthy brown water. Angered by what they saw as the incompetence of the Federal Emergency Management Agency (FEMA), they resolved to restore what had been lost. Since then, they have worked tirelessly to try to rebuild what was once a tightly knit community (many of whom, like DiFatta himself, are descended from settlers who came to Louisiana from the Canary Islands). But persuading thousands of refugees to come back to Saint Bernard has proved far from easy; two years later the parish still has only one third of its pre-Katrina population. A large part of the problem turns out to be insurance. Today, insuring a house in Saint Bernard and other low-lying parts of New Orleans is virtually impossible. And without buildings insurance, it is virtually impossible to get a mortgage.

Nearly all the survivors of Katrina lost property in the disaster, since nearly three quarters of the city's total housing stock were damaged. There were no fewer than 1.75 million property and casualty claims, with estimated insurance losses in excess of $41 billion, making Katrina the costliest catastrophe in modern American history.[1] But Katrina not only submerged New Orleans.

New Orleans after Katrina: where insurance failed

It also laid bare the defects of a system of insurance that divided responsibility between private insurance companies, which offered protection against wind damage, and the federal government, which offered protection against flooding, under a scheme that had been introduced after Hurricane Betsy in 1965. In the aftermath of the 2005 disaster, thousands of insurance company assessors fanned out along the Louisiana and Mississippi coastline. According to many residents, their job was not to help stricken policy-holders but to avoid paying out to them by asserting that the damage their properties had suffered was due to flooding and not to wind.* The insurance companies did not

* A typical Gulf Coast homeowner's policy has a Hurricane Deductible Endorsement, with a percentage deduction applying to any claim for 'direct physical loss or damage to covered property caused by wind, wind gust, hail, rain, tornadoes, or cyclones caused by or resulting from a hurricane'.

reckon with one of their policy-holders, former US Navy pilot and celebrity lawyer Richard F. Scruggs, the man once known as the King of Torts.

'Dickie' Scruggs first hit the headlines in the 1980s, when he represented shipyard workers whose lungs had been fatally damaged by exposure to asbestos, winning a $50 million settlement. But that was small change compared with what he later made the tobacco companies pay: over $200 billion to Mississippi and forty-five other states as compensation for Medicaid costs arising from tobacco-related illnesses. The case (immortalized in the film *The Insider*) made Scruggs a rich man. His fee in the tobacco class action is said to have been $1.4 billion, or $22,500 for every hour his law firm worked. It was money he used to acquire a waterfront house on Pascagoula's Beach Boulevard, a short commute (by private jet, naturally) from his Oxford, Mississippi, offices. All that remained of that house after Katrina was a concrete base plus a few ruined walls so badly damaged that they had to be bulldozed. Although his insurance company (wisely) paid out, Scruggs was dismayed to hear of the treatment of other policy-holders. Among those he offered to represent was his brother-in-law Trent Lott, the former Republican majority leader in the Senate, and his friend Mississippi Congressman

---

However, there is usually an exclusion along these lines: 'We do not insure . . . for any loss which would not have occurred in the absence of one or more of the following excluded events', such as 'Water Damage, meaning . . . flood, surface water, waves, tidal water, tsunami, seiche [lake wave], overflow of a body of water, or spray from any of these, all whether driven by wind or not'. Moreover, 'We do not insure for such loss regardless of: (a) the cause of the excluded event; or (b) other causes of the loss; or (c) whether other causes acted concurrently or in any sequence with the excluded event to produce the loss; or (d) whether the event occurs suddenly or gradually . . .' This is a classic example of small print designed to limit the insurer's liability in a way not readily intelligible to the policy-holder.

Gene Taylor, both of whom had also lost homes to Katrina and had received short shrift from their insurers.[2] In a series of cases on behalf of policy-holders, Scruggs alleged that the insurers (principally State Farm and All State) were trying to renege on their legal obligations.[3] He and his 'Scruggs Katrina Group' conducted detailed meteorological research to show that nearly all the damage in places like Pascagoula was caused by the wind, hours before the floodwaters struck. Scruggs was also approached by two whistle-blowing insurance adjusters, who claimed the company they worked for had altered reports in order to attribute damage to flooding rather than wind. The insurance companies' record profits in 2005 and 2006 only whetted Scruggs's appetite for redress.* As he told me when we met in the wasteland where his house used to stand: 'This [town] was home for fifty years; where I raised my family; what I was proud of. It makes me somewhat emotional when I see this.' By that time, State Farm had already settled 640 cases brought by Scruggs on behalf of clients whose claims had initially been turned down, paying out $80 million; and had agreed to review 36,000 other claims.[4] It seemed as if the insurers were retreating. Scruggs's campaign against them collapsed in November 2007, however, when he, his son Zachary and three associates were indicted on charges of trying to bribe a state-court judge in a case arising from a dispute over Katrina-related legal fees.† Scruggs now faces a prison sentence of up to five years.[5]

---

* US property and casualty insurance companies had net after-tax income of $43 billion in 2005 and $64 billion in 2006, compared with an average of less than $24 billion in the preceding three years.
† Scruggs's associate Timothy Balducci was taped offering $40,000 to Judge Lackey. 'The only person in the world outside of me and you that has discussed this is me and Dick,' Mr Balducci told Lackey. 'We, uh, like I say, it ain't but three people in this world that know anything about this . . . and two of them are sitting here, and the other one, uh, being Scruggs . . . He and I, um, how shall I say, for over the last five or six years there, there are bodies

It may sound like just another story of Southern moral laxity – or proof that those who live by the tort, die by the tort. Yet, regardless of Scruggs's descent from good fellow to bad felon, the fact remains that both State Farm and All State have now declared a large part of the Gulf of Mexico coast a 'no insurance' zone. Why risk renewing policies here, where natural disasters happen all too often and where, after the disaster, companies have to contend with the likes of Dickie Scruggs? The strong implication would seem to be that providing coverage to the inhabitants of places like Pascagoula and Saint Bernard is no longer something the private sector is prepared to do. Yet it is far from clear that American legislators are ready to take on the liabilities implied by a further extension of public insurance. Total non-insured damages arising from hurricanes in 2005 are likely to end up costing the federal government at least $109 billion in post-disaster assistance and $8 billion in tax relief, nearly three times the estimated insurance losses.[6] According to Naomi Klein, this is symptomatic of a dysfunctional 'Disaster Capitalism Complex', which generates private profits for some, but leaves taxpayers to foot the true costs of catastrophe.[7] In the face of such ruinous bills, what is the right way to proceed? When insurance fails, is the only alternative, in effect, to nationalize all natural disasters – creating a huge open-ended liability for governments?

Of course, life has always been dangerous. There have always been hurricanes, just as there have always been wars, plagues and

buried that, that you know, that he and I know where.' On 1 November 2007 Balducci called Scruggs to tell him that the Judge now felt 'a little more exposed on the facts and the law than he was before' and to ask if Scruggs 'would do a little something else, you know, to 'bout 10 or so more'. Scruggs said he would 'take care of it'.

famines. And disasters can be small private affairs as well as big public ones. Every day, men and women fall ill or are injured and suddenly can no longer work. We all get old and lose the strength to earn our daily bread. An unlucky few are born unable to fend for themselves. And sooner or later we all die, often leaving one or more dependants behind us. The key point is that few of these calamities are random events. The incidence of hurricanes has a certain regularity like the incidence of disease and death. In every decade since the 1850s the United States has been struck by between one and ten major hurricanes (defined as a storm with wind speeds above 110 mph and a storm surge above 8 feet). It is not yet clear that the present decade will beat the record of the 1940s, which saw ten such hurricanes.[8] Because there are data covering a century and a half, it is possible to attach probabilities to the incidence and scale of hurricanes. The US Army Corps of Engineers described Hurricane Katrina as a 1-in-396 storm, meaning that there is a 0.25 per cent chance of such a large hurricane striking the United States in any given year.[9] A rather different view was taken by the company Risk Management Solutions, which judged a Katrina-sized hurricane to be a once-in-forty-years event just a few weeks before the storm struck.[10] These different assessments indicate that, like earthquakes and wars, hurricanes may belong more in the realm of uncertainty than of risk properly understood.* Such probabilities can be calculated with greater precision for most of the other risks that people face mainly because they are more frequent, so statistical patterns are easier to discern. The average American's lifetime risk of death from exposure to forces of nature, including all kinds of natural disaster, has been estimated at 1 in 3,288. The equivalent figure

---

* For a further discussion of this crucial distinction see the Afterword, pp. 343–4.

for death due to a fire in a building is 1 in 1,358. The odds of the average American being shot to death are 1 in 314. But he or she is even more likely to commit suicide (1 in 119); more likely still to die in a fatal road accident (1 in 78); and most likely of all to die of cancer (1 in 5).[11]

In pre-modern agricultural societies, nearly everyone was at substantial risk from premature death due to malnutrition or disease, to say nothing of war. People in those days could do much less than later generations in the way of prophylaxis. They relied much more on seeking to propitiate the gods or God who, they conjectured, determined the incidence of famines, plagues and invasions. Only slowly did men appreciate the significance of measurable regularities in the weather, crop yields and infections. Only very belatedly – in the eighteenth and nineteenth centuries – did they begin systematically to record rainfall, harvests and mortality in a way that made probabilistic calculation possible. Yet, even before they did so, they understood the wisdom of saving: putting money aside for the proverbial (and in agricultural societies literal) extreme rainy day. Most primitive societies at least attempt to hoard food and other provisions to tide them over hard times. And our tribal species intuitively grasped from the earliest times that it makes sense to pool resources, since there is genuine safety in numbers. Appropriately, given our ancestors' chronic vulnerability, the earliest forms of insurance were probably burial societies, which set aside resources to guarantee a tribe member a decent interment. (Such societies remain the only form of financial institution in some of the poorest parts of East Africa.) Saving in advance of probable future adversity remains the fundamental principle of insurance, whether it is against death, the effects of old age, sickness or accident. The trick is knowing how much to save and what to do with those savings to ensure that, unlike in New Orleans after Katrina, there is enough money in the kitty to cover the costs of catastrophe when it strikes. But to do that, you need to be more than usually canny. And that provides an important clue as to just where the history of insurance had its origins. Where else but in bonny, canny Scotland?

Taking Cover

They say we Scots are a pessimistic people. Maybe it has to do with the weather – all those dreary, rainy days. Maybe it's the endless years of sporting disappointment. Or maybe it was the Calvinism that Lowlanders like my family embraced at the time of the Reformation. Predestination is not an especially cheering article of faith, logical though it may be to assume that an omniscient God already knows which of us ('the Elect') will go to heaven, and which of us (a rather larger number of hopeless sinners) will go to hell. For whatever reason, two Church of Scotland ministers deserve the credit for inventing the first true insurance fund more than two hundred and fifty years ago, in 1744.

It is true that insurance companies existed prior to that date. 'Bottomry' – the insurance of merchant ships' 'bottoms' (hulls) – was where insurance originated as a branch of commerce. Some say that the first insurance contracts date from early fourteenth-century Italy, when payments for *securitas* begin to appear in business documents. But the earliest of these arrangements had the character of conditional loans to merchants (as in ancient Babylon), which could be cancelled in case of a mishap, rather than policies in the modern sense;[12] in *The Merchant of Venice*, Antonio's 'argosies' are conspicuously uninsured, leaving him exposed to Shylock's murderous intent. It was not until the 1350s that true insurance contracts began to appear, with premiums ranging between 15 and 20 per cent of the sum insured, falling below 10 per cent by the fifteenth century. A typical contract in the archives of the merchant Francesco Datini (c. 1335–1410) stipulates that the insurers agree to assume the risks 'of God, of the sea, of men of war, of fire, of jettison, of detainment by princes, by cities, or by any other person, of reprisals, of arrest, of whatever loss, peril, misfortune, impediment or sinister that might occur, with the exception of packing and customs' until the insured goods are safely unloaded at their destination.[13] Gradually such contracts became standardized – a standard that would endure for centuries after it became incorporated into the *lex mercatoria* (mercantile law). These insurers were, however, not specialists, but merchants who also engaged in trade on their own account.

Beginning in the late seventeenth century, something more like a dedicated insurance market began to form in London. Minds were doubtless focused by the Great Fire of 1666, which destroyed more than 13,000 houses.* Fourteen years later Nicholas Barbon established the first fire insurance company. At around the same time, a specialized marine insurance market began to coalesce in Edward Lloyd's coffee house in London's Tower Street (later in Lombard Street). Between the 1730s and the 1760s, the practice of exchanging information at Lloyd's became more routinized until in 1774 a Society of Lloyd's was formed at the Royal Exchange, initially bringing together seventy-

* The human propensity to shut stable doors after horses have bolted is well illustrated by the history of fire insurance. It was *after* the New York fire of 1835 that American states began to insist that insurance companies maintain adequate reserves. It was *after* the Hamburg fire of 1842 that reinsurance was developed as a way for insurance companies to share the risk of major disasters.

nine life members, each of whom paid a £15 subscription. Compared with the earlier monopoly trading companies, Lloyd's was an unsophisticated entity, essentially an unincorporated association of market participants. The liability of the underwriters (who literally wrote their names under insurance contracts, and were hence also known as Lloyd's Names) was unlimited. And the financial arrangements were what would now be called pay as you go – that is, the aim was to collect sufficient premiums in any given year to cover that year's payments out and leave a margin of profit. Limited liability came to the insurance business with the founding of the Sun Insurance Office (1710), a fire insurance specialist and, ten years later (at the height of the South Sea Bubble), the Royal Exchange Assurance Corporation and the London Assurance Corporation, which focused on life and maritime insurance. However, all three firms still operated on a pay-as-you-go basis. Figures from London Assurance show premium income usually, but not always, exceeding payments out, with periods of war against France causing huge spikes in both. (This was not least because before 1793 it was quite normal for London insurers to sell cover to French merchants.[14] In peacetime the practice resumed, so that on the eve of the First World War most of Germany's merchant marine was insured by Lloyd's.[15])

Life insurance, too, existed in medieval times. The Florentine merchant Bernardo Cambi's account books contain references to insurance on the life of the pope (Nicholas V), of the doge of Venice (Francesco Foscari) and of the king of Aragon (Alfonso V). It seems, however, that these were little more than wagers, comparable with the bets Cambi made on horse races.[16] In truth, all these forms of insurance – including even the most sophisticated shipping insurance – were a form of gambling. There did not yet exist an adequate theoretical basis for evaluating the risks that were being covered. Then, in a remarkable rush of intellectual innovation, beginning in around 1660, that theoretical basis was created. In essence, there were six crucial breakthroughs:

1. *Probability*. It was to a monk at Port-Royal that the French mathematician Blaise Pascal attributed the insight (published in Pascal's *Ars Cogitandi*) that 'fear of harm ought to be proportional not merely to the gravity of the harm, but also to the probability of the event.' Pascal and his friend Pierre de Fermat had been toying with problems of probability for many years, but for the evolution of insurance, this was to be a critical point.

2. *Life expectancy*. In the same year that *Ars Cogitandi* appeared (1662), John Graunt published his 'Natural and Political Observations . . . Made upon the Bills of Mortality', which sought to estimate the likelihood of dying from a particular cause on the basis of official London mortality statistics. However, Graunt's data did not include ages at death, limiting what could legitimately be inferred from them. It was his fellow member of the Royal Society, Edmund Halley, who made the critical breakthrough using data supplied to the Society from the Prussian town of Breslau (today Wrocław in Poland). Halley's life table, based on 1,238 recorded births and 1,174 recorded deaths, gives the odds of not dying in a given year: 'It being 100 to 1 that a Man of 20 dies not in a year, and but 38 to 1 for a Man of 50 . . .' This was to be one of the founding stones of actuarial mathematics.[17]

3. *Certainty*. Jacob Bernoulli proposed in 1705 that 'Under similar conditions, the occurrence (or non-occurrence) of an event in the future will follow the same pattern as was observed in the past.' His Law of Large Numbers stated that inferences could be drawn with a degree of certainty about, for example, the total contents of a jar filled with two kinds of ball on the basis of a sample. This provides the basis for the concept of statistical

significance and modern formulations of probabilities at specified confidence intervals (for example, the statement that 40 per cent of the balls in the jar are white, at a confidence interval of 95 per cent, implies that the precise value lies somewhere between 35 and 45 per cent – 40 plus or minus 5 per cent).

4. *Normal distribution*. It was Abraham de Moivre who showed that outcomes of any kind of iterated process could be distributed along a curve according to their variance around the mean or standard deviation. 'Tho' Chance produces Irregularities,' wrote de Moivre in 1733, 'still the Odds will be infinitely great, that in process of Time, those Irregularities will bear no proportion to recurrency of that Order which naturally results from Original Design.' The bell curve that we encountered in Chapter 3 represents the normal distribution, in which 68.2 per cent of outcomes are within one standard deviation (plus or minus) of the mean.

5. *Utility*. In 1738 the Swiss mathematician Daniel Bernoulli proposed that 'The value of an item must not be based on its price, but rather on the utility that it yields', and that the 'utility resulting from any small increase in wealth will be inversely proportionate to the quantity of goods previously possessed' – in other words $100 is worth more to someone on the median income than to a hedge fund manager.

6. *Inference*. In his 'Essay Towards Solving a Problem in the Doctrine of Chances' (published posthumously in 1764), Thomas Bayes set himself the following problem: 'Given the number of times in which an unknown event has happened and failed; Required the chance that the probability of its happening in a single trial lies somewhere between any two degrees of probability that can be named.' His resolution of the problem – 'The probability of any event is the ratio between the value at which an expectation depending on the happening of the event ought to be computed, and the chance of the thing expected upon it's [*sic*]

happening' – anticipates the modern formulation that expected utility is the probability of an event times the payoff received in case of that event.[18]

In short, it was not merchants but mathematicians who were the true progenitors of modern insurance. Yet it took clergymen to turn theory into practice.

Greyfriars Kirkyard, on the hill that is the heart of Edinburgh's Old Town, is best known today for Greyfriars Bobby, the loyal Skye terrier who refused to desert his master's grave, and also for the grave robbers – the so-called 'Resurrection Men' – who went there in the early nineteenth century to supply the medical school at Edinburgh University with corpses for dissection. But Greyfriars's importance in the history of finance lies in the earlier mathematical work of its minister, Robert Wallace, and his friend Alexander Webster, who was minister of Tolbooth. Along with Colin Maclaurin, Professor of Mathematics at Edinburgh, it was their achievement to create the first modern insurance fund, based on correct actuarial and financial principles, rather than mercantile gambling.

Living in Auld Reekie, as the distinctly smelly Scottish capital was then known, Wallace and Webster had a keen sense of the fragility of the human condition. They themselves lived to ripe old ages: 74 and 75 respectively. But Maclaurin died at the age of just 48, having fallen from his horse and suffered exposure while trying to evade the Jacobites during the 1745 rising. Invasions of Papist Highlanders were only one of the hazards inhabitants of Edinburgh faced in the mid eighteenth century. Average life expectancy at birth is unlikely to have been better than it was in England, where it was just 37 until the 1800s. It may even have been as bad as in London, where it was 23 in the late eighteenth century – perhaps even worse, given the Scottish

The spirit of insurance: Alexander Webster
preaching in Edinburgh

capital's notoriously bad hygiene.[19] For Wallace and Webster,
one group of people seemed especially vulnerable to the consequences of premature death. Under the Law of Ann (1672), the
widow and children of a deceased minister of the Church of
Scotland received only half a year's stipend in the year of the
minister's death. After that, they faced penury. A supplementary
scheme had been set up by the Bishop of Edinburgh in 1711,
but on the traditional pay-as-you-go basis. Wallace and Webster
knew this to be unsatisfactory.

We tend to think of Scottish clergymen as the epitome of
prudence and thrift, weighed down with an anticipation of
impending divine retribution for every tiny transgression. In

reality, Robert Wallace was a hard drinker as well as a mathematical prodigy, who loved to knock back claret with his bibulous
buddies at the Rankenian Club, which met in what used to be
Ranken's Inn.* Alexander Webster's nickname was Bonum Mag-
num; it was said to be 'hardly in the power of liquor to affect Dr
Webster's understanding or his limbs'. Yet no one was more sober
when it came to calculations of life expectancy. The plan Webster
and Wallace came up with was ingenious, reflecting the fact that
they were as much products of Scotland's eighteenth-century
Enlightenment as of the Calvinist Reformation that had preceded
it. Rather than merely having ministers pay an annual premium,
which could be used to take care of widows and orphans as and
when ministers died, they argued that the premiums should be
used to create a fund that could then be profitably invested.
Widows and orphans would be paid out of the returns on the
investment, not just the premiums themselves. All that was
required for the scheme to work was an accurate projection of
how many beneficiaries there would be in the future, and how
much money could be generated to support them. Modern actuaries still marvel at the precision with which Webster and Wallace
did their calculations.[20] 'It is experience alone & nice calculation
that must determine the proportional sum the widow is to have
after the husband's death,' wrote Wallace in an early draft, 'but
a beginning may be made by allowing triple the sum the husband
payed [sic] in [yearly] during his life . . .' Wallace then turned to
the evidence that he and Webster had been able to gather from
presbyteries all over Scotland. It seemed that there tended to be
'930 ministers in life at all times':

* Wallace was also a member of the Philosophical Society of Edinburgh, to
which he presented his 'Dissertation on the Numbers of Mankind in Ancient
and Modern Times', a work which in some respects anticipated Thomas
Malthus's later *Essay on the Principle of Population*.

. . . 'tis found by a Medium of 20 years back, that 27 [of 930] ministers die yearly, 18 of them leave Widows, 5 of them Children without a Widow, 2 of them who leave Widows, leave also Children of a former Marriage, under the Age of 16; and when the whole Number of Widows shall be complete, 3 Annuitants will die, or marry, leaving Children under 16.

Wallace originally estimated the maximum number of widows living at any one time to be 279; but Maclaurin was able to correct this, pointing out that it was wrong to assume a constant mortality rate for the widows, since they would not all be the same age. To arrive at the correct, higher figure, he turned to Halley's life tables.[21]

Time was to be the test of their calculations. According to the final version of the scheme, each minister was to pay an annual premium of between £2 12s 6d and £6 11s 3d (there were four levels of premium to choose from). The proceeds would then be used to create a fund that could be profitably invested (initially in loans to younger ministers) to yield sufficient income to pay annuities to new widows of between £10 and £25, depending on the level of premium paid, and to cover the fund's management costs. In other words, the 'Fund for a Provision for the Widows and Children of the Ministers of the Church of Scotland' was the first insurance fund to operate on the maximum principle, with capital being accumulated until interest and contributions would suffice to pay the maximum amount of annuities and expenses likely to arise. If the projections were wrong, the fund would either overshoot or, more problematically, undershoot the amount required. After at least five attempts to estimate the rate of growth of the fund, Wallace and Webster agreed figures that projected a rise from £18,620 at the inception in 1748 to £58,348 in 1765. They were out by just

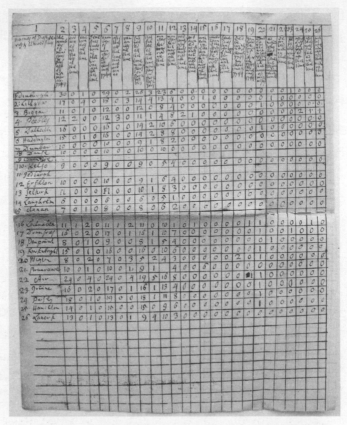

Calculations for the original Scottish Ministers'
Widows' Fund (1)

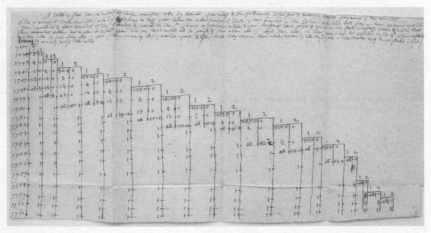

Calculations for the original Scottish Ministers' Widows'
Fund (2)

one pound. The actual free capital of the fund in 1765 was £58,347. Both Wallace and Webster lived to see their calculations vindicated.

In 1930 the German insurance expert Alfred Manes concisely defined insurance as:

An economic institution resting on the principle of mutuality, established for the purpose of supplying a fund, the need for which arises from a chance occurrence whose probability can be estimated.[22]

The Scottish Ministers' Widows' Fund was the first such fund, and its foundation was truly a milestone in financial history. It established a model not just for Scottish clergymen, but for everyone who aspired to provide against premature death. Even before the fund was fully operational, the universities of Edinburgh, Glasgow and St Andrews had applied to join. Within the next twenty years similar funds sprang up on the same model all over the English-speaking world, including the Presbyterian Ministers' Fund of Philadelphia (1761) and the English Equitable Company (1762), as well as the United Incorporations of St Mary's Chapel (1768), which provided for the widows of Scottish artisans. By 1815 the principle of insurance was so widespread that it was adopted even for those men who lost their lives fighting against Napoleon. A soldier's odds of being killed at Waterloo were roughly 1 in 4. But if he was insured, he had the consolation of knowing, even as he expired on the field of battle, that his wife and children would not be thrown out onto the streets (giving a whole new meaning to the phrase 'take cover'). By the middle of the nineteenth century, being insured was as much a badge of respectability as going to Church on a Sunday. Even novelists, not generally renowned for their financial prudence, could join. Sir Walter Scott[23] took out a policy in 1826 to reassure his creditors that they would still get their money back in the event of his death.* A fund that had originally been intended to support the widows of a few hundred clergymen grew steadily to become the general insurance and pension fund we know today as Scottish Widows. Although it is now just another financial services provider, having been taken over by Lloyds Bank in 1999, Scottish Widows is still seen as exemplifying the benefits of Calvinist thrift, thanks in no small measure to one of the most successful advertising campaigns in financial history.†

What no one anticipated back in the 1740s was that by constantly increasing the number of people paying premiums, insurance companies and their close relatives the pension funds would rise to become some of the biggest investors in the world – the so-called institutional investors who today dominate global financial markets. When, after the Second World War, insurance companies were allowed to start investing in the stock market, they quickly snapped up huge chunks of the British economy, owning

* Scott was a victim of the financial crisis triggered by the first Latin American debt crisis (see Chapter 2). Perhaps he was also a victim of his own appetite for real estate. To help finance the cost of his beloved country seat at Abbotsford, the author had become a sleeping partner in the printers that published his books, James Ballantyne and Co., and the associated publishing house of John Ballantyne & Co. He was also an investor in his own publisher, Archibald Constable, believing that the returns on these equity stakes would be superior to traditional royalties. He kept these business interests secret, believing them to be incompatible with his standing as a Clerk to the Court of Sessions and a Sheriff. The failure of Ballantyne and Constable in 1825 left Scott with debts of between £117,000 and £130,000. Rather than sell Abbotsford, Scott vowed to write his way back into the black. He succeeded, but at considerable cost to his own health, dying in 1832. Had he died earlier, the creditors would have been the beneficiaries of the Scottish Widows policy.
† The original 1986 advertisement was photographed by David Bailey with the actor Roger Moore's daughter Deborah as the improbably alluring Scottish Widow.

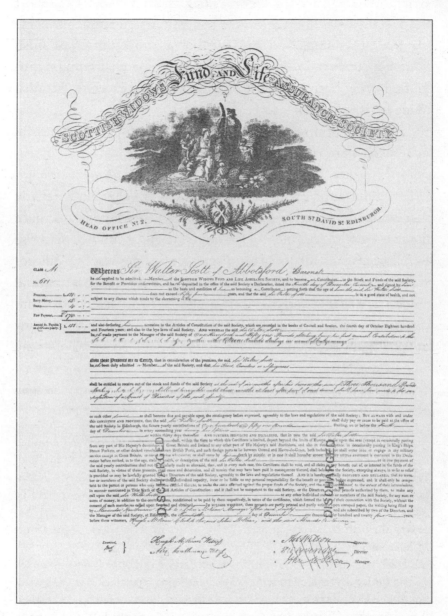

Sir Walter Scott's life insurance policy

around a third of major UK companies by the mid 1950s.[24] Today Scottish Widows alone has over £100 billion under management. Insurance premiums have risen steadily as a proportion of gross domestic product in developed economies, from around 2 per cent on the eve of the First World War to just under 10 per cent today.

As Robert Wallace realized more than 250 years ago, size matters in insurance because the more people who pay into a fund the easier it becomes, by the law of averages, to predict what will have to be paid out each year. Although no individual's date of death can be known in advance, actuaries can calculate the likely life expectancies of a large group of individuals with astonishing precision using the principles first applied by Wallace, Webster and Maclaurin. In addition to how long the policy-holders are likely to live, insurers also need to know what the investment of their funds will bring in. What should they buy with the premiums their policy-holders pay? Relatively safe bonds, as recommended by Victorian authorities such as A. H. Bailey, head actuary of the London Assurance Corporation? Or riskier but probably higher yielding stocks? Insurance, in other words, is where the risks and uncertainties of daily life meet the risks and uncertainties of finance. To be sure, actuarial science gives insurance companies an in-built advantage over policy-holders. Before the dawn of modern probability theory, insurers were the gamblers; now they are the casino. The case can be made, as it was by Dickie Scruggs before his fall from grace, that the odds are now stacked unjustly against the punters/policy-holders. But as the economist Kenneth Arrow long ago pointed out, most of us prefer a gamble that has a 100 per cent chance of a small loss (our annual premium) and a small chance of a large gain (the insurance payout after disaster) to a gamble that has a 100 per cent chance of a small gain (no premiums) but an uncertain chance of a huge loss (no payout after a disaster). That is why the guitarist Keith Richards insured his fingers and the singer Tina Turner her legs. Only if insurance companies systematically fail to pay out to those who have placed their bets will their long-standing reputation for Scottish prudence become a reputation for stinginess and lack of scruple.

Yet there remains a puzzle. It may seem appropriate that, as the inventors of modern insurance, the British remain the world's most insured people, paying more than 12 per cent of GDP on premiums, roughly a third more than Americans spend on insurance and nearly twice what the Germans spend.[25] A moment's reflection, however, prompts the question, why should that be? Unlike the United States, Britain rarely suffers extreme weather events; the nearest thing to a hurricane in my lifetime was the storm of October 1987. No British city stands on a fault-line, as San Francisco does. And, compared with Germany, Britain's history since the foundation of Scottish Widows has been one of almost miraculous political stability. Why, then, do the British take out so much insurance?

The answer lies in the rise and fall of an alternative form of protection against risk: the welfare state.

From Warfare to Welfare

No matter how many private funds like Scottish Widows were set up, there were always going to be people beyond the reach of insurance, who were either too poor or too feckless to save for that rainy day. Their lot was a painfully hard one: dependence on private charity or the austere regime of the workhouse. At the large Marylebone Workhouse on London's Northumberland Street, the 'poor being lame impotent old and blind' numbered up to 1,900 in hard times. When the weather was bitter, work scarce and food dear, men and women 'casuals' would submit to a prison-like regime. As the *Illustrated London News* described it in 1867:

They are washed with plenty of hot and cold water and soap, and receive six ounces of bread and a pint of gruel for supper; after which, their clothes being taken to be cleaned and fumigated, they are furnished with warm woollen night-shirts and sent to bed. Prayers are read by Scripture-readers; strict order and silence are maintained all night in the dormitory . . . The bed consists of a mattress stuffed with coir, a flock pillow, and a pair of rugs. At six o'clock in the morning in summer, and at seven in winter, they are aroused and ordered to work. The women are set to clean the wards, or to pick oakum; the men to break stones, but none are detained longer than four hours after their breakfast which is of the same kind and quantity as their supper. Their clothes, disinfected and freed of vermin, being restored to them in the morning, those who choose to mend their ragged garments are supplied with needles, thread, and patches of cloth for that purpose. If any are ill, the medical officer of the workhouse attends to them; if too ill to travel, they are admitted into the infirmary.

The author of the report concluded that 'the "Amateur Casual" would find nothing to complain of . . . A board of Good Samaritans could do no more.'[26] By the later nineteenth century, however, a feeling began to grow that life's losers deserved better. The seeds began to be planted of a new approach to the problem of risk – one that would ultimately grow into the welfare state. These state systems of insurance were designed to exploit the ultimate economy of scale, by covering literally every citizen from birth to death.

We tend to think of the welfare state as a British invention. We also tend to think of it as a socialist or at least liberal invention.

Two scenes from a London workhouse, 1902: Oakum-picking
involved teasing fibres out of old hemp ropes for re-use in
ship-building

In fact, the first system of compulsory state health insurance and old age pensions was introduced not in Britain but in Germany, and it was an example the British took more than twenty years to follow. Nor was it a creation of the Left; rather the opposite. The aim of Otto von Bismarck's social insurance legislation, as he himself put it in 1880, was 'to engender in the great mass of the unpropertied the conservative state of mind that springs from the feeling of entitlement to a pension.' In Bismarck's view, 'A man who has a pension for his old age is . . . much easier to deal with than a man without that prospect.' To the surprise of his liberal opponents, Bismarck openly acknowledged that this was 'a state-socialist idea! The generality must undertake to assist the unpropertied.' But his motives were far from altruistic. 'Whoever embraces this idea', he observed, 'will come to power.'[27] It was not until 1908 that Britain followed the Bismarckian example, when the Liberal Chancellor of the Exchequer David Lloyd George introduced a modest and means-tested state pension for those over 70. A National Health Insurance Act followed in 1911. Though a man of the Left, Lloyd George shared Bismarck's insight that such measures were vote-winners in a system of rapidly widening electoral franchises. The rich were outnumbered by the poor. When Lloyd George raised direct taxes to pay for the state pension, he relished the label that stuck to his 1909 budget: 'The People's Budget.'

If the welfare state was conceived in politics, however, it grew to maturity in war. The First World War expanded the scope of government activity in nearly every field. With German submarines sending no less than 7,759,000 gross tons of merchant shipping to the bottom of the ocean, there was clearly no way that war risk could be covered by the private marine insurers. The standard Lloyd's policy had in fact already been modified (in 1898) to exclude 'the consequences of hostilities or warlike

Men dining in the St Marylebone workhouse. God's justice and goodness may not have been immediately obvious to the inmates

operations' (the so-called f.c.s. clause: 'free of capture and seiz-ure'). But even those policies that had been altered to remove that exclusion were cancelled when war broke out.[28] The state stepped in, virtually nationalizing merchant shipping in the case of the United States,[29] and (predictably) enabling insurance companies to claim that any damage to ships between 1914 and 1918 was a consequence of the war.[30] With the coming of peace, politicians in Britain also hastened to cushion the effects of demobilization on the labour market by introducing an Unemployment Insurance Scheme in 1920.[31] This process repeated itself during and after the Second World War. The British version of social insurance was radically expanded under the terms of the 1942 Report of the Inter-Departmental Committee on Social Insurance and Allied Services, chaired by the economist William Beveridge, which recommended a broad assault on 'Want, Disease, Ignorance, Squalor and Idleness' through a variety of state schemes. In a March 1943 broadcast, Churchill summarized these as: 'national compulsory insurance for all classes for all purposes from the cradle to the grave'; the abolition of unemployment by govern-ment policies which would 'exercise a balancing influence upon development which can be turned on or off as circumstances require'; 'a broadening field for State ownership and enterprise'; more publicly provided housing; reforms to public education and greatly expanded health and welfare services.[32]

The arguments for state insurance extended beyond mere social equity. First, state insurance could step in where private insurers feared to tread. Second, universal and sometimes compulsory membership removed the need for expensive advertising and sales campaigns. Third, as one leading authority observed in the 1930s, 'the larger numbers combined should form more stable averages for the statistical experience'.[33] State insurance exploited econo-mies of scale, in other words; so why not make it as comprehensive as possible? The enthusiasm with which the Beveridge Report was greeted not just in Britain but around the world helps explain why the welfare state is still thought of as having 'Made in Britain' stamped on it. However, the world's first welfare superpower, the country that took the principle furthest and with the greatest success, was not Britain but Japan. Nothing illustrates more clearly than the Japanese experience the intimate links between the welfare state and the warfare state.

Disaster kept striking Japan in the first half of the twentieth century. On 1 September 1923, a huge earthquake (7.9 on the Richter scale) struck the Kantō region, devastating the cities of Yokohama and Tokyo. More than 128,000 houses completely collapsed, around the same number half-collapsed, 900 were swept away by the sea and nearly 450,000 were burnt down in fires that broke out almost immediately after the quake.[34] The Japanese were insured; between 1879 and 1914 their insurance industry had grown from nothing into a vibrant sector of the economy, offering cover against loss at sea, death, fire, conscription, transport accident and burglary, to name just some of the thirteen distinct forms of insurance sold by more than thirty companies. In the year of the earthquake, for example, Japanese citizens had purchased ¥699,634,000 ($328 million) worth of new life insurance for 1923, with an average policy amount of ¥1,280 ($600).[35] But the total losses caused by the earthquake were in the region of $4.6 billion. Six years later the Great Depression struck, pushing some rural areas to the brink of starvation (at this time 70 per cent of the population was engaged in agriculture, of whom 70 per cent tilled an average of just one and a half acres).[36] In 1937 the country embarked on an expensive and ultimately futile war of conquest in China. Then, in December 1941, Japan went to war with the world's economic colossus, the United States, and eventually paid the ultimate price at Hiroshima and Nagasaki. Quite apart from the nearly three million lives lost in Japan's doomed bid for empire, by the end in 1945 the value of Japan's entire capital stock seemed to have been reduced to zero by American bombers. In aggregate, according to the US Strategic Bombing Survey, at least 40 per cent of the built-up areas of more than sixty cities had been destroyed; 2.5 million homes had been lost, leaving 8.3 million people homeless.[37] Practically the only city to survive intact (though not wholly unscathed) was Kyoto, the former imperial capital – a city which still embodies the ethos of pre-modern Japan, as it is one of the last places where the traditional wooden townhouses known as *machiya* can still be seen. One look at these long, thin structures, with their sliding doors, paper screens, polished beams and straw mats, makes it clear why Japanese cities were so vulnerable to fire.

In Japan, as in most combatant countries, the lesson was clear: the world was just too dangerous a place for private insurance markets to cope with. (Even in the United States, the federal government took over 90 per cent of the risk for war damage through the War Damage Corporation, one of the most profitable public sector entities in history for the obvious reason that no war damage befell the mainland United States.)[38] With the best will in the world, individuals could not be expected to insure themselves against the US Air Force. The answer adopted more or less everywhere was for the government to take over, in effect to nationalize risk. When the Japanese set out to devise a system of universal welfare in 1949, their Advisory Council for Social Security acknowledged a debt to the British example. In the eyes of Bunji Kondo, a convinced believer in universal welfare coverage, it was time to have *bebariji no nihonhan*: Beveridge for the Japanese.[39] But they took the idea even further than Beveridge had intended. The aim, as the report of the Advisory Council put it, was to create a system in which measures are taken for economic security for sickness, injury, childbirth, disability, death, old age, unemployment, large families and other causes of impoverishment through . . . payment by governments . . . [and] in which the needy will be guaranteed the minimum standard of living by national assistance.[40]

From now on, the welfare state would cover people against all the vagaries of modern life. If they were born sick, the state would pay. If they could not afford education, the state would pay. If they could not find work, the state would pay. If they were too ill to work, the state would pay. When they retired, the state would pay. And when they finally died, the state would pay their dependants. This certainly chimed with one of the objectives of the post-war American occupation: 'To replace a feudal economy by a welfare economy'.[41] Yet it would be wrong to assume (as a number of post-war commentators did) that Japan's welfare state was 'imposed wholesale by an alien power'.[42] In reality, the Japanese set up their own welfare state – and they began to do so long before the end of the Second World War. It was the mid twentieth-century state's insatiable appetite for able-bodied young soldiers and workers, not social altruism, that was the real driver. As the American political scientist Harold D. Lasswell put it, Japan in the 1930s became a garrison state.[43] But it was one which carried within it the promise of a 'warfare-welfare state', offered social security in return for military sacrifice.

There had been some basic social insurance in Japan before the 1930s: factory accident insurance and health insurance (introduced for factory workers in 1927). But this covered less than two fifths of the industrial workforce.[44] Significantly, the plan for a Japanese Welfare Ministry (*Kōseishō*) was approved by Japan's imperial government on 9 July 1937, just two months after the outbreak of war with China.[45] Its first step was to introduce a new system of universal health insurance to supplement the existing programme for industrial employees. Between the end of 1938 and the end of 1944, the number of citizens covered by the scheme increased nearly a hundred-fold, from just over 500,000 to over 40 million. The aim was explicit: a healthier populace would ensure healthier recruits to the Emperor's armed forces. The wartime slogan of 'all people are soldiers' (*kokumin kai hei*) was adapted to become 'all people should have insurance' (*kokumin kai hoken*). And to ensure universal coverage, the medical profession and pharmaceutical industry were essentially subordinated to the state.[46] The war years also saw the introduction of compulsory pension schemes for seamen and workers, with the state covering 10 per cent of the costs, while employers and employees each contributed 5.5 per cent of the latter's wages. The first steps towards the large-scale provision of public housing were also taken. So what happened after the war in Japan was in large measure the extension of the warfare-welfare state. Now 'all people should have pensions', *kokumin kai nenkin*. Now there should be unemployment insurance, rather than the earlier paternalistic practice of keeping workers on payrolls even in lean times. Small wonder some Japanese tended to think of welfare in nationalistic terms, a kind of peaceful mode of national aggrandisement. The 1950 report, with its British-style recommendations, was in fact rejected by the government. Only in 1961, long after the end of American control, were most of its recommendations adopted. By the late 1970s a Japanese politician, Nakagawa Yatsuhiro, could boast that Japan had become 'The Welfare Super-Power' (*fukushi chōdaikoku*), precisely because its system was different from (and superior to) Western models.[47]

There was in fact nothing institutionally unique about Japan's system, of course. Most welfare states aimed at universal, cradle-to-grave coverage. Yet the Japanese welfare state seemed to be a miracle of effectiveness. In terms of life expectancy, the country led the world. In education, too, it was ahead of the field. Around 90 per cent of the population had graduated from high school in the mid seventies, compared with just 32 per cent in England.[48] Japan was also a much more equal society than any in the West, with the sole exception of Sweden. And Japan had the largest state pension fund in the world, so that every Japanese who retired could count on a generous bonus as well as a regular income throughout his (generally rather numerous) years of well-earned rest. The welfare superpower was also a miracle of parsimony. In 1975 just 9 per cent of national income went on social security, compared with 31 per cent in Sweden.[49] The burden of tax and social welfare was roughly half that in England. Run on this basis, the welfare state seemed to make perfect sense. Japan had achieved security for all – the elimination of risk – while at the same time its economy grew so rapidly that by 1968 it was the second largest in the world. A year before, Herman Kahn had predicted that Japan's per capita income would overtake America's by 2000. Indeed, Nakagawa Yatsuhiro argued that, when fringe benefits were taken into account, 'the actual income of the Japanese worker [was already] at least three times more than that of the American'.[50] Warfare had failed to make Japan Top Nation, but welfare was succeeding. The key turned out to be not a foreign empire, but a domestic safety net.[51]

Yet there was a catch, a fatal flaw in the design of the post-warfare welfare state. The welfare state might have worked smoothly enough in 1970s Japan. But the same could not be said of its counterparts in the Western world. Despite their superficial topographical and historical resemblances (archipelagos off Eurasia, imperial pasts, buttoned-up behaviour when sober) the Japanese and the British had quite different cultures. Outwardly, their welfare systems might seem similar: state pensions financed out of taxation on the old pay-as-you-go model; standardized retirement ages; universal health insurance; unemployment benefits; subsidies to farmers; quite heavily restricted labour markets. But these institutions worked in quite different ways in the two countries. In Japan egalitarianism was a prized goal of policy, while a culture of social conformism encouraged compliance with the rules. English individualism, by contrast, inclined people cynically to game the system. In Japan, firms and families continued to play substantial supporting roles in the welfare system. Employers offered supplementary benefits and were reluctant to fire workers. As recently as the 1990s, two thirds of Japanese older than 64 lived with their children.[52] In Britain, by contrast, employers did not hesitate to slash payrolls in hard times, while people were much more likely to leave elderly parents to the tender mercies of the National Health Service. The welfare state might have made Japan an economic superpower, but in the 1970s it appeared to be having the opposite effect in Britain.

According to British conservatives, what had started out as a system of national insurance had degenerated into a system of state handouts and confiscatory taxation which disastrously skewed economic incentives. Between 1930 and 1980, social transfers in Britain had risen from just 2.2 per cent of gross domestic product to 10 per cent in 1960, 13 per cent in 1970 and nearly 17 per cent in 1980, more than 6 per cent higher than in Japan.[53] Health care, social services and social security were consuming three times more than defence as a share of total managed government expenditure. Yet the results were dismal. Increased expenditure on UK welfare had been accompanied by low growth and inflation significantly above the developed world average. A particular problem was chronically slow productivity growth (real GDP per person employed grew by just 2.8 per cent between 1960 and 1979, compared with 8.1 per cent in Japan),[54] which in turn seemed closely related to the bloody-minded bargaining techniques of British trade unions ('go slows' being a favourite alternative to outright 'downing tools'). Meanwhile, marginal tax rates in excess of 100 per cent on higher incomes and capital gains discouraged traditional forms of saving and investment. The British welfare state, it seemed, had removed the incentives without which a capitalist economy simply could not function: the carrot of serious money for those who strove, the stick of hardship for those who slacked. The result was 'stagflation': stagnant growth plus high inflation. Similar problems were afflicting the US economy, where expenditure on health, Medicare, income security and social security had risen from 4 per cent of GDP in 1959 to 9 per cent in 1975, outstripping defence spending for the first time. In America, too, productivity was scarcely growing and stagflation was rampant. What was to be done?

One man, and his pupils, thought they knew the answer. Thanks in large measure to their influence, one of the most pronounced economic trends of the past twenty-five years has been for the Western welfare state to be dismantled, reintroducing people with a sharp shock to the unpredictable monster they thought they had escaped from: risk.

The Big Chill

In 1976 a diminutive professor working at the University of Chicago won the Nobel Prize in economics. Milton Friedman's reputation as an economist rested in large measure on his reinstatement of the idea that inflation was due to an excessive increase in the supply of money. As we have seen, he co-wrote perhaps the single most important book on US monetary policy

Milton Friedman

of all time, firmly laying the blame for the Great Depression on mistakes by the Federal Reserve.[55] But the question that had come to preoccupy him by the mid-seventies was: what had gone wrong with the welfare state? In March 1975, Friedman flew from Chicago to Chile to answer that question.

Only eighteen months earlier, in September 1973, tanks had rolled through the capital Santiago to overthrow the government of the Marxist President Salvador Allende, whose attempt to turn Chile into a Communist state had ended in total economic chaos and a call by the parliament for a military takeover. Air force jets bombed the presidential Moneda Palace, watched from the balcony of the nearby Carera Hotel by opponents of Allende who celebrated with champagne. Inside the palace, the president himself fought a hopeless rearguard action armed with an AK47 – a gift from Fidel Castro, the man he had sought to emulate. As the tanks rumbled towards him, Allende realized it was all over and, cornered in what was left of his quarters, shot himself.

The coup epitomized a world-wide crisis of the post-war welfare state and posed a stark choice between rival economic systems. With output collapsing and inflation rampant, Chile's system of universal benefits and state pensions was essentially bankrupt. For Allende, the answer had been full blown Marxism, a complete Soviet-style takeover of every aspect of economic life. The generals and their supporters knew they were against that. But what were they actually for, since the status quo was clearly unsustainable? Enter Milton Friedman. Amid his lectures and seminars, he spent three quarters of an hour with the new president General Pinochet and later wrote him an assessment of the Chilean economic situation, urging him to reduce the government deficit that he had identified as the main cause of the country's sky-high inflation, then running at an annual rate of 900 per cent.[56] A month after Friedman's visit, the Chilean junta announced that inflation would be stopped 'at any cost'. The regime cut government spending by 27 per cent and set fire to bundles of banknotes. But Friedman was offering more than his patent monetarist shock therapy. In a letter to Pinochet written after his return to Chicago, he argued that 'this problem' of inflation arose 'from trends toward socialism that started forty years ago, and reached their logical – and terrible – climax in the Allende regime'. As he later recalled, 'The general line I was taking . . . was that their present difficulties were due almost entirely to the forty-year trend toward collectivism, socialism, and the welfare state . . .'[57] And he assured Pinochet: 'The end of inflation will lead to a rapid expansion of the capital market, which will greatly facilitate the transfer of enterprises and activities still in the hands of the government to the private sector.'[58]

For tendering this advice Friedman found himself denounced by the American press. After all, he was acting as a consultant to a military dictator responsible for the executions of more than two thousand real and suspected Communists and the torture of nearly 30,000 more. As the *New York Times* asked: '. . . if the pure Chicago economic theory can be carried out in Chile only at the price of repression, should its authors feel some responsibility?'*

Chicago's role in the new regime consisted of more than just one visit by Milton Friedman. Since the 1950s, there had been a regular stream of bright young Chilean economists studying at Chicago on an exchange programme with the Universidad Católica in Santiago, and they went back convinced of the need to balance the budget, tighten the money supply and liberalize trade.[59] These were the so-called Chicago Boys, Friedman's foot-soldiers: Jorge Cauas, Pinochet's finance minister and later economics 'superminister', Sergio de Castro, his successor as finance minister, Miguel Kast, labour minister and later central bank chief, and at least eight others who studied in Chicago and went on to serve in government. Even before the fall of Allende, they had devised a detailed programme of reforms known as *El Ladrillo* (The Brick) because of the thickness of the manuscript. The most radical measures, however, would come from a Catholic University student who had opted to study at Harvard, not Chicago. What he had in mind was the most profound challenge to the welfare state in a generation. Thatcher and

* Friedman noted in 1988 that he had given much the same advice on inflation to the Chinese government, yet found that he received no 'avalanche of protests for [his] having been willing to give advice to so evil a government', despite the fact that it 'has been and still is more repressive than the Chilean military junta'.

Reagan came later. The backlash against welfare started in Chile.

For José Piñera, just 24 when Pinochet seized power, the invitation to return to Chile from Harvard posed an agonizing dilemma. He had no illusions about the nature of Pinochet's regime. Yet he also believed there was an opportunity to put into practice ideas that had been taking shape in his mind ever since his arrival in New England. The key, as he saw it, was not just to reduce inflation. It was also essential to foster that link between property rights and political rights which had been at the heart of the successful North American experiment with capitalist democracy. There was no surer way to do this, Piñera believed, than radically to overhaul the welfare state, beginning with the pay-as-you-go system of funding state pensions and other benefits. As he saw it:

What had begun as a system of large-scale insurance had simply become a system of taxation, with today's contributions being used to pay today's benefits, rather than to accumulate a fund for future use. This 'pay-as-you-go' approach had replaced the principle of thrift with the practice of entitlement ... [But this approach] is rooted in a false conception of how human beings behave. It destroys, at the individual level, the link between contributions and benefits. In other words, between effort and reward. Wherever that happens on a massive scale and for a long period of time, the final result is disaster.[60]

Between 1979 and 1981, as minister of labour (and later minister of mining), Piñera created a radically new pension system for Chile, offering every worker the chance to opt out of the state pension system. Instead of paying a payroll tax, they would put an equivalent amount (10 per cent of their wages) into an individual Personal Retirement Account, to be managed by private and competing companies known as *Administradora de Fondos de Pensiones* (AFPs).[61] On reaching retirement age, a participant would withdraw his money and use it to buy an annuity; or, if he preferred, he could keep working and contributing. In addition to a pension, the scheme also included a disability and life insurance premium. The idea was to give the Chilean worker a sense that the money being set aside was really his own capital. In the words of Hernán Büchi (who helped Piñera draft the social security legislation and went on to implement the reform of health care), 'Social programmes have to include some incentive for individual effort and for persons gradually to be responsible for their own destiny. There is nothing more pathetic than social programmes that encourage social parasitism.'[62]

Piñera gambled. He gave workers a choice: stick with the old system of pay-as-you-go, or opt for the new Personal Retirement Accounts. He cajoled, making regular television appearances to reassure workers that 'Nobody will take away your grandmother's cheque' (from the old state system). He held firm, sarcastically dismissing a proposal that the country's trade unions, rather than individual workers, should be responsible for choosing their members' AFPs. Finally, on 4 November 1980, the reform was approved, coming into effect at Piñera's mischievous suggestion on 1 May, international Labour Day, the following year.[63] The public response was enthusiastic. By 1990 more than 70 per cent of workers had made the switch to the private system.[64] Each one received a shiny new book in which the contributions and investment returns were recorded. By the end of 2006, around 7.7 million Chileans had a Personal Retirement Account; 2.7 million were also covered by private health schemes, under the so-called ISAPRE system, which allowed workers to opt out of the state health insurance system in favour of a private provider. It may not sound like it, but – along with the other Chicago-inspired reforms implemented under Pinochet – this represented as big a revolution as anything the Marxist Allende had planned back in 1973. Moreover, the reform had to be introduced at a time of extreme economic instability, a consequence of the ill-judged decision to peg the Chilean currency to the dollar in 1979, when the inflation dragon appeared to have been slain. When US interest rates rose shortly afterwards, the deflationary pressure plunged Chile into a recession that threatened to derail the Chicago-Harvard express altogether. The economy contracted 13 per cent in 1982, seemingly vindicating the left-wing critics of Friedman's 'shock treatment'. Only towards the end of 1985 could the crisis really be regarded as over. By 1990 it was clear that the reform had been a success: welfare reforms were responsible for fully half the decline of total government expenditure from 34 per cent of GDP to 22 per cent.

Was it worth it? Was it worth the huge moral gamble that the Chicago and Harvard boys made, of getting into bed with a murderous, torturing military dictator? The answer depends on whether or not you think these economic reforms helped pave the way back to a sustainable democracy in Chile. In 1980, just seven years after the coup, Pinochet conceded a new constitution that prescribed a ten-year transition back to democracy. In 1990, having lost a referendum on his leadership, he stepped down as president (though he remained in charge of the army for a further eight years). Democracy was restored, and by that time the economic miracle was under way that helped to ensure its survival. For the pension reform not only created a new class of property-owners, each with his own retirement nest egg. It also gave the Chilean economy a massive shot in the arm, since the effect was significantly to increase the savings rate (to 30 per cent of GDP by 1989, the highest in Latin America). Initially, a cap was imposed that prevented the AFPs from investing more than 6 per cent (later 12 per cent) of the new pension funds outside Chile.[65] The effect of this was to ensure that Chile's new source of savings was channelled into the country's own economic development. In January 2008 I visited Santiago and watched brokers at the Banco de Chile busily investing the pension contributions of Chilean workers in their own stock market. The results have been impressive. The annual rate of return on the Personal Retirement Accounts has been over 10 per cent, reflecting the soaring performance of the Chilean stock market, which has risen by a factor of 18 since 1987.

There is a shadow side to the system, to be sure. The administrative and fiscal costs of the system are sometimes said to be too high.[66] Since not everyone in the economy has a regular full-time job, not everyone ends up participating in the system. The self-employed were not obliged to contribute to Personal Retirement Accounts, and the casually employed do not contribute either. That leaves a substantial proportion of the population with no pension coverage at all, including many of the people living in La Victoria, once a hotbed of popular resistance to the Pinochet regime – and still the kind of place where Che Guevara's face is spray-painted on the walls. On the other hand, the government stands ready to make up the difference for those whose savings do not suffice to pay a minimum pension, provided they have done at least twenty years of work. And there is also a Basic Solidarity pension for those who do not qualify for this.[67] Above all, the improvement in Chile's economic performance since the Chicago Boys' reforms is very hard to argue with. The growth rate in the fifteen years before Friedman's visit was 0.17 per cent. In the fifteen years that followed, it was 3.28 per cent, nearly twenty times higher. The poverty rate has declined dramatically to just 15 per cent, compared with 40 per cent in the rest of Latin America.[68] Santiago today is the shining city of the Andes, easily the continent's most prosperous and attractive city.

It is a sign of Chile's success that the country's pension reforms have been imitated all across the continent, and indeed around the world. Bolivia, El Salvador and Mexico copied the Chilean scheme to the letter. Peru and Colombia introduced private pensions as an alternative to the state system.[69] Kazakhstan, too, has followed the Chilean example. Even British MPs have beaten a path from Westminster to Piñera's door. The irony is that the Chilean reform was far more radical than anything that has been attempted in the United States, the heartland of free market economics. Yet welfare reform is coming to North America, whether anyone wants it or not.

When Hurricane Katrina struck New Orleans, it laid bare some realities about the American system that many people had been doing their best to ignore. Yes, America had a welfare state. No, it didn't work. The Reagan and Clinton administrations had implemented what seemed like radical welfare reforms, reducing unemployment benefits and the periods for which they could be claimed. But no amount of reform could insulate the system from the ageing of the American population and the spiralling cost of private health care.

The US has a unique welfare system. Social Security provides a minimal state pension to all retirees, while at the same time the Medicare system covers all the health costs of the elderly and disabled. Income support and other health expenditures push up the total cost of federal welfare programmes to 11 per cent of GDP. American healthcare, however, is almost entirely provided by the private sector. At its best it is state-of-the-art, but it is very far from cheap. And, if you want treatment before you retire, you need a private insurance policy – something an estimated 47 million Americans do not have, since such policies tend to be available only to those in regular, formal employment. The result is a welfare system which is not comprehensive, is much less redistributive than European systems, but is still hugely expensive. Since 1993 Social Security has been more expensive than National Security. Public expenditure on education is higher as a percentage of GDP (5.9 per cent) than in Britain, Germany or Japan. Public health expenditures are equivalent to around 7 per cent of GDP, the same as in Britain; but private health care spending accounts for more (8.5 per cent, compared with a paltry 1.1 per cent in Britain).[70]

Such a welfare system is ill prepared to cope with a rapid increase in the number of claimants. But that is precisely what Americans face as the members of the so-called 'Baby Boomer' generation, born after the Second World War, begin to retire.[71] According to the United Nations, between now and 2050 male life expectancy in the United States is likely to rise from 75 to 80. Over the next forty years, the share of the American population that is aged 65 or over is projected to rise from 12 per cent to nearly 21 per cent. Unfortunately, many of the soon-to-be-retired have made inadequate provision for life after work. According to the 2006 Retirement Confidence Survey, six in ten American workers say they are saving for retirement and just four in ten say they have actually calculated how much they should be saving. Many of those without sufficient savings imagine that they will compensate by working for longer. The average worker plans to work until age 65. But it turns out that he or she actually ends up retiring at 62; indeed, around four in ten American workers end up leaving the workforce earlier than they planned.[72] This has grave implications for the federal budget, since those who make these miscalculations are likely to end up a charge on taxpayers in one way or another. Today the average retiree receives Social Security, Medicare and Medicaid benefits totalling $21,000 a year. Multiply this by the current 36 million elderly and you see why these programmes already consume such a large proportion of federal tax revenues. And that proportion is bound to rise, not only because the number of retirees is going up but also because the costs of benefits like Medicare are out of control, rising at double the rate of inflation. The 2003 extension of Medicare to cover prescription drugs only made matters worse. According to one projection, by the aptly named Medicare Trustee Thomas R. Saving, the cost of Medicare alone will absorb 24 per cent of all federal income taxes by 2019. Current figures also imply that the federal government has much larger unfunded liabilities than official data imply. The Government Accountability Office's latest estimate of the implicit 'exposures' arising from unfunded future Social Security and Medicare benefits is $34 trillion.[73] That is nearly four times the size of the official federal debt.

Ironically, there's only one country where the problem of an ageing population has more serious economic implications than the United States. That country is Japan. So successful was the Japanese 'welfare superpower' that by the 1970s life expectancy in Japan had become the longest in the world. But that, combined with a falling birth rate, has produced the world's oldest society, with more than 21 per cent of the population already over the age of 65. According to Nakamae International Economic Research, the elderly population will be equal to that of the working population by 2044.[74] As a result, Japan is now grappling with a profound structural crisis of its welfare system, which was not designed to cope with what the Japanese call the longevity society (*chôju shakai*).[75] Despite raising the retirement age, the government has not yet resolved the problems of the state pension system. (Matters are not helped by the fact that many self-employed people and students – not to mention some eminent politicians – are failing to make their required social security contributions.) Public health insurers, meanwhile, have been in

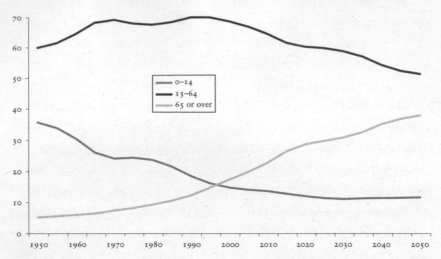

The demographics of a welfare crisis: Japan, 1950–2050
(percentage shares of population by age group)

deficit since the early 1990s.[76] Japan's welfare budget is now equal to three quarters of tax revenues. Its debt exceeds one quadrillion yen, around 170 per cent of GDP.[77] Yet private sector institutions are in no better shape. Life insurance companies have been struggling since the 1990 stock market crash; three major insurers failed between 1997 and 2000. Pension funds are in equally dire straits. As most countries in the developed world are moving in the same direction, it gives a new meaning to that old 1980s pop song about 'turning Japanese'. Assets at the world's largest pension funds (which include the Japanese government's own fund, its Dutch counterpart and the California Public Employees' fund) now exceed $10 trillion, having risen by 60 per cent between 2004 and 2007.[78] But are their liabilities ultimately going to grow so large that perhaps even these huge sums will not suffice?

Longer life is good news for individuals, but it is bad news for the welfare state and the politicians who have to persuade voters to reform it. The even worse news is that, even as the world's population is getting older, the world itself may be getting more dangerous.[79]

The Hedged and the Unhedged

What if international terrorism strikes more frequently and/or lethally, as Al Qaeda continues its quest for weapons of mass destruction? There is in fact good reason to fear this. Given the relatively limited impact of the 2001 attacks, Al Qaeda has a strong incentive to attempt a 'nuclear 9/11'.[80] The organization's spokesmen do not deny this; on the contrary, they openly boast of their ambition 'to kill 4 million Americans – 2 million of them children – and to exile twice as many and wound and cripple hundreds of thousands'.[81] This cannot be dismissed as mere rhetoric. According to Graham Allison, of Harvard University's Belfer Center, 'if the US and other governments just keep doing what they are doing today, a nuclear terrorist attack in a major city is more likely than not by 2014'. In the view of Richard Garwin, one of the designers of the hydrogen bomb, there is already a '20 per cent per year probability of a nuclear explosion with American cities and European cities included'. Another estimate, by Allison's colleague Matthew Bunn, puts the odds of a nuclear terrorist attack over a ten-year period at 29 per cent.[82] Even a small 12.5-kiloton nuclear device would kill up to 80,000 people if detonated in an average American city; a 1.0 megaton hydrogen bomb could kill as many as 1.9 million. A successful biological attack using anthrax spores could be nearly as lethal.[83]

What if global warming is increasing the incidence of natural disasters? Here, too, there are some grounds for unease. According to the scientific experts on the Intergovernmental Panel on Climate Change 'the frequency of heavy precipitation events has increased over most areas' as a result of man-made global warming. There is also 'observational evidence of an increase in intense tropical cyclone activity in the North Atlantic since about 1970'. The rising sea levels forecast by the IPCC would inevitably increase the flood damage caused by storms like Katrina.[84] Not all scientists accept the notion that hurricane activity along the US Atlantic coast is on the increase (as claimed by Al Gore in his film *An Inconvenient Truth*). But it would clearly be a mistake blithely to assume that this is not the case, especially given the continued growth of residential construction in vulnerable states. For governments that are already tottering under the weight of ever-increasing welfare commitments, an increase in the frequency or scale of catastrophes could be fiscally fatal. The insurance (and reinsurance) losses arising from the 9/11 attacks were in the region of $30–58 billion, close to the insurance losses due to Katrina.[85] In both cases, the US federal government had to step in to help private insurers meet their commitments, providing emergency federal terrorism insurance in the aftermath of 9/11, and absorbing the bulk of the costs of emergency relief and reconstruction along the coast of the Gulf of Mexico. In other words, just as happened during the world wars, the welfare state steps in when the insurers are overwhelmed. But this has a perverse result in the case of natural disasters. In effect, taxpayers in relatively safer parts of the country are subsidizing those who choose to live in hurricane-prone regions. One possible way of correcting this imbalance would be to create a federal reinsurance programme to cover mega-catastrophes. Rather than looking to taxpayers to pick up the tab for big disasters, insurers would charge differential premiums (higher for those closest to hurricane zones), laying off the risk of another Katrina by reinsuring the risk through the government.[86] But there is another way.

*

Insurance and welfare are not the only way of buying protection against future shocks. The smart way to do it is by being hedged. Everyone today has heard of hedge funds like Kenneth C. Griffin's Chicago-based Citadel. As founder of the Citadel Investment Group, now one of the twenty biggest hedge funds in the world, Griffin currently manages around $16 billion in assets. Among them are many so-called distressed assets, which Griffin picks up from failed companies like Enron for knock-down prices. It would not be too much to say that Ken Griffin loves risk. He lives and breathes uncertainty. Since he began trading convertible bonds from his Harvard undergraduate dormitory, he has feasted on 'fat tails'. Citadel's main offshore fund has generated annual returns of 21 per cent since 1998.[87] In 2007, when other financial institutions were losing billions in the credit crunch, he personally made more than a billion dollars. Among the artworks that decorate his penthouse apartment on North Michigan Avenue is Jasper Johns's *False Start*, for which he paid $80 million, and a Cézanne which cost him $60 million. When Griffin got married, the wedding was at Versailles (the French château, not the small Illinois town of the same name).[88] Hedging is clearly a good business in a risky world. But what exactly does it mean, and where did it come from?

The origins of hedging, appropriately enough, are agricultural. For a farmer planting a crop, nothing is more crucial than the price it will fetch after it has been harvested and taken to market. But that could be lower than he expects or higher. A futures contract allows him to protect himself by committing a merchant to buy his crop when it comes to market at a price agreed when the seeds are being planted. If the market price on the day of delivery is lower than expected, the farmer is protected; the merchant who sells him the contract naturally hopes it will be higher, leaving him with a profit. As the American prairies were ploughed and planted, and as canals and railways connected them to the major cities of the industrial Northeast, they became the nation's breadbasket. But supply and demand, and hence prices, fluctuated wildly. Between January 1858 and May 1867, partly as a result of the Civil War, the price of wheat soared from 55 cents to $2.88 per bushel, before plummeting back to 77 cents in March 1870. The earliest forms of protection for farmers were known as forward contracts, which were simply bilateral agreements between seller and buyer. A true futures contract, however, is a standardized instrument issued by a futures exchange and hence tradable. With the development of a standard 'to arrive' futures contract, along with a set of rules to enforce settlement and, finally, an effective clearinghouse, the first true futures market was born. Its birthplace was the Windy City: Chicago. The creation of a permanent futures exchange in 1874 – the Chicago Produce Exchange, the ancestor of today's Chicago Mercantile Exchange – created a home for 'hedging' in the US commodity markets.[89]

A pure hedge eliminates price risk entirely. It requires a speculator as a counter-party to take on the risk. In practice, however, most hedgers tend to engage in some measure of speculative activity, looking for ways to profit from future price movements. Partly because of public unease about this – the feeling that futures markets were little better than casinos – it was not until the 1970s that futures could also be issued for currencies and interest rates; and not until 1982 that futures contracts on the stock market became possible.

At Citadel, Griffin has brought together mathematicians, physicists, engineers, investment analysts and advanced computer technology. Some of what they do is truly the financial equivalent of rocket science. But the underlying principles are simple. Because they are all derived from the value of underlying assets, all futures contracts are forms of 'derivative'. Closely related, though distinct from futures, are the financial contracts known as options. In essence, the buyer of a call option has the right, but not the obligation, to buy an agreed quantity of a particular commodity or financial asset from the seller ('writer') of the option at a certain time (the expiration date) for a certain price (known as the strike price). Clearly, the buyer of a call option expects the price of the commodity or underlying instrument to rise in the future. When the price passes the agreed strike price, the option is 'in the money' – and so is the smart guy who bought it. A put option is just the opposite: the buyer has the right, but not the obligation, to sell an agreed quantity of something to the seller of the option. A third kind of derivative is the swap, which is effectively a bet between two parties on, for example, the future path of interest rates. A pure interest rate swap allows two parties already receiving interest payments literally to swap them, allowing someone receiving a variable rate of interest to exchange it for a fixed rate, in case interest rates decline. A credit default swap, meanwhile, offers protection against a company's defaulting on its bonds. Perhaps the most intriguing kind of derivative, however, are the weather derivatives like natural catastrophe bonds, which allow insurance companies and others to offset the effects of extreme temperatures or natural disasters by selling the so-called tail risk to hedge funds like Fermat Capital. In effect, the buyer of a 'cat bond' is selling insurance; if the disaster specified in the bond happens, the buyer has to pay out an agreed sum or forfeit his principal. In return, the seller pays an attractive rate of interest. In 2006 the total notional value of weather-risk derivatives was around $45 billion.

There was a time when most such derivatives were standardized instruments produced by exchanges like the Chicago Mercantile, which has pioneered the market for weather derivatives. Now, however, the vast proportion are custom-made and sold 'over-the-counter' (OTC), often by banks which charge attractive commissions for their services. According to the Bank for International Settlements, the total notional amounts outstanding of OTC derivative contracts – arranged on an ad hoc basis between two parties – reached a staggering $596 trillion in December 2007, with a gross market value of just over $14.5 trillion.* Though they have famously been called financial weapons of mass destruction by more traditional investors like Warren Buffett (who has, nonetheless, made use of them), the view in Chicago is that the world's economic system has never been better protected against the unexpected.

The fact nevertheless remains that this financial revolution has effectively divided the world in two: those who are (or can be) hedged, and those who are not (or cannot be). You need money to be hedged. Hedge funds typically ask for a minimum six- or seven-figure investment and charge a management fee of at least 2 per cent of your money (Citadel charges four times that) and 20 per cent of the profits. That means that most big corporations can afford to be hedged against unexpected increases in interest rates, exchange rates or commodity prices. If they want to, they can also hedge against future hurricanes or terrorist attacks by selling cat bonds and other derivatives. By comparison, most ordinary households cannot afford to hedge at all and would not know how to even if they could. We lesser mortals still have to rely on the relatively blunt and often expensive instrument of insurance policies to protect us against life's nasty surprises; or hope for the welfare state to ride to the rescue.

There is, of course, a third and much simpler strategy: the old

---

* That is to say, the notional amount outstanding if all derivatives paid out is roughly four and a half times the contracts' estimated market value.

one of simply saving for that rainy day. Or, rather, borrowing to buy assets whose future appreciation in value will supposedly afford a cushion against calamity. For many families in recent years, making provision for an uncertain future has taken the very simple form of an investment (usually leveraged, that is debt-financed) in a house, the value of which is supposed to keep increasing until the day the breadwinners need to retire. If the pension plan falls short, never mind. If you run out of health insurance, don't panic. There is always home, sweet home.

As an insurance policy or a pension plan, however, this strategy has one very obvious flaw. It represents a one-way, totally unhedged bet on one market: the property market. Unfortunately, as we shall see in the next chapter, a bet on bricks and mortar is very far from being as safe as houses. And you do not need to live in New Orleans to find that out the hard way.

5

Safe as Houses

It is the English-speaking world's favourite economic game: property. No other facet of financial life has such a hold on the popular imagination. No other asset-allocation decision has inspired so many dinner-party conversations. The real estate market is unique. Every adult, no matter how economically illiterate, has a view on its future prospects. Even children are taught how to climb the property ladder, long before they have money of their own.* And the way we teach them is literally to play a property game.

The game we know today as Monopoly was first devised in 1903 by an American woman, Elizabeth ('Lizzie') Phillips, a devotee of the radical economist Henry George. Her Utopian dream was of a world in which the only tax would be a levy on land values. The game's intended purpose was to expose the iniquity of a social system in which a small minority of landlords profited from the rents they collected from tenants. Originally known as The Landlord's Game, this proto-Monopoly had a number of familiar features – the continuous rectangular path, the Go to Jail corner – but it appeared too complex and didactic

* Arousing expectations which it may be impossible to fulfil. The fifteen-fold increase of house prices in England between 1975 and 2006 has put home ownership out of reach for nearly all those first-time buyers who cannot get financial assistance from their parents.

to have mass appeal. Indeed, its early adopters included a couple of eccentric university professors, Scott Nearing at Wharton and Guy Tugwell at Columbia, who modified it for classroom use. It was an unemployed plumbing engineer named Charles Darrow who saw the game's commercial potential after he was introduced by friends to a version based on the streets of Atlantic City, the New Jersey seaside resort. Darrow redesigned the board so that each property square had a brightly coloured band across it and hand-carved the little houses and hotels that players could 'build' on the squares they acquired. Darrow was good with his hands (he could turn out a single game in eight hours), but he also had the salesman's 'moxie', persuading the Philadelphia department store John Wanamaker and the toy retailer F. A. O. Schwartz to buy his game for the 1934 Christmas season. Soon he was selling more than he could make by himself. In 1935 the board-games company Parker Brothers (which had passed on the earlier Landlord's Game) bought him out.[1]

The Great Depression might have seemed an unpropitious time to launch what had by now mutated into a game for would-be property owners. But perhaps all that fake multicoloured money was part of Monopoly's appeal. 'As the name of the game suggests,' announced Parker Brothers in April 1935:

the players deal in real estate, railroads and public utilities in an endeavor to obtain a monopoly on a piece of property so as to obtain rent from the other players. Excitement runs high when such familiar problems are encountered as mortgages, taxes, a Community Chest, options, rentals, interest money, undeveloped real estate, hotels, apartment houses, power companies and other transactions, for which scrip money is supplied.[2]

The game was a phenomenal success. By the end of 1935 a quarter of a million sets had been sold. Within four years, versions had been created in Britain (where Waddington's created the London version that I first played), France, Germany, Italy and Austria – though fascist governments were at best ambivalent about its now unapologetically capitalist character.[3] By the time of the Second World War, the game was so ubiquitous that British intelligence could use Monopoly boards supplied by the Red Cross to smuggle escape kits – including maps and genuine European currencies – to British prisoners of war in German camps.[4] Unemployed Americans and captive Britons enjoyed Monopoly for the same reason. In real life, times may be hard, but when we play Monopoly we can dream of buying whole streets. What the game tells us, in complete contradiction to its original inventor's intention, is that it's smart to own property. The more you own, the more money you make. In the English-speaking world particularly, it has become a truth universally acknowledged that nothing beats bricks and mortar as an investment.

'Safe as houses': the phrase tells you all you need to know about why people all over the world yearn to own their own homes. But that phrase means something more precise in the world of finance. It means that there is nothing safer than lending money to people with property. Why? Because if they default on the loan, you can repossess the house. Even if they run away, the house can't. As the Germans say, land and buildings are 'immobile' property. So it is no coincidence that the single most important source of funds for a new business in the United States is a mortgage on the entrepreneur's house. Correspondingly, financial institutions have become ever less inhibited about lending money to people who want to buy property. Since 1959, the total mortgage debt outstanding in the US has risen seventy-five fold. Altogether, American owner-occupiers owed a sum equivalent to 99 per cent of US gross domestic product by the end of 2006, compared with just 38 per cent fifty years before. This upsurge in borrowing helped to finance a boom in residential investment, which reached a fifty-year peak in 2005. For a time, the supply of new housing seemed unable to keep pace with accelerating demand. About half of all the growth in US GDP in the first half of 2005 was housing related.

The English-speaking world's passion for property has also been the foundation for a political experiment: the creation of the world's first true property-owning democracies, with between 65 and 83 per cent of households owning the home they live in.* A majority of voters, in other words, are also property owners. Some say this is a model the whole world should adopt. Indeed, in recent years it has been spreading fast, with house price booms not only in the 'Anglosphere' (Australia, Canada, Ireland, the United Kingdom and the United States), but also in China, France, India, Italy, Russia, South Korea and Spain. In 2006 nominal house price inflation exceeded 10 per cent in eight out of eighteen countries in the Organization for Economic Cooperation and Development. The United States did not in fact experience an exceptional housing bubble between 2000 and 2007; prices rose further in the Netherlands and Norway.[5]

But is property really as safe as houses? Or is the real estate game more like a house of cards?

---

* Ireland leads the field with 83 per cent of households owning their own homes, followed by Australia and the United Kingdom (both 69 per cent), Canada (67 per cent) and the United States (65 per cent). The figure for Japan is 60 per cent, for France 54 per cent and for Germany 43 per cent. Note, however, that these figures are for 2000. Since then, the figure for the United States has risen to above 68 per cent. Note also the regional variation: Midwesterners and Southerners are significantly more likely to own their own homes (72 per cent do) than people living in the West and the Northeast. Housing is more affordable in the Midwest and South. 78 per cent of West Virginians own their own homes; just 46 per cent of New Yorkers do.

The Property-owning Aristocracy

Home ownership is now the exception only in the poorest parts of Britain and the United States, like the East End of Glasgow or the East Side of Detroit. For most of history, however, it was the exclusive privilege of an aristocratic elite. Estates were passed down from father to son, along with honorific titles and political privileges. Everyone else was a mere tenant, paying rent to their landlord. Even the right to vote in elections was originally a function of property ownership. In rural England before 1832, according to statutes passed in the fifteenth century, only men who owned freehold property worth at least forty shillings a year in a particular county were entitled to vote there. That meant, at most, 435,000 people in England and Wales – the majority of whom were bound to the wealthiest landowners by an intricate web of patronage. Of the 514 Members of Parliament representing England and Wales in the House of Commons in the early 1800s, about 370 were selected by nearly 180 land-owning patrons. More than a fifth of MPs were the sons of peers.

In one respect, not much has changed in Britain since those days. Around forty million acres out of sixty million are owned by just 189,000 families.[6] The Duke of Westminster remains the third-richest man in the UK, with estimated assets of £7 billion; also in the top fifty of the 'rich list' are Earl Cadogan (£2.6 billion) and Baroness Howard de Walden (£1.6 billion). The difference is that the aristocracy no longer monopolizes the political system. The last aristocrat to serve as Prime Minister was Alec Douglas-Home, the 14th Earl of Home, who left office in 1964 (defeated by, as he put it, 'the 14th Mr Wilson'). Indeed, thanks to the reform of the House of Lords, the hereditary peerage is in the process of finally being phased out of the British parliamentary system.

The decline of the aristocracy as a political force has been explained in many ways. At its heart, however, was finance. Until the 1830s fortune smiled on the elite, the thirty or so families with gross annual income from their lands above £60,000 a year. Land values had soared during the Napoleonic Wars, as the combination of demographic pressure and wartime inflation caused the price of wheat to double. Thereafter, industrialization brought windfalls to those who happened to be sitting on coalfields or urban real estate, while the aristocratic dominance of the political system ensured a steady stream of remuneration from the public purse. As if that were not enough, the great magnates took full advantage of their ability to borrow to the hilt. Some did so to 'improve' their estates, draining fields and enclosing common land. Others borrowed to finance a lifestyle of conspicuous consumption. The Dukes of Devonshire, for example, spent between 40 and 55 per cent of their annual income on interest payments, so enormous were their borrowings during the nineteenth century. 'All that you want,' complained one of their solicitors, 'is the power of self-restraint.'[7]

The trouble is that property, no matter how much you own, is a security only to the person who lends you money. As Miss Demolines says in Trollope's *Last Chronicle of Barset*, 'the land can't run away'.* This was why so many nineteenth-century investors – local solicitors, private banks and insurance companies – were attracted to mortgages as a seemingly risk-free investment.

* 'Life is always uncertain, Miss Demolines.'
'You're quizzing now, I know. But don't you feel now, really, that City money is always very chancy? It comes and goes so quick.'
'As regards the going, I think that's the same with all money,' said Johnny.
'Not with land, or the funds. Mamma has every shilling laid out in a first-class mortgage on land at four per cent. That does make one feel so secure! The land can't run away.' (Ch. 25)

By contrast, the borrower's sole security against the loss of his property to such creditors is his income. Unfortunately for the great landowners of Victorian Britain, that suddenly fell away. From the late 1840s onwards, the combination of increasing grain production around the world, plummeting transport costs and falling tariff barriers – exemplified by the repeal of the Corn Laws in 1846 – eroded the economic position of landowners. As grain prices slid from a peak of $3 a bushel in 1847 to a nadir of 50 cents in 1894, so did the income from agricultural land. Rates of return on rural property slumped from 3.65 per cent in 1845 to just 2.51 per cent in 1885.[8] As *The Economist* put it: 'No security was ever relied upon with more implicit faith, and few have lately been found more sadly wanting than English land.' For those with estates in Ireland, the problem was compounded by mounting political unrest. This economic decline and fall was exemplified by the fortunes of the family that built Stowe House, in Buckinghamshire.

There is something undeniably magnificent about Stowe House. With its sweeping colonnades, its impressive Vanbrugh portico and its delightful 'Capability' Brown gardens, it is one of the finest surviving examples of eighteenth-century aristocratic architecture. Yet there is something missing from Stowe today – or rather many things. In each of the alcoves of the elliptical Marble Saloon, there was once a Romanesque statue. The splendid Georgian fireplaces in the State Rooms have been replaced by cheap and diminutive Victorian substitutes. Rooms that were once crammed full of the finest furniture now lie empty. Why? The answer is that this house once belonged to the most distinguished victim of the first modern property crash, Richard Plantagenet Temple-Nugent-Brydges-Chandos-Grenville, 6th Viscount Cobham and 2nd Duke of Buckingham.

Stowe was only part of the vast empire of real estate acquired by the Duke of Buckingham and his ancestors, who had propelled

Stowe House: aristocratic grandeur, mortgaged to the hilt

themselves from a barony to a dukedom in the space of 125 years by a combination of political patronage and strategic marriage.[9] In all, the Duke owned around 67,000 acres in England, Ireland and Jamaica. It seemed a more than adequate basis for his extravagant lifestyle. He spent money as if it might go out of fashion: on mistresses, on illegitimate children, on suing his father-in-law's executors, on buying his way into the Order of the Garter, on opposing the Great Reform Bill and the Repeal of the Corn Laws – on anything he felt was compatible with his standing as a duke of the realm and the living embodiment of The Land. He prided himself on 'resisting any measure injurious to the agricultural interests, no matter by what Government it should be brought forward'. Indeed, he resigned as Lord Privy Seal in Sir Robert Peel's government rather than support Corn Law Repeal.[10] By 1845, however – even before the mid-century slump in grain prices, in other words – his debts were close to overwhelming him. With a gross annual income of £72,000, he was spending £109,140 a year and had accumulated debts of £1,027,282.[11] Most of his income was absorbed by interest payments (with rates on some of his debts as high as 15 per cent) and life insurance premiums on a policy that was probably his creditors' best hope of seeing their money.[12] Yet there was to be one final folly.

In preparation for a much-sought-after visit by Queen Victoria and Prince Albert in January 1845, the Duke refurbished Stowe House from top to bottom. The entire house was filled with the very latest in luxury furniture. There were even tiger skins in the royal bathroom. Queen Victoria remarked waspishly: 'I have no such splendour in either of my two palaces.' As if that were not enough, the Duke called out the entire Regiment of Yeomanry (at his own expense) to fire welcoming salvoes of artillery as the Queen and her Consort entered his estate. Four hundred tenants lined up on horseback to greet them, as well as several hundred smartly dressed labourers, three brass bands and a special detachment of police brought down from London for the day.[13] It was the last straw for the ducal finances. To avert the complete ruin of the family, Buckingham's son, the Marquis of Chandos, was advised to take control of his father's estates as soon as he came of age. After painful legal wrangles, the son won the upper hand.[14] In August 1848, to the Duke's horror, the entire contents of Stowe House were auctioned off. Now his ancestral stately home was thrown open for throngs of bargain hunters to bid for the plate, the wine, the china, the works of art and the rare books, for all the world (as *The Economist* sneered) as if the Duke were 'a bankrupt earthenware dealer'.[15] The total proceeds from the sale were £75,000. Nothing could better have symbolized the new age of aristocratic decline.

Three generations of aristocracy:

TOP LEFT: Richard Grenville,
1st Duke of Buckingham
TOP RIGHT: Richard Grenville,
2nd Duke of Buckingham
BOTTOM LEFT: Richard Grenville,
3rd Duke of Buckingham

Divorced by his long-suffering, much-betrayed Scottish wife, whose entire wardrobe had been seized by sheriff's officers in London, the Duke was forced to move out of Stowe House into rented lodgings. He eked out his days at his London club, the Carlton, writing a succession of highly unreliable memoirs and incorrigibly chasing actresses and other men's wives. Accustomed to what had once seemed a limitless overdraft facility, he bitterly grumbled that his son allowed him 'scarcely the pay of an officer upon full pay of my own rank who has nothing beyond his own expenses to pay for':[16]

In the hour of distress [he] forced his Father into the world, neglected, forsaken & persecuted ... Having got possession of his estates & property, [he] held them to his detriment & loss, & against every principle of honour and justice, & ... lived to witness his Father's dishonour and degradation.[17]

'You find me poisoned and robbed,' he lamented to anyone at the Carlton who would listen.[18] When the Duke finally expired in 1861 he was living at his son's expense in the Great Western Hotel at Paddington railway station. Symbolically, his more parsimonious son was by now chairman of the London and North-western Railway Company.[19] In the modern world, it turned out, a regular job mattered more than an inherited title, no matter how many acres you owned.

The fall of the Duke of Buckingham was a harbinger of a new, democratic age. Electoral reform acts in 1832, 1867 and 1884 eroded what remained of the aristocratic stranglehold on British politics. By the end of the nineteenth century, paying £10 a year in rent qualified you to vote just as legitimately as earning £10 a year from property. The electorate now numbered 5.5 million – 40 per cent of adult males. In 1918 that last economic qualification was finally removed and after 1928 all adults, male and female, had the vote. Yet the advent of universal suffrage did not mean that property ownership had become universal. On the contrary: as late as 1938, less than a third of the UK housing stock was in the hands of owner-occupiers. It was on the other side of the Atlantic that the first true property-owning democracy would emerge. And it would come out of the deepest financial crisis ever known.

Home-owning Democracy

An Englishman's home is his castle, or so the saying goes. Americans, too, know that (as Dorothy says in *The Wizard of Oz*) there's no place like home – even if the homes do all look rather similar. But the origins of the Anglo-American model of the highly geared home-owning family lie as much in the realm of government policy as in the realm of culture. If the old class system based on elite property ownership was distinctively British, the property-owning democracy was made in America.

Before the 1930s, little more than two fifths of American households were owner-occupiers. Unless you were a farmer, mortgages were the exception, not the rule. The few people who did borrow money to buy their own houses in the 1920s found themselves in deep difficulties when the Great Depression struck, especially if the main breadwinner was among the millions who lost their jobs and their incomes. Mortgages were short-term, usually for three to five years, and they were not amortized. In other words, people paid interest, but did not repay the sum they had borrowed (the principal) until the end of the loan's term, so that they ended up facing a balloon-sized final payment. The average difference (spread) between mortgage rates and high-grade corporate bond yields was about two percentage points during the 1920s, compared with about half a per cent (50 basis points) in the past twenty years. There were substantial regional variations in mortgage rates, too.[20] When the economy nose-dived, nervous lenders simply refused to renew. In 1932 and 1933 there were over a half million foreclosures. By mid 1933, over a thousand mortgages were being foreclosed every day. House prices plummeted by more than a fifth.[21] The construction indus-try collapsed, revealing (as in all future recessions of the twentieth century) the extent to which the wider US economy relied on residential investment as an engine of growth.[22] While the effect of the Depression was perhaps most devastating in the countryside, where land prices fell below half of their 1920 peak, the predica-ment of America's cities was little better. Tenants, too, struggled to pay the rent when all they had coming in was the dole. In Detroit, for example, the automobile industry employed only half the number of workers it had in 1929, and at half the wages. The effects of the Depression are scarcely imaginable today: the abject misery of ubiquitous unemployment, the wretchedness of the soup kitchens, the desperate nomadic search for non-existent work. By 1932 the dispossessed of the Depression had had enough.

On 7 March 1932 five thousand unemployed workers laid off by the Ford Motor Company marched through central Detroit to demand relief. As the unarmed crowd reached Gate 4 of the company's River Rouge plant in Dearborn, scuffles broke out. Suddenly the factory gates opened and a group of armed police and security men rushed out and fired into the crowd. Five workers were killed. Days later, 60,000 people sang 'The Inter-nationale' at their funeral. The Communist Party newspaper accused Edsel Ford, son of the firm's founder Henry, of allowing a massacre: 'You, a patron of the arts, a pillar of the Episcopal Church, stood on the bridge at the Rouge Plant and saw the workers killed. You did not lift a hand to stop it.' Could anything be done to defuse what was beginning to seem like a revolutionary situation?

In a remarkable gesture of conciliation, Edsel Ford turned to the Mexican artist Diego Rivera, who had been invited by the Detroit Institute of Arts to paint a mural that would show Detroit's economy as a place of cooperation, not class conflict. The site chosen for the work was the Institute's imposing Garden Court, a space which so appealed to Rivera that he proposed to paint not just two of its panels, as had originally been suggested, but all twenty-seven. Ford, impressed by Rivera's preliminary sketches, agreed to fund the entire scheme, at a cost of around $25,000. Work began in May 1932, just two months after the clashes at the River Rouge plant, and by March 1933 Rivera had finished. As Ford well knew, Rivera was a Communist (though an unorthodox Trotskyite who had been expelled from the Mexican Party).[23] His ideal was of a society in which there would be no private property; in which the means of production would be commonly owned. In Rivera's eyes, Ford's River Rouge plant was the very opposite: a capitalist society where the workers worked and the property owners, who reaped the rewards from their efforts, just stood and watched. Rivera also sought to explore the racial divisions that were such a striking feature of Detroit, anthropomorphizing the elements necessary to make steel. As he himself explained the allegory:

The yellow race represents the sand, because it is most numerous. And the red race, the first in this country, is like the iron ore, the first thing necessary for the steel. The black race is like coal, because it has a great native aesthetic sense, a real flame of feeling and beauty in its ancient sculpture, its native rhythm and music. So its aesthetic sense is like the fire, and its labor furnished the hardness which the carbon

Hunger march in Detroit, March 1932

Police use tear gas against the hunger marchers

'Smash Ford-Murphy Police Terror': protest following the deaths
of five demonstrators

in the coal gives to steel. The white race is like the lime, not only
because it is white, but because lime is the organizing agent in the
making of steel. It binds together the other elements and so you see
the white race as the great organizer of the world.

When the murals were unveiled in 1933, the city's dignitaries
were appalled. In the words of Dr George H. Derry, president of
Marygrove College:

Senor Rivera has perpetrated a heartless hoax on his capitalist
employer, Edsel Ford. Rivera was engaged to interpret Detroit; he has
foisted on Mr Ford and the museum a Communist manifesto. The
key panel that first strikes the eye, when you enter the room, betrays
the Communist motif that animates and alone explains the whole
ensemble. Will the women of Detroit feel flattered when they realize
that they are embodied in the female with the hard, masculine, unsexed

face, ecstatically staring for hope and help across the panel to the languorous and grossly sensual Asiatic sister on the right?[24]

One city councillor argued that whitewash was too good for the murals, as it could still be removed in future. He wanted Rivera's work to be completely stripped off as 'a travesty on the spirit of Detroit'. That was more or less what happened to Rivera's next commission – to decorate the walls of New York's Rockefeller Center for John D. Rockefeller Jr. – after the artist insisted on including a portrait of Lenin as well as Communist slogans like 'Down With Imperialistic Wars!', 'Workers Unite!' and, most shocking of all, 'Free Money!' These were to be carried by demonstrators marching down Wall Street itself. A scandalized Rockefeller ordered the mural to be destroyed.

The power of art is a wonderful thing. But clearly something more powerful than art was going to be needed to put together a society that had been split in two by the Depression. Many other countries swung to the extremes of totalitarianism. But in the United States the answer was the New Deal. Franklin D. Roosevelt's first administration saw a proliferation of new federal government agencies and initiatives intended to re-inject confidence into the prostrate US economy. In the flood of acronyms the New Deal produced, it is easy to miss the fact that its most successful and enduring component was the new deal it offered with respect to housing. By radically increasing the opportunity for Americans to own their own homes, the Roosevelt administration pioneered the idea of a property-owning democracy. It proved to be the perfect antidote to red revolution.

At one level, the New Deal was an attempt by government to step in where the market had failed. Some New Dealers favoured the increased provision of public housing, the model that was adopted in most European countries. Indeed, the Public Works

Administration spent nearly 15 per cent of its budget on low-cost homes and slum clearance. But of far more importance was the Roosevelt administration's lifeline to the rapidly sinking mortgage market. A new Home Owners' Loan Corporation stepped in to refinance mortgages on longer terms, up to fifteen years. A Federal Home Loan Bank Board had already been set up in 1932 to encourage and oversee local mortgage lenders known as Savings and Loans (or thrifts), mutual associations like British building societies, which took in deposits and lent to home buyers. To reassure depositors, who had been traumatized by the bank failures of the previous three years, Roosevelt introduced federal deposit insurance. The idea was that putting money in mortgages would be even safer than houses, because if borrowers defaulted, the government would simply compensate the savers.[25] In theory, there could never be another run on a Savings and Loan like the run on the family-owned Bailey Building & Loan which George Bailey (played by Jimmy Stewart) struggled to keep afloat in Frank Capra's classic 1946 movie *It's a Wonderful Life*. 'You know, George,' his father tells him, 'I feel that in a small way we are doing something important. Satisfying a fundamental urge. It's deep in the race for a man to want his own roof and walls and fireplace, and we're helping him get those things in our shabby little office.' George gets the message, as he passionately explains to the villainous slum landlord Potter after Bailey senior's death:

[My father] never once thought of himself . . . But he did help a few people get out of your slums, Mr Potter. And what's wrong with that? Doesn't it make them better citizens? Doesn't it make them better customers? . . . You said . . . they had to wait and save their money before they even ought to think of a decent home. Wait! Wait for what? Until their children grow up and leave them? Until they're so

It's a Wonderful Life: Frank Capra's celebration of the virtues of the local 'thrift' or Savings and Loan, with Jimmy Stewart as the lovable mortgage lender

old and broken-down that they . . . Do you know how long it takes a working man to save five thousand dollars? Just remember this, Mr Potter, that this rabble you're talking about . . . they do most of the working and paying and living and dying in this community. Well, is it too much to have them work and pay and live and die in a couple of decent rooms and a bath?

This radical affirmation of the virtue of home ownership was new. But it was the Federal Housing Administration that really made the difference for American homebuyers. By providing federally backed insurance for mortgage lenders, the FHA sought to encourage large (up to 80 per cent of the purchase price), long (twenty-year), fully amortized and low-interest loans. This did more than merely revive the mortgage market; it reinvented it.

By standardizing the long-term mortgage and creating a national system of official inspection and valuation, the FHA laid the foundation for a national secondary market. This market came to life in 1938, when a new Federal National Mortgage Association – nicknamed Fannie Mae – was authorized to issue bonds and use the proceeds to buy mortgages from the local Savings and Loans, which were now restricted by regulation both in terms of geography (they could not lend to borrowers more than fifty miles from their offices) and in terms of the rates they could offer depositors (the so-called Regulation Q, which imposed a low ceiling). Because these changes tended to reduce the average monthly payment on a mortgage, the FHA made home ownership viable for many more Americans than ever before. Indeed, it is not too much to say that the modern United States, with its seductively samey suburbs, was born here.

From the 1930s onwards, then, the US government was effectively underwriting the mortgage market, encouraging lenders and borrowers to get together. That was what caused property ownership – and mortgage debt – to soar after the Second World War, driving up the home ownership rate from 40 per cent to 60 per cent by 1960. There was only one catch. Not everyone in American society was entitled to join the property-owning party.

In 1941 a real estate developer built a six-foot high wall right across Detroit's 8 Mile district. He had to build it to qualify for subsidized loans from the Federal Housing Administration. The loans were to be given out for construction only on the side of the wall where the residents were mainly white. In the predominantly black part of town, there was to be no federal lending, because African-Americans were regarded as uncreditworthy.[26] It was part of a system that divided the whole city, in theory by credit-rating, in practice by colour. Segregation, in other words, was not accidental, but a direct consequence of government policy. Federal Home Loan Bank Board maps showed the predominantly black areas of Detroit – the Lower East Side and some so-called colonies on the West Side and 8 Mile – marked with a D and coloured red. The areas marked A, B or C were mainly white. The distinction explains why the practice of giving whole areas a negative credit-rating came to be known as red-lining.[27] As a result, when people in D areas wanted to take out mortgages, they paid significantly higher interest rates than the people from areas A to C. In the 1950s, one in five black mortgage-borrowers paid 8 per cent or more, whereas virtually no whites paid more than 7 per cent.[28] This was the hidden financial dimension of the Civil Rights struggle.

Detroit was home to successful black entrepreneurs like Berry Gordy, the founder of the Motown record label, which appropriately enough had its very first hit in 1960 with Barrett Strong's 'Money, That's What I Want'. Other Motown stars like Aretha Franklin and Marvin Gaye still lived in the city. Yet throughout the 1960s the prejudice persisted that black neighbourhoods were a bad credit risk. Anger at such economic discrimination lay behind the riots that broke out in Detroit's 12th Street on 23 July 1967. In five days of mayhem after a police raid on a 'blind pig' (an unlicensed bar), forty-three people were killed, 467 injured, over 7,200 arrested and nearly 3,000 buildings looted or burned – a potent symbol of black rejection of a property-owning democracy that still treated them as second-class citizens.[29] Even today, you can still see the empty lots that the riots left in their wake. It took regular army troops with tanks and machine-guns to quell what was officially recognized as an insurrection.

As in the 1930s, the challenge of violence brought a political response. In the wake of the Civil Rights legislation of the 1960s, new steps were taken to broaden access to home ownership. In

1968 Fannie Mae was split in two: the Government National Mortgage Association (Ginnie Mae), which was to cater to poor borrowers like military veterans, and a rechartered Fannie Mae, now a privately owned government sponsored enterprise (GSE), which was permitted to buy conventional as well as government-guaranteed mortgages. Two years later, to provide some competition in the secondary market, the Federal Home Loan Mortgage Corporation (Freddie Mac) was set up. The effect was once again to broaden the secondary market for mortgages, and in theory at least to lower mortgage rates. Red-lining on the basis of racial discrimination did not cease overnight, needless to say; but it became a federal offence.[30] Indeed, with the Community Reinvestment Act of 1977, American banks came under statutory pressure to lend to poorer minority communities. With the US housing market now underwritten by what sounded like a financial version of the Mamas and the Papas – Fannie, Ginnie and Freddie – the political winds were set fair for the property owning democracy. Those who ran Savings and Loans could live by the comfortable 3-6-3 rule: pay 3 per cent on deposits, lend money at 6 per cent and be on the golf course by 3 o'clock every afternoon.

The rate of home ownership caught up more slowly with the representation of the people on the other side of the Atlantic. In post-war Britain the conventional wisdom among Conservative as well as Labour politicians was that the state should provide or at least subsidize housing for the working classes. Indeed, Harold Macmillan sought to out-build Labour with a target of 300,000 (later 400,000) new houses a year. Between 1959 and 1964, roughly a third of new houses in Britain were built by local councils, rising to half in the subsequent six years of Labour rule. The ugly and socially dysfunctional tower blocks and housing 'estates' that today blight most of Britain's cities can be blamed on both parties. The only real difference between Right and Left was the readiness of the Conservatives to deregulate the private rental market, in the hope of encouraging private landlords, and the equal and opposite resolve of Labour to reimpose rent controls and stamp out 'Rachmanism' (exploitative behaviour by landlords), exemplified by Peter Rachman, who used intimidation to evict the sitting tenants of rent-controlled properties, replacing them with West Indian immigrants who had to pay market rents.[31] As late as 1971, fewer than half of British homes were owner-occupied.

In the United States, where public housing was never so important, mortgage interest payments were always tax deductible, from the inception of the federal income tax in 1913.[32] As Ronald Reagan said when the rationality of this tax break was challenged, mortgage interest relief was 'part of the American dream'.* It played a much smaller role in Britain until 1983, when a more radically Conservative government led by Margaret Thatcher introduced Mortgage Interest Relief At Source (MIRAS) for the first £30,000 of a qualifying mortgage. When her Chancellor of the Exchequer Nigel Lawson sought to limit the deduction (so that multiple borrowers could not all take advantage of it for a single property), he soon 'ran up against the brick wall of Margaret [Thatcher]'s passionate devotion to the preservation of every last ounce of mortgage interest relief'.[33] Nor was MIRAS the only way that Thatcher sought to encourage home ownership. By selling off council houses at bargain-basement prices to a million and a half aspirant working-class families, she ensured that more and more British men and women had a home of their own. The result was a leap in the share of owner-occupiers from

* Today, around 37 million American individuals and couples claim the deduction on mortgages of up to $1,000,000, at a cost of $76 billion to the US Treasury.

54 per cent in 1981 to 67 per cent ten years later. The stock of owner-occupied properties has soared from just over 11 million in 1980 to more than 17 million today.[34]

Up until the 1980s, government incentives to borrow and buy a house made a good deal of sense for ordinary households. Indeed, the tendency for inflation rates to rise above interest rates in the late 1960s and 1970s gave debtors a free lunch as the real value of their debts and interest payments declined. While American home purchasers in the mid seventies anticipated an inflation rate of at least 12 per cent by 1980, mortgage lenders were offering thirty-year fixed-rate loans at 9 per cent or less.[35] For a time, lenders were effectively paying people to borrow their money. Meanwhile, property prices roughly trebled between 1963 and 1979, while consumer prices rose by a factor of just 2.5. But there was a sting in the tail. The same governments that avowed their faith in the 'property-owning democracy' also turned out to believe in price stability, or at least lower inflation. Achieving that meant higher interest rates. The unintended consequence was one of the most spectacular booms and busts in the history of the property market.

From S&L to Subprime

Take a drive along Interstate 30 from Dallas, Texas, and you cannot fail to notice mile after mile of half-built houses and condominiums. Their existence is one of the last visible traces of one of the biggest financial scandals in American history, a scam that made a mockery of the whole idea of property as a safe investment. What follows is a story not so much about real estate as about surreal estate.

Savings and Loan (S&L) associations – the American version

of Britain's building societies – were the foundation on which America's property-owning democracy had come to rest. Owned mutually by their depositors, they were simultaneously protected and constrained by a framework of government regulation.[36] Deposits of up to $40,000 were insured by government for a premium of just one twelfth of one per cent of total deposits. On the other hand, they could lend only to home buyers within fifty miles of their main office. And from 1966, under Regulation Q, there was a ceiling of 5.5 per cent on their deposit rates, a quarter of a per cent more than banks were allowed to pay. In the late 1970s, this sleepy sector was hit first by double-digit inflation – which reached 13.3 per cent in 1979 – and then by sharply rising interest rates as the newly appointed Federal Reserve Chairman Paul Volcker sought to break the wage-price spiral by slowing monetary growth. This double punch was lethal. The S&Ls were simultaneously losing money on long-term fixed-rate mortgages, because of inflation, and haemorrhaging deposits to higher-interest money market funds. The response in Washington from both the Carter and Reagan administrations was to try to salvage the entire sector with tax breaks and deregulation,* in the belief that market forces could solve the problem.[37] When the new legislation was passed, President Reagan declared: 'All in all, I think we hit the jackpot.'[38] Some people certainly did.

On the one hand, S&Ls could now invest in whatever they liked, not just long-term mortgages. Commercial property, stocks, junk bonds: anything was allowed. They could even issue credit cards. On the other, they could now pay whatever interest rate they liked to depositors. Yet all their deposits were still effectively insured, with the maximum covered amount raised

* The crucial legislation was the Depository Institutions Deregulation and Monetary Control Act of 1980 and the Garn-St Germain Depository Institutions Act of 1982.

from $40,000 to $100,000. And, if ordinary deposits did not suffice, the S&Ls could raise money in the form of brokered deposits from middlemen, who packaged and sold 'jumbo' $100,000 certificates of deposit.[39] Suddenly the people running Savings and Loans had nothing to lose – a clear case of what economists call moral hazard.[40] What happened next perfectly illustrated the great financial precept first enunciated by William Crawford, the Commissioner of the California Department of Savings and Loans: 'The best way to rob a bank is to own one.'[41] Some S&Ls bet their depositors' money on highly dubious projects. Many simply stole it, as if deregulation meant that the law no longer applied to them. Nowhere were these practices more rife than in Texas.

When they weren't whooping it up at their Southfork-style ranches, the Dallas property cowboys liked to do their deals at the Wise Circle Grill.[42] Regulars for Sunday brunch included Don Dixon, whose Vernon S&L was nicknamed Vermin by regulators,[43] Ed McBirney of Sunbelt ('Gunbelt') and Tyrell Barker, owner and CEO of State Savings and Loan, who liked to tell property developers: 'You bring the dirt, I bring the money.'[44] One individual who brought both dirt and money was Mario Renda, a New York broker for the Teamsters Union who allegedly used Savings and Loans to launder Mafia funds. When he needed more cash, he even advertised in the *New York Times*:

MONEY FOR RENT: BORROWING OBSTACLES NEUTRALIZED
BY HAVING US DEPOSIT FUNDS WITH YOUR LOCAL BANK:
NEW TURNSTILE APPROACH TO FINANCING.[45]

If you want to build a property empire, why not just say so? For one group of Dallas developers, it was Empire Savings and Loan that offered the perfect opportunity to make a fortune out of thin air – or, rather, flat Texan earth. The surrealism began when Empire chairman Spencer H. Blain Jr. teamed up with James Toler, the mayor of the town of Garland, and a flamboyant high school dropout turned property developer named Danny Faulkner, whose speciality was extravagant generosity with other people's money. The money in question came in the form of brokered deposits, on which Empire paid alluringly high interest rates. Faulkner's Point, located near the bleak artificial lake known as Lake Ray Hubbard, twenty miles east of Dallas, was the first outpost of a property empire that would later encompass Faulkner Circle, Faulkner Creek, Faulkner Oaks – even Faulkner Fountains. Faulkner's favourite trick was 'the flip', whereby he would acquire a plot of land for peanuts, and then sell it on at vastly inflated prices to investors, who borrowed the money from Empire Savings and Loan. One parcel of land was bought by Faulkner for $3 million and sold just a few days later for $47 million. Danny Faulkner claimed to be illiterate. He was certainly not innumerate.

By 1984 development in the Dallas area was out of control. There were new condos under construction for miles along Interstate 30. The city's skyline had been transformed with what locals referred to as 'see-through' office buildings – see-through because they were still mostly empty. The building just kept on going, paid for by federally insured deposits that were effectively going straight into the developers' pockets. On paper at least, the assets of Empire had grown from $12 million to $257 million in just over two years. By January 1984 they stood at $309 million. Many investors never even got a chance to view their properties close up; Faulkner would simply fly them over in his helicopter without landing. Everyone was making money: Faulkner with his $4 million Learjet, Toler with his white Rolls-Royce, Blain with his $4,000 Rolex – not to mention the property appraisers, the sports star investors and the local regulators. There were gold

The master of the real estate 'flip': Danny Faulkner with
his helicopter

bracelets for the men and fur coats for the wives.[46] 'It was', one
of those involved acknowledged, 'like a money machine, and all
of it was geared to what Danny needed. If Danny needed a new
jet, we did a land deal. If Danny wanted to buy a new farm, we
did another. Danny ran the whole thing for Danny, right down
to the last detail.'[47] The line between thrift and theft is supposed
to be a wide one. Faulkner & Co. reduced it to a hair's breadth.

The trouble was that the demand for condos on Interstate 30
could never possibly have kept pace with the vast supply being
built by Faulkner, Blain and their cronies. By the early 1980s
estate agents were joking that the difference between venereal
disease and condominiums was that you could get rid of VD.
Moreover, the mismatch between the assets and liabilities of most
Savings and Loans had now become disastrous, with ever more

long-term loans being made (to insiders) using money borrowed short-term (from outsiders). When the regulators belatedly sought to act in 1984, these realities could no longer be ignored. On 14 March Edwin J. Gray, then chairman of the Federal Home Loan Bank Board, ordered the closure of Empire. The cost to the Federal Savings and Loan Insurance Corporation, which was supposed to insure S&L deposits, was $300 million. But this was just the beginning. As other firms came under scrutiny, legislators hesitated, particularly those who had received generous campaign contributions from S&Ls.* Yet the longer they waited, the more money got burned. By 1986 it was clear that the FSLIC was itself insolvent.

In 1991, after two trials (the first of which ended with a hung jury), Faulkner, Blain and Toler were convicted of civil racketeering and looting $165 million from Empire and other S&Ls through fraudulent land deals. Each was sentenced to twenty years in jail and ordered to pay millions of dollars in restitution. One investigator called Empire 'one of the most reckless and fraudulent land investment schemes' he had ever seen.[48] Much the same could be said for the Savings and Loans crisis as a whole; Edwin Gray called it 'the most widespread, reckless and fraudulent era in this nation's banking history'. In all, nearly five hundred S&Ls collapsed or were forced to close down; roughly the same number were merged out of existence under the auspices of the Resolution Trust Corporation set up by Congress to clear up the mess. According to one official estimate, nearly half of the insolvent institutions had seen 'fraud and potentially criminal

* The most notorious case was that of Charles Keating, whose Lincoln Savings and Loan in Irvine, California, received support from five Senators, among them John McCain, when it came under pressure from the Federal Home Loan Bank. McCain had previously accepted political contributions from Keating but was cleared of acting improperly by the Senate Ethics Committee.

conduct by insiders'. By May 1991, 764 people had been charged
with a variety of offences, of whom 550 were convicted and 326
sentenced to jail. Fines of $8 million were imposed.[49] The final
cost of the Savings and Loans crisis between 1986 and 1995 was
$153 billion (around 3 per cent of GDP), of which taxpayers had
to pay $124 billion, making it the most expensive financial crisis
since the Depression.[50] Strewn all over Texas are the archaeolog-
ical remains of the debacle: derelict housing estates, built on the
cheap with stolen money, and subsequently bulldozed or burned
down. Twenty-four years later, much of the I-30 corridor is still
just another Texan wasteland.

For American taxpayers, the Savings and Loans debacle was a
hugely expensive lesson in the perils of ill-considered deregulation. But even as the S&Ls were going belly up, they offered
another very different group of Americans a fast track to megabucks. To the bond traders at Salomon Brothers, the New York
investment bank, the breakdown of the New Deal mortgage
system was not a crisis but a wonderful opportunity. As profit-
hungry as their language was profane, the self-styled 'Big Swing-
ing Dicks' at Salomon saw a way of exploiting the gyrating
interest rates of the early 1980s. It was the chief mortgage trader
Lewis Ranieri at Salomon who stepped up when desperate
Savings and Loans began to sell their mortgages in a vain bid to
stay solvent. Needless to say, 'Lou' bought them up at rock-
bottom prices. With his broad girth, cheap shirts and Brooklyn
wisecracks, Ranieri (who had started working for Salomon in
the mailroom) personified the new Wall Street, the antithesis
of the preppie investment bankers in their Brooks Brothers
suits and braces. The idea was to reinvent mortgages by bund-
ling thousands of them together as the backing for new and
alluring securities that could be sold as alternatives to traditional

government and corporate bonds – in short, to convert mortgages into bonds. Once lumped together, the interest payments due on the mortgages could be subdivided into 'strips' with different maturities and credit risks. The first issue of this new kind of mortgage-backed security (known as a collateralized mortgage obligation) happened in June 1983.[51] It was the dawn of a new era in American finance.

The process was called securitization and it was an innovation that fundamentally transformed Wall Street, blowing the dust off a previously sleepy bond market and ushering in a new era in which anonymous transactions would count for more than personal relationships. Once again, however, it was the federal government that stood ready to pick up the tab in a crisis. For the majority of mortgages continued to enjoy an implicit guarantee from the government-sponsored trio of Fannie, Freddie or Ginnie, meaning that bonds which used those mortgages as collateral could be represented as virtually government bonds, and hence 'investment grade'. Between 1980 and 2007 the volume of such GSE-backed mortgage-backed securities grew from $200 million to $4 trillion. With the advent of private bond insurers, firms like Salomon could also offer to securitize so-called nonconforming loans not eligible for GSE guarantees. By 2007 private pools of capital sufficed to securitize $2 trillion in residential mortgage debt.[52] In 1980 only 10 per cent of the home mortgage market had been securitized; by 2007 it had risen to 56 per cent.*

It was not only human vanities that ended up on the bonfire

---

* At the end of 2006 the GSEs held the largest share of mortgages, amounting to 30 per cent of the total debt outstanding. Commercial banks held 22 per cent; residential mortgage-backed securities (RMBS), CDOs and other asset-backed securities accounted for 14 per cent of the total; savings institutions for 13 per cent; state and local governments for 8 per cent of the total; and life insurance companies for 6 per cent. Individuals held the rest.

that was 1980s Wall Street. It was also the last vestiges of the business model depicted in *It's a Wonderful Life*. Once there had been meaningful social ties between mortgage lenders and borrowers. Jimmy Stewart knew both the depositors and the debtors. By contrast, in a securitized market (just like in space) no one can hear you scream – because the interest you pay on your mortgage is ultimately going to someone who has no idea you exist. The full implications of this transition for ordinary homeowners would become apparent only twenty years later.

We tend to assume in the English-speaking world that property is a one-way bet. The way to get rich is to play the property market. In fact, you're a mug to invest in anything else. The remarkable thing about this supposed truth is how often reality gives it the lie. Suppose you had put $100,000 into the US property market back in the first quarter of 1987. According to either the Office of Federal Housing Enterprise Oversight index or the Case-Shiller national home price index, you would have roughly trebled your money by the first quarter of 2007, to between $275,000 and $299,000. But if you had put the same money into the S&P 500 (the benchmark US stock market index), and had continued to reinvest the dividend income in that index, you would have ended up with $772,000 to play with, more than double what you would have made on bricks and mortar. In the UK the differential is similar. If you had put £100,000 into property in 1987, according to the Nationwide house price index, you would have more than quadrupled your money after twenty years. But if you had put it in the FTSE All Share index you would be nearly seven times richer. There is, of course, an important difference between a house and a stock market index: you cannot live inside a stock market index. (On the other hand, local property taxes usually fall on real estate not financial assets.) For the sake of a fair comparison, allowance must therefore be made for the rent you save by owning your house (or the rent you can collect if you own two properties and let the other out). A simple way to proceed is simply to strip out both dividends and rents. In that case the difference is somewhat reduced. In the two decades after 1987 the S&P 500, excluding dividends, rose by a factor of just over five, still comfortably beating housing. The differential is also narrowed, but again not eliminated, if you add rental income to the property portfolio and include dividends on the stock portfolio, since average rental yields in the period declined from around 5 per cent to just 3.5 per cent at the peak of the real estate boom (in other words, a typical $100,000 property would have brought in an average monthly rent of less than $416).[53] In the British case, by contrast, stock market capitalization has grown less slowly than in the US, while dividends have been a more important source of income to investors. At the same time, restrictions on the supply of new housing (such as laws protecting 'greenbelt' areas) have bolstered rents. To omit dividends and rents is therefore to remove the advantage of stocks over property. In terms of pure capital appreciation between 1987 and 2007, bricks and mortar (up by a factor of 4.5) out-performed shares (up by a factor of just 3.3). Only if one takes the story back to 1979 do British stocks beat British bricks.*

There are, however, three other considerations to bear in mind when trying to compare housing with other forms of capital asset.

---

* In the long-standing argument I have had with my wife about the unwisdom of a large-scale leveraged play on the UK property market (her favoured financial strategy), she therefore emerges as the winner on the assumption that I would have preferred to live in rented university accommodation and played the UK stock market. The optimal strategy would of course have been to own a diversified portfolio of real estate and global stocks, financed with a moderate amount of leverage.

US stocks versus real estate, 1987–2007

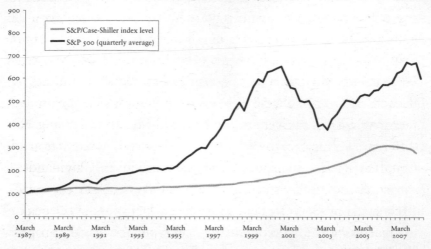

The first is depreciation. Stocks do not wear out and require new roofs; houses do. The second is liquidity. As assets, houses are a great deal more expensive to convert into cash than stocks. The third is volatility. Housing markets since the Second World War have been far less volatile than stock markets (not least because of the transactions costs associated with the real estate market). Yet that is not to say that house prices have never deviated from a steady upward path. In Britain between 1989 and 1995, for example, the average house price fell by 18 per cent or in real, inflation-adjusted terms by more than a third (37 per cent). In London the real decline was closer to 47 per cent.[54] In Japan between 1990 and 2000, property prices fell by over 60 per cent. And, of course, in the time that I have been writing this book, property prices in the United States – for the first time in a generation – have been going down. And down. From its peak in July 2006, the Case-Shiller 'composite 20' index of home prices in twenty big American cities had declined 15 per cent by February 2008. In that month the annualized rate of decline reached 13 per cent, a figure not seen since the early 1930s. In some cities

– Phoenix, San Diego, Los Angeles and Miami – the total decline was as much as a fifth or a quarter. Moreover, at the time of writing (May 2008), a majority of experts still anticipated further falls.

In depressed Detroit, the housing slide started earlier, in December 2005, and had already dragged house prices down by more than ten per cent when I visited the city in July 2007. I went to Detroit because I had the feeling that what was happening there was the shape of things to come in the United States as a whole and perhaps throughout the English-speaking world. In the space of ten years, house prices in Detroit – which probably possesses the worst housing stock of any American city other than New Orleans – had risen by nearly 50 per cent; not much compared with the nationwide bubble (which saw average house prices rise 180 per cent), but still hard to explain given the city's chronically depressed economic state. As I discovered, the explanation lay in fundamental changes in the rules of the housing game, changes exemplified by the experience of Detroit's West Outer Drive, a busy but respectable middle-class thoroughfare of substantial detached houses with large lawns and garages. Once the home of Motown's finest, today it is just another street in a huge sprawling country within a country: the developing economy *within* the United States,[55] otherwise known as Subprimia.

'Subprime' mortgage loans are aimed by local brokers at families or neighbourhoods with poor or patchy credit histories. Just as jumbo mortgages are too big to qualify for Fannie Mae's seal of approval (and implicit government guarantee), subprime mortgages are too risky. Yet it was precisely their riskiness that made them seem potentially lucrative to lenders. These were not the old thirty-year fixed-rate mortgages invented in the New Deal. On the contrary, a high proportion were adjustable-rate mortgages (ARMs) – in other words, the interest rate could vary according to changes in short-term lending rates. Many were also interest-only mortgages, without amortization (repayment of principal), even when the principal represented 100 per cent of the assessed value of the mortgaged property. And most had introductory 'teaser' periods, whereby the initial interest payments – usually for the first two years – were kept artificially low, back-loading the cost of the loan. All of these devices were intended to allow an immediate reduction in the debt-servicing costs of the borrower. But the small print of subprime contracts implied major gains for the lender. One particularly egregious subprime loan in Detroit carried an interest rate of 9.75 per cent for the first two years, but after that a margin of 9.125 percentage points over the benchmark short-term rate at which banks lend each other money: conventionally the London interbank offered rate (Libor). Even before the subprime crisis struck, that already stood above 5 per cent, implying a huge upward leap in interest payments in the third year of the loan.

Subprime lending hit Detroit like an avalanche of Monopoly money. The city was bombarded with radio, television, direct-mail advertisements and armies of agents and brokers, all offering what sounded like attractive deals. In 2006 alone, subprime lenders injected more than a billion dollars into twenty-two Detroit ZIP codes. In the 48235 ZIP code, which includes the 5100 block of West Outer Drive, subprime mortgages accounted for more than half of all loans made between 2002 and 2006. Seven of the twenty-six households on the 5100 block took out subprime loans.[56] Note that only a minority of these loans were going to first-time buyers. They were nearly all refinancing deals, which allowed borrowers to treat their homes as cash machines, converting their existing equity into cash. Most used the proceeds to pay off credit card debts, carry out renovations or buy new consumer durables.* Elsewhere, however, the combination of declining long-term interest rates and ever more alluring mortgage deals did attract new buyers into the housing market. By 2005, 69 per cent of all US households were home-owners, compared with 64 per cent ten years before. Around half of that increase can be attributed to the subprime lending boom. Significantly, a disproportionate number of subprime borrowers belonged to ethnic minorities. Indeed, I found myself wondering as I drove around Detroit if subprime was in fact a new financial euphemism for black. This was no idle supposition. According to a study by the Massachusetts Affordable Housing Alliance, 55 per cent of black and Latino borrowers in metropolitan Boston who had obtained loans for single-family homes in 2005 had been given subprime mortgages, compared with just 13 per cent of white borrowers. More than three quarters of black and Latino borrowers from Washington Mutual were classed as subprime, compared with just 17 per cent of white borrowers.[57] According to the Department of Housing and Urban Development (HUD), minority ownership increased by 3.1 million between 2002 and 2007.

Here, surely, was the zenith of the property-owning democracy. The new mortgage market seemed to be making the American dream of home ownership a reality for hundreds of thousands of people who had once been excluded from mainstream finance by credit-rating agencies and thinly veiled racial prejudice.

Criticism would subsequently be levelled at Alan Greenspan for failing adequately to regulate mortgage lending in his last years as Federal Reserve chairman. Yet, despite his notorious

* Between 1997 and 2006, US consumers withdrew an estimated $9 trillion in cash from the equity in their homes. By the first quarter of 2006 home equity extraction accounted for nearly 10 per cent of disposable personal income.

(and subsequently retracted) endorsement of adjustable-rate mortgages in a 2004 speech, Greenspan was not the principal proponent of wider home ownership. Nor is it credible to blame all the excesses of recent years on monetary policy.

'We want everybody in America to own their own home,' President George W. Bush had said in October 2002. Having challenged lenders to create 5.5 million new minority home-owners by the end of the decade, Bush signed the American Dream Downpayment Act in 2003, a measure designed to subsidize first-time house purchases among lower income groups. Lenders were encouraged by the administration not to press subprime borrowers for full documentation. Fannie Mae and Freddie Mac also came under pressure from HUD to support the subprime market. As Bush put it in December 2003: 'It is in our national interest that more people own their home.'[58] Few dissented. Writing in the *New York Times* in November 2007, Henry Louis ('Skip') Gates Jr., Alphonse Fletcher University Professor at Harvard and Director of the W. E. B. Du Bois Institute for African and African-American Research, appeared to welcome the trend, pointing out that fifteen out of twenty successful African-Americans he had studied (among them Oprah Winfrey and Whoopi Goldberg) were the descendants of 'at least one line of former slaves who managed to obtain property by 1920'. Heedless of the bursting of the property bubble months before, Gates suggested a surprising solution to the problem of 'black poverty and dysfunction' – namely 'to give property to the people who had once been defined as property':

Perhaps Margaret Thatcher, of all people, suggested a program that might help. In the 1980s, she turned 1.5 million residents of public housing projects in Britain into homeowners. It was certainly the most liberal thing Mrs Thatcher did, and perhaps progressives should borrow a leaf from her playbook ... A bold and innovative approach to the problem of black poverty ... would be to look at ways to turn tenants into homeowners ... For the black poor, real progress may come only once they have an ownership stake in American society. People who own property feel a sense of ownership in their future and their society. They study, save, work, strive and vote. And people trapped in a culture of tenancy do not ...[59]

Beanie Self, a black community leader in the Frayser area of Memphis, identified the fatal flaw in Gates's argument: 'The American Dream is home ownership, and one of the things that concerns me is – while the dream is wonderful – we are not really prepared for it. People don't realize you have a real estate industry, an appraisal industry, a mortgage industry now that can really push to put people into houses that a lot of times they really can't afford.'[60]

As a business model subprime lending worked beautifully – as long as interest rates stayed low, as long as people kept their jobs and as long as real estate prices continued to rise. Of course, such conditions could not be relied upon to last, least of all in a city like Detroit. But that did not worry the subprime lenders. They simply followed the trail blazed by mainstream mortgage lenders in the 1980s. Instead of putting their own money at risk, they pocketed fat commissions on signature of the original loan contracts and then resold their loans in bulk to Wall Street banks. The banks, in turn, bundled the loans into high-yielding residential mortgage-backed securities (RMBS) and sold them on to investors around the world, all eager for a few hundredths of a percentage point more return on their capital. Repackaged as collateralized debt obligations (CDOs), these subprime securities could be transformed from risky loans to flaky borrowers into triple-A rated investment-grade securities. All that was required was certification from one of the two dominant rating agencies, Moody's or Standard & Poor's, that at least the top tier of these securities was unlikely to go into default. The lower 'mezzanine' and 'equity' tiers were admittedly more risky; then again, they paid higher interest rates.

The key to this financial alchemy was that there could be thousands of miles between the mortgage borrowers in Detroit and the people who ended up receiving their interest payments. The risk was spread across the globe from American state pension funds to public health networks in Australia and even to town councils beyond the Arctic Circle. In Norway, for example, the municipalities of Rana, Hemnes, Hattjelldal and Narvik invested some $120 million of their taxpayers' money in CDOs secured on American subprime mortgages. At the time, the sellers of these 'structured products' boasted that securitization was having the effect of allocating risk 'to those best able to bear it'. Only later did it turn out that risk was being allocated to those least able to understand it. Those who knew best the flakiness of subprime loans – the people who dealt directly with the borrowers and knew their economic circumstances – bore the least risk. They could make a 100 per cent loan-to-value 'NINJA' loan (to someone with No Income No Job or Assets) and sell it on the same day to one of the big banks in the CDO business. In no time at all, the risk was floating up a fjord.

In Detroit the rise of subprime mortgages had in fact coincided with a new slump in the inexorably declining automobile industry that cost the city 20,000 jobs. This anticipated a wider American slowdown, an almost inevitable consequence of a tightening of monetary policy as the Federal Reserve raised short-term interest rates from 1 per cent to 5¼ per cent; this had a modest but nevertheless significant impact on average mortgage rates, which went up by roughly a quarter (from 5.34 to 6.66 per cent). The effect on the subprime market of this seemingly innocuous change in credit conditions was devastating. As soon as the teaser rates expired and the mortgages reset at new and much higher interest rates, hundreds of Detroit households swiftly fell behind with their mortgage payments. As early as March 2007, about one in three subprime mortgages in the 48235 ZIP code were more than sixty days in arrears, effectively on the verge of foreclosure. The effect was to burst the real estate bubble, causing house prices to start falling for the first time since the early 1990s. As soon as this began to happen, those who had taken out 100 per cent mortgages found their debts worth more than their homes. The further house prices fell, the more homeowners found themselves with negative equity, a term familiar in Britain since the early 1990s. In this respect, West Outer Drive was a harbinger of a wider crisis of the American real estate market, the ramifications of which would rock the financial system of the Western world to its foundations.

On a sultry Friday afternoon, shortly after arriving in Memphis from Detroit, I watched more than fifty homes being sold off on the steps of the Memphis courthouse. In each case it was because mortgage lenders had foreclosed on the owners for failing to keep up with their interest payments.* Not only is Memphis the bankruptcy capital of America (as we saw in Chapter 1). By the summer of 2007 it was also fast becoming the foreclosure capital.

---

* It is an important feature of American law that in many states (though not all) mortgages are generally 'no recourse' loans, meaning that when there is a default the mortgage lender can only collect the value of the property and cannot seize other property (e.g. a car or money in the bank) or put a lien on future wages. According to some economists, this gives borrowers a strong incentive to default.

Over the last five years, I was told, one in four households in the city had received a notice threatening foreclosure. And once again subprime mortgages were the root of the problem. In 2006 alone subprime finance companies had lent $460 million to fourteen Memphis ZIP codes. What I was witnessing was just the beginning of a flood of foreclosures. In March 2007 the Center for Responsible Lending predicted that the number of foreclosures could reach 2.4 million.[61] This may turn out to have been an under-estimate. At the time of writing (May 2008), around 1.8 million mortgages are in default, but an estimated 9 million American households, or the occupants of one in every ten single-family homes, have already fallen into negative equity. About 11 per cent of subprime ARMs are already in foreclosure. According to Crédit Suisse, the total number of foreclosures on all types of mortgages could end up being 6.5 million over the next five years. That could put 8.4 per cent of all American homeowners, or 12.7 per cent of those with mortgages, out of their homes.[62]

Since the subprime mortgage market began to turn sour in the early summer of 2007, shockwaves have been spreading through all the world's credit markets, wiping out some hedge funds and costing hundreds of billions of dollars to banks and other finan-cial companies. The main problem lay with CDOs, over half a trillion dollars of which had been sold in 2006, of which around half contained subprime exposure. It turned out that many of these CDOs had been seriously over-priced, as a result of erroneous estimates of likely subprime default rates. As even triple-A-rated securities began going into default, hedge funds that had specialized in buying the highest-risk CDO tranches were the first to suffer. Although there had been signs of trouble since February 2007, when HSBC admitted to heavy losses on US mortgages, most analysts would date the beginning of the subprime crisis from June of that year, when two hedge funds owned by Bear Stearns* were asked to post additional collateral by Merrill Lynch, another investment bank that had lent them money but was now concerned about their excessive exposure to subprime-backed assets. Bear bailed out one fund, but let the other collapse. The following month the ratings agencies began to downgrade scores of RMBS CDOs (short for 'residential mortgage-backed security collateralized debt obligations', the very term testifying to the over-complex nature of these products). As they did so, all kinds of financial institutions holding such assets found themselves staring huge losses in the face. The problem was greatly magnified by the amount of leverage (debt) in the system. Hedge funds in particular had borrowed vast sums from their prime brokers – banks – in order to magnify the returns they could generate. The banks, meanwhile, had been disguising their own exposure by parking subprime-related assets in off-balance-sheet entities known as conduits and strategic investment vehicles (SIVs, surely the most apt of all the acronyms of the crisis), which relied for funding on short-term borrowings on the markets for commercial paper and overnight interbank loans. As fears rose about counterparty risk (the danger that the other party in a financial transaction may go bust), those credit markets seized up. The liquidity crisis that some commentators had been warning about for at least a year struck in August 2007, when American Home Mortgage filed for bankruptcy, BNP Paribas suspended three mortgage investment funds and Countrywide Financial drew down its entire $11 billion credit line. What scarcely anyone had anticipated was that defaults on subprime mortgages by low-income households in cities like Detroit and Memphis could unleash so much financial

* One of which gloried in the name High-Grade Structured Credit Strategies Enhanced Leverage Fund.

havoc:* one bank (Northern Rock) nationalized; another (Bear Stearns) sold off cheaply to a competitor in a deal underwritten by the Fed; numerous hedge funds wound up; 'write-downs' by banks amounting to at least $318 billion; total anticipated losses in excess of one trillion dollars. The subprime butterfly had flapped its wings and triggered a global hurricane.

Among the many ironies of the crisis is that it could ultimately deal a fatal blow to the government-sponsored mother of the property-owning democracy: Fannie Mae.[63] One consequence of government policy has been to increase the proportion of mortgages held by Fannie Mae and her younger siblings Freddie and Ginnie, while at the same time reducing the importance of the original government guarantees that were once a key component of the system. Between the 1955 and 2006 the proportion of non-farm mortgages underwritten by the government fell from 35 to 5 per cent. But over the same period the share of mortgages held by these government-sponsored enterprises rose from 4 per cent to a peak of 43 per cent in 2003.[64] The Office of Federal Housing Enterprise Oversight has been egging on Fannie and Freddie to acquire even more RMBS (including subprime-backed securities) by relaxing the rules that regulate their capital/assets ratio. But the two institutions have only $84 billion of capital between them, a mere 5 per cent of the $1.7 trillion of assets on their balance sheets, to say nothing of the further $2.8 trillion of RMBS that they have guaranteed.[65] Should these institutions get into difficulties, it seems a reasonable assumption that government sponsorship could turn into government ownership, with major implications for the federal budget.†

So no, it turns out that houses are not a uniquely safe investment.

* Few dissented when the International Monetary Fund called it 'the largest financial shock since the Great Depression'.
† Events subsequent to this writing have indeed borne this out.

Their prices can go down as well as up. And, as we have seen, houses are pretty illiquid assets – which means they are hard to sell quickly when you are in a financial jam. House prices are 'sticky' on the way down because sellers hate to cut the asking price in a downturn; the result is a glut of unsold properties and people who would otherwise move stuck looking at their For Sale signs. That in turn means that home ownership can tend to reduce labour mobility, thereby slowing down recovery. These turn out to be the disadvantages of the idea of property-owning democracy, appealing though it once seemed to turn all tenants into homeowners. The question that remains to be answered is whether or not we have any business exporting this high-risk model to the rest of the world.

As Safe as Housewives

Quilmes, a sprawling slum on the southern outskirts of Buenos Aires, seems a million miles from the elegant boulevards of the Argentine capital's centre. But are the people who live there really as poor as they look? As Peruvian economist Hernando de Soto sees it, shanty towns like Quilmes, despite their ramshackle appearance, represent literally trillions of dollars of unrealized wealth. De Soto has calculated that the total value of the real estate occupied by the world's poor amounts to $9.3 trillion. That, he points out, is very nearly the total market capitalization of all the listed companies in the world's top twenty economies – and roughly ninety times all the foreign aid paid to developing countries over between 1970 and 2000. The problem is that the people in Quilmes, and in countless shanty towns the world over, do not have secure legal title to their homes. And without some kind of legal title, property cannot be used as collateral for a loan. The result is a fundamental constraint on economic growth, de Soto reasons, because if you can't borrow, you can't raise the capital to start a business. Potential entrepreneurs are thwarted. Capitalist energies are smothered.[66]

A large part of the trouble is that it is so bureaucratically difficult to establish legal title to property in places like South America. In Argentina today, according to the World Bank, it takes around thirty days to register a property, but it used to be much longer. In some countries – Bangladesh and Haiti are the worst – it can take closer to three hundred days. When de Soto and his researchers tried to secure legal authorization to build a house on state-owned land in Peru, it took six years and eleven months, during which they had to deal with fifty-two different government offices. In the Philippines, formalizing home owner-ship was until recently a 168-step process involving fifty-three public and private agencies and taking between thirteen and twenty-five years. In the English-speaking world, by contrast, it can take as little as two days and seldom more than three weeks. In de Soto's eyes, bureaucratic obstacles to securing legal ownership make the assets of the poor so much 'dead capital . . . like water in a lake high up in the Andes – an untapped stock of potential energy'. Breathing life into this capital, he argues, is the key to providing countries like Peru with a more prosperous future. Only with a working system of property rights can the value of a house be properly established by the market; can it easily be bought and sold; can it legally be used as collateral for loans; can its owner be held to account in other transactions he may enter into. Moreover, excluding the poor from the pale of legitimate property ownership ensures that they operate at least partially in a grey or black economic zone, beyond the reach of the state's dead hand. This is doubly damaging. It prevents effective taxation. And it reduces the legitimacy of the state in the eyes of the populace.

Poor countries are poor, in other words, because they lack secure property rights, the 'hidden architecture' of a successful economy. 'Property law is not a silver bullet,' de Soto admits, 'but it is the missing link . . . Without property law, you will never be able to accomplish other reforms in a sustainable manner.' And poor countries are also more likely to fail as democracies because they lack an electorate of stakeholders. 'Property rights will eventually lead to democracy,' de Soto has argued, 'because you can't sustain a market-oriented property system unless you provide a democratic system. That's the only way investors can feel secure.'[67]

To some – like the Maoist terrorist group Shining Path, who tried to assassinate him in 1992 in a bomb attack that killed three people – de Soto is a villain.[68] Other critics denounced him as the Rasputin behind the now disgraced Peruvian President Alberto Fujimori. To others, de Soto's efforts to globalize the property-owning democracy have made him a hero. Former President Bill Clinton has called him 'probably the greatest living economist', while his Russian counterpart, Vladimir Putin, has called de Soto's achievements 'extraordinary'. In 2004 the American libertarian think-tank the Cato Institute awarded him the biennial Milton Friedman Prize for work that 'exemplifies the spirit and practice of liberty'. De Soto and his Institute for Liberty and Democracy have advised governments in Egypt, El Salvador, Ghana, Haiti, Honduras, Kazakhstan, Mexico, the Philippines and Tanzania. The critical question is, of course, does his theory work in practice?

Quilmes provides a natural experiment to find out if de Soto really has unravelled the 'mystery of capital'. It was here in 1981 that a group of 1,800 families defied the military junta then ruling Argentina by occupying a stretch of wasteland. After the restoration of democracy the provincial government expropriated the original owners of the land to give the squatters legal title to their homes. However, only eight of the thirteen landowners accepted the compensation they were offered; the others (one of whom settled in 1998) fought a protracted legal battle. The result was that some of the Quilmes squatters became property owners by paying a nominal sum for leases, which, after ten years, became full deeds of ownership; while others remained as squatters. Today you can tell the owner-occupied houses from the rest by their better fences and painted walls. The houses whose ownership remains contested are, by contrast, seedy shacks. As everyone (including 'Skip' Gates) knows, owners generally take better care of properties than tenants do.

There is no doubt that home ownership has changed people's attitudes in Quilmes. According to one recent study, those who have acquired property titles have become significantly more individualist and materialist in their attitudes than those who are still squatting. For example, when asked 'Do you think money is important for happiness?', the property owners were 34 per cent more likely than the squatters to say that it was.[69] Yet there seems to be a flaw in the theory, for owning their homes has not made it significantly easier for people in Quilmes to borrow money. Only 4 per cent have managed to secure a mortgage.[70] In de Soto's native Peru, too, ownership alone doesn't seem to be enough to resuscitate dead capital. True, after his initial recommendations were accepted by the Peruvian government in 1988, there was a drastic reduction in the time it took to register a property (to just one month) and an even steeper 99 per cent cut in the costs of the transaction. Further efforts were made after the creation of the Commission for the Formalization of Informal Property in 1996 so that, within four years, 1.2 million buildings on urban land had been brought into the legal system. Yet economic progress of the sort de Soto promised has been disappointingly slow. Out of more than 200,000 Lima households awarded land titles in 1998 and 1999, only around a quarter had secured any kind of loans by 2002. In other places where de Soto's approach has been tried, notably Cambodia, granting legal title to urban properties simply encouraged unscrupulous developers and speculators to buy out – or turf out – poor residents.[71]

Remember: it's not owning property that gives you security; it just gives your creditors security. Real security comes from having a steady income, as the Duke of Buckingham found out in the 1840s, and as Detroit homeowners are finding out today. For that reason, it may not be necessary for every entrepreneur in the developing world to raise money by mortgaging his house. Or her house. In fact, home ownership may not be the key to wealth generation at all.

I met Betty Flores on a rainy Monday morning in a street market in El Alto, the Bolivian town next to (or rather above) the capital La Paz. I was on my way to the El Alto offices of the microfinance organization Pro Mujer, but I was feeling tired because of the high altitude and suggested we stop for some coffee. And there she was, busily brewing up and distributing pots and cups of thick, strong Bolivian coffee for shoppers and other stall-keepers throughout the market. I was immediately struck by her energy and vivacity. In marked contrast to the majority of indigenous Bolivian women, she seemed quite uninhibited about talking to an obvious foreigner. It turned out that she was in fact one of Pro Mujer's clients, having taken out a loan to enlarge her coffee stall – something her husband, a mechanic, had not been able to do. And it had worked; I only had to look at Betty's perpetual motion to see that. Did she plan any further expansion? Yes indeed. The business was helping her put their daughters through school.

Betty Flores is not what would conventionally be thought of

as a good credit risk. She has modest savings and does not own her own home. Yet she and thousands of women like her in poor countries around the world are being lent money by institutions like Pro Mujer as part of a revolutionary effort to unleash female enterpreneurial energies. The great revelation of the microfinance movement in countries like Bolivia is that women are actually a better credit risk than men, with or without a house as security for their loans. That certainly flies in the face of the conventional image of the spendthrift female shopper. Indeed, it goes against the grain of centuries of prejudice which, until as recently as the 1970s, systematically rated women as less creditworthy than men. In the United States, for example, married women used to be denied credit, even when they were themselves employed, if their husbands were not in work. Deserted and divorced women fared even worse. When I was growing up, credit was still emphatically male. Microfinance, however, suggests that credit-worthiness may in fact be a female trait.

The founder of the microfinance movement, the Nobel prize winner Muhammad Yunus, came to understand the potential of making small loans to women when studying rural poverty in his native Bangladesh. His mutually owned Grameen ('Village') Bank, founded in the village of Jobra in 1983, has made micro-loans to nearly seven and a half million borrowers, nearly all of them women who have no collateral. Virtually all the borrowers take out their loans as members of a five-member group (*koota*), which meets on a weekly basis and informally shares responsibil-ity for loan repayments. Since its inception, Grameen Bank has made microloans worth more than $3 billion, initially financing its operations with money from aid agencies, but now attracting sufficient deposits (nearly $650 billion by January 2007) to be entirely self-reliant and, indeed, profitable.[72] Pro Mujer, founded in 1990 by Lynne Patterson and Carmen Velasco, is among the most successful of Grameen Bank's South American imitators.* Loans start at around $200 for three months. Most women use the money to buy livestock for their farms or, like Betty, to fund their own micro-businesses, selling anything from tortillas to Tupperware.

By the time I tore myself away from Betty's coffee stall, the Pro Mujer offices in El Alto were already a hive of activity. I found it hard not to be impressed by the sight of dozens of Bolivian women, nearly all in traditional costume (each with a miniature bowler hat, pinned at a jaunty angle), lining up to make their regular loan payments. As they told stories about their experiences, I began wondering if it might just be time to change an age-old catchphrase from 'As safe as houses' to 'As safe as housewives'. For what I saw in Bolivia has its equivalents in poor countries all over the world, from the slums of Nairobi to the villages of Andhra Pradesh in India. And not only in the developing world. Microfinance can also work in enclaves of poverty in the developed world – like Castlemilk, in Glasgow, where a whole network of lending agencies called credit unions has been set up as an antidote to predatory lending by loan sharks (of the sort we encountered in Chapter 1). In Castlemilk, too, the recipients of loans are local women. In both El Alto and Castlemilk I heard how men were much more likely to spend their wages in the pub or the betting shop than to worry about making interest payments. Women, I was told repeatedly, were better at managing money than their husbands.

Of course, it would be a mistake to assume that microfinance is the holy grail solution to the problem of global poverty, any more than is Hernando de Soto's property rights prescription.

* So impressed have Bill and Melinda Gates been by Pro Mujer that their Foundation is giving the organization $3.1 million.

Roughly two fifths of the world's population is effectively outside the financial system, without access to bank accounts, much less credit. But just giving them loans won't necessarily consign poverty to the museum, in Yunus's phrase, whether or not you ask for collateral. Nor should we forget that some people in the microfinance business are in it to make money, not to end poverty.[73] It comes as something of a shock to discover that some microfinance firms are charging interest rates as high as 80 or even 125 per cent a year on their loans – rates worthy of loan sharks. The justification is that this is the only way to make money, given the cost of administering so many tiny loans.

Glasgow has come a long way since my fellow Scotsman Adam Smith wrote the seminal case for the free market, *The Wealth of Nations*, in 1776. Like Detroit, it rose on the upswing of the industrial age. The age of finance has been less kind to it. But in Glasgow, as in North and South America, and as in South Asia, people are learning the same lesson. Financial illiteracy may be ubiquitous, but somehow we were all experts on one branch of economics: the property market. We all knew that property was a one-way bet. Except that it wasn't. (In the last quarter of 2007, Glasgow house prices fell by 2.1 per cent. The only consolation was that in Edinburgh they fell by 5.8 per cent.) In cities all over the world, house prices soared far above what was justified in terms of rental income or construction costs. There was, as the economist Robert Shiller has said, simply a 'widespread perception that houses are a great investment', which generated a 'classic speculative bubble' via the same feedback mechanism which has more commonly affected stock markets since the days of John Law. In short, there was irrational exuberance about bricks and mortar and the capital gains they could yield.[74]

This perception, as we have seen, was partly political in origin. But while encouraging home ownership may help build a political constituency for capitalism, it also distorts the capital market by forcing people to bet the house on, well, the house. When financial theorists warn against 'home bias', they mean the tendency for investors to keep their money in assets produced by their own country. But the real home bias is the tendency to invest nearly all our wealth in our own homes. Housing, after all, represents two thirds of the typical US household's portfolio, and a higher proportion in other countries.[75] From Buckinghamshire to Bolivia, the key to financial security should be a properly diversified portfolio of assets.[76] To acquire that we are well advised to borrow in anticipation of future earnings. But we should not be lured into staking everything on a highly leveraged play on the far from risk-free property market. There has to be a sustainable spread between borrowing costs and returns on investment, and a sustainable balance between debt and income.

These rules, needless to say, do not apply exclusively to households. They also apply to national economies. The final question that remains to be answered is how far – as a result of the process we have come to call globalization – the biggest economy in the world has been tempted to ignore them. What price, in short, a subprime superpower?

The Tokyo-Yokohama earthquake of 1923, one of many disasters to befall Japan's insurance industry in the mid twentieth century.

(*above*) Erstwhile 'King of Torts' and scourge of the insurers Richard 'Dickie' Scruggs in the ruins of his beachfront house at Pascagoula following Hurricane Katrina.

(*left*) Ken Griffin, founder and CEO of the Chicago-based hedge fund Citadel: grand master of modern risk management.

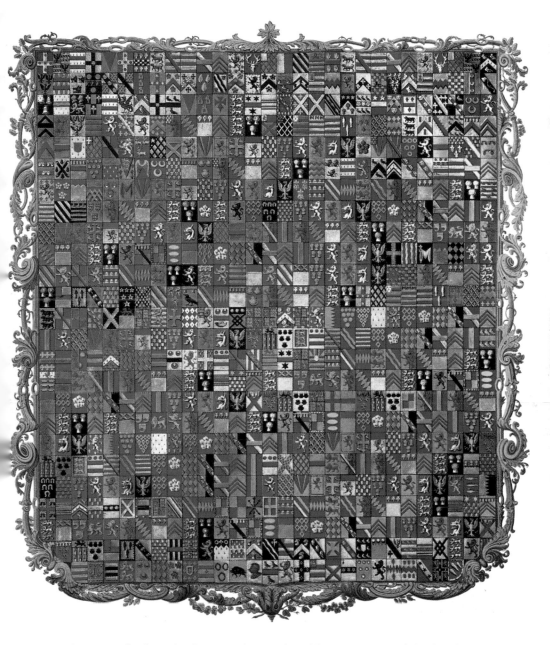

The Grenville diptych, showing the 719 heraldic quarterings of the family at
the time of the 2nd Duke of Buckingham. No amount of inherited status could
protect his estate from the consequences of excessive leverage.

(*above*) A Marxist view of Motor City: Diego Rivera's Garden Court mural, north wall.

(*right*) Diego Rivera's Garden Court mural, south wall (detail).

Detail from Charles Darrow's original Atlantic City version of *Monopoly*.

Two faces of real estate: the original Mr Monopoly and Go To Jail.

Chongqing before …

... and Chongqing after China's economic ascent.

6

From Empire to Chimerica

Just ten years ago, during the Asian Crisis of 1997–8, it was conventional wisdom that financial crises were more likely to happen on the periphery of the world economy – in the so-called emerging markets (formerly known as less developed countries) of East Asia or Latin America. Yet the biggest threats to the global financial system in this new century have come not from the periphery but from the core. In the two years after Silicon Valley's dot-com bubble peaked in August 2000, the US stock market fell by almost half. It was not until May 2007 that investors in the Standard & Poor's 500 had recouped their losses. Then, just three months later, a new financial storm blew up, this time in the credit market rather than the stock market. As we have seen, this crisis also originated in the United States as millions of American households discovered they could not afford to service billions of dollars' worth of subprime mortgages. There was a time when American crises like these would have plunged the rest of the global financial system into recession, if not depression. Yet at the time of writing Asia seems scarcely affected by the credit crunch in the US. Indeed, some analysts like Jim O'Neill, Head of Global Research at Goldman Sachs, say the rest of the world, led by booming China, is 'decoupling' itself from the American economy.

If O'Neill is correct, we are living through one of the most astonishing shifts there has ever been in the global balance of financial power; the end of an era, stretching back more than a century, when the financial tempo of the world economy was set by English-speakers, first in Britain, then in America. The Chinese economy has achieved extraordinary feats of growth in the past thirty years, with per capita GDP increasing at a compound annual growth rate of 8.4 per cent. But in recent times the pace has, if anything, intensified. When O'Neill and his team first calculated projections of gross domestic product for the so-called BRICs (Brazil, Russia, India and China, or Big Rapidly Industrializing Countries), they envisaged that China could overtake the United States in around 2040.[1] Their most recent estimates, however, have brought the date forward to 2027.[2] The Goldman Sachs economists do not ignore the challenges that China undoubtedly faces, not least the demographic time bomb planted by the Communist regime's draconian one-child policy and the environmental consequences of East Asia's supercharged industrial revolution.[3] They are aware, too, of the inflationary pressures in China, exemplified by soaring stock prices in 2007 and surging food prices in 2008. Yet the overall assessment is still strikingly positive. And it implies, quite simply, that history has changed direction in our lifetimes.

Three or four hundred years ago there was little to choose between per capita incomes in the West and in the East. The average North American colonist, it has been claimed, had a standard of living not significantly superior to that of the average Chinese peasant cultivator. Indeed, in many ways the Chinese civilization of the Ming era was more sophisticated than that of early Massachusetts. Beijing, for centuries the world's largest city, dwarfed Boston, just as Admiral Zheng He's early-fifteenth-century treasure ship had dwarfed Christopher Columbus's *Santa*

Maria. The Yangtze delta seemed as likely a place as the Thames Valley to produce major productivity-enhancing technological innovations.[4] Yet between 1700 and 1950 there was a 'great divergence' of living standards between East and West. While China may have suffered an absolute decline in per capita income in that period, the societies of the North West – in particular Britain and its colonial offshoots – experienced unprecedented growth thanks, in large part, to the impact of the industrial revolution. By 1820 per capita income in the United States was roughly twice that of China; by 1870, nearly five times higher; by 1913 nearly ten times; by 1950 nearly twenty-two times. The average annual growth rate of per capita GDP in the United States was 1.57 per cent between 1820 and 1950. The equivalent figure for China was –0.24 per cent.[5] In 1973 the average Chinese income was at best one twentieth of the average American. Calculated in terms of international dollars at market exchange rates, the differential was even wider. As recently as 2006, the ratio of US to Chinese per capita income by this measure was still 22.9 to 1.

What went wrong in China between the 1700s and the 1970s? One argument is that China missed out on two major macroeconomic strokes of good luck that were indispensable to the North-West's eighteenth-century take-off. The first was the conquest of the Americas and particularly the conversion of the islands of the Caribbean into sugar-producing colonies, 'ghost acres' which relieved the pressure on a European agricultural system that might otherwise have suffered from Chinese-style diminishing returns. The second was the proximity of coalfields to locations otherwise well suited for industrial development. Besides cheaper calories, cheaper wood and cheaper wool and cotton, imperial expansion brought other unintended economic benefits, too. It encouraged the development of militarily useful technologies – clocks, guns, lenses and navigational instruments – that turned out to have big spin-offs for the development of industrial machinery.[6] Many other explanations have, needless to say, been offered for the great East–West divergence: differences in topography, resource endowments, culture, attitudes towards science and technology, even differences in human evolution.[7] Yet there remains a credible hypothesis that China's problems were as much financial as they were resource-based. For one thing, the unitary character of the Empire precluded that fiscal competition which proved such a driver of financial innovation in Renaissance Europe and subsequently. For another, the ease with which the Empire could finance its deficits by printing money discouraged the emergence of European-style capital markets.[8] Coinage, too, was more readily available than in Europe because of China's trade surplus with the West. In short, the Middle Kingdom had far fewer incentives to develop commercial bills, bonds and equities. When modern financial institutions finally came to China in the late nineteenth century, they came as part of the package of Western imperialism and, as we shall see, were always vulnerable to patriotic backlashes against foreign influence.[9]

Globalization, in the sense of a rapid integration of international markets for commodities, manufactures, labour and capital, is not a new phenomenon. In the three decades before 1914, trade in goods reached almost as large a proportion of global output as in the past thirty years.[10] In a world of less regulated borders, international migration was almost certainly larger relative to world population; more than 14 per cent of the US population was foreign born in 1910 compared with less than 12 per cent in 2003.[11] Although, in gross terms, stocks of international capital were larger in relation to global GDP during the 1990s than they were a century ago, in net terms the amounts invested abroad – particularly by rich countries in poor countries – were much larger in the earlier period.[12] Over a century ago, enterprising businessmen in Europe and North America could see that there were enticing opportunities throughout Asia. By the middle of the nineteenth century, the key technologies of the industrial revolution could be transferred anywhere. Communication lags had been dramatically reduced thanks to the laying of an international undersea cable network. Capital was abundantly available and, as we shall see, British investors were more than ready to risk their money in remote countries. Equipment was affordable, energy available and labour so abundant that manufacturing textiles in China or India ought to have been a hugely profitable line of business.[13] Yet, despite the investment of over a billion pounds of Western funds, the promise of Victorian globalization went largely unfulfilled in most of Asia, leaving a legacy of bitterness towards what is still remembered to this day as colonial exploitation. Indeed, so profound was the mid-century reaction against globalization that the two most populous Asian countries ended up largely cutting themselves off from the global market from the 1950s until the 1970s.

Moreover, the last age of globalization had anything but a happy ending. On the contrary, less than a hundred years ago, in the summer of 1914, it ended not with a whimper, but with a deafening bang, as the principal beneficiaries of the globalized economy embarked on the most destructive war the world had ever witnessed. We think we know why international capital failed to produce self-sustaining growth in Asia before 1914. But was there also some connection between the effects of global economic integration and the outbreak of the First World War? It has recently been suggested that the war should be understood as a kind of backlash against globalization, heralded by rising tariffs and immigration restrictions in the decade before 1914, and welcomed most ardently by Europe's agrarian elites, whose position had been undermined for decades by the decline in agricultural prices and emigration of surplus rural labour to the New World.[14] Before blithely embracing today's brave, new and supposedly 'post-American' world,[15] we must be sure that similar unforeseen reactions could not pull the geopolitical rug out from under the latest version of globalization.

Globalization and Armageddon

It used to be said that emerging markets were the places where they had emergencies. Investing in far-away countries could make you rich but, when things went wrong, it could be a fast track to financial ruin. As we saw in Chapter 2, the first Latin American debt crisis happened as long ago as the 1820s. It was another emerging market crisis, in Argentina, that all but bankrupted the house of Baring in 1890, just as it was a rogue futures trader in Singapore, Nick Leeson, who finally finished Barings off 105 years later. The Latin American debt crisis of the 1980s and the Asian crisis of the 1990s were scarcely unprecedented events. Financial history suggests that many of today's emerging markets would be better called re-emerging markets.* These days, the ultimate re-emerging market is China. According to Sinophile investors like Jim Rogers, there is almost no limit to the amount of money to be made there.[16] Yet this is not the first time that foreign investors have poured money into Chinese securities, dreaming of the vast sums to be made from the world's most populous country. The last time around, it is worth remembering, they lost as many shirts as Hong Kong's famous tailors can stitch together in a month.

* The term 'emerging markets' was first used in the 1980s by the World Bank economist Antoine van Agtmael.

The key problem with overseas investment, then as now, is that it is hard for investors in London or New York to see what a foreign government or an overseas manager is up to when they are an ocean or more away. Moreover, most non-Western countries had, until quite recently, highly unreliable legal systems and differing accounting rules. If a foreign trading partner decided to default on its debts, there was little that an investor situated on the other side of the world could do. In the first era of globalization, the solution to this problem was brutally simple but effective: to impose European rule.

William Jardine and James Matheson were buccaneering Scotsmen who had set up a trading company in the southern Chinese port of Guangzhou (then known as Canton) in 1832. One of their best lines of business was importing government-produced opium from India. Jardine was a former East India Company surgeon, but the opium he was bringing into China was for distinctly non-medicinal purposes. This was a practice that the Emperor Yongzheng had prohibited over a century before, in 1729, because of the high social costs of opium addiction. On 10 March 1839 an imperial official named Lin Zexu arrived in Canton under orders from the Daoguang Emperor to stamp out the trade once and for all. Lin blockaded the Guangzhou opium godowns (warehouses) until the British merchants acceded to his demands. In all, around 20,000 chests of opium valued at £2 million were surrendered. The contents were adulterated to render it unusable and literally thrown in the sea.[17] The Chinese also insisted that henceforth British subjects in Chinese territory should submit to Chinese law. This was not to Jardine's taste at all. Known to the Chinese as 'Iron-Headed Old Rat', he was in Europe during the crisis and hastened to London to lobby the British government. After three meetings with the Foreign Secretary, Viscount Palmerston, Jardine seems to have persuaded him

'Iron-Headed Old Rat': William Jardine, co-founder of
Jardine, Matheson

that a show of strength was required, and that 'the want of power
of their war junks' would ensure an easy victory for a 'sufficient'
British force. On 20 February 1840 Palmerston gave the order.
By June 1840 all the naval preparations were complete. The Qing
Empire was about to feel the full force of history's most successful
narco-state: the British Empire.

Just as Jardine had predicted, the Chinese authorities were

James Matheson, Jardine's partner in the opium trade

no match for British naval power. Guangzhou was blockaded; Chusan (Zhoushan) Island was captured. After a ten-month stand off, British marines seized the forts that guarded the mouth of the Pearl River, the waterway between Hong Kong and Guangzhou. Under the Convention of Chuenpi, signed in January 1841 (but then repudiated by the Emperor), Hong Kong became a British possession. The Treaty of Nanking, signed a year later after another bout of one-sided fighting, confirmed this cession and also gave free rein to the opium trade in five so-called treaty ports: Canton, Amoy (Xiamen), Foochow (Fuzhou), Ningbo and Shanghai. According to the principle of extraterritoriality, British subjects could operate in these cities with complete immunity from Chinese law.

For China, the first Opium War ushered in an era of humiliation. Drug addiction exploded. Christian missionaries destabilized traditional Confucian beliefs. And in the chaos of the Taiping Rebellion – a peasant revolt against a discredited dynasty led by the self-proclaimed younger brother of Christ – between 20 and 40 million people lost their lives. But for Jardine and Matheson, who hastened to acquire land in Hong Kong and soon moved their head office to the island's East Point, the glory days of Victorian globalization had arrived. Jardine's Lookout, one of the highest points on Hong Kong island, was where the company used to keep a watchman permanently stationed, to spy the sails of the firm's clippers as they sailed in from Bombay, Calcutta or London. As Hong Kong flourished as an entrepôt, opium soon ceased to be the company's sole line of business. By the early 1900s Jardine, Matheson had its own breweries, its own cotton mills, its own insurance company, its own ferry company and even its own railways, including the Kowloon to Canton line, built between 1907 and 1911.

Back in London, an investor had myriad foreign investment opportunities open to him. Nothing illustrates this better than the ledgers of N. M. Rothschild & Sons, which reveal the extraordinary array of securities that the Rothschild partners held in their multi-million-pound portfolio. A single page lists no fewer than twenty different securities, including bonds issued by the governments of Chile, Egypt, Germany, Hungary, Italy, Japan, Norway, Spain and Turkey, as well as securities issued by eleven different railways, among them four in Argentina, two in Canada and one in China.[18] Nor was it only members of the rarefied financial elite who could engage in this kind of international diversification. As early as 1909, for the modest outlay of 2s 6d, British investors could buy Henry Lowenfeld's book *Investment: An Exact Science*, which recommended 'a sound system of averages, based upon the Geographical Distribution of Capital'

as a means of 'reduc[ing] to a minimum the taint of speculation from the act of investment'.[19] As Keynes later recalled,
in a justly famous passage in his *Economic Consequences of the
Peace*, it required scarcely any effort for a Londoner of moderate means to 'adventure his wealth in the natural resources
and new enterprises of any quarter of the world, and share,
without exertion or even trouble, in their prospective fruits and
advantages'.[20]

At that time there were around forty foreign stock exchanges
scattered throughout the world, of which seven were regularly
covered in the British financial press. The London Stock Exchange
listed bonds issued by fifty-seven sovereign and colonial governments. Following the money from London to the rest of the world
reveals the full extent of this first financial globalization. Around
45 per cent of British investment went to the United States,
Canada and the Antipodes, 20 per cent to Latin America, 16 per
cent to Asia, 13 per cent to Africa and 6 per cent to the rest of
Europe.[21] If you add together all the British capital raised through
public issues of securities between 1865 and 1914, you see that
the majority went overseas; less than a third was invested in
the United Kingdom itself.[22] By 1913 an estimated $158 billion
in securities were in existence worldwide, of which around
$45 billion (28 per cent) were internationally held. Of all the
securities quoted on the London Stock Exchange in 1913 nearly
half (48 per cent) were foreign bonds.[23] Gross foreign assets in
1913 were equivalent to around 150 per cent of UK GDP and
the annual current account surplus rose as high as 9 per cent of
GDP in 1913 – evidence of what might now be called a British
savings glut. Significantly, a much higher proportion of pre-1914
capital export went to relatively poor countries than has been the
case more recently. In 1913, 25 per cent of the world's stock of
foreign capital was invested in countries with per capita incomes

of a fifth or less of US per capita GDP; in 1997 the proportion was just 5 per cent.[24]

It may be that British investors were attracted to foreign markets simply by the prospect of higher returns in capital-poor regions.[25] It may be that they were encouraged by the spread of the gold standard, or by the increasing fiscal responsibility of foreign governments. Yet it is hard to believe there would have been so much overseas investment before 1914 had it not been for the rise of British imperial power. Somewhere between two fifths and half of all this British overseas investment went to British-controlled colonies. A substantial proportion also went to countries like Argentina and Brazil over which Britain exercised considerable informal influence. And British foreign investment was disproportionately focused on assets that increased London's political leverage: not only government bonds but also the securities issued to finance the construction of railways, port facilities and mines. Part of the attraction of colonial securities was the explicit guarantees some of them carried.[26] The Colonial Loans Act (1899) and the Colonial Stock Act (1900) also gave colonial bonds the same trustee status as the benchmark British government perpetual bond, the consol, making them eligible investments for Trustee Savings Banks.[27] But the real appeal of colonial securities was implicit rather than explicit.

The Victorians imposed a distinctive set of institutions on their colonies that was very likely to enhance their appeal to investors. These extended beyond the Gladstonian trinity of sound money, balanced budgets and free trade to include the rule of law (specifically, British-style property rights) and relatively non-corrupt administration – among the most important 'public goods' of late-nineteenth-century liberal imperialism. Debt contracts with colonial borrowers were, quite simply, more likely to be enforceable than those with independent states. This was why, as Keynes later noted, 'Southern Rhodesia – a place in the middle of Africa with a few thousand white inhabitants and less than a million black ones – can place an unguaranteed loan on terms not very different from our own [British] War Loan', while investors could prefer 'Nigeria stock (which has no British Government guarantee) [to] . . . London and North-Eastern Railway debentures'.[28] The imposition of British rule (as in Egypt in 1882) practically amounted to a 'no default' guarantee; the only uncertainty investors had to face concerned the expected duration of British rule. Before 1914, despite the growth of nationalist movements in possessions as different as Ireland and India, political independence still seemed a distinctly remote prospect for most subject peoples. At this point even the major colonies of white settlement had been granted only a limited political autonomy. And no colony seemed further removed from gaining its independence than Hong Kong.

Between 1865 and 1914 British investors put at least £74 million into Chinese securities, a tiny proportion of the total £4 billion that they held abroad by 1914, but a significant sum for impoverished China.[29] No doubt it reassured investors that, from 1854, Britain not only ruled Hong Kong as a crown colony but also controlled the entire Chinese system of Imperial Maritime Customs, ensuring that at least a portion of the duties collected at China's ports was earmarked to pay the interest on British-owned bonds. Yet even in the European quarters of the so-called treaty ports, where the Union Jack fluttered and the *taipan* sipped his gin and tonic, there were dangers. No matter how tightly the British controlled Hong Kong, they could do nothing to prevent China from becoming embroiled first in a war with Japan in 1894–5, then in the Boxer Rebellion of 1900 and finally in the revolution that overthrew the Qing dynasty in 1911 – a revolution partly sparked by widespread Chinese disgust at the extent of foreign domination of their economy. Each of these political upheavals hit foreign investors where it hurts them the most: in their wallets. Much as happened in later crises – the Japanese invasion of 1941 or, for that matter, the Chinese takeover in 1997 – investors in Hong Kong saw steep declines in the value of their Chinese bonds and stocks.[30] This vulnerability of early globalization to wars and revolutions was not peculiar to China. It turned out to be true of the entire world financial system.

The three decades before 1914 were golden years for international investors – literally. Communications with foreign markets dramatically improved: by 1911, a telegraphic message took just thirty seconds to travel from New York to London, and the cost of sending it was a mere 0.5 per cent of the 1866 level. Europe's central banks had nearly all committed themselves to the gold standard by 1908; that meant that they nearly all had to target their gold reserves, raising rates (or otherwise intervening) if they experienced a specie outflow. At the very least, this simplified life for investors, by reducing the risk of large exchange rate fluctuations.[31] Governments around the world also seemed to be improving their fiscal positions as the deflation of the 1870s and 1880s gave way to gentle inflation from the mid 1890s, which reduced debt burdens in real terms. Higher growth also raised tax revenues.[32] Long-term interest rates nevertheless remained low. Although the yield on the benchmark British consol rose by over a percentage point between 1897 and 1914, that was from an all-time nadir of 2.25 per cent. What we would now call emerging market spreads narrowed dramatically, despite major episodes of debt default in the 1870s and 1890s. With the exception of securities issued by improvident Greece and Nicaragua, none of the sovereign or colonial bonds that were traded in London in 1913 yielded more than two percentage points above consols, and most paid considerably less. That meant that anyone who had bought a portfolio of foreign bonds in, say, 1880 had enjoyed handsome capital gains.[33]

The yields and volatility of the bonds of the other great powers, which accounted for about half the foreign sovereign debt quoted in London, also declined steadily after 1880, suggesting that political risk premiums were falling too. Before 1880, Austrian, French, German and Russian bonds had tended to fluctuate quite violently in response to political news; but the various diplomatic alarums and excursions of the decade before 1914, like those over Morocco and the Balkans, caused scarcely a tremor in the London bond market. Although the UK stock market remained fairly flat following the bursting of the 1895–1900 Kaffir (gold mine) bubble, the volatility of returns trended downwards. There is at least some evidence to connect these trends with a long-run rise in liquidity, due partly to increased gold production and, more importantly, to financial innovation, as joint-stock banks expanded their balance sheets relative to their reserves, and savings banks successfully attracted deposits from middle-class and lower-class households.[34]

All these benign economic trends encouraged optimism. To many businessmen – from Ivan Bloch in Tsarist Russia to Andrew Carnegie in the United States – it was self-evident that a major war would be catastrophic for the capitalist system. In 1898 Bloch published a massive six-volume work entitled *The Future of War* which argued that, because of technological advances in the destructiveness of weaponry, war essentially had no future. Any attempt to wage it on a large scale would end in 'the bankruptcy of nations'.[35] In 1910, the same year that Carnegie established his Endowment for International Peace, the left-leaning British journalist Norman Angell published *The Great Illusion*, in which he argued that a war between the great powers had become an economic impossibility precisely because of 'the delicate interdependence of our credit-built finance'.[36] In the spring of 1914 an international commission published its report into the outrages committed during the Balkan Wars of 1912–13. Despite the evidence he and his colleagues confronted of wars waged *à l'outrance* between entire populations, the commission's chairman noted in his introduction that the great powers of Europe (unlike the petty Balkan states) 'had discovered the obvious truth that the richest country has the most to lose by war, and each country wishes for peace above all things'. One of the British members of the commission, Henry Noel Brailsford – a staunch supporter of the Independent Labour Party and author of a fierce critique of the arms industry (*The War of Steel and Gold*) – declared:

In Europe the epoch of conquest is over and save in the Balkans and perhaps on the fringes of the Austrian and Russian empires, it is as certain as anything in politics that the frontiers of our national states are finally drawn. My own belief is that there will be no more wars among the six great powers.[37]

Financial markets had initially shrugged off the assassination by Gavrilo Princip of the heir to the Austrian throne, the Archduke Franz Ferdinand, in the Bosnian capital Sarajevo on 28 June 1914. Not until 22 July did the financial press express any serious anxiety that the Balkan crisis might escalate into something bigger and more economically threatening. When investors belatedly grasped the likelihood of a full-scale European war, however, liquidity was sucked out of the world economy as if the bottom had dropped out of a bath. The first symptom of the crisis was a rise in shipping insurance premiums in the wake of the Austrian ultimatum to Serbia (which demanded, among other things, that Austrian officials be allowed into Serbia to seek evidence of

Belgrade's complicity in the assassination). Bond and stock prices began to slip as prudent investors sought to increase the liquidity of their positions by shifting into cash. European investors were especially quick to start selling their Russian securities, followed by Americans. Exchange rates went haywire as a result of efforts by cross-border creditors to repatriate their money: sterling and the franc surged, while the ruble and dollar slumped.[38] By 30 July panic reigned on most financial markets.[39] The first firms to come under pressure in London were the so-called jobbers on the Stock Exchange, who relied heavily on borrowed money to finance their purchases of equities. As sell orders flooded in, the value of their stocks plunged below the value of their debts, forcing a number (notably Derenberg & Co.) into bankruptcy. Also under pressure were the commercial bill brokers in London, many of whom were owed substantial sums by continental counterparties now unable or unwilling to remit funds. Their difficulties in turn impacted on the acceptance houses (the elite merchant banks), who were first in line if the foreigners defaulted, since they had accepted the bills. If the acceptance houses went bust, the bill brokers would go down with them, and possibly also the larger joint-stock banks, which lent millions every day short-term to the discount market. The joint-stock banks' decision to call in loans deepened what we would now call the credit crunch.[40] As everyone scrambled to sell assets and increase their liquidity, stock prices fell, compromising brokers and others who had borrowed money using shares as collateral. Domestic customers began to fear a banking crisis. Queues formed as people sought to exchange banknotes for gold coins at the Bank of England.[41] The effective suspension of London's role as the hub of international credit helped spread the crisis from Europe to the rest of the world.

Perhaps the most remarkable feature of the crisis of 1914 was the closure of the world's major stock markets for periods of up to five months. The Vienna market was the first to close (on 27 July). By 30 July all the continental European exchanges had shut their doors. The next day London and New York felt compelled to follow suit. Although a belated settlement day went ahead smoothly on 18 November, the London Stock Exchange did not reopen until 4 January 1915. Nothing like this had happened since its foundation in 1773.[42] The New York market reopened for limited trading (bonds for cash only) on 28 November, but wholly unrestricted trading did not resume until 1 April 1915.[43] Nor were stock exchanges the only markets to close in the crisis. Most US commodity markets had to suspend trading, as did most European foreign exchange markets. The London Royal Exchange, for example, remained shut until 17 September.[44] It seems likely that, had the markets not closed, the collapse in prices would have been as extreme as in 1929, if not worse. No act of state-sponsored terrorism has had greater financial consequences than Gavrilo Princip's in 1914.

The near-universal adoption of the gold standard had once been seen as a comfort to investors. In the crisis of 1914, however, it tended to exacerbate the liquidity crisis. Some central banks (notably the Bank of England) actually raised their discount rates in the initial phase of the crisis, in a vain attempt to deter foreigners from repatriating their capital and thereby draining gold reserves. The adequacy of gold reserves in the event of an emergency had been hotly debated before the war; indeed, these debates are almost the only evidence that the financial world had given any thought whatever to the trouble that lay ahead.[45] Yet the gold standard was no more rigidly binding than today's informal dollar pegs in Asia and the Middle East; in the emergency of war, a number of countries, beginning with Russia, simply suspended the gold convertibility of their currencies. In both

Britain and the United States formal convertibility was maintained, but it could have been suspended if that had been thought necessary. (The Bank of England was granted suspension of the 1844 Bank Act, which imposed a fixed relationship between the Bank's reserve and note issue, but this was not equivalent to suspending specie payments, which could easily be maintained with a lower reserve.) In each case, the crisis prompted the issue of emergency paper money: in Britain, £1 and 10s Treasury notes; in the United States, the emergency currency that banks were authorized to issue under the Aldrich-Vreeland Act of 1908.[46] Then, as now, the authorities reacted to a liquidity crisis by printing money.

Nor were these the only measures deemed necessary. In London the bank holiday of Monday 3 August was extended until Thursday the 6th. Payments due on bills of exchange were postponed for a month by royal proclamation. A month-long moratorium on all other payments due (except wages, taxes, pensions and the like) was rushed onto the statute books. (These moratoria were later extended until, respectively, 19 October and 4 November.) On 13 August the Chancellor of the Exchequer gave the Bank of England a guarantee that, if the Bank discounted all approved bills accepted before 4 August (when war was declared) 'without recourse against the holders', then the Treasury would bear the cost of any loss the Bank might incur. This amounted to a government rescue of the discount houses; it opened the door for a massive expansion of the monetary base, as bills poured into the Bank to be discounted. On 5 September assistance was also extended to the acceptance houses.[47] Arrangements varied from country to country, but the expedients were broadly similar and quite unprecedented in their scope: temporary closures of markets; moratoria on debts; emergency money issued by governments; bailouts for the most vulnerable institutions. In all these respects, the authorities were prepared to go much further than they had previously gone in purely financial crises. As had happened during the previous 'world war' (against revolutionary and then Napoleonic France more than a century before), the war of 1914 was understood to be a special kind of emergency, justifying measures that would have been inconceivable in peacetime, including (as one Conservative peer put it) 'the release of the bankers . . . from all liability'.[48]

The closure of the stock market and the intervention of the authorities to supply liquidity almost certainly averted a catastrophic fire-sale of assets. The London stock market was already down 7 per cent on the year when trading was suspended, and that was before the fighting had even begun. Fragmentary data on bond transactions (conducted literally in the street during the period of stock market closure) give a sense of the losses investors had to contemplate, despite the authorities' efforts. By the end of 1914, Russian bonds were down 8.8 per cent, British consols 9.3 per cent, French *rentes* 13.2 per cent and Austrian bonds 23 per cent.[49] In the words of Patrick Shaw-Stewart of Barings, it was 'one of the most terrific things London had been up against since finance existed'.[50] This, however, was merely the beginning. Contrary to the 'short war' illusion (which was more widespread in financial than in military circles), there were another four years of carnage still to go, and an even longer period of financial losses. Any investor unwise or patriotic enough to hang on to gilt-edged securities (consols or the new UK War Loans) would have suffered inflation-adjusted losses of –46 per cent by 1920. Even the real returns on British equities were negative (–27 per cent).[51] Inflation in France and hyperinflation in Germany inflicted even more severe punishment on anyone rash enough to maintain large franc or Reichsmark balances. By 1923 holders of all kinds of German securities had lost everything, though subsequent revaluation legislation restored some of their original capital.

Those with substantial holdings of Austrian, Hungarian, Ottoman and Russian bonds also lost heavily – even when these were gold-denominated – as the Habsburg, Ottoman and Romanov empires fell apart under the stresses of total war. The losses were especially sudden and severe in the case of Russian bonds, on which the Bolshevik regime defaulted in February 1918. By the time this happened, Russian 5 per cent bonds of the 1906 vintage were trading at below 45 per cent of their face value. Hopes of some kind of settlement with foreign creditors lingered on throughout the 1920s, by which time the bonds were trading at around 20 per cent of par. By the 1930s they were all but worthless.[52]

Despite the best efforts of the bankers, who indefatigably floated loans for such unpromising purposes as the payment of German reparations, it proved impossible to restore the old order of free capital mobility between the wars. Currency crises, defaults, arguments about reparations and war debts and then the onset of the Depression led more and more countries to impose exchange and capital controls as well as protectionist tariffs and other trade restrictions, in a vain bid to preserve national wealth at the expense of international exchange. On 19 October 1921, for example, the Chinese government declared bankruptcy, and proceeded to default on nearly all China's external debts. It was a story repeated all over the world, from Shanghai to Santiago, from Moscow to Mexico City. By the end of the 1930s, most states in the world, including those that retained political freedoms, had imposed restrictions on trade, migration and investment as a matter of course. Some achieved near-total economic self-sufficiency (autarky), the ideal of a de-globalized society. Consciously or unconsciously, all governments applied in peacetime the economic restrictions that had first been imposed between 1914 and 1918.

*

The origins of the First World War became clearly visible – as soon as it had broken out. Only then did the Bolshevik leader Lenin see that war was an inevitable consequence of imperialist rivalries. Only then did American liberals grasp that secret diplomacy and the tangle of European alliances were the principal causes of conflict. The British and French naturally blamed the Germans; the Germans blamed the British and French. Historians have been refining and modifying these arguments for more than ninety years now. Some have traced the origins of the war back to the naval race of the mid 1890s; others to events in the Balkans after 1907. So why, when its causes today seem so numerous and so obvious, were contemporaries so oblivious of Armageddon until just days before its advent? One possible answer is that their vision was blurred by a mixture of abundant liquidity and the passage of time. The combination of global integration and financial innovation had made the world seem reassuringly safe to investors. Moreover, it had been thirty-four years since the last major European war, between France and Germany, and that had been mercifully short. Geopolitically, of course, the world was anything but a safe place. Any reader of the *Daily Mail* could see that the European arms race and imperial rivalry might one day lead to a major war; indeed, there was an entire subgenre of popular fiction based on imaginary Anglo-German wars. Yet the lights in financial markets were flashing green, not red, until the very eve of destruction.

There may be a lesson here for our time, too. The first era of financial globalization took at least a generation to achieve. But it was blown apart in a matter of days. And it would take more than two generations to repair the damage done by the guns of August 1914.

Economic Hit Men

From the 1930s until the late 1960s, international finance and the idea of globalization slumbered – some even considered it dead.[53] In the words of the American economist Arthur Bloomfield, writing in 1946:

It is now highly respectable doctrine, in academic and banking circles alike, that a substantial measure of *direct* control over private capital movements, especially of the so-called hot money varieties, will be desirable for most countries not only in the years immediately ahead but also in the long run as well . . . This doctrinal *volte-face* represents a widespread disillusionment resulting from the destructive behaviour of these movements in the interwar years.[54]

At Bretton Woods, in New Hampshire's White Mountains, the soon-to be-victorious Allies met in July 1944 to devise a new financial architecture for the post-war world. In this new order, trade would be progressively liberalized, but restrictions on capital movements would remain in place. Exchange rates would be fixed, as under the gold standard, but now the anchor – the international reserve currency – would be the dollar rather than gold (though the dollar itself would notionally remain convertible into gold, vast quantities of which sat, immobile but totemic, in Fort Knox). In the words of Keynes, one of the key architects of the Bretton Woods system, 'control of capital movements' would be 'a permanent feature of the post-war system'.[55] Even tourists could be prevented from going abroad with more than a pocketful of currency if governments felt unable to make their currencies convertible. When capital sums did flow across national borders, they would go from government to government, like the Marshall

Aid* that helped revive devastated Western Europe between 1948 and 1952.[56] The two guardian 'sisters' of this new order were to be established in Washington, DC, the capital of the 'free world': the International Monetary Fund and the International Bank for Reconstruction and Development, later (in combination with the International Development Association) known as the World Bank. In the words of current World Bank President Robert Zoellick, 'The IMF was supposed to regulate exchange rates. What became the World Bank was supposed to help rebuild countries shattered by the war. Free trade would be revived. But free capital flows were out.' Thus, for the next quarter century, did governments resolve the so-called 'trilemma', according to which a country can choose any two out of three policy options:

1. full freedom of cross-border capital movements;
2. a fixed exchange rate;
3. an independent monetary policy oriented towards domestic objectives.[57]

Under Bretton Woods, the countries of the Western world opted for 2 and 3. Indeed, the trend was for capital controls to be tightened rather than loosened as time went on. A good example is the Interest Equalization Act passed by the United

---

* The total amount disbursed under the Marshall Plan was equivalent to roughly 5.4 per cent of US gross national product in the year of General George Marshall's seminal speech, or 1.1 per cent spread over the whole period of the programme, which dated from April 1948, when the Foreign Assistance Act was passed, to June 1952, when the last payment was made. If there had been a Marshall Plan between 2003 and 2007, it would have cost $550 billion. By comparison, actual foreign economic aid under the Bush administration between 2001 and 2006 totalled less than $150 billion, an average of below 0.2 per cent of GDP.

States in 1963, which was expressly designed to discourage Americans from investing in foreign securities.

Yet there was always an unsustainable quality to the Bretton Woods system. For the so-called Third World, the various attempts to replicate the Marshall Plan through government-to-government aid programmes proved deeply disappointing. Over time, American aid in particular became hedged around with political and military conditions that were not always in the best interests of the recipients. Even if that had not been the case, it is doubtful that capital injections of the sort envisaged by American economists like Walt Rostow* were the solution to the problems of most African, Asian and Latin American economies. Much aid was disbursed to poor countries, but the greater part of it was either wasted or stolen.[58] In so far as Bretton Woods did succeed in generating new wealth by expediting the recovery of Western Europe, it could only frustrate those investors who saw the risk in excessive home bias. And, in so far as it allowed countries to subordinate monetary policy to the goal of full employment, it created potential conflicts even between options 2 and 3 of the trilemma. In the late 1960s, US public sector deficits were negligible by today's standards, but large enough to prompt complaints from France that Washington was exploiting its reserve currency status in order to collect seigniorage from America's foreign creditors by printing dollars, much as medieval monarchs had exploited their monopoly on minting to debase the currency. The decision of the Nixon administration to sever the final link with the gold standard (by ending gold convertibility of the dollar)

* Rostow, the author of *The Stages of Economic Growth: A Non-Communist Manifesto* (1960), offered economic and strategic advice in roughly equal measure to the Democratic administrations of the 1960s. As the equivalent of National Security Adviser to Lyndon Johnson, he was closely associated with the escalation of the Vietnam War.

sounded the death knell for Bretton Woods in 1971.[59] When the Arab-Israeli War and the Arab oil embargo struck in 1973, most central banks tended to accommodate the price shock with easier credit, leading to precisely the inflationary crisis that General de Gaulle's adviser Jacques Rueff had feared.[60]

With currencies floating again and offshore markets like the Eurobond market flourishing, the 1970s saw a revival of non-governmental capital export. In particular, there was a rush by Western banks to recycle the rapidly growing surpluses of the oil-exporting countries. The region where the bankers chose to lend the Middle Eastern petrodollars was an old favourite. Between 1975 and 1982, Latin America quadrupled its borrowings from foreigners from $75 billion to more than $315 billion. (Eastern European countries also entered the capital debt market, a sure sign of the Communist bloc's impending doom.) Then, in August 1982, Mexico declared that it would no longer be able to service its debt. An entire continent teetered on the verge of declaring bankruptcy. Yet the days had gone when investors could confidently expect their governments to send a gunboat when a foreign government misbehaved. Now the role of financial policing had to be played by two unarmed bankers, the International Monetary Fund and the World Bank. Their new watchword became 'conditionality': no reforms, no money. Their preferred mechanism was the structural adjustment programme. And the policies the debtor countries had to adopt became known as the Washington Consensus, a wish-list of ten economic policies that would have gladdened the heart of a British imperial administrator a hundred years before.* Number one was to impose fiscal

* Here is a brief overview of the ten points, based on John Williamson's original 1989 formulation: 1. Impose fiscal discipline; 2. Reform taxation; 3. Liberalize interest rates; 4. Raise spending on health and education; 5. Secure property rights; 6. Privatize state-run industries; 7. Deregulate

discipline to reduce or eliminate deficits. The tax base was to be broadened and tax rates lowered. The market was to set interest and exchange rates. Trade was be liberalized and so, crucially, were capital flows. Suddenly 'hot' money, which had been out-lawed at Bretton Woods, was hot again.

To some critics, however, the World Bank and the IMF were no better than agents of the same old Yankee imperialism. Any loans from the IMF or World Bank, it was claimed, would simply be used to buy American goods from American firms – often arms to keep ruthless dictators or corrupt oligarchies in power. The costs of 'structural adjustment' would be borne by their hapless subjects. And Third World leaders who stepped out of line would soon find themselves in trouble. These became popular arguments, particularly in the 1990s, when anti-globalization protests became regular features of international gatherings. When articulated on placards or in rowdy chants by crowds of well-fed Western youths such notions are relatively easy to dis-miss. But when similar charges are levelled at the Bretton Woods institutions by former insiders, they merit closer scrutiny.

When he was chief economist of the Boston-based company Chas. T. Main, Inc., John Perkins claims he was employed to ensure that the money lent to countries like Ecuador and Panama by the IMF and World Bank would be spent on goods supplied by US corporations. 'Economic hit men' like himself, according to Perkins, 'were trained ... to build up the American empire ... to create situations where as many resources as possible flow into this country, to our corporations, and our governments':

This empire, unlike any other in the history of the world, has been built primarily through economic manipulation, through cheating,

---

markets; 8. Adopt a competitive exchange rate; 9. Remove barriers to trade; 10. Remove barriers to foreign direct investment.

through fraud, through seducing people into our way of life, through the economic hit men . . . My real job . . . was giving loans to other countries, huge loans, much bigger than they could possibly repay . . . So we make this big loan, most of it comes back to the United States, the country is left with debt plus lots of interest, and they basically become our servants, our slaves. It's an empire. There's no two ways about it. It's a huge empire.[61]

According to Perkins's book, *The Confessions of an Economic Hit Man*, two Latin American leaders, Jaime Roldós Aguilera of Ecuador and Omar Torrijos of Panama, were assassinated in 1981 for opposing what he calls 'that fraternity of corporate, government, and banking heads whose goal is global empire'.[62] There is, admittedly, something about his story that seems a little odd. It is not as if the United States had lent much money to Ecuador and Panama. In the 1970s the totals were just $96 million and $197 million, less than 0.4 per cent of total US grants and loans. And it is not as if Ecuador and Panama were major customers for the United States. In 1990 they accounted for, respectively, 0.17 per cent and 0.22 per cent of total US exports. Those do not seem like figures worth killing for. As Bob Zoellick puts it, 'The IMF and the World Bank lend money to countries in crisis, not countries that offer huge opportunities to corporate America.'

Nevertheless, the charge of neo-imperialism refuses to go away. According to Nobel prize-winning economist Joseph Stiglitz, who was chief economist at the World Bank between 1997 and 2000, the IMF in the 1980s not only 'champion[ed] market supremacy with ideological fervour' but also 'took a rather imperialistic view' of its role. Moreover, Stiglitz argues, 'many of the policies that the IMF has pushed, in particular premature capital market liberalization, have contributed to global instability . . . Jobs have

Jaime Roldós Aguilera of Ecuador . . .

. . . and Omar Torrijos of Panama: Allegedly
victims of the 'economic hit men'

been systematically destroyed ... [because] the influx of hot money into and out of the country that so frequently follows after capital market liberalization leaves havoc in its wake ... Even those countries that have experienced some limited growth have seen the benefits accrue to the well-off, and especially the very well-off.'[63] In his animus against the IMF (and Wall Street), Stiglitz overlooks the fact that it was not just those institutions that came to favour a return to free capital movements in the 1980s. It was actually the Organization for Economic Cooperation and Development that blazed the liberalizing trail, followed (after the conversion of French socialists like Jacques Delors and Michel Camdessus) by the European Commission and European Council. Indeed, there was arguably a Paris Consensus before there was a Washington Consensus (though in many ways it was building on a much earlier Bonn Consensus in favour of free capital markets).[64] In London, too, Margaret Thatcher's government pressed ahead with unilateral capital account liberalization without any prompting from the United States. Rather, it was the Reagan administration that followed Thatcher's lead.

Stiglitz's biggest complaint against the IMF is that it responded the wrong way to the Asian financial crisis of 1997, lending a total of $95 billion to countries in difficulty, but attaching Washington Consensus-style conditions (higher interest rates, smaller government deficits) that actually served to worsen the crisis. It is a view that has been partially echoed by, among others, the economist and columnist Paul Krugman.[65] There is no doubting the severity of the 1997–8 crisis. In countries such as Indonesia, Malaysia, South Korea and Thailand there was a very severe recession in 1998. Yet neither Stiglitz nor Krugman offers a convincing account of how the East Asian crisis might have been better managed on standard Keynesian lines, with currencies being allowed to float and government deficits to rise.

In the acerbic words of an open letter to Stiglitz by Kenneth Rogoff, who became chief economist at the IMF after the Asian crisis:

Governments typically come to the IMF for financial assistance when they are having trouble finding buyers for their debt and when the value of their money is falling. The Stiglitzian prescription is to raise ... fiscal deficits, that is, to issue more debt and to print more money. You seem to believe that if a distressed government issues more currency, its citizens will suddenly think it more valuable. You seem to believe that when investors are no longer willing to hold a government's debt, all that needs to be done is to increase the supply and it will sell like hot cakes. We at the – no, make that we on planet Earth – have considerable experience suggesting otherwise. We earthlings have found that when a country in fiscal distress tries to escape by printing more money, inflation rises, often uncontrollably ... The laws of economics may be different in your part of the gamma quadrant, but around here we find that when an almost bankrupt government fails to credibly constrain the time profile of its fiscal deficits, things generally get worse instead of better.[66]

Nor is it clear that Malaysia's temporary imposition of capital controls in 1997 made a significant difference to the economy's performance during the crisis. Krugman at least acknowledges that the East Asian financial institutions, which had borrowed short-term in dollars but lent out long-term in local currency (often to political cronies), bore much of the responsibility for the crisis. Yet his talk of a return of Depression economics now looks overdone. There never was a Depression in East Asia (except perhaps in Japan, which could hardly be portrayed as a victim of IMF malfeasance). After the shock of 1998 all the economies affected returned swiftly to rapid growth – growth so rapid, indeed, that by 2004 some commentators were wondering if the 'two sisters' of Bretton Woods any longer had a role to play as international lenders.[67]

In truth, the 1980s saw the rise of an altogether different kind of economic hit man, far more intimidating than those portrayed by Perkins precisely because they never even had to contemplate resorting to violence to achieve their objective. To this new generation, making a hit meant making a billion dollars on a single successful speculation. As the Cold War drew to its close, these hit men had no real interest in pursuing an American imperialist agenda; on the contrary, their stated political inclinations were more often liberal than conservative. They did not work for public sector institutions like the IMF or the World Bank. On the contrary, they ran businesses that were entirely private, to the extent that they were not even quoted on the stock market. These businesses were called hedge funds, which we first encountered as an alternative form of risk manager in Chapter 4. Like the rise of China, the even more rapid rise of the hedge funds has been one of the biggest changes the global economy has witnessed since the Second World War. As pools of lightly regulated,* highly mobile capital, hedge funds exemplify the return of hot money after the big chill that prevailed between the onset of the Depression and the end of Bretton Woods. And the acknowledged *capo dei capi* of the new economic hit men has been George Soros. It was no coincidence that when the Malaysian prime minister Mahathir bin Mohamad wanted to blame someone other than himself for

* Since the term was first used, in 1966, to describe the long-short fund set up by Alfred Winslow Jones in 1949 (which took both long and short positions on the US stock market), most hedge funds have been limited liability partnerships. As such they have been exempted from the provisions of the 1933 Securities Act and the 1940 Investment Company Act, which restrict the operations of mutual funds and investment banks with respect to leverage and short selling.

George Soros: hedge fund *capo dei capi*
and master of reflexivity

the currency crisis that struck the ringgit in August 1997, it was Soros rather than the IMF that he called 'a moron'.

A Hungarian Jew by birth, though educated in London, George Soros emigrated to the United States in 1956. There he made his reputation as an analyst and then head of research at the venerable house of Arnhold & S. Bleichroeder (a direct descendant of the Berlin private bank that had once managed Bismarck's money).[68] As might be expected of a Central European intellectual – who named his fund the Quantum Fund in honour of the physicist Werner Heisenberg's Uncertainty Principle – Soros regards himself as more a philosopher than a hit man. His book

The Alchemy of Finance (1987) begins with a bold critique of the fundamental assumptions of economics as a subject, reflecting the influence on his early intellectual development of the philosopher Karl Popper.[69] According to Soros's pet theory of 'reflexivity', financial markets cannot be regarded as perfectly efficient, because prices are reflections of the ignorance and biases, often irrational, of millions of investors. 'Not only do market participants operate with a bias', Soros argues, 'but their bias can also influence the course of events. This may create the impression that markets anticipate future developments accurately, but in fact it is not present expectations that correspond to future events but future events that are shaped by present expectations.'[70] It is the feedback effect – as investors' biases affect market outcomes, which in turn change investors' biases, which again affect market outcomes – that Soros calls reflexivity. As he puts it in his most recent book:

... markets never reach the equilibrium postulated by economic theory. There is a two-way reflexive connection between perception and reality which can give rise to initially self-reinforcing but eventually self-defeating boom-bust processes, or bubbles. Every bubble consists of a trend and a misconception that interact in a reflexive manner.[71]

Originally devised to hedge against market risk with short positions,* which make money if a security goes down in price, a hedge fund provided the perfect vehicle for Soros to exploit his insights about reflexive markets. Soros knew how to make money from long positions too, it should be emphasized – that is, from buying assets in the expectation of future prices rises. In 1969 he

* Technically, according to the US Securities and Exchange Commission, a short sale is 'any sale of a security which the seller does not own or any sale which is consummated by the delivery of a security borrowed by, or for the account of, the seller'.

was long real estate. Three years later he backed bank stocks to take off. He was long Japan in 1971. He was long oil in 1972. A year later, when these bets were already paying off, he deduced from Israeli complaints about the quality of US-supplied hardware in the Yom Kippur War that there would need to be some heavy investment in America's defence industries. So he went long defence stocks too.[72] Right, right, right, right and right again. But Soros's biggest coups came from being right about losers, not winners: for example, the telegraph company Western Union in 1985, as fax technology threatened to destroy its business, as well as the US dollar, which duly plunged after the Group of Five's Plaza accord of 22 September 1985.[73] That year was an *annus mirabilis* for Soros, who saw his fund grow by 122 per cent. But the greatest of all his shorts proved to be one of the most momentous bets in British financial history.

I admit I have a vested interest in the events of Wednesday 16 September 1992. In those days, moonlighting as a newspaper leader writer while I was a junior lecturer at Cambridge, I became convinced that speculators like Soros could beat the Bank of England if it came to a showdown. It was simple arithmetic: a trillion dollars being traded on foreign exchange markets every day, versus the Bank's meagre hard currency reserves. Soros reasoned that the rising costs of German reunification would drive up interest rates and hence the Deutschmark. This would make the Conservative government's policy of shadowing the German currency – formalized when Britain had joined the European Exchange Rate Mechanism (ERM) in 1990 – untenable. As interest rates rose, the British economy would tank. Sooner or later, the government would be forced to withdraw from the ERM and devalue the pound. So sure was Soros that the pound would drop that he ultimately bet $10 billion, more than the entire capital of his fund, on a series of transactions whereby he

The force of destiny: Chancellor the Exchequer Norman Lamont
announces sterling's exit from the European Exchange Rate
Mechanism, 16 September 1992

effectively borrowed sterling in the UK and invested in German
currency at the pre-16 September price of around 2.95 Deutsch-
marks).[74] I was equally sure that the pound would be devalued,
though all I had to bet was my credibility. As it happened, the
City editor of the newspaper I wrote for disagreed. That night,
having been given something of a browbeating at the leader
writers' morning conference with the editor, I went to the English
National Opera, to hear Verdi's *The Force of Destiny*. It proved
a highly appropriate choice. Someone announced at the interval
that Britain had withdrawn from the ERM. How we all cheered
– and no one louder than me (except possibly George Soros). His
fund made more than a billion dollars as sterling slumped –
ultimately by as much as 20 per cent – allowing Soros to repay
the sterling he had borrowed but at the new lower exchange rate

and to pocket the difference. And that trade accounted for just 40 per cent of the year's profits.[75]

The success of the Quantum Fund was staggering. If someone had invested $100,000 with Soros when he established his second fund (Double Eagle, the earlier name of Quantum) in 1969 and had reinvested all the dividends, he would have been worth $130 million by 1994, an average annual growth rate of 35 per cent.[76] The essential differences between the old and the new economic hit men were twofold: first, the cold, calculating absence of loyalty to any particular country – the dollar and the pound could both be shorted with impunity; second, the sheer scale of the money the new men had to play with. 'How big a position do you have?' Soros once asked his partner Stanley Druckenmiller. 'One billion dollars,' Druckenmiller replied. 'You call that a position?' was Soros's sardonic retort.[77] For Soros, if a bet looked as good as his bet against the pound in 1992, then maximum leverage should be applied to it. His hedge fund pioneered the technique of borrowing from investment banks in order to take speculative long or short positions far in excess of the fund's own capital.

Yet there were limits to the power of the hedge funds. At one level, Soros and his ilk had proved that the markets were mightier than any government or central bank. But that was not the same as saying that the hedge funds could always command the markets. Soros owed his success to a gut instinct about the direction of the 'electronic herd'. However, even his instincts (often signalled by a spasm of back pain) could sometimes be wrong. Reflexivity, as he himself acknowledges, is a special case; it does not rule the markets every week of the year. What, then, if instincts could somehow be replaced by mathematics? What if you could write an infallible algebraic formula for double-digit returns? On the other side of the world – indeed on the other side of the financial galaxy – it seemed as if that formula had just been discovered.

Short-Term Capital Mismanagement

Imagine another planet – a planet without all the complicating frictions caused by subjective, sometimes irrational human beings. One where the inhabitants were omniscient and perfectly rational; where they instantly absorbed all new information and used it to maximize profits; where they never stopped trading; where markets were continuous, frictionless and completely liquid. Financial markets on this planet would follow a 'random walk', meaning that each day's prices would be quite unrelated to the previous day's but would reflect all the relevant information available. The returns on the planet's stock market would be normally distributed along the bell curve (see Chapter 3), with most years clustered closely around the mean, and two thirds of them within one standard deviation of the mean. In such a world, a 'six standard deviation' sell-off would be about as common as a person shorter than one and a half feet in our world. It would happen only once in four million years of trading.[78] This was the planet imagined by some of the most brilliant financial economists of modern times. Perhaps it is not altogether surprising that it turned out to look like Greenwich, Connecticut, one of the blandest places on Earth.

In 1993 two mathematical geniuses came to Greenwich with a big idea. Working closely with Fisher Black of Goldman Sachs, Stanford's Myron Scholes had developed a revolutionary new theory of pricing options. Now he and a third economist, Harvard Business School's Robert Merton, hoped to turn the so-called Black-Scholes model into a money-making machine. The starting point of their work as academics was the long-established financial instrument known as an option contract, which (as we saw in Chapter 4) works like this. If a particular stock is worth, say, $100 today and I believe that it may be worth more in the future, say, in a year's time, $200, it would be nice to have the option to buy it at that future date for, say, $150. If I am right, I make a profit. If not, well, it was only an option, so forget about it. The only cost was the price of the option, which the seller pockets. The big question was what that price should be.

'Quants' – the mathematically skilled analysts with the PhDs – sometimes refer to the Black Scholes model of options pricing as a black box. It is worth taking a look inside this particular box. The question, to repeat, is how to price an option to buy a particular stock on a particular date in the future, taking into account the unpredictable movement of the price of the stock in the intervening period. Work out that option price accurately, rather than just relying on guesswork, and you truly deserve the title 'rocket scientist'. Black and Scholes reasoned that the option's value depended on five variables: the current market price of the stock (S), the agreed future price at which the option could be exercised (X), the expiration date of the option (T), the risk-free rate of return in the economy as a whole (r) and – the crucial variable – the expected annual volatility of the stock, that is, the likely fluctuations of its price between the time of purchase and the expiration date (σ – the Greek letter sigma). With wonderful mathematical wizardry, Black and Scholes reduced the price of the option (C) to this formula:

$$C = SN(d_1) - Xe^{-rT}N(d_2)$$

where

$$d_1 = \frac{\log\left(\frac{S}{X}\right)+\left(r+\frac{\sigma^2}{2}\right)T}{\sigma\sqrt{T}} \text{ and } d_2 = d_1 - \sigma\sqrt{T}$$

Feeling a bit baffled? Can't follow the algebra? To be honest, I am baffled too. But that was just fine by the quants. To make money from this insight, they needed markets to be full of people who didn't have a clue how to price options but relied instead on their (seldom accurate) gut instincts. They also needed a great deal of computing power, a force which had been transforming the financial markets since the early 1980s. All they required now was a partner with some market savvy and they could make the leap from the faculty club to the trading floor. Struck down by cancer, Fisher Black could not be that partner. Instead, Merton and Scholes turned to John Meriwether, the former head of the bond arbitrage group at Salomon Brothers, who had made his first fortune out of the Savings and Loans meltdown of the late 1980s. The firm they created in 1994 was called Long-Term Capital Management.

It seemed like the dream team: two of academia's hottest quants teaming up with the ex-Salomon superstar plus a former Federal Reserve vice-chairman, David Mullins, another ex-Harvard professor, Eric Rosenfeld, and a bevy of ex-Salomon traders (Victor Haghani, Larry Hilibrand and Hans Hufschmid). The investors LTCM attracted to its fund were mainly big banks, among them the New York investment bank Merrill Lynch and the Swiss private bank Julius Baer. A latecomer to the party was another Swiss bank, UBS.[79] The minimum investment was $10 million. As compensation, the partners would take 2 per cent of the assets under management and 25 per cent of the profits (most hedge funds now charge 2 and 20, rather than 2 and 25).[80] Investors would be locked in for three years before they could exit. And another Wall Street firm, Bear Stearns, would stand ready to execute whatever trades Long-Term wanted to make.

In its first two years, the fund managed by LTCM made megabucks, posting returns (even after its hefty fees) of 43 and 41 per cent. If you had invested $10 million in Long-Term in March 1994, it would have been worth just over $40 million four years later. By September 1997 the fund's net capital stood at $6.7 billion. The partners' stakes had increased by a factor of more than ten. Admittedly, to generate these huge returns on an ever-growing pool of assets under management, Long-Term had to borrow, like George Soros. This additional leverage allowed them to bet more than just their own money. At the end of August 1997 the fund's capital was $6.7 billion, but the debt-financed assets on its balance sheet amounted to $126.4 billion, a ratio of assets to capital of 19 to 1.[81] By April 1998 the balance sheet had reached $134 billion. When we talk about being highly geared, most academics are referring to their bicycles. But when Merton and Scholes did so, they meant Long-Term was borrowing most of the money it traded with. Not that this pile of debt scared them. Their mathematical models said there was next to no risk involved. For one thing, they were simultaneously pursuing multiple, uncorrelated trading strategies: around a hundred of them, with a total of 7,600 different positions.[82] One might go wrong, or even two. But all these different bets just could not go wrong simultaneously. That was the beauty of a diversified portfolio – another key insight of modern financial theory, which had been formalized by Harry M. Markowitz, a Chicago-trained economist at the Rand Corporation, in the early 1950s, and further developed in William Sharpe's Capital Asset Pricing Model (CAPM).[83]

Long-Term made money by exploiting price discrepancies in multiple markets: in the fixed-rate residential mortgage market; in the US, Japanese and European government bond markets; in the more complex market for interest rate swaps* – anywhere, in

* A swap is a kind of derivative: a contractual arrangement in which one party agrees to pay another a fixed interest rate, in exchange for a floating rate (usually the London interbank offered rate, or Libor), applied to a notional amount.

fact, where their models spotted a pricing anomaly, whereby two fundamentally identical assets or options had fractionally different prices. But the biggest bet the firm put on, and the one most obviously based on the Black–Scholes formula, was selling long-dated options on American and European stock markets; in other words giving other people options which they would exercise if there were big future stock price movements. The prices these options were fetching in 1998 implied, according to the Black–Scholes formula, an abnormally high future volatility of around 22 per cent per year. In the belief that volatility would actually move towards its recent average of 10–13 per cent, Long-Term piled these options high and sold them cheap. Banks wanting to protect themselves against higher volatility – for example, another 1987-style stock market sell-off – were happy buyers. Long-Term sold so many such options that some people started calling it the Central Bank of Volatility.[84] At peak, they had $40 million riding on each percentage point change in US equity volatility.[85]

Sounds risky? The quants at Long-Term didn't think so. Among Long-Term's selling points was the claim that they were a market neutral fund – in other words they could not be hurt by a significant movement in any of the major stock, bond or currency markets. So-called dynamic hedging allowed them to sell options on a particular stock index while avoiding exposure to the index itself. What was more, the fund had virtually no exposure to emerging markets. It was as if Long-Term really was on another planet, far from the mundane ups and downs of terrestrial finance. Indeed, the partners started to worry that they weren't taking enough risks. Their target was a risk level corresponding to an annual variation (standard deviation) of 20 per cent of their assets. In practice, they were operating at closer to half that (meaning that their assets were fluctuating up and down by no more than 10 per cent).[86] According to the firm's Value at Risk models, it would take a ten-sigma (in other words, ten standard deviation) event to cause the firm to lose all its capital in a single year. But the probability of such an event, the quants calculated, was 1 in 10^{24} – effectively zero.[87]

In October 1997, as if to prove that LTCM really was the ultimate Brains Trust, Merton and Scholes were awarded the Nobel Prize in economics. So self-confident were they and their partners that on 31 December 1997 they returned $2.7 billion to outside investors (strongly implying that they would much rather focus on investing their own money).[88] It seemed as if intellect had triumphed over intuition, rocket science over risk-taking. Equipped with their magic black box, the partners at LTCM seemed poised to make fortunes beyond even George Soros's wildest dreams. And then, just five months later, something happened that threatened to blow the lid right off the Nobel winners' black box. For no immediately apparent reason, equity markets dipped, so that volatility went up instead of down. And the higher volatility went – it hit 27 in June, more than double the Long-Term projection – the more money was lost. May 1998 was Long-Term's worst month ever: the fund dropped by 6.7 per cent. But this was just the beginning. In June it was down 10.1 per cent. And the less the fund's assets were worth, the higher its leverage – the ratio of debt to capital – rose. In June it hit 31 to 1.[89]

In evolution, big extinctions tend to be caused by outside shocks, like an asteroid hitting the earth. A large meteor struck Greenwich in July 1998, when it emerged that Salomon Smith Barney (as Salomon Brothers had been renamed following its takeover by Travelers) was closing down its US bond arbitrage group, the place where Meriwether had made his Wall Street reputation, and an outfit that had been virtually replicating

LTCM's trading strategies. Clearly, the firm's new owners did not like the losses they had been seeing since May. Then, on Monday 17 August 1998, that was followed by a giant asteroid – not from outer space, but from one of earth's flakiest emerging markets as, weakened by political upheaval, declining oil revenues and a botched privatization, the ailing Russian financial system collapsed. A desperate Russian government was driven to default on its debts (including rouble-denominated domestic bonds), fuelling the fires of volatility throughout the world's financial markets.[90] Coming in the wake of the Asian crisis of the previous year, the Russian default had a contagious effect on other emerging markets, and indeed some developed markets too. Credit spreads blew out.* Stock markets plunged. Equity volatility hit 29 per cent. At peak it reached 45 per cent, which implied that the indices would move 3 per cent each day for the next five years.[91] Now, that just wasn't supposed to happen, not according to the Long-Term risk models. The quants had said that Long-Term was unlikely to lose more than $45 million in a single day.[92] On Friday 21 August 1998, it lost $550 million – 15 per cent of its entire capital, driving its leverage up to 42:1.[93] The traders in Greenwich stared, slack-jawed and glassy-eyed, at their screens. It couldn't be happening. But it was. Suddenly all the different markets where Long-Term had exposure were moving in sync, nullifying the protection offered by diversification. In quant-speak, the correlations had gone to one. By the end of the month, Long-Term was down 44 per cent: a total loss of over $1.8 billion.[94]

August is usually a time of thin trading in financial markets. Most people are out of town. John Meriwether was on the other

* For example, the spread over US Treasuries of the JP Morgan emerging market bond index rose from 3.3 per cent in October 1997, to 6.6 per cent in July 1998, to 17.05 per cent on 10 September 1998.

side of the world, in Beijing. Dashing home, he and his partners desperately sought a white knight to rescue them. They tried Warren Buffett in Omaha, Nebraska – despite the fact that just months before LTCM had been aggressively shorting shares in Buffett's company Berkshire Hathaway. He declined. On 24 August they reluctantly sought a meeting with none other than George Soros.[95] It was the ultimate humiliation: the quants from Planet Finance begging for a bail-out from the earthling prophet of irrational, unquantifiable reflexivity. Soros recalls that he 'offered Meriwether $500 million if he could find another $500 million from someone else. It didn't seem likely...' JP Morgan offered $200 million. Goldman Sachs also offered to help. But others held back. Their trading desks scented blood. If Long-Term was going bust, they just wanted their collateral, not to buy Long-Term's positions. And they didn't give a damn if volatility went through the roof. In the end, fearful that Long-Term's failure could trigger a generalized meltdown on Wall Street, the Federal Reserve Bank of New York hastily brokered a $3.625 billion bail-out by fourteen Wall Street banks.[96] But the original investors – who included some of the self-same banks, but also some smaller players like the University of Pittsburgh – had meanwhile seen their holdings cut from $4.9 billion to just $400 million. The sixteen partners were left with $30 million between them, a fraction of the fortune they had anticipated.

What had happened? Why was Soros so right and the giant brains at Long-Term so wrong? Part of the problem was precisely that LTCM's extraterrestrial founders had come back down to Planet Earth with a bang. Remember the assumptions underlying the Black–Scholes formula? Markets are efficient, meaning that the movement of stock prices cannot be predicted; they are continuous, frictionless and completely liquid; and returns on stocks follow the normal, bell-curve distribution. Arguably, the more traders learned to employ the Black–Scholes formula, the more efficient financial markets would become.[97] But, as John Maynard Keynes once observed, in a crisis 'markets can remain irrational longer than you can remain solvent'. In the long term, it might be true that the world would become more like Planet Finance, always coolly logical. Short term, it was still dear old Planet Earth, inhabited by emotional human beings, capable of flipping suddenly from greed to fear. When losses began to mount, many participants simply withdrew from the market, leaving LTCM with a largely illiquid portfolio of assets that couldn't be sold at any price. Moreover, this was an ever more integrated Planet Earth, in which a default in Russia could cause volatility to spike all over the world. 'Maybe the error of Long Term', mused Myron Scholes in an interview, 'was . . . that of not realizing that the world is becoming more and more global over time.' Meriwether echoed this view: 'The nature of the world had changed, and we hadn't recognized it.'[98] In particular, because many other firms had begun trying to copy Long-Term's strategies, when things went wrong it was not just the Long-Term portfolio that was hit; it was as if an entire super-portfolio was haemorrhaging.[99] There was a herd-like stampede for the exits, with senior managers at the big banks insisting that positions be closed down at any price. Everything suddenly went down at once. As one leading London hedge fund manager later put it to Meriwether: 'John, you were the correlation.'

There was, however, another reason why LTCM failed. The firm's value at risk (VaR) models had implied that the loss Long-Term suffered in August was so unlikely that it ought never to have happened in the entire life of the universe. But that was because the models were working with just five years' worth of data. If the models had gone back even eleven years, they would have captured the 1987 stock market crash. If they had gone back eighty years they would have captured the last great Russian default, after the 1917 Revolution. Meriwether himself, born in 1947, ruefully observed: 'If I had lived through the Depression, I would have been in a better position to understand events.'[100] To put it bluntly, the Nobel prize winners had known plenty of mathematics, but not enough history. They had understood the beautiful theory of Planet Finance, but overlooked the messy past of Planet Earth. And that, put very simply, was why Long-Term Capital Management ended up being Short-Term Capital Mismanagement.

It might be assumed that after the catastrophic failure of LTCM, quantitative hedge funds would have vanished from the financial scene. After all, the failure, though spectacular in scale, was far from anomalous. Of 1,308 hedge funds that were formed between 1989 and 1996, more than a third (36.7 per cent) had ceased to exist by the end of the period. In that period the average life span of a hedge fund was just forty months.[101] Yet the very reverse has happened. Far from declining, in the past ten years hedge funds of every type have exploded in number and in the volume of assets they manage. In 1990, according to Hedge Fund Research, there were just over 600 hedge funds managing some $39 billion in assets. By 2000 there were 3,873 funds with $490 billion in assets. The latest figures (for the first quarter of 2008) put the total at 7,601 funds with $1.9 trillion in assets. Since 1998 there has been a veritable stampede to invest in hedge funds (and in the 'funds of funds' that aggregate the performance of multiple firms). Where once they were the preserve of 'high net worth' individuals and investment banks, hedge funds are now attracting growing numbers of pension funds and university endowments.[102] This trend is all the more striking given that the attrition rate remains high; only a quarter of the 600 funds reporting in 1996 still existed at the end of 2004. In 2006, 717 ceased to trade; in the first nine months of 2007, 409.[103] It is not widely recognized that large numbers of hedge funds simply fizzle out, having failed to meet investors' expectations.

The obvious explanation for this hedge fund population explosion is that they perform relatively well as an asset class, with relatively low volatility and low correlation to other investment vehicles. But the returns on hedge funds, according to Hedge Fund Research, have been falling, from 18 per cent in the 1990s to just 7.5 per cent between 2000 and 2006. Moreover, there is increasing scepticism that hedge fund returns truly reflect 'alpha' (skill of asset management) as opposed to 'beta' (general market movements that could be captured with an appropriate mix of indices).[104] An alternative explanation is that, while they exist, hedge funds enrich their managers in a uniquely alluring way. In 2007 George Soros made $2.9 billion, ahead of Ken Griffin of Citadel and James Simons of Renaissance, but behind John Paulson, who earned a staggering $3.7 billion from his bets against subprime mortgages. As John Kay has pointed out, if Warren Buffett had charged investors in Berkshire Hathaway '2 and 20', he would have kept for himself $57 billion of the $62 billion his company has made for its shareholders over the past forty-two years.[105] Soros, Griffin and Simons are clearly exceptional fund managers (though surely not more so than Buffett). This explains why their funds, along with other superior performers, have grown enormously over the past decade. Today around 390 funds have assets under management in excess of $1 billion. The top hundred now account for 75 per cent of all hedge fund assets; and the top ten alone manage $324 billion.[106] But a quite mediocre conman could make a good deal of money by setting up a hedge fund, taking $100 million off gullible investors and running the simplest possible strategy:

1. He parks the $100 million in one-year Treasury bills yielding 4 per cent.
2. This then allows him to sell for 10 cents on the dollar 100 million covered options, which will pay out if the S&P 500 falls by more than 20 per cent in the coming year.
3. He takes the $10 million from the sale of the options and buys some more Treasury bills, which enables him to sell another 10 million options, which nets him another $1 million.
4. He then takes a long vacation.
5. At the end of the year the probability is 90 per cent that the S&P 500 has not fallen by 20 per cent, so he owes the option-holders nothing.
6. He adds up his earnings – $11 million from the sale of the options plus 4 per cent on the $110 million of T-bills – a handsome return of 15.4 per cent before expenses.
7. He pockets 2 per cent of the funds under management ($2 million) and 20 per cent of the returns above, say, a 4 per cent benchmark, which comes to over $4 million gross.
8. The chances are nearly 60 per cent that the fund will run smoothly on this basis for more than five years without the S&P 500 falling by 20 per cent, in which case he makes $15 million even if no new money comes into his fund, and even without leveraging his positions.[107]

Could an LTCM-style crisis replay itself today, ten years on – only this time on such a scale, and involving so many such bogus hedge funds, that it would simply be too big to bail out? Are the banks of the Western world now even more exposed to hedge fund losses, and related counterparty risks, than they were in 1998?*

---

* It is surely no coincidence that it was reports of losses at hedge funds run by Bear Stearns and by Goldman Sachs that signalled the onset of the credit crunch in the summer of 2007.

And, if they are, then who will bail them out this time around? The answers to those questions lie not on another planet, but on the other side of this one.

Chimerica

To many, financial history is just so much water under the bridge – ancient history, like the history of imperial China. Markets have short memories. Many young traders today did not even experience the Asian crisis of 1997–8. Those who went into finance after 2000 lived through seven heady years. Stock markets the world over boomed. So did bond markets, commodity markets and derivatives markets. In fact, so did all asset classes – not to mention those that benefit when bonuses are big, from vintage Bordeaux to luxury yachts. But these boom years were also mystery years, when markets soared at a time of rising short-term interest rates, glaring trade imbalances and soaring political risk, particularly in the economically crucial, oil-exporting regions of the world. The key to this seeming paradox lay in China.[108]

Chongqing, on the undulating banks of the mighty earth-brown River Yangtze, is deep in the heart of the Middle Kingdom, over a thousand miles from the coastal enterprise zones most Westerners visit. Yet the province's 32 million inhabitants are as much caught up in today's economic miracle as those in Hong Kong or Shanghai. At one level, the breakneck industrialization and urbanization going on in Chongqing are the last and greatest feat of the Communist planned economy. The thirty bridges, the ten light railways, the countless towerblocks all appear through the smog like monuments to the power of the centralized one-party state. Yet the growth of Chongqing is also the result of unfettered private enterprise. In many ways, Wu Yajun is the personification of China's newfound wealth. As one of Chong-qing's leading property developers, she is among the wealthiest women in China, worth over $9 billion – the living antithesis of those Scotsmen who made their fortunes in Hong Kong a century ago. Or take Yin Mingsha. Imprisoned during the Cultural Revolution, Mr Yin discovered his true vocation in the early 1990s, after the liberalization of the Chinese economy. In just fifteen years he has built up a $900 million business. Last year his Lifan company sold more than 1.5 million motorcycle engines and bikes; now he is exporting to the United States and Europe. Wu and Yin are just two of more than 345,000 dollar millionaires who now live in China.

Not only has China left its imperial past far behind. So far, the fastest growing economy in the world has also managed to avoid the kind of crisis that has periodically blown up other emerging markets. Having already devalued the renminbi in 1994, and having retained capital controls throughout the period of economic reform, China suffered no currency crisis in 1997–8. When the Chinese wanted to attract foreign capital, they insisted that it take the form of direct investment. That meant that instead of borrowing from Western banks to finance their industrial development, as many other emerging markets did, they got foreigners to build factories in Chinese enterprise zones – large, lumpy assets that could not easily be withdrawn in a crisis. The crucial point, though, is that the bulk of Chinese investment has been financed from China's own savings (and from the overseas Chinese diaspora). Cautious after years of instability and unused to the panoply of credit facilities we have in the West, Chinese households save an unusually high proportion of their rising incomes, in marked contrast to Americans, who in recent years have saved almost none at all. Chinese corporations save an even larger proportion of their soaring profits. So plentiful are savings that, for the first time in centuries, the direction of capital flow is now not from West to East, but from East to West. And it is a mighty flow. In 2007, the United States needed to borrow around $800 billion from the rest of the world; more than $4 billion every working day. China, by contrast, ran a current account surplus of $262 billion, equivalent to more than a quarter of the US deficit. And a remarkably large proportion of that surplus has ended up being lent to the United States. In effect, the People's Republic China has become banker to the United States of America.

At first sight, it may seem bizarre. Today the average American earns more than $34,000 a year. Despite the wealth of people like Wu Yajun and Yin Mingsha, the average Chinese lives on less than $2,000. Why would the latter want, in effect, to lend money to the former, who is twenty-two times richer? The answer is that, until recently, the best way for China to employ its vast population was through exporting manufactures to the insatiably spendthrift US consumer. To ensure that those exports were irresistibly cheap, China had to fight the tendency for the Chinese currency to strengthen against the dollar by buying literally billions of dollars on world markets – part of a system of Asian currency pegs that some commentators dubbed Bretton Woods II.[109] In 2006 Chinese holdings of dollars almost certainly passed the trillion dollar mark. (Significantly, the net increase of China's foreign exchange reserves almost exactly matched the net issuance of US Treasury and government agency bonds.) From America's point of view, meanwhile, the best way of keeping the good times rolling in recent years has been to import cheap Chinese goods. More-over, by out-sourcing manufacturing to China, US corporations have been able to reap the benefits of cheap labour too. And, crucially, by selling billions of dollars of bonds to the People's Bank

Net national savings as a percentage of gross national income, 1970–2006

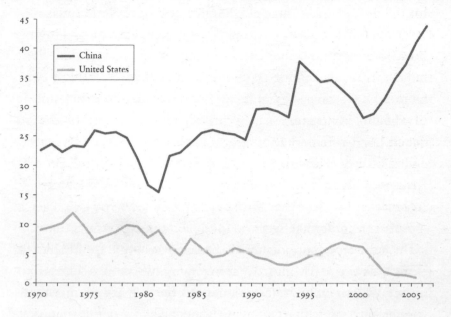

of China, the United States has been able to enjoy significantly lower interest rates than would otherwise have been the case.

Welcome to the wonderful dual country of 'Chimerica' – China plus America – which accounts for just over a tenth of the world's land surface, a quarter of its population, a third of its economic output and more than half of global economic growth in the past eight years. For a time it seemed like a marriage made in heaven. The East Chimericans did the saving. The West Chimericans did the spending. Chinese imports kept down US inflation. Chinese savings kept down US interest rates. Chinese labour kept down US wage costs. As a result, it was remarkably cheap to borrow money and remarkably profitable to run a corporation. Thanks to Chimerica, global real interest rates – the cost of borrowing, after inflation – sank by more than a third below their average over the past fifteen years. Thanks to Chimerica, US corporate profits in 2006 rose by about the same proportion above their average share of GDP. But there was a catch. The more China was willing to lend to the United States, the more Americans were willing to borrow. Chimerica, in other words, was the underlying cause of the surge in bank lending, bond issuance and new derivative contracts that Planet Finance witnessed after 2000. It was the underlying cause of the hedge fund population explosion. It was the underlying reason why private equity partnerships were able to borrow money left, right and centre to finance leveraged buyouts. And Chimerica – or the Asian 'savings glut', as Ben Bernanke called it[110] – was the underlying reason why the US mortgage market was so awash with cash in 2006 that you could get a 100 per cent mortgage with no income, no job or assets.

The subprime mortgage crisis of 2007 was not so difficult to predict, as we have already seen. What was much harder to predict was the way a tremor caused by a spate of mortgage defaults in America's very own, home-grown emerging market would cause a financial earthquake right across the Western financial system. Not many people understood that defaults on subprime mortgages would destroy the value of exotic new asset-backed instruments like collateralized debt obligations. Not many people saw that, as the magnitude of these losses soared, interbank lending would simply seize up, and that the interest rates charged to issuers of short-term commercial paper and corporate bonds would leap upwards, leading to a painful squeeze for all kinds of private sector borrowers. Not many people foresaw that this credit crunch would cause a British bank to suffer the first run since 1866 and end up being nationalized. Back in July 2007, before the trouble started, one American hedge fund manager had bet me 7 to 1 that there would be no recession in the United States in the next five years. 'I bet that the world wasn't going to come to an end,' he admitted six months later. 'We lost.' Certainly, by the end of May 2008, a US recession seemed already to have begun. But the end of the world?

True, it seemed unlikely in May 2008 that China (to say nothing of the other BRICs) would be left wholly unscathed by an American recession. The United States remains China's biggest trading partner, accounting for around a fifth of Chinese exports. On the other hand, the importance of net exports to Chinese growth has declined considerably in recent years.[111] Moreover, Chinese reserve accumulation has put Beijing in the powerful position of being able to offer capital injections to struggling American banks. The rise of the hedge funds was only a part of the story of the post-1998 reorientation of global finance. Even more important was the growth of sovereign wealth funds, entities created by countries running large trade surpluses to manage their accumulating wealth. By the end of 2007 sovereign wealth funds had around $2.6 trillion under management, more than all the world's hedge funds, and not far behind government pension funds and central bank reserves. According to a forecast by Morgan Stanley, within fifteen years they could end up with assets of $27 trillion – just over 9 per cent of total global financial assets. Already in 2007, Asian and Middle Eastern sovereign wealth funds had moved to invest in Western financial companies, including Barclays, Bear Stearns, Citigroup, Merrill Lynch, Morgan Stanley, UBS and the private equity firms Blackstone and Carlyle. For a time it seemed as if the sovereign wealth funds might orchestrate a global bail-out of Western finance; the ultimate role reversal in financial history. For the proponents of what George Soros has disparaged as 'market fundamentalism', here was a painful anomaly: among the biggest winners of the latest crisis were state-owned entities.*

* Some sovereign wealth funds in fact have a relatively long history. The Kuwait Investment Authority was set up in 1953; Singapore's Temasek in 1974; ADIA, the United Arab Emirates' fund, in 1976; Singapore's GIC in 1981.

And yet there are reasons why this seemingly elegant, and quintessentially Chimerican, resolution of the American crisis has failed to happen. Part of the reason is simply that the initial Chinese forays into US financial stocks have produced less than stellar results.* There are justifiable fears in Beijing that the worst may be yet to come for Western banks, especially given the unknowable impact of a US recession on outstanding credit default swaps with a notional value of $62 trillion. But there is also a serious political tension now detectable at the very heart of Chimerica. For some time, concern has been mounting in the US Congress about what is seen as unfair competition and currency manipulation by China, and the worse the recession gets in the United States, the louder the complaints are likely to grow. Yet US monetary loosening since August 2007 – the steep cuts in the federal funds and discount rates, the various auction and lending 'facilities' that have directed $150 billion to the banking system, the underwriting of JP Morgan's acquisition of Bear Stearns – has amounted to an American version of currency manipulation.[112] Since the onset of the American crisis, the dollar has depreciated roughly 25 per cent against the currencies of its major trading partners, including 9 per cent against the renminbi. Because this has coincided with simultaneous demand and supply pressures in nearly all markets for commodities, the result has been a significant spike in the prices of food, fuel and raw materials. Rising commodity prices, in turn, are intensifying inflationary pressures for China, necessitating the imposition of

* Having paid $5 billion for a 9.9 per cent stake in Morgan Stanley in December 2007, the China Investment Corporation's chairman Lou Jiwei compared the opportunity to a rabbit appearing in front of a farmer. 'If we see a big fat rabbit,' he said, 'we will shoot at it.' But he added (referring to the subsequent decline in Morgan Stanley's share price), 'Some people may say we were shot by Morgan Stanley.'

price controls and export prohibitions and encouraging an extra-ordinary scramble for natural resources in Africa and elsewhere that, to Western eyes, has an unnervingly imperial undertone.[113] Maybe, as its name was always intended to hint, Chimerica is nothing more than a chimera – the mythical beast of ancient legend that was part lion, part goat, part dragon.

Perhaps, on reflection, we have been here before. A hundred years ago, in the first age of globalization, many investors thought there was a similarly symbiotic relationship between the world's financial centre, Britain, and continental Europe's most dynamic industrial economy. That economy was Germany's. Then, as today, there was a fine line between symbiosis and rivalry.[114] Could anything trigger another breakdown of globalization like the one that happened in 1914? The obvious answer is a deterior-ation of political relations between the United States and China, whether over trade, Taiwan, Tibet or some other as yet subliminal issue.[115] The scenario may seem implausible. Yet it is easy to see how future historians could retrospectively construct plausible chains of causation to explain such a turn of events. The advo-cates of 'war guilt' would blame a more assertive China, leaving others to lament the sins of omission of a weary American titan. Scholars of international relations would no doubt identify the systemic origins of the war in the breakdown of free trade, the competition for natural resources or the clash of civilizations. Couched in the language of historical explanation, a major con-flagration can start to seem unnervingly probable in our time, just as it turned out to be in 1914. Some may even be tempted to say that the surge of commodity prices in the period from 2003 until 2008 reflected some unconscious market anticipation of the coming conflict.

One important lesson of history is that major wars can arise even when economic globalization is very far advanced and the hegemonic position of an English-speaking empire seems fairly secure. A second important lesson is that the longer the world goes without a major conflict, the harder one becomes to imagine (and, perhaps, the easier one becomes to start). A third and final lesson is that when a crisis strikes complacent investors it causes much more disruption than when it strikes battle-scarred ones. As we have seen repeatedly, the really big crises come just seldom enough to be beyond the living memory of today's bank executives, fund managers and traders. The average career of a Wall Street CEO is just over twenty-five years,[116] which means that first-hand memories at the top of the US banking system do not extend back beyond 1983 – ten years after the beginning of the last great surge in oil and gold prices. That fact alone provides a powerful justification for the study of financial history.

Afterword:
The Descent of Money

Today's financial world is the result of four millennia of economic evolution. Money – the crystallized relationship between debtor and creditor – begat banks, clearing houses for ever larger aggregations of borrowing and lending. From the thirteenth century onwards, government bonds introduced the securitization of streams of interest payments; while bond markets revealed the benefits of regulated public markets for trading and pricing securities. From the seventeenth century, equity in corporations could be bought and sold in similar ways. From the eighteenth century, insurance funds and then pension funds exploited economies of scale and the laws of averages to provide financial protection against calculable risk. From the nineteenth, futures and options offered more specialized and sophisticated instruments: the first derivatives. And, from the twentieth, households were encouraged, for political reasons, to increase leverage and skew their portfolios in favour of real estate.

Economics that combined all these institutional innovations – banks, bond markets, stock markets, insurance and property-owning democracy – performed better over the long run than those that did not, because financial intermediation generally permits a more efficient allocation of resources than, say, feudalism or central planning. For this reason, it is not wholly surprising that the Western financial model tended to spread around the world, first in the guise of imperialism, then in the guise of globalization.[1] From ancient Mesopotamia to present-day China, in short, the ascent of money has been one of the driving forces behind human progress: a complex process of innovation, intermediation and integration that has been as vital as the advance of science or the spread of law in mankind's escape from the drudgery of subsistence agriculture and the misery of the Malthusian trap. In the words of former Federal Reserve Governor Frederic Mishkin, 'the financial system [is] the brain of the economy . . . It acts as a coordinating mechanism that allocates capital, the lifeblood of economic activity, to its most productive uses by businesses and households. If capital goes to the wrong uses or does not flow at all, the economy will operate inefficiently, and ultimately economic growth will be low.'[2]

Yet money's ascent has not been, and can never be, a smooth one. On the contrary, financial history is a roller-coaster ride of ups and downs, bubbles and busts, manias and panics, shocks and crashes.[3] One recent study of the available data for gross domestic product and consumption since 1870 has identified 148 crises in which a country experienced a cumulative decline in GDP of at least 10 per cent and eighty-seven crises in which consumption suffered a fall of comparable magnitude, implying a probability of financial disaster of around 3.6 per cent per year.[4] Even today, despite the unprecedented sophistication of our institutions and instruments, Planet Finance remains as vulnerable as ever to crises. It seems that, for all our ingenuity, we are doomed to be 'fooled by randomness'[5] and surprised by 'black swans'.[6] It may even be that we are living through the deflation of a multi-decade 'super bubble'.[7]

There are three fundamental reasons for this. The first is that so much about the future – or, rather, futures, since there is never a singular future – lies in the realm of uncertainty, as opposed to calculable risk. As Frank Knight argued in 1921, 'Uncertainty must be taken in a sense radically distinct from the familiar notion of Risk, from which it has never been properly separated ... A *measurable* uncertainty, or "risk" proper ... is so far different from an *unmeasurable* one that it is not in effect an uncertainty at all.' To put it simply, much of what happens in life isn't like a game of dice. Again and again an event will occur that is 'so entirely unique that there are no others or not a sufficient number to make it possible to tabulate enough like it to form a basis for any inference of value about any real probability ...'[8] The same point was brilliantly expressed by Keynes in 1937. 'By "uncertain" knowledge,' he wrote in a response to critics of his *General Theory*,

... I do not mean merely to distinguish what is known for certain from what is only probable. The game of roulette is not subject, in this sense, to uncertainty ... The expectation of life is only slightly uncertain. Even the weather is only moderately uncertain. The sense in which I am using the term is that in which the prospect of a European war is uncertain, or ... the rate of interest twenty years hence ... About these matters there is no scientific basis on which to form any calculable probability whatever. We simply do not know.*

Keynes went on to hypothesize about the ways in which investors 'manage in such circumstances to behave in a manner which saves our faces as rational, economic men':

* As Peter Bernstein has said, 'We pour in data from the past ... but past data ... constitute a sequence of events rather than a set of independent observations, which is what the laws of probability demand. History provides us with only one sample of the ... capital markets, not with thousands of separate and randomly distributed numbers.' The same problem – that the sample size is effectively one – is of course inherent in geology, a more advanced historical science than financial history, as Larry Neal has observed.

(1) We assume that the present is a much more serviceable guide to the future than a candid examination of past experience would show it to have been hitherto. In other words we largely ignore the prospect of future changes about the actual character of which we know nothing.

(2) We assume that the *existing* state of opinion as expressed in prices and the character of existing output is based on a *correct* summing up of future prospects . . .

(3) Knowing that our own individual judgment is worthless, we endeavor to fall back on the judgment of the rest of the world which is perhaps better informed. That is, we endeavor to conform with the behavior of the majority or the average.[9]

Though it is far from clear that Keynes was correct in his interpretation of investors' behaviour, he was certainly thinking along the right lines. For there is no question that the heuristic biases of individuals play a critical role in generating volatility in financial markets.

This brings us to the second reason for the inherent instability of the financial system: human behaviour. As we have seen, all financial institutions are at the mercy of our innate inclination to veer from euphoria to despondency; our recurrent inability to protect ourselves against 'tail risk'; our perennial failure to learn from history. In a famous article, Daniel Kahneman and Amos Tversky demonstrated with a series of experiments the tendency that people have to miscalculate probabilities when confronted with simple financial choices. First, they gave their sample group 1,000 Israeli pounds each. Then they offered them a choice between either a) a 50 per cent chance of winning an additional 1,000 pounds or b) a 100 per cent chance of winning an additional 500 pounds. Only 16 per cent of people chose a); everyone else (84 per cent) chose b). Next, they asked the same group to imagine having received 2,000 Israeli pounds each and confronted them with another choice: between either c) a 50 per cent chance of losing 1,000 pounds or b) a 100 per cent chance of losing 500 pounds. This time the majority (69 per cent) chose a); only 31 per cent chose b). Yet, viewed in terms of their payoffs, the two problems are identical. In both cases you have a choice between a 50 per cent chance of ending up with 1,000 pounds and an equal chance of ending up with 2,000 pounds (a and c) or a certainty of ending up with 1,500 pounds (b and d). In this and other experiments, Kahneman and Tversky identify a striking asymmetry: risk aversion for positive prospects, but risk seeking for negative ones. A loss has about two and a half times the impact of a gain of the same magnitude.[10]

This 'failure of invariance' is only one of many heuristic biases (skewed modes of thinking or learning) that distinguish real human beings from the *homo oeconomicus* of neoclassical economic theory, who is supposed to make his decisions rationally, on the basis of all the available information and his expected utility. Other experiments show that we also succumb too readily to such cognitive traps as:

1. *Availability bias*, which causes us to base decisions on information that is more readily available in our memories, rather than the data we really need;
2. *Hindsight bias*, which causes us to attach higher probabilities to events after they have happened (*ex post*) than we did before they happened (*ex ante*);
3. *The problem of induction*, which leads us to formulate general rules on the basis of insufficient information;
4. *The fallacy of conjunction* (or disjunction), which means we tend to overestimate the probability that seven events of 90 per cent probability will *all* occur, while underestimating

the probability that *at least one* of seven events of 10 per cent probability will occur;

5. *Confirmation bias*, which inclines us to look for confirming evidence of an initial hypothesis, rather than falsifying evidence that would disprove it;

6. *Contamination effects*, whereby we allow irrelevant but proximate information to influence a decision;

7. *The affect heuristic*, whereby preconceived value-judgements interfere with our assessment of costs and benefits;

8. *Scope neglect*, which prevents us from proportionately adjusting what we should be willing to sacrifice to avoid harms of different orders of magnitude;

9. *Overconfidence in calibration*, which leads us to underestimate the confidence intervals within which our estimates will be robust (e.g. to conflate the 'best case' scenario with the 'most probable'); and

10. *Bystander apathy*, which inclines us to abdicate individual responsibility when in a crowd.[11]

If you still doubt the hard-wired fallibility of human beings, ask yourself the following question. A bat and ball, together, cost a total of £1.10 and the bat costs £1 more than the ball. How much is the ball? The wrong answer is the one that roughly one in every two people blurts out: 10 pence. The correct answer is 5 pence, since only with a bat worth £1.05 and a ball worth 5 pence are both conditions satisfied.[12]

If any field has the potential to revolutionize our understanding of the way financial markets work, it must surely be the burgeoning discipline of behavioural finance.[13] It is far from clear how much of the body of work derived from the efficient markets hypothesis can survive this challenge.[14] Those who put their faith in the 'wisdom of crowds'[15] mean no more than that a large group of people is more likely to make a correct assessment than a small group of supposed experts. But that is not saying much. The old joke that 'Macroeconomists have successfully predicted nine of the last five recessions' is not so much a joke as a dispiriting truth about the difficulty of economic forecasting.[16] Meanwhile, serious students of human psychology will expect as much madness as wisdom from large groups of people.[17] A case in point must be the near-universal delusion among investors in the first half of 2007 that a major liquidity crisis could not occur (see Introduction). To adapt an elegant summation by Eliezer Yudkowsky:

People may be overconfident and over-optimistic. They may focus on overly specific scenarios for the future, to the exclusion of all others. They may not recall any past [liquidity crises] in memory. They may overestimate the predictability of the past, and hence underestimate the surprise of the future. They may not realize the difficulty of preparing for [liquidity crises] without the benefit of hindsight. They may prefer . . . gambles with higher payoff probabilities, neglecting the value of the stakes. They may conflate positive information about the benefits of a technology [e.g. bond insurance] and negative information about its risks. They may be contaminated by movies where the [financial system] ends up being saved . . . Or the extremely unpleasant prospect of [a liquidity crisis] may spur them to seek arguments that [liquidity] will *not* [dry up], without an equally frantic search for reasons why [it should]. But if the question is, specifically, 'Why aren't more people doing something about it?', one possible component is that people are asking that very question – darting their eyes around to see if anyone else is reacting . . . meanwhile trying to appear poised and unflustered.[18]

Most of our cognitive warping is, of course, the result of evolution. The third reason for the erratic path of financial history is also related to the theory of evolution, though by analogy. It is commonly said that finance has a Darwinian quality. 'The survival of the fittest' is a phrase that aggressive traders like to use; as we have seen, investment banks like to hold conferences with titles like 'The Evolution of Excellence'. But the American crisis of 2007 has increased the frequency of such language. US Assistant Secretary of the Treasury Anthony W. Ryan was not the only person to talk in terms of a wave of financial extinctions in the second half of 2007. Andrew Lo, director of the Massachusetts Institute of Technology's Laboratory for Financial Engineering, is in the vanguard of an effort to re-conceptualize markets as adaptive systems.[19] A long-run historical analysis of the development of financial services also suggests that evolutionary forces are present in the financial world as much as they are in the natural world.[20]

The notion that Darwinian processes may be at work in the economy is not new, of course. Evolutionary economics is in fact a well-established sub-discipline, which has had its own dedicated journal for the past sixteen years.[21] Thorstein Veblen first posed the question 'Why is Economics Not an Evolutionary Science?' (implying that it really should be) as long ago as 1898.[22] In a famous passage in his *Capitalism, Socialism and Democracy*, which could equally well apply to finance, Joseph Schumpeter characterized industrial capitalism as 'an evolutionary process':

This evolutionary character ... is not merely due to the fact that economic life goes on in a social and natural environment which changes and by its change alters the data of economic action; this fact is important and these changes (wars, revolutions and so on) often condition industrial change, but they are not its prime movers. Nor is this evolutionary character due to quasi-autonomic increase in population and capital or to the vagaries of monetary systems of which exactly the same thing holds true. The fundamental impulse that sets and keeps the capitalist engine in motion comes from the new consumers' goods, the new methods of production or transportation, the new markets, the new forms of industrial organization that capitalist enterprise creates . . . The opening up of new markets, foreign or domestic, and the organizational development from the craft shop and factory to such concerns as US Steel illustrate the same process of industrial mutation – if I may use the biological term – that incessantly revolutionizes the economic structure *from within*, incessantly destroying the old one, incessantly creating a new one. This process of Creative Destruction is the essential fact about capitalism.[23]

A key point that emerges from recent research is just how much destruction goes on in a modern economy. Around one in ten US companies disappears each year. Between 1989 and 1997, to be precise, an average of 611,000 businesses a year vanished out of a total of 5.73 million firms. Ten per cent is the average extinction rate, it should be noted; in some sectors of the economy it can rise as high as 20 per cent in a bad year (as in the District of Columbia's financial sector in 1989, at the height of the Savings and Loans crisis).[24] According to the UK Department of Trade and Industry, 30 per cent of tax-registered businesses disappear after three years.[25] Even if they survive the first few years of existence and go on to enjoy great success, most firms fail eventually. Of the world's 100 largest companies in 1912, 29 were bankrupt by 1995, 48 had disappeared, and only 19 were still in the top 100.[26] Given that a good deal of what banks and stock markets do is to provide finance to companies, we should not be surprised to find a similar pattern of creative destruction in the financial world. We have already noted the high attrition rate among hedge funds. (The only reason that more banks do not fail, as we shall see, is that they are explicitly and implicitly protected from collapse by governments.)

What are the common features shared by the financial world and a true evolutionary system? Six spring to mind:

- 'Genes', in the sense that certain business practices perform the same role as genes in biology, allowing information to be stored in the 'organizational memory' and passed on from individual to individual or from firm to firm when a new firm is created.
- The potential for spontaneous mutation, usually referred to in the economic world as innovation and primarily, though by no means always, technological.
- Competition between individuals within a species for resources, with the outcomes in terms of longevity and proliferation determining which business practices persist.
- A mechanism for natural selection through the market allocation of capital and human resources and the possibility of death in cases of under-performance, i.e. 'differential survival'.
- Scope for speciation, sustaining biodiversity through the creation of wholly new species of financial institutions.
- Scope for extinction, with species dying out altogether.

Financial history is essentially the result of institutional mutation and natural selection. Random 'drift' (innovations/mutations that are not promoted by natural selection, but just happen) and 'flow' (innovations/mutations that are caused when, say, American practices are adopted by Chinese banks) play a part. There can also be 'co-evolution', when different financial species work and adapt together (like hedge funds and their prime brokers). But market selection is the main driver. Financial organisms are in competition with one another for finite resources. At certain times and in certain places, certain species may become dominant. But innovations by competitor species, or the emergence of altogether new species, prevent any permanent hierarchy or monoculture from emerging. Broadly speaking, the law of the survival of the fittest applies. Institutions with a 'selfish gene' that is good at self-replication and self-perpetuation will tend to proliferate and endure.[27]

Note that this may not result in the evolution of the perfect organism. A 'good enough' mutation will achieve dominance if it happens in the right place at the right time, because of the sensitivity of the evolutionary process to initial conditions; that is, an initial slim advantage may translate into a prolonged period of dominance, without necessarily being optimal. It is also worth bearing in mind that in the natural world, evolution is not progressive, as used to be thought (notably by the followers of Herbert Spencer). Primitive financial life-forms like loan sharks are not condemned to oblivion, any more than the microscopic prokaryotes that still account for the majority of earth's species. Evolved complexity protects neither an organism nor a firm against extinction – the fate of most animal and plant species.

The evolutionary analogy is, admittedly, imperfect. When one organism ingests another in the natural world, it is just eating; whereas, in the world of financial services, mergers and acquisitions can lead directly to mutation. Among financial organisms, there is no counterpart to the role of sexual reproduction in the animal world (though demotic sexual language is often used to describe certain kinds of financial transaction). Most financial mutation is deliberate, conscious innovation, rather than random change. Indeed, because a firm can adapt within its own lifetime to change going on around it, financial evolution (like cultural evolution) may be more Lamarckian than Darwinian in character. Two other key differences will be discussed below.

Nevertheless, evolution certainly offers a better model for under-standing financial change than any other we have.

Ninety years ago, the German socialist Rudolf Hilferding pre-dicted an inexorable movement towards more concentration of ownership in what he termed finance capital.[28] The conventional view of financial development does indeed see the process from the vantage point of the big, successful survivor firm. In Citi-group's official family tree, numerous small firms – dating back to the City Bank of New York, founded in 1812 – are seen to converge over time on a common trunk, the present-day conglom-erate. However, this is precisely the wrong way to think about financial evolution over the long run, which *begins* at a common trunk. Periodically, the trunk branches outwards as new kinds of bank and other financial institution evolve. The fact that a particular firm successfully devours smaller firms along the way is more or less irrelevant. In the evolutionary process, animals eat one another, but that is not the driving force behind evolutionary mutation and the emergence of new species and sub-species. The point is that economies of scale and scope are not always the driving force in financial history. More often, the real drivers are the process of speciation – whereby entirely new types of firm are created – and the equally recurrent process of creative destruc-tion, whereby weaker firms die out.

Take the case of retail and commercial banking, where there remains considerable biodiversity. Although giants like Citigroup and Bank of America exist, North America and some European markets still have relatively fragmented retail banking sectors. The cooperative banking sector has seen the most change in recent years, with high levels of consolidation (especially following the Savings and Loans crisis of the 1980s), and most institutions moving to shareholder ownership. But the only species that is now close to extinction in the developed world is the state-owned bank, as privatization has swept the world (though the nationaliz-ation of Northern Rock suggests the species could make a come-back). In other respects, the story is one of speciation, the proliferation of new types of financial institution, which is just what we would expect in a truly evolutionary system. Many new 'mono-line' financial services firms have emerged, especially in consumer finance (for example, Capital One). A number of new 'boutiques' now exist to cater to the private banking market. Direct banking (telephone and Internet) is another relatively recent and growing phenomenon. Likewise, even as giants have formed in the realm of investment banking, new and nimbler species such as hedge funds and private equity partnerships have evolved and proliferated. And, as we saw in Chapter 6, the rapidly accruing hard currency reserves of exporters of manufactured goods and energy are producing a new generation of sovereign wealth funds.

Not only are new forms of financial firm proliferating; so too are new forms of financial asset and service. In recent years, investors' appetite has grown dramatically for mortgage-backed and other asset-backed securities. The use of derivatives has also increased enormously, with the majority being bought and sold 'over the counter', on a one-to-one bespoke basis, rather than through public exchanges – a tendency which, though profitable for the sellers of derivatives, may have unpleasant as well as unintended consequences because of the lack of standardization of these instruments and the potential for legal disputes in the event of a crisis.

In evolutionary terms, then, the financial services sector appears to have passed through a twenty-year Cambrian explosion, with existing species flourishing and new species increasing in number. As in the natural world, the existence of giants has not precluded the evolution and continued existence of smaller species. Size isn't everything, in finance as in nature. Indeed, the very difficulties that arise as publicly owned firms become larger and more complex – the diseconomies of scale associated with bureaucracy, the pressures associated with quarterly reporting – give opportunities to new forms of private firm. What matters in evolution is not your size or (beyond a certain level) your complexity. All that matters is that you are good at surviving and reproducing your genes. The financial equivalent is being good at generating returns on equity and generating imitators employing a similar business model.

In the financial world, mutation and speciation have usually been evolved responses to the environment and competition, with natural selection determining which new traits become widely disseminated. Sometimes, as in the natural world, the evolutionary process has been subject to big disruptions in the form of geopolitical shocks and financial crises. The difference is, of course, that whereas giant asteroids (like the one that eliminated 85 per cent of species at the end of the Cretaceous period) are exogenous shocks, financial crises are endogenous to the financial system. The Great Depression of the 1930s and the Great Inflation of the 1970s stand out as times of major discontinuity, with 'mass extinctions' such as the bank panics of the 1930s and the Savings and Loans failures of the 1980s.

Could something similar be happening in our time? Certainly, the sharp deterioration in credit conditions in the summer of 2007 created acute problems for many hedge funds, leaving them vulnerable to redemptions by investors. But a more important feature of the recent credit crunch has been the pressure on banks and insurance companies. Losses on asset-backed securities and other forms of risky debt are thought likely to be in excess of $1 trillion. At the time of writing (May 2008), around $318 billion of write-downs (booked losses) have been acknowledged, which means that more than $600 billion of losses have yet to come to light. Since the onset of the crisis, financial institutions have raised around $225 billion of new capital, leaving a shortfall of slightly less than $100 billion. Since banks typically target a constant capital/assets ratio of less than 10 per cent, that implies that balance sheets may need to be shrunk by as much as $1 trillion. However, the collapse of the so-called shadow banking system of off-balance-sheet entities such as structured investment vehicles and conduits is making that contraction very difficult indeed.

It remains to be seen whether the major Western banks can navigate their way through this crisis without a fundamental change to the international accords (Basel I and II)* governing capital adequacy. In Europe, for example, average bank capital is now equivalent to significantly less than 10 per cent of assets (perhaps as little as 4), compared with around 25 per cent towards the beginning of the twentieth century. The 2007 crisis has dashed the hopes of those who believed that the separation of risk origination and balance sheet management would distribute risk optimally throughout the financial system. It seems inconceivable that this crisis will pass without further mergers and acquisitions, as the relatively strong devour the relatively weak. Bond insurance companies seem destined to disappear. Some hedge funds,

---

* Under the Basel I rules agreed in 1988, assets of banks are divided into five categories according to credit risk, carrying risk weights ranging from zero (for example, home country government bonds) to 100 per cent (corporate debt). International banks are required to hold capital equal to 8 per cent of their risk-weighted assets. Basel II, first published in 2004 but only gradually being adopted around the world, sets out more complex rules, distinguishing between credit risk, operational risk and market risk, the last of which mandates the use of value at risk (VaR) models. Ironically, in the light of 2007–8, liquidity risk is combined with other risks under the heading 'residual risk'. Such rules inevitably conflict with the incentive all banks have to minimize their capital and hence raise their return on equity.

by contrast, are likely to thrive on the return of volatility.* It also seems likely that new forms of financial institution will spring up in the aftermath of the crisis. As Andrew Lo has suggested: 'As with past forest fires in the markets, we're likely to see incredible flora and fauna springing up in its wake.'[29]

There is another big difference between nature and finance. Whereas evolution in biology takes place in the natural environment, where change is essentially random (hence Richard Dawkins's image of the blind watchmaker), evolution in financial services occurs within a regulatory framework where – to borrow a phrase from anti-Darwinian creationists – 'intelligent design' plays a part. Sudden changes to the regulatory environment are rather different from sudden changes in the macroeconomic environment, which are analogous to environmental changes in the natural world. The difference is once again that there is an element of endogeneity in regulatory changes, since those responsible are often poachers turned gamekeepers, with a good insight into the way that the private sector works. The net effect, however, is similar to climate change on biological evolution. New rules and regulations can make previously good traits suddenly disadvantageous. The rise and fall of Savings and Loans, for example, was due in large measure to changes in the regulatory environment in the United States. Regulatory changes in the wake of the 2007 crisis may have comparably unforeseen consequences.

The stated intention of most regulators is to maintain stability within the financial services sector, thereby protecting the consumers whom banks serve and the 'real' economy which the

* In Andrew Lo's words: 'Hedge funds are the Galapagos Islands of finance ... The rate of innovation, evolution, competition, adaptation, births and deaths, the whole range of evolutionary phenomena, occurs at an extraordinarily rapid clip.'

industry supports. Companies in non-financial industries are seen as less systemically important to the economy as a whole and less critical to the livelihood of the consumer. The collapse of a major financial institution, in which retail customers lose their deposits, is therefore an event which any regulator (and politician) wishes to avoid at all costs. An old question that has raised its head since August 2007 is how far implicit guarantees to bail out banks create a problem of moral hazard, encouraging excessive risk-taking on the assumption that the state will intervene to avert illiquidity and even insolvency if an institution is considered too big to fail – meaning too politically sensitive or too likely to bring a lot of other firms down with it. From an evolutionary perspective, however, the problem looks slightly different. It may, in fact, be undesirable to have any institutions in the category of 'too big to fail', because without occasional bouts of creative destruction the evolutionary process will be thwarted. The experience of Japan in the 1990s stands as a warning to legislators and regulators that an entire banking sector can become a kind of economic dead hand if institutions are propped up despite under-performance, and bad debts are not written off.

Every shock to the financial system must result in casualties. Left to itself, natural selection should work fast to eliminate the weakest institutions in the market, which typically are gobbled up by the successful. But most crises also usher in new rules and regulations, as legislators and regulators rush to stabilize the financial system and to protect the consumer/voter. The critical point is that the possibility of extinction cannot and should not be removed by excessively precautionary rules. As Joseph Schumpeter wrote more than seventy years ago, 'This economic system cannot do without the *ultima ratio* of the complete destruction of those existences which are irretrievably associated with the hopelessly unadapted.' This meant, in his view, nothing less than the disappearance of 'those firms which are unfit to live'.[30]

In writing this book, I have frequently been asked if I gave it the wrong title. *The Ascent of Money* may seem to sound an incongruously optimistic note (especially to those who miss the allusion to Bronowski's *Ascent of Man*) at a time when a surge of inflation and a flight into commodities seem to signal a literal descent in public esteem and purchasing power of fiat moneys like the dollar. Yet it should by now be obvious to the reader just how far our financial system has ascended since its distant origins among the moneylenders of Mesopotamia. There have been great reverses, contractions and dyings, to be sure. But not even the worst has set us permanently back. Though the line of financial history has a saw-tooth quality, its trajectory is unquestionably upwards.

Still, I might equally well have paid homage to Charles Darwin by calling the book *The Descent of Finance*, for the story I have told is authentically evolutionary. When we withdraw banknotes from automated telling machines, or invest portions of our monthly salaries in bonds and stocks, or insure our cars, or remortgage our homes, or renounce home bias in favour of emerging markets, we are entering into transactions with many historical antecedents.

I remain more than ever convinced that, until we fully under-stand the origin of financial species, we shall never understand the fundamental truth about money: that, far from being 'a mon-ster that must be put back in its place', as the German president recently complained,[31] financial markets are like the mirror of mankind, revealing every hour of every working day the way we value ourselves and the resources of the world around us.

It is not the fault of the mirror if it reflects our blemishes as clearly as our beauty.

Acknowledgements

Though writing is a solitary activity, no book is a solo venture. I am grateful to the staff at the following archives: the Amsterdam Historical Museum; the National Library, Paris; the British Museum, London; the Cotton Museum at the Memphis Cotton Exchange; the Dutch National Archives, The Hague; the Louisiana State Museum, New Orleans; the Medici Archives, Florentine City Archive; the National Archives of Scotland, Edinburgh; the National Library, Venice; the Rothschild Archive, London; and the Scottish Widows Archive, Edinburgh. A number of scholars and librarians generously responded to my requests for assistance. In particular, I would like to thank Melanie Aspey, Tristram Clarke, Florence Groshens, Francesco Guidi-Bruscoli, Greg Lambousy, Valerie Moar, Liesbeth Strasser, Jonathan Taylor and Lodewijk Wagenaar. I have had invaluable research assistance from Andrew Novo.

Special thanks go to the select group of financial experts who agreed to be interviewed on the record: Domingo Cavallo, Joseph DiFatta, John Elick, Kenneth Griffin, William Gross, José Piñera, Lord Rothschild, Sir Evelyn de Rothschild, Richard Scruggs, George Soros, George Stevenson, Carmen Velasco, Paul Volcker, Sherron Watkins and Robert Zoellick. I have also learned much from informal conversations with participants at events organized by Morgan Stanley and GLG Partners.

This is a Penguin book on both sides of the Atlantic. In New York it was a pleasure and privilege to be edited for the first time by Ann Godoff. In London Simon Winder made sure that no unintelligible jargon made it into print. Michael Page did a superb job as copy-editor. Thanks are also due to Richard Duguid, Ruth Stimson, Rosie Glaisher, Alice Dawson, Helen Fraser, Stefan McGrath, Ruth Pinkney and Penelope Vogler.

Like my last three books, *The Ascent of Money* was from its earliest inception a television series as well as a book. At Channel 4 I owe debts to Julian Bellamy, Ralph Lee, Kevin Lygo and, above all, Hamish Mykura. Our occasional tensions were always creative. At W-NET/Channel 13 in New York Stephen Segaller has been an invaluable supporter. I am especially grateful to the Channel 13 fund-raising team, led by Barbara Bantivoglio, for all their efforts. Neither series nor book could have been made without the extraordinary team of people assembled by Chimerica Media: Dewald Aukema, our peerless cinematographer, Rosalind Bentley, our researcher, Vaughan Matthews, our additional cameraman, Paul Paragon and Ronald van der Speck, our occasional sound men, Joanna Potts, our assistant producer, Vivienne Steel, our production manager, and Charlotte Wilkins, our production co-ordinator – not forgetting her predecessor Hedda Archbold. As for Melanie Fall and Adrian Pennink, my fellow Chimericans, suffice to say that without them *The Ascent of Money* would never have got off the ground.

Among the many people who helped us film the series, a number of 'fixers' went out of their way to help. My thanks go to Sergio Ballivian, Rudra Banerji, Matias de Sa Moreira, Makarena Gagliardi, Laurens Grant, Juan Harrington, Fernando Mecklenburg, Alexandra Sanchez, Tiziana Tortarolo, Khaliph Troup, Sebastiano Venturo and Eelco Vijzelaar. My friend Chris Wilson ensured that I missed no planes.

I am extremely fortunate to have in Andrew Wylie the best literary agent in the world and in Sue Ayton his counterpart in the realm of British television. My thanks also go to James Pullen and all the other staff in the London and New York offices of the Wylie Agency.

A number of historians, economists and financial practitioners generously read all or part of the manuscript in draft or discussed key issues. I would like to thank Rawi Abdelal, Ewen Cameron Watt, Richart Carty, Rafael DiTella, Mohamed El-Erian, Benjamin Friedman, Brigitte Granville, Laurence Kotlikoff, Robert Litan, George Magnus, Ian Mukherjee, Greg Peters, Richard Roberts, Emmanuel Roman, William Silber, André Stern, Lawrence Summers, Richard Sylla, Nassim Taleb, Peter Temin and

James Tisch. Needless to say, all errors of fact and interpretation that remain are my fault alone.

This book was researched and written at a time of considerable personal upheaval. Without the understanding and support of three academic institutions it would quite simply have been impossible. At Oxford University I would like to thank the Principal and Fellows of Jesus College, their counterparts at Oriel College and the librarians of the Bodleian. At the Hoover Institution, Stanford, I owe debts to John Raisian, the Director, and his excellent staff, particularly Jeff Bliss, William Bonnett, Noel Kolak, Richard Sousa, Celeste Szeto, Deborah Ventura and Dan Wilhelmi. Hoover Fellows who have helped or inspired this work include Robert Barro, Stephen Haber, Alvin Rabushka and Barry Weingast.

My biggest debts, however, are to my colleagues at Harvard. It would take much too long to thank every member of the Harvard History Department individually, so let me confine myself to those who directly contributed to this project. Charles Maier has been a constant source of inspiration and friendship. Jim Hankins offered hospitality and help in Florence. I would also like to thank David Armitage, Erez Manela, Ernest May and Daniel Sargent (now, alas, lost to Berkeley) for establishing International History as the perfect milieu for interdisciplinary historical research. Andrew Gordon and his successor James Kloppenberg have chaired the Department with exceptional skill and sensitivity. And without Janet Hatch and her staff, at least one of the three spinning plates of administration, research and teaching would have crashed to the ground.

At the Centre of European Studies I have been lucky to share space and thoughts with, among others, David Blackbourn, Patricia Craig, Paul Dzus, Patrice Higonnet, Stanley Hoffman, Maya Jasanoff, Katiana Orluc, Anna Popiel, Sandy Selesky, Cindy Skach, Michelle Weitzel and Daniel Ziblatt.

It was above all my colleagues at Harvard Business School who had to take the strain during 2006–7. First and foremost, I thank Dean Jay Light for being so kind to me at a time of crisis. But I am equally grateful to all the members of the Business and Government in the International Economy unit for tolerating my unscheduled absences, in particular Richard

ACKNOWLEDGEMENTS

Vietor, whom I left in the lurch, as well as Rawi Abdelal, Laura Alfaro, Diego Comin, Arthur Daemmrich, Rafael DiTella, Catherine Duggan, Lakshmi Iyer, Noel Maurer, David Moss, Aldo Musacchio, Forest Reinhardt, Julio Rotemberg, Debora Spar, Gunnar Trumbull, Louis Wells and Eric Werker. Zac Pelleriti has provided vital administrative assistance.

Thanks are also due to Steven Bloomfield and his colleagues at the Weatherhead Center for International Affairs; Graham Allison and everyone at the Belfer Center for Science and International Affairs; Claudia Goldin and other participants at the Workshop in Economic History; and, last but not least, Dorothy Austin and Diana Eck and all the other denizens of Lowell House.

Finally, I thank all my students on both sides of the Charles River, particularly those in my classes 10b, 1961, 1964 and 1965. I have learned from their many papers and from the countless formal and informal conversations that make working at Harvard such a joy.

In the time that this book was written, my wife Susan fought her way back from a severe accident and other reverses. To her and to our children, Felix, Freya and Lachlan, I owe the biggest debt. I only wish that I were able to repay them in a sounder currency.

Cambridge, Massachusetts, June 2008

Notes

Introduction

1. To be precise, this was the increase in per capita disposable personal income between the third quarter of 2006 and the third quarter of 2007. It has since been static, rising barely at all between March 2007 and March 2008. Data from *Economic Report of the President 2008*, table B-31: *http://www.gpoaccess.gov/eop/*.
2. Carmen DeNavas-Walt, Bernadette D. Proctor and Jessica Smith, *Income, Poverty and Health Insurance Coverage in the United States: 2006* (Washington, DC, August 2007), p. 4.
3. *We See Opportunity: Goldman Sachs 2007 Annual Report* (New York, 2008).
4. Paul Collier, *The Bottom Billion: Why the Poorest Countries Are Failing and What Can Be Done About It* (Oxford, 2007).
5. David Wessel, 'A Source of our Bubble Trouble', *Wall Street Journal*, 17 January 2008.
6. Stephen Roach, 'Special Compendium: Lyford Cay 2006', *Morgan Stanley Research* (21 November 2006), p. 4.
7. Milton Friedman and Anna J. Schwartz, *A Monetary History of the United States, 1867–1960* (Princeton, 1963).
8. Princeton Survey Research Associates International, prepared for the National Foundation for Credit Counseling, 'Financial Literacy Survey', 19 April 2007: *http://www.nfcc.org/NFCC_Summary Report_ToplineFinal.pdf*.

9. Alexander R. Konrad, 'Finance Basics Elude Citizens', *Harvard Crimson*, 2 February 2008.

10. Associated Press, 'Teens Still Lack Financial Literacy, Survey Finds', 5 April, 2006: *http://www.msnbc.msn.com/id/12168872/*.

1. Dreams of Avarice

1. 'A World without Money', *Socialist Standard* (July 1979). The passage was a translated extract from 'Les Amis de Quatre Millions de Jeune Travailleurs', *Un Monde sans Argent: Le Communisme* (Paris, 1975–6): *http://www.geocities.com/~johngray/stanmond.htm*.

2. Indeed, Marx and Engels had themselves recommended not the abolition of money but 'Centralization of credit in the hands of the state, by means of a national bank with state capital and an exclusive monopoly': clause 5 of *The Communist Manifesto*.

3. Juan Forero, 'Amazonian Tribe Suddenly Leaves Jungle Home', 11 May 2006: *http://www.entheology.org/edoto/anmviewer.asp?a=244*.

4. Clifford Smyth, *Francisco Pizarro and the Conquest of Peru* (Whitefish, Montana, 2007 [1931]).

5. Michael Wood, *Conquistadors* (London, 2001), p. 128.

6. For a vivid account from the conquistadors' vantage point, which makes it clear that gold was their prime motive, see the November 1533 letter from Hernando Pizarro to the Royal Audience of Santo Domingo, in Clements R. Markham (ed.), *Reports on the Discovery of Peru* (London, 1872), pp. 113–27.

7. M. A. Burkholder, *Colonial Latin America* (2nd edn., Oxford, 1994), p. 46.

8. J. Hemming, *Conquest of the Incas* (London, 2004), p. 77.

9. Ibid., p. 355.

10. Wood, *Conquistadors*, pp. 38, 148.

11. Hemming, *Conquest*, p. 392.

12. P. Bakewell, *A History of Latin America* (2nd edn., Oxford, 2004), p. 186.

13. Hemming, *Conquest*, pp. 356ff.

14. See Alexander Murray, *Reason and Society in the Middle Ages* (Oxford, 2002), pp. 25–58.

15. See Thomas J. Sargent and François R. Velde, *The Big Problem of Small Change* (Princeton, NJ, 2002).

16. Bakewell, *History of Latin America*, p. 182.

17. Mauricio Drelichman and Hans-Joachim Voth, 'Institutions and the Resource Curse in Early Modern Spain', paper presented at the CIAR Institutions, Organizations, and Growth Program Meeting in Toronto, 16–18 March 2007.

18. Hans J. Nissen, Peter Damerow and Robert K. Englund, *Archaic Bookkeeping: Early Writing and Techniques of Economic Administration in the Ancient Near East* (London, 1993).

19. I am grateful to Dr John Taylor of the British Museum for his expert guidance and assistance with deciphering the cuneiform inscriptions. I also learned much from Martin Schubik's 'virtual museum' at Yale: *http://www.museumofmoney.org/babylon/*.

20. Glyn Davies, *A History of Money: From Ancient Times to the Present Day* (Cardiff, 1994); Jonathan Williams, with Joe Cribb and Elizabeth Errington (eds.), *Money: A History* (London, 1997)

21. See Marc Van De Mieroop, *Society and Enterprise in Old Babylonian Ur* (Berlin, 1992) and the essays in Michael Hudson and Marc Van De Mieroop (eds.), *Debt and Economic Renewal in the Ancient Near East*, vol. III (Bethesda, MD, 1998); Jack M. Sassoon, Gary Beckman and Karen S. Rubinson, *Civilizations of the Ancient Near East*, vol. III (London, 2000).

22. William N. Goetzmann, 'Fibonacci and the Financial Revolution', NBER Working Paper 10352 (March 2004).

23. John H. Munro, 'The Medieval Origins of the Financial Revolution: Usury, Rentes, and Negotiability', *International History Review*, 25, 3 (September 2003), pp. 505–62.

24. On the advantages to Italian cities of nurturing Jewish communities, see Maristella Botticini, 'A Tale of "Benevolent" Governments: Private Credit Markets, Public Finance, and the Role of Jewish Lenders in Renaissance Italy', *Journal of Economic History*, 60, 1 (March 2000), pp. 164–189.

25. Frederic C. Lane, *Venice: A Maritime Republic* (Baltimore, 1973), p. 300.

26. *Idem*, 'Venetian Bankers, 1496–1533: A Study in the Early Stages of

Deposit Banking', *Journal of Political Economy*, 45, 2 (April 1937), pp. 187–206.

27. Benjamin C. I. Ravid, 'The First Charter of the Jewish Merchants of Venice', *AJS Review*, 1 (1976), pp. 190ff.

28. *Idem*, 'The Legal Status of the Jewish Merchants of Venice, 1541–1638', *Journal of Economic History*, 35, 1 (March 1975), pp. 274–9.

29. Rhiannon Edward, 'Loan Shark Charged 11m per cent Interest', *Scotsman*, 18 August 2006.

30. John Hale, *The Civilization of Europe in the Renaissance* (London, 1993), p. 83.

31. Gene A. Brucker, 'The Medici in the Fourteenth Century', *Speculum*, 32, 1 (January 1957), p. 13.

32. John H. Munro, 'The Medieval Origins of the Financial Revolution: Usury, Rentes, and Negotiability', *International History Review*, 25, 3 (September 2003), pp. 505–62.

33. Richard A. Goldthwaite, 'The Medici Bank and the World of Florentine Capitalism', *Past and Present*, 114 (Feb. 1987), pp. 3–31. On the background to the Medicis' rise, see Raymond de Roover, *The Rise and Decline of the Medici Bank, 1397–1494* (Cambridge, MA, 1963), pp. 9–34.

34. Venetian State Archives, Mediceo Avanti Principato, MAP 133, 134, 153.

35. Franz-Josef Arlinghaus, 'Bookkeeping, Double-entry Bookkeeping', in Christopher Kleinhenz (ed.), *Medieval Italy: An Encyclopedia*, vol. 1 (New York, 2004). The first book to describe the method was Benedetto Cotrugli's *Il libro dell'arte di mercatura*, published in 1458.

36. Raymond de Roover, 'The Medici Bank: Organization and Management', *Journal of Economic History*, 6, 1 (May 1946), pp. 24–52.

37. Venetian State Archives, Archivio del Monte, Catasto of 1427. I am grateful to Dr Francesco Guidi for his guidance regarding the Medici papers in the Florence State Archives.

38. Raymond de Roover, 'The Decline of the Medici Bank', *Journal of Economic History*, 7, 1 (May 1947), pp. 69–82.

39. Stephen Quinn and William Roberds, 'The Big Problem of Large Bills: The Bank of Amsterdam and the Origins of Central Banking', Federal Reserve Bank of Atlanta Working Paper, 2005-16 (August 2005).

40. See for example Peter L. Rousseau and Richard Sylla, 'Financial Systems, Economic Growth, and Globalization', in Michael D. Bordo, Alan M. Tayor and Jeffrey G. Williamson (eds.), *Globalization in Historical Perspective* (Chicago / London, 2003), pp. 373–416.

41. See Charles P. Kindleberger, *A Financial History of Western Europe* (London, 1984), p. 94.

42. Walter Bagehot, *Lombard Street: A Description of the Money Market* (London, 1873).

43. Quoted in Kindleberger, *Financial History*, p. 87.

44. Niall Ferguson and Oliver Wyman, *The Evolution of Financial Services: Making Sense of the Past, Preparing for the Future* (London / New York, 2007), p. 34. See also p. 40 for a composite measure of global liquidity.

45. Ibid., p. 63.

46. Ibid., p. 48.

47. *http://www.bis.org/statistics/bankstats.htm*.

48. Lord [Victor] Rothschild, *Meditations of a Broomstick* (London, 1977), p. 17.

2. Of Human Bondage

1. David Wessel and Thomas T. Vogel Jr., 'Arcane World of Bonds is Guide and Beacon to a Populist President', *Wall Street Journal*, 25 February 1993, p. A1.

2. Raymond Goldsmith, *Premodern Financial Systems* (Cambridge, 1987), pp. 157ff., 164–9.

3. See M. Veseth, *Mountains of Debt: Crisis and Change in Renaissance Florence, Victorian Britain and Postwar America* (New York / Oxford, 1990).

4. John H. Munro, 'The Origins of the Modern Financial Revolution: Responses to Impediments from Church and State in Western Europe, 1200–1600', University of Toronto Working Paper, 2 (6 July 2001), p. 7.

5. James Macdonald, *A Free Nation Deep in Debt: The Financial Roots of Democracy* (New York, 2003), pp. 81ff.

6. Jean-Claude Hocquet, 'City-State and Market Economy', in Richard

Bonney (ed.), *Economic Systems and State Finance* (Oxford, 1995), pp. 87–91.

7. Jean-Claude Hocquet, 'Venice', in Richard Bonney (ed.), *The Rise of the Fiscal State in Europe, c. 1200–1815* (Oxford, 1999), p. 395.

8. Frederic C. Lane, *Venice: A Maritime Republic* (Baltimore, 1973), p. 323.

9. *Idem*, 'Venetian Bankers, 1496–1533: A Study in the Early Stages of Deposit Banking', *Journal of Political Economy*, 45, 2 (April 1937), pp. 197f.

10. Munro, 'Origins of the Modern Financial Revolution', pp. 15f.

11. Martin Körner, 'Public Credit', in Richard Bonney (ed.), *Economic Systems and State Finance* (Oxford, 1995), pp. 520f., 524f. See also Juan Gelabert, 'Castile, 1504–1808', in Richard Bonney (ed.), *The Rise of the Fiscal State in Europe, c. 1200–1815* (Oxford, 1999), pp. 208ff.

12. Marjolein 't Hart, 'The United Provinces 1579–1806', in Richard Bonney (ed.), *The Rise of the Fiscal State in Europe, c. 1200–1815* (Oxford, 1999), pp. 311ff.

13. Douglass C. North and Barry R. Weingast, 'Constitutions and Commitment: The Evolution of Institutions Governing Public Choice in Seventeenth-Century England', *Journal of Economic History*, 49, 4 (1989), pp. 803–32. The classic account of Britain's financial revolution is P. G. M. Dickson, *The Financial Revolution in England: A Study in the Development of Public Credit, 1688–1756* (London, 1967).

14. The best account of the financial crisis of the *ancien régime* is J. F. Bosher, *French Finances, 1770–1795* (Cambridge, 1970).

15. Larry Neal, *The Rise of Financial Capitalism: International Capital Markets in the Age of Reason* (Cambridge, 1990).

16. *Hansard*, New Series, vol. XVIII, pp. 540–43.

17. For a detailed account, see Niall Ferguson, *The World's Banker: The History of the House of Rothschild* (London, 1998). See also *Herbert H. Kaplan, Nathan Mayer Rothschild and the Creation of a Dynasty: The Critical Years, 1806–1816* (Stanford, 2006).

18. Rothschild Archive, London, XI/109, Nathan Rothschild to his brothers Amschel, Carl and James, 2 January 1816.

19. Rothschild Archive, London, XI/109/2/2/156, Salomon, Paris, to Nathan, London, 29 October 1815.

20. See Lord [Victor] Rothschild, *The Shadow of a Great Man* (London, 1982).

21. Philip Ziegler, *The Sixth Great Power: Barings, 1762–1929* (London, 1988), pp. 94f.

22. Heinrich Heine, *Ludwig Börne – ein Denkschrift: Sämtliche Schriften*, vol. IV (Munich, 1971), p. 27.

23. Heinrich Heine, 'Lutetia', in *Sämtliche Schriften*, vol. V (Munich, 1971), pp. 321ff., 353.

24. Anon., *The Hebrew Talisman* (London 1840), pp. 28ff.

25. Henry Iliowzi, *'In the Pale': Stories and Legends of the Russian Jews* (Philadelphia, 1897).

26. Richard McGregor, 'Chinese Buy into Conspiracy Theory', *Financial Times*, 26 September 2007.

27. Marc Flandreau and Juan H. Flores, 'Bonds and Brands: Lessons from the 1820s', Center for Economic Policy Research Discussion Paper, 6420 (August 2007).

28. For a more complete list of all the bond issues with which the Rothschilds were in any way associated, see J. Ayer, *A Century of Finance, 1804 to 1904: The London House of Rothschild* (London, 1904), pp. 14–42

29. On Amsterdam, see James C. Riley, *International Government Finance and the Amsterdam Capital Market* (Cambridge, 1980), pp. 119–94.

30. Niall Ferguson, 'The first "Eurobonds": The Rothschilds and the Financing of the Holy Alliance, 1818–1822', in William N. Goetzmann and K. Geert Rouwenhorst (eds.), *The Origins of Value: The Financial Innovations that Created Modern Capital Markets* (Oxford, 2005), pp. 311–23.

31. Johann Heinrich Bender, *Über den Verkehr mit Staatspapieren in seinen Hauptrichtungen ... Als Beylageheft zum Archiv für die Civilist[ische] Praxis*, vol. VIII (Heidelberg, 1825), pp. 6ff.

32. Heine, *Ludwig Börne*, p. 28.

33. Alfred Rubens, *Anglo-Jewish Portraits* (London, 1935), p. 299.

34. *The Times*, 15 January 1821.

35. Bertrand Gille, *Histoire de la Maison Rothschild*, vol. I: *Des origines à 1848* (Geneva, 1965), p. 487.

36. Richard Hofstadter, *The Age of Reform from Bryan to F.D.R.* (London, 1962), pp. 75ff.

37. Hermann Fürst Pückler, *Briefe eines Verstorbenen*, ed. Heinz Ohff (Kupfergraben, 1986), p. 7.

38. J. A. Hobson, *Imperialism: A Study* (London, 1902), Part I, ch. 4.

39. See e.g. Douglas B. Ball, *Financial Failure and Confederate Defeat* (Urbana, 1991).

40. Irving Katz, *August Belmont: A Political Biography* (New York, 1968), esp. pp. 96–9.

41. S. Diamond (ed.), *A Casual View of America: The Home Letters of Salomon de Rothschild, 1859–1861* (London, 1962).

42. See Rudolf Glanz, 'The Rothschild Legend in America', *Jewish Social Studies*, 19 (1957), pp. 3–28.

43. Marc D. Weidenmier, 'The Market for Confederate Cotton Bonds', *Explorations in Economic History*, 37 (2000), pp. 76–97. See also *idem*, 'Turning Points in the U.S. Civil War: Views from the Grayback Market', *Southern Economic Journal*, 68, 4 (2002), pp. 875–90.

44. See W. O. Henderson, *The Lancashire Cotton Famine: 1861–1865* (Manchester, 1934); Thomas Ellison, *The Cotton Trade of Great Britain* (New York, 1968 [1886]).

45. Marc D. Weidenmier, 'Comrades in Bonds: The Subsidized Sale of Confederate War Debt to British Leaders', Claremont McKenna College Working Paper (February 2003).

46. Richard Roberts, *Schroders: Merchants and Bankers* (Basingstoke, 1992), pp. 66f.

47. Richard C. K. Burdekin and Marc D. Weidenmier, 'Inflation is Always and Everywhere a Monetary Phenomenon: Richmond vs. Houston in 1864', *American Economic Review*, 91, 5 (December 2001), pp. 1621–30.

48. Richard Burdekin and Marc Weidenmier, 'Suppressing Asset Price Inflation: The Confederate Experience, 1861–1865', *Economic Inquiry*, 41, 3 (July 2003), 420–32. Cf. Eugene M. Lerner, 'Money, Prices and Wages in the Confederacy, 1861–65', *Journal of Political Economy*, 63, 1 (February 1955), pp. 20–40.

49. Frank Griffith Dawson, *The First Latin American Debt Crisis* (London, 1990).

50. Kris James Mitchener and Marc Weidenmier, 'Supersanctions and Sovereign Debt Repayment', NBER Working Paper 11472 (2005).
51. Niall Ferguson and Moritz Schularick, 'The Empire Effect: The Determinants of Country Risk in the First Age of Globalization, 1880–1913', *Journal of Economic History*, 66, 2 (June 2006), pp. 283–312.
52. Kris James Mitchener and Marc Weidenmier, 'Empire, Public Goods, and the Roosevelt Corollary', *Journal of Economic History*, 65 (2005), pp. 658–92.
53. William Cobbett, *Rural Rides* (London, 1985 [1830]), p. 117.
54. Ibid., pp. 34, 53.
55. M. de Cecco, *Money and Empire: The International Gold Standard, 1890–1914* (Oxford, 1973).
56. Theo Balderston, 'War Finance and Inflation in Britain and Germany, 1914–1918', *Economic History Review*, 42, 2 (May 1989), pp. 222–44.
57. Calculated from B. R. Mitchell, *International Historical Statistics: Europe, 1750–1993* (London, 1998), pp. 358ff.
58. Jay Winter and Jean-Louis Robert (eds.), *Capital Cities at War: Paris, London, Berlin 1914–1919*, Studies in the Social and Cultural History of Modern Warfare, No. 2 (Cambridge, 1997), p. 259.
59. Gerald D. Feldman, *The Great Disorder: Politics, Economy and Society in the German Inflation, 1914–1924* (Oxford / New York, 1997), pp. 211–54.
60. Elias Canetti, *Crowds and Power* (New York, 1988), p. 186.
61. John Maynard Keynes, *A Tract on Monetary Reform*, reprinted in *Collected Writings*, vol. IV (Cambridge, 1971), pp. 3, 29, 36.
62. John Maynard Keynes, *The Economic Consequences of the Peace* (London, 1919), pp. 220–33.
63. Frank Whitson Fetter, 'Lenin, Keynes and Inflation', *Economica*, 44, 173 (February 1977), p. 78.
64. William C. Smith, 'Democracy, Distributional Conflicts and Macroeconomic Policymaking in Argentina, 1983–89', *Journal of Interamerican Studies and World Affairs*, 32, 2 (Summer 1990), pp. 1–42. Cf. Rafael Di Tella and Ingrid Vogel, 'The Argentine Paradox: Economic Growth and Populist Tradition', Harvard Business School Case 9–702–001 (2001).

65. Jorge Luis Borges, 'The Garden of Forking Paths', in *idem*, *Labyrinths: Selected Stories and Other Writings*, ed. Donald A. Yates and James E. Irby (Harmondsworth, 1970), pp. 50ff.

66. Ferguson, *World's Banker*, ch. 27.

67. Further details in Gerardo della Paolera and Alan M. Taylor, *Straining at the Anchor: The Argentine Currency Board and the Search for Macroeconomic Stability, 1880–1935* (Chicago, 2001).

68. 'A Victory by Default', *Economist*, 3 March 2005.

69. For a recent discussion of the issue, see Michael Tomz, *Reputation and International Cooperation: Sovereign Debt across Three Centuries* (Princeton, 2007).

70. On the Great Inflation, see Fabrice Collard and Harris Dellas, 'The Great Inflation of the 1970s', Working Paper (1 October 2003); Edward Nelson, 'The Great Inflation of the Seventies: What Really Happened?', Federal Reserve Bank of St Louis Working Paper, 2004-001 (January 2004); Allan H. Meltzer, 'Origins of the Great Inflation', *Federal Reserve Bank of St Louis Review*, Part 2 (March / April 2005), pp. 145–75.

71. The eleven markets are Australia, Canada, France, Germany, Hong Kong, Ireland, Japan, Netherlands, Switzerland, the United Kingdom and the United States. See Watson Wyatt, 'Global Pension Fund Assets Rise and Fall': *http://www.watsonwyatt.com/news/press.asp?ID=18579*.

72. CNN, 9 July 2000.

73. Testimony of Chairman Alan Greenspan, Federal Reserve Board's semi-annual Monetary Policy Report to the Congress, before the Committee on Banking, Housing, and Urban Affairs, US Senate, 16 February 2005.

3. Blowing Bubbles

1. For a recent contribution to a vast literature, see Timothy Guinnane, Ron Harris, Naomi R. Lamoreaux, and Jean-Laurent Rosenthal, 'Putting the Corporation in its Place', NBER Working Paper 13109 (May 2007).

2. See especially Robert J. Shiller, *Irrational Exuberance* (2nd edn., Princeton, 2005).

3. See Charles P. Kindleberger, *Manias, Panics and Crashes: A History of Financial Crises* (3rd edn., New York / Chichester / Brisbane / Toronto / Singapore, 1996), pp. 12–16. Kindleberger owed a debt to the pioneering work of Hyman Minsky. For two of his key essays, see Hyman P. Minsky, 'Longer Waves in Financial Relations: Financial Factors in the More Severe Depressions', *American Economic Review*, 54, 3 (May 1964), pp. 324–35; *idem*, 'Financial Instability Revisited: The Economics of Disaster', in *idem* (ed.), *Inflation, Recession and Economic Policy* (Brighton, 1982), pp. 117–61.

4. Kindleberger, *Manias*, p. 14.

5. 'The Death of Equities', *Business Week*, 13 August 1979.

6. 'Dow 36,000', *Business Week*, 27 September 1999.

7. William N. Goetzmann and Philippe Jorion, 'Global Stock Markets in the Twentieth Century', *Journal of Finance*, 54, 3 (June 1999), pp. 953–80.

8. Jeremy J. Siegel, *Stocks for the Long Run: The Definitive Guide to Financial Market Returns and Long-Term Investment Strategies* (New York, 2000).

9. Elroy Dimson, Paul Marsh and Mike Stanton, *Triumph of the Optimists: 101 Years of Global Investment Returns* (Princeton, 2002).

10. Paul Frentrop, *A History of Corporate Governance 1602–2002* (Brussels, 2003), pp. 49–51.

11. Ronald Findlay and Kevin H. O'Rourke, *Power and Plenty: Trade, War, and the World Economy in the Second Millennium* (Princeton, 2007), p. 178.

12. Frentrop, *Corporate Governance*, p. 59.

13. On the ambivalence of the Calvinist capitalist Dutch Republic, see Simon Schama, *The Embarrassment of Riches: An Interpretation of Dutch Culture in the Golden Age* (New York, 1997 [1987]).

14. John P. Shelton, 'The First Printed Share Certificate: An Important Link in Financial History', *Business History Review*, 39, 3 (Autumn 1965), p. 396.

15. Shelton, 'First Printed Share Certificate', pp. 400f.

16. Engel Sluiter, 'Dutch Maritime Power and the Colonial Status Quo, 1585–1641', *Pacific Historical Review*, 11, 1 (March 1942), p. 33.
17. Ibid., p. 34.
18. Frentrop, *Corporate Governance*, pp. 69f.
19. Larry Neal, 'Venture Shares of the Dutch East India Company', in William N. Goetzmann and K. Geert Rouwenhorst (eds.), *The Origins of Value: The Financial Innovations that Created Modern Capital Markets* (Oxford, 2005), p. 167.
20. Neal, 'Venture Shares', p. 169.
21. Schama, *Embarrassment of Riches*, p. 349.
22. Ibid., p. 339.
23. Neal, 'Venture Shares', p. 169.
24. Frentrop, *Corporate Governance*, p. 85.
25. Ibid., pp. 95f.
26. Ibid., p. 103. Cf. Neal, 'Venture Shares', p. 171.
27. Neal, 'Venture Shares', p. 166.
28. Findlay and O'Rourke, *Power and Plenty*, p. 178.
29. Ibid., pp. 179–83. Cf. Sluiter, 'Dutch Maritime Power', p. 32.
30. Findlay and O'Rourke, *Power and Plenty*, p. 208.
31. Femme S. Gaastra, 'War, Competition and Collaboration: Relations between the English and Dutch East India Company in the Seventeenth and Eighteenth Centuries', in H. V. Bowen, Margarette Lincoln and Nigel Ribgy (eds.), *The Worlds of the East India Company* (Leicester, 2002), p. 51.
32. Gaastra, 'War, Competition and Collaboration', p. 58.
33. Ann M. Carlos and Stephen Nicholas, '"Giants of an Earlier Capitalism": The Chartered Trading Companies as Modern Multinationals', *Business History Review*, 62, 3 (Autumn 1988), pp. 398–419.
34. Gaastra, 'War, Competition and Collaboration', p. 51.
35. Findlay and O'Rourke, *Power and Plenty*, p. 183.
36. Ibid., p. 185, figure 4.5.
37. Gaastra, 'War, Competition and Collaboration', p. 55.
38. Jan de Vries and A. van der Woude, *The First Modern Economy: Success, Failure and Perseverance of the Dutch Economy, 1500–1815* (Cambridge, 1997), p. 396.

39. Andrew McFarland Davis, 'An Historical Study of Law's System', *Quarterly Journal of Economics*, 1, 3 (April 1887), p. 292.

40. H. Montgomery Hyde, *John Law: The History of an Honest Adventurer* (London, 1969), p. 83.

41. Earl J. Hamilton, 'Prices and Wages at Paris under John Law's System', *Quarterly Journal of Economics*, 51, 1 (November 1936), p. 43.

42. Davis, 'Law's System', p. 300.

43. Ibid., p. 305.

44. Thomas E. Kaiser, 'Money, Despotism, and Public Opinion in Early Eighteenth-Century Finance: John Law and the Debate on Royal Credit', *Journal of Modern History*, 63, 1 (March 1991), p. 6.

45. Max J. Wasserman and Frank H. Beach, 'Some Neglected Monetary Theories of John Law', *American Economic Review*, 24, 4 (December 1934), p. 653.

46. James Macdonald, *A Free Nation Deep in Debt: The Financial Roots of Democracy* (New York, 2003), p. 192.

47. Kaiser, 'Money', p. 12.

48. Ibid., p. 18.

49. Hamilton, 'Prices and Wages', p. 47.

50. Davis, 'Law's System', p. 317.

51. Antoin E. Murphy, *John Law: Economic Theorist and Policy-Maker* (Oxford, 1997), p. 233.

52. Hamilton, 'Prices and Wages', p. 55.

53. Murphy, *John Law*, p. 201.

54. Ibid., p. 190.

55. See Larry Neal, *The Rise of Financial Capitalism: International Capital Markets in the Age of Reason* (Cambridge, 1990), p. 74.

56. Kaiser, 'Money', p. 22.

57. For evidence of English speculators exiting Paris in November and December, see Neal, *Financial Capitalism*, p. 68.

58. Murphy, *John Law*, pp. 213f.

59. Ibid., p. 205.

60. Lord Wharncliffe (ed.), *The Letters and Works of Lady Mary Wortley Montagu* (Paris, 1837), pp. 321f.

61. Earl J. Hamilton, 'John Law of Lauriston: Banker, Gamester,

Merchant, Chief?', *American Economic Review*, 57, 2 (May 1967), p. 273.

62. Murphy, *John Law*, pp. 201–2.
63. Hamilton, 'John Law', p. 276.
64. Murphy, *John Law*, p. 239. Cf. Hamilton, 'Prices and Wages', p. 60.
65. Kaiser, 'Money', pp. 16, 20.
66. Ibid., p. 22.
67. Murphy, *John Law*, p. 235.
68. Ibid., p. 250.
69. Hyde, *Law*, p. 159.
70. Schama, *Embarrassment of Riches*, pp. 366ff.
71. Ibid., pp. 367ff.
72. For contrasting accounts see Neal, *Financial Capitalism*, pp. 89–117; Edward Chancellor, *Devil Take the Hindmost: A History of Financial Speculation* (London, 1999), pp. 58–95.
73. Chancellor, *Devil Take the Hindmost*, p. 64.
74. Ibid., p. 84.
75. Neal, *Financial Capitalism*, pp. 90, 111f. As Neal has observed, an investor who had bought South Sea stock at the beginning of 1720 and sold it at the end of the year, ignoring the intervening bubble, would still have realized a 56 per cent annual return.
76. Julian Hoppitt, 'The Myths of the South Sea Bubble', *Transactions of the Royal Historical Society*, 12 (2002), pp. 141–65.
77. Tom Nicholas, 'Trouble with a Bubble', Harvard Business School Case N9-807-146 (28 February 2007), p. 1.
78. William L. Silber, *When Washington Shut Down Wall Street: The Great Financial Crisis of 1914 and the Origins of America's Monetary Supremacy* (Princeton, 2006).
79. Niall Ferguson, 'Political Risk and the International Bond Market between the 1848 Revolution and the Outbreak of the First World War', *Economic History Review*, 59, 1 (February 2006), pp. 70–112.
80. *New York Times*, 23 October 1929.
81. Nicholas, 'Trouble with a Bubble', p. 4.
82. Ibid., p. 6.
83. Chancellor, *Devil Take the Hindmost*, pp. 199ff.

84. See Milton Friedman and Anna J. Schwartz, *A Monetary History of the United States, 1867–1960* (Princeton, 1963), pp. 299–419. This chapter, 'The Great Contraction', should be required reading for all financial practitioners.

85. Ibid., pp. 309f., n. 9. Anyone who reads this footnote will understand why the Fed moved so swiftly and open-handedly to ensure that JP Morgan bought Bear Stearns in March 2007.

86. Ibid., p. 315.

87. Ibid., p. 317.

88. Ibid., p. 396.

89. Ibid., p. 325.

90. Ibid., p. 328.

91. US Department of Commerce Bureau of the Census, *Historical Statistics of the United States: Colonial Times to 1970* (Washington, DC, 1975), p. 1019.

92. Barry Eichengreen, *Golden Fetters: The Gold Standard and the Great Depression, 1919–1939* (New York / Oxford, 1992). See also *idem*, 'The Origins and Nature of the Great Slump Revisited', *Economic History Review*, 45, 2 (May 1992), pp. 213–39.

93. See e.g. Ben S. Bernanke, 'The Macroeconomics of the Great Depression: A Comparative Approach', NBER Working Paper 4814 (August 1994).

94. Hyman P. Minsky, 'Introduction: Can "It" Happen Again? A Reprise', in *idem* (ed.), *Inflation, Recession and Economic Policy* (Brighton, 1982), p. xi.

95. The index has fallen by 10 per cent or more in 23 out of 113 years.

96. See Nicholas Brady, James C. Cotting, Robert G. Kirby, John R. Opel and Howard M. Stein, *Report of the Presidential Task Force on Market Mechanisms, submitted to the President of the United States, the Secretary of the Treasury and the Chairman of the Federal Reserve Board* (Washington, DC, January 1988). Of especial interest to the historian is the comparison with 1929: see Appendix VIII, pp. 1–13.

97. James Dale Davidson and William Rees-Mogg, *The Great Reckoning: How the World Will Change in the Depression of the 1990's* (London, 1991).

98. For Greenspan's own version of events, see Alan Greenspan, *The Age of Turbulence: Adventures in a New World* (New York, 2007), pp. 100–110.

99. Greenspan, *Age of Turbulence*, p. 166.

100. Ibid., p. 167.

101. Ibid., pp. 190–5.

102. Ibid., pp. 200f.

103. The best account remains Bethany McLean and Peter Elkind, *The Smartest Guys in the Room: The Amazing Rise and Scandalous Fall of Enron* (New York, 2003).

104. Ibid., p. 55.

105. See her own account of events in Mimi Swartz and Sherron Watkins, *Power Failure: The Inside Story of the Collapse of Enron* (New York, 2003).

4. The Return of Risk

1. Rawle O. King, 'Hurricane Katrina: Insurance Losses and National Capacities for Financing Disaster Risks', Congressional Research Service Report for Congress, 31 January 2008, table 1.

2. Joseph B. Treaster, 'A Lawyer Like a Hurricane: Facing Off Against Asbestos, Tobacco and Now Home Insurers', *New York Times*, 16 March 2007.

3. For details, see Richard F. Scruggs, 'Hurricane Katrina: Issues and Observations', American Enterprise Institute–Brookings Judicial Symposium, 'Insurance and Risk Allocation in America: Economics, Law and Regulation', Georgetown Law Center, 20–22 September 2006.

4. Details from *http://www.usa.gov/Citizen/Topics/PublicSafety/Hurricane_Katrina_Recovery.shtml*, *http://katrina.louisiana.gov/index.html* and *http://www.ldi.state.la.us/HurricaneKatrina.htm*.

5. Peter Lattman, 'Plaintiffs Laywer Scruggs is Indicted on Bribery Charges', *Wall Street Journal*, 29 November 2007; Ashby Jones and Paulo Prada, 'Richard Scruggs Pleads Guilty', ibid., 15 March 2008.

6. King, 'Hurricane Katrina', p. 4.

7. Naomi Klein, *The Shock Doctrine: The Rise of Disaster Capitalism* (New York, 2007).

8. *http://www.nhc.noaa.gov/pastdec.shtml*.

9. John Schwartz, 'One Billion Dollars Later, New Orleans is Still at Risk', *New York Times*, 17 August 2007.

10. Michael Lewis, 'In Nature's Casino', *New York Times Magazine*, 26 August 2007.

11. National Safety Council, 'What are the Odds of Dying?': *http://www.nsc.org/lrs/statinfo/odds.htm*. For the cancer statistic, see the National Cancer Institute, 'SEER Cancer Statistics Review, 1975–2004', table I-17: *http://srab.cancer.gov./devcan/*. The precise lifetime probability of dying from cancer in the United States between 2002 and 2004 was 21.29 per cent, with a 95 per cent confidence interval.

12. Florence Edler de Roover, 'Early Examples of Marine Insurance', *Journal of Economic History*, 5, 2 (November 1945), pp. 172–200.

13. Ibid., pp. 188f.

14. A. H. John, 'The London Assurance Company and the Marine Insurance Market of the Eighteenth Century', *Economica*, New Series, 25, 98 (May 1958), p. 130.

15. Paul A. Papayoanou, 'Interdependence, Institutions, and the Balance of Power', *International Security*, 20, 4 (Spring 1996), p. 55.

16. Roover, 'Early Examples of Marine Insurance', p. 196.

17. M. Greenwood, 'The First Life Table', *Notes and Records of the Royal Society of London*, 1, 2 (October 1938), pp. 70–2.

18. The preceding paragraph owes a great debt to Peter L. Bernstein, *Against the Gods: The Remarkable Story of Risk* (New York, 1996).

19. Gregory Clark, *A Farewell to Alms: A Brief Economic History of the World* (Princeton, 2007).

20. See the essays in A. Ian Dunlop (ed.), *The Scottish Ministers' Widows' Fund, 1743–1993* (Edinburgh, 1992) for details.

21. The key documents are to be found in the Robert Wallace papers, National Archives of Scotland: CH/9/17/6-13.

22. G. W. Richmond, 'Insurance Tendencies in England', *Annals of the American Academy of Political and Social Science*, 161 (May 1932), p. 183.

23. A. N. Wilson, *A Life of Walter Scott: The Laird of Abbotsford* (London: Pimlico, 2002), pp. 169–71.

24. G. Clayton and W. T. Osborne, 'Insurance Companies and the Finance of Industry', *Oxford Economic Papers*, New Series, 10, 1 (February 1958), pp. 84–97.

25. 'American Exceptionalism', *Economist*, 10 August 2006.

26. *http://www.workhouses.org.uk/index.html?StMarylebone/ StMarylebone.shtml*.

27. Lothar Gall, *Bismarck: The White Revolutionary*, vol. II: *1879– 1898*, trans. J. A. Underwood (London, 1986), p. 129.

28. H. G. Lay, *Marine Insurance: A Text Book of the History of Marine Insurance, including the Functions of Lloyd's Register of Shipping* (London, 1925), p. 137.

29. Richard Sicotte, 'Economic Crisis and Political Response: The Political Economy of the Shipping Act of 1916', *Journal of Economic History*, 59, 4 (December 1999), pp. 861–84.

30. Anon., 'Allocation of Risk between Marine and War Insurer', *Yale Law Journal*, 51, 4 (February 1942), p. 674; C., 'War Risks in Marine Insurance', *Modern Law Review*, 10, 2 (April 1947), pp. 211–14.

31. Alfred T. Lauterbach, 'Economic Demobilization in Great Britain after the First World War', *Political Science Quarterly*, 57, 3 (September 1942), pp. 376–93.

32. Correlli Barnett, *The Audit of War* (London, 2001), pp. 31f.

33. Richmond, 'Insurance Tendencies', p. 185.

34. Charles Davison, 'The Japanese Earthquake of 1 September', *Geographical Journal*, 65, 1 (January 1925), pp. 42f.

35. Yoshimichi Miura, 'Insurance Tendencies in Japan', *Annals of the American Academy of Political and Social Science*, 161 (May 1932), pp. 215–19.

36. Herbert H. Gowen, 'Living Conditions in Japan', *Annals of the American Academy of Political and Social Science*, 122 (November 1925), p. 163.

37. Kenneth Hewitt, 'Place Annihilation: Area Bombing and the Fate of Urban Places', *Annals of the Association of American Geographers*, 73 (1983), p. 263.

38. Anon., 'War Damage Insurance', *Yale Law Journal*, 51, 7 (May 1942), pp. 1160–1. It made $210 million, having collected premiums from 8 million policies and paid out only a modest amount.

39. Kingo Tamai, 'Development of Social Security in Japan', in Misa Izuhara (ed.), *Comparing Social Policies: Exploring New Perspectives in Britain and Japan* (Bristol, 2003), pp. 35–48. See also Gregory J. Kasza, 'War and Welfare Policy in Japan', *Journal of Asian Studies*, 61, 2 (May 2002), p. 428.

40. Recommendation of the Council of Social Security System (1950).

41. W. Macmahon Ball, 'Reflections on Japan', *Pacific Affairs*, 21, 1 (March 1948), pp. 15f.

42. Beatrice G. Reubens, 'Social Legislation in Japan', *Far Eastern Survey*, 18, 23 (16 November 1949), p. 270.

43. Keith L. Nelson, 'The "Warfare State": History of a Concept', *Pacific Historical Review*, 40, 2 (May 1971), pp. 138f.

44. Kasza, 'War and Welfare Policy', pp. 418f.

45. Ibid., p. 423.

46. Ibid., p. 424.

47. Nakagawa Yatsuhiro, 'Japan, the Welfare Super-Power', *Journal of Japanese Studies*, 5, 1 (Winter 1979), pp. 5–51.

48. Ibid., p. 21.

49. Ibid., p. 9.

50. Ibid., p. 18.

51. For comparative studies, see Gregory J. Kasza, *One World of Welfare: Japan in Comparative Perspective* (Ithaca, 2006) and Neil Gilbert and Ailee Moon, 'Analyzing Welfare Effort: An Appraisal of Comparative Methods', *Journal of Policy Analysis and Management*, 7, 2 (Winter 1988), pp. 326–40.

52. Kasza, *One World of Welfare*, p. 107.

53. Peter H. Lindert, *Growing Public: Social Spending and Economic Growth since the Eighteenth Century* (Cambridge, 2004), vol. I, table I.2.

54. Hiroto Tsukada, *Economic Globalization and the Citizens' Welfare State* (Aldershot / Burlington / Singapore / Sydney, 2002), p. 96.

55. Milton Friedman and Anna J. Schwartz, *A Monetary History of the United States, 1867–1960* (Princeton, 1963).

56. Milton Friedman and Rose D. Friedman, *Two Lucky People: Memoirs* (Chicago / London, 1998), p. 399.
57. Ibid., p. 400.
58. Ibid., p. 593.
59. Patricio Silva, 'Technocrats and Politics in Chile: From the Chicago Boys to the CEIPLAN Monks', *Journal of Latin American Studies*, 23, 2 (May 1991), pp. 385–410.
60. Bill Jamieson, '25 Years On, Chile Has a Pensions Message for Britain', *Sunday Business*, 14 December 2006.
61. Rossana Castiglioni, 'The Politics of Retrenchment: The Quandaries of Social Protection under Military Rule in Chile, 1973–1990', *Latin American Politics and Society*, 43, 4 (Winter 2001), pp. 39ff.
62. Ibid., p. 55.
63. José Piñera, 'Empowering Workers: The Privatization of Social Security in Chile', *Cato Journal*, 15, 2–3 (Fall / Winter 1995/96), pp. 155–166.
64. Ibid., p. 40.
65. Teresita Ramos, 'Chile: The Latin American Tiger?', Harvard Business School Case 9-798-092 (21 March 1999), p. 6.
66. Laurence J. Kotlikoff, 'Pension Reform as the Triumph of Form over Substance', *Economists' Voice* (January 2008), pp. 1–5.
67. Armando Barrientos, 'Pension Reform and Pension Coverage in Chile: Lessons for Other Countries', *Bulletin of Latin American Research*, 15, 3 (1996), p. 312.
68. 'Destitute No More', *Economist*, 16 August 2007.
69. Barrientos, 'Pension Reform', pp. 309f. See also Raul Madrid, 'The Politics and Economics of Pension Privatization in Latin America', *Latin American Research Review*, 37, 2 (2002), pp. 159–82.
70. All figures are for 2004, the latest comparative data available from the World Bank's World Development Indicators database.
71. I am indebted here to Laurence J. Kotlikoff and Scott Burns, *The Coming Generational Storm: What You Need to Know about America's Economic Future* (Cambridge, 2005). See also Peter G. Peterson, *Running on Empty: How the Democratic and Republican Parties Are Bankrupting Our Future and What Americans Can Do about It* (New York, 2005).

72. Ruth Helman, Craig Copeland and Jack VanDerhei, 'Will More of Us Be Working Forever? The 2006 Retirement Confidence Survey', Employee Benefit Research Institute Issue Brief, 292 (April 2006).

73. Gene L. Dodaro, Acting Comptroller General of the United States, 'Working to Improve Accountability in an Evolving Environment', address to the 2008 Maryland Association of CPAs' Government and Not-for-profit Conference (18 April 2008).

74. James Brooke, 'A Tough Sell: Japanese Social Security', New York Times, 6 May 2004.

75. See Mutsuko Takahashi, The Emergence of Welfare Society in Japan (Aldershot / Brookfield / Hong Kong / Singapore / Sydney, 1997), pp. 185f. See also Kasza, One World of Welfare, pp. 179–82.

76. Alex Kerr, Dogs and Demons: The Fall of Modern Japan (London, 2001), pp. 261–66.

77. Gavan McCormack, Client State: Japan in the American Embrace (London, 2007), pp. 45–69.

78. Lisa Haines, 'World's Largest Pension Funds Top $10 Trillion', Financial News, 5 September 2007.

79. 'Living Dangerously', Economist, 22 January 2004.

80. Philip Bobbitt, Terror and Consent: The Wars for the Twenty-first Century (New York, 2008), esp. pp. 98–179.

81. Suleiman abu Gheith, quoted in ibid., p. 119.

82. Graham Allison, 'Time to Bury a Dangerous Legacy, Part 1', Yale Global, 14 March 2008. Cf. idem, Nuclear Terrorism: The Ultimate Preventable Catastrophe (Cambridge, MA, 2004).

83. Michael D. Intriligator and Abdullah Toukan, 'Terrorism and Weapons of Mass Destruction', in Peter Kotana, Michael D. Intriligator and John P. Sullivan (eds.), Countering Terrorism and WMD: Creating a Global Counter-terrorism Network (New York, 2006), table 4.1A.

84. See IPCC, Climate Change 2007: Synthesis Report (Valencia, 2007).

85. Robert Looney, 'Economic Costs to the United States Stemming from the 9/11 Attacks', Center for Contemporary Conflict Strategic Insight (5 August 2002).

86. Robert E. Litan, 'Sharing and Reducing the Financial Risks of Future

Mega-Catastrophes', *Brookings Issues in Economic Policy*, 4 (March 2006).

87. William Hutchings, 'Citadel Builds a Diverse Business', *Financial News*, 3 October 2007.

88. Marcia Vickers, 'A Hedge Fund Superstar', *Fortune*, 3 April 2007.

89. Joseph Santos, 'A History of Futures Trading in the United States', South Dakota University MS, n.d.

5. Safe as Houses

1. Philip E. Orbanes, *Monopoly: The World's Most Famous Game – And How It Got That Way* (New York, 2006), pp. 10–71.

2. Ibid., p. 50.

3. Ibid., pp. 86f.

4. Ibid., p. 90.

5. Robert J. Shiller, 'Understanding Recent Trends in House Prices and Home Ownership', paper presented at Federal Reserve Bank of Kansas City's Jackson Hole Conference (August 2007).

6. *http://www.canongate.net/WhoOwnsBritain/DoTheMathsOnLand Ownership*.

7. David Cannadine, *Aspects of Aristocracy: Grandeur and Decline in Modern Britain* (New Haven, 1994), p. 170.

8. I am grateful to Gregory Clark for these statistics.

9. Frederick B. Heath, 'The Grenvilles, in the Nineteenth Century: The Emergence of Commercial Affiliations', *Huntington Library Quarterly*, 25, 1 (November 1961), p. 29.

10. Heath, 'Grenvilles', pp. 32f.

11. Ibid., p. 35.

12. David Spring and Eileen Spring, 'The Fall of the Grenvilles', *Huntington Library Quarterly*, 19, 2 (February 1956), p. 166.

13. Ibid., pp. 177f.

14. Details in Spring and Spring, 'Fall of the Grenvilles', pp. 169–74.

15. Ibid., p. 185.

16. Heath, 'Grenvilles', p. 39.

17. Spring and Spring, 'Fall of the Grenvilles', p. 183.

18. Heath, 'Grenvilles', p. 40.

19. Ibid., p. 46.
20. Ben Bernanke, 'Housing, Housing Finance, and Monetary Policy', speech at the Kansas City Federal Reserve Bank's Jackson Hole Conference (31 August 2007).
21. Louis Hyman, 'Debtor Nation: How Consumer Credit Built Postwar America', unpublished Ph.D. thesis (Harvard University, 2007), ch. 1.
22. Edward E. Leamer, 'Housing and the Business Cycle', paper presented at Federal Reserve Bank of Kansas City's Jackson Hole Conference (August 2007).
23. Saronne Rubyan-Ling, 'The Detroit Murals of Diego Rivera', *History Today*, 46, 4 (April 1996), pp. 34–8.
24. Donald Lochbiler, 'Battle of the Garden Court', *Detroit News*, 15 July 1997.
25. Hyman, 'Debtor Nation', ch. 2.
26. Thomas J. Sugrue, *The Origins of the Urban Crisis: Race and Inequality in Postwar Detroit* (Princeton, 1996), p. 64.
27. Ibid., pp. 38–43.
28. Hyman, 'Debtor Nation', ch. 5.
29. Sugrue, *Origins of the Urban Crisis*, p. 259.
30. For a recent case in Detroit, see Ben Lefebvre, 'Justice Dept. Accuses Detroit Bank of Bias in Lending', *New York Times*, 20 May 2004.
31. Glen O'Hara, *From Dreams to Disillusionment: Economic and Social Planning in 1960s Britain* (Basingstoke, 2007), ch. 5.
32. Bernanke, 'Housing, Housing Finance, and Monetary Policy'. See also Roger Loewenstein, 'Who Needs the Mortgage-Interest Deduction?', *New York Times Magazine*, 5 March 2006.
33. Nigel Lawson, *The View from No. 11: Memoirs of a Tory Radical* (London, 1992), p. 821.
34. *Living in Britain: General Household Survey 2002* (London, 2003), p. 30: *http://www.statistics.gov.uk/cci/nugget.asp?id=821*.
35. Ned Eichler, 'Homebuilding in the 1980s: Crisis or Transition?', *Annals of the American Academy of Political and Social Science*, 465 (January 1983), p. 37.
36. Maureen O'Hara, 'Property Rights and the Financial Firm', *Journal of Law and Economics*, 24 (October 1981), pp. 317–32.

37. Eichler, 'Homebuilding', p. 40. See also Henry N. Pontell and Kitty Calavita, 'White-Collar Crime in the Savings and Loan Scandal', *Annals of the American Academy of Political and Social Science*, 525 (January 1993), pp. 31–45; Marcia Millon Cornett and Hassan Tehranian, 'An Examination of the Impact of the Garn-St Germain Depository Institutions Act of 1982 on Commercial Banks and Savings and Loans', *Journal of Finance*, 45, 1 (March 1990), pp. 95–111.

38. Henry N. Pontell and Kitty Calavita, 'The Savings and Loan Industry', *Crime and Justice*, 18 (1993), p. 211.

39. Ibid., pp. 208f.

40. F. Stevens Redburn, 'The Deeper Structure of the Savings and Loan Disaster', *Political Science and Politics*, 24, 3 (September 1991), p. 439.

41. Pontell and Calavita, 'White-Collar Crime', p. 37.

42. Allen Pusey, 'Fast Money and Fraud', *New York Times*, 23 April 1989.

43. K. Calavita, R. Tillman, and H. N. Pontell, 'The Savings and Loan Debacle, Financial Crime and the State', *Annual Review of Sociology*, 23 (1997), p. 23.

44. Pontell and Calavita, 'Savings and Loans Industry', p. 215.

45. Calavita, Tillman and Pontell, 'Savings and Loan Debacle', p. 24.

46. Allen Pusey and Christi Harlan, 'Bankers Shared in Profits from I--30 Deals', *Dallas Morning News*, 29 January 1986.

47. Allen Pusey and Christi Harlan, 'I–30 Real Estate Deals: A "Virtual Money Machine"', *Dallas Morning News*, 26 January 1986.

48. Pusey, 'Fast Money and Fraud'.

49. Pontell and Calavita, 'White-Collar Crime', p. 43. See also Kitty Calavita and Henry N. Pontell, 'The State and White-Collar Crime: Saving the Savings and Loans', *Law Society Review*, 28, 2 (1994), pp. 297–324.

50. The losses were initially feared to be higher. In 1990 the General Accounting Office foresaw costs of up to $500 billion. Others estimated costs of a trillion dollars or more: Pontell and Calavita, 'Savings and Loan Industry', p. 203.

51. For a vivid account, see Michael Lewis, *Liar's Poker* (London, 1989), pp. 78–124.

52. Bernanke, 'Housing, Housing Finance, and Monetary Policy'.

53. I am grateful to Joseph Barillari for his assistance with these calculations. Morris A. Davisa, Andreas Lehnert and Robert F. Martin, 'The Rent–Price Ratio for the Aggregate Stock of Owner-Occupied Housing', Working paper (December 2007).

54. Shiller, 'Recent Trends in House Prices'.

55. Carmen M. Reinhart and Kenneth S. Rogoff, 'Is the 2007 Sub-Prime Financial Crisis So Different? An International Historical Comparison', Draft Working Paper (14 January 2008).

56. Mark Whitehouse, 'Debt Bomb: Inside the "Subprime" Mortgage Debacle', *Wall Street Journal*, 30 May 2007, p. A1.

57. See Kimberly Blanton, 'A "Smoking Gun" on Race, Subprime Loans', *Boston Globe*, 16 March 2007.

58. 'U.S. Housing Bust Fuels Blame Game', *Wall Street Journal*, 19 March 2008. See also David Wessel, 'Housing Bust Offers Insights', *Wall Street Journal*, 10 April 2008.

59. Henry Louis Gates Jr., 'Forty Acres and a Gap in Wealth', *New York Times*, 18 November 2007.

60. Andy Meek, 'Frayser Foreclosures Revealed', *Daily News*, 21 September 2006.

61. *http://www.responsiblelending.org/page.jsp?itemID=32032031*.

62. Credit Suisse, 'Foreclosure Trends – A Sobering Reality', *Fixed Income Research* (23 April 2008).

63. See Prabha Natarajan, 'Fannie, Freddie Could Hurt U.S. Credit', *Wall Street Journal*, 15 April 2008.

64. *Economic Report of the President 2007*, tables B-77 and B-76: *http://www.gpoaccess.gov/eop/*.

65. George Magnus, 'Managing Minsky', UBS research paper, 27 March 2008.

66. Hernando de Soto, *The Mystery of Capital: Why Capitalism Triumphs in the West and Fails Everywhere Else* (London, 2001).

67. *Idem*, 'Interview: Land and Freedom', *New Scientist*, 27 April 2002.

68. *Idem*, *The Other Path* (New York, 1989).

69. Rafael Di Tella, Sebastian Galiani and Ernesto Schargrodsky, 'The Formation of Beliefs: Evidence from the Allocation of Land Titles to Squatters', *Quarterly Journal of Economics*, 122, 1 (February 2007), pp. 209–41.

70. 'The Mystery of Capital Deepens', *The Economist*, 26 August 2006.

71. See John Gravois, 'The De Soto Delusion', *Slate*, 29 January 2005: *http://state.msn.com/id/2112792/*.

72. The entire profit is transferred to a Rehabilitation Fund created to cope with emergency situations, in return for an exemption from corporate income tax.

73. Connie Black, 'Millions for Millions', *New Yorker*, 30 October 2006, pp. 62–73.

74. Shiller, 'Recent Trends in House Prices'.

75. Edward L. Glaeser and Joseph Gyourko, 'Housing Dynamics', NBER Working Paper 12787 (revised version, 31 March 2007).

76. Robert J. Shiller, *The New Financial Order: Risk in the 21st Century* (Princeton, 2003).

6. From Empire to Chimerica

1. Dominic Wilson and Roopa Purushothaman, 'Dreaming with the BRICs: The Path to 2050', *Goldman Sachs Global Economics Paper*, 99 (1 October 2003). See also Jim O'Neill, 'Building Better Global Economic BRICs', *Goldman Sachs Global Economics Paper*, 66 (30 November 2001); Jim O'Neill, Dominic Wilson, Roopa Purushothaman and Anna Stupnytska, 'How Solid are the BRICs?', *Goldman Sachs Global Economics Paper*, 134 (1 December 2005).

2. Dominic Wilson and Anna Stupnytska, 'The N-11: More than an Acronym', *Goldman Sachs Global Economics Paper*, 153 (28 March 2007).

3. Goldman Sachs Global Economics Group, *BRICs and Beyond* (London, 2007), esp. pp. 45–72, 103–8.

4. The argument is made in Kenneth Pomeranz, *The Great Divergence: China, Europe and the Making of the Modern World Economy* (Princeton / Oxford, 2000). For a more sceptical view of China's position in 1700, see *inter alia* Angus Maddison, *The World Economy: A Millennial Perspective* (Paris, 2001).

5. Calculated from the estimates for per capita gross domestic product in Maddison, *World Economy*, table B-21.

6. Pomeranz, *Great Divergence*.

7. Among the most important recent works on the subject are Eric Jones, *The European Miracle: Environments, Economies and Geopolitics in the History of Europe and Asia* (Cambridge, 1981); David S. Landes, *The Wealth and Poverty of Nations: Why Some are So Rich and Some So Poor* (New York, 1998); Joel Mokyr, *The Gifts of Athena: Historical Origins of the Knowledge Economy* (Princeton, 2002); Gregory Clark, *A Farewell to Alms: A Brief Economic History of the World* (Princeton, 2007).

8. William N. Goetzmann, 'Fibonacci and the Financial Revolution', NBER Working Paper 10352 (March 2004).

9. William N. Goetzmann, Andrey D. Ukhov and Ning Zhu, 'China and the World Financial Markets, 1870–1930: Modern Lessons from Historical Globalization', *Economic History Review* (forthcoming).

10. Nicholas Crafts, 'Globalisation and Growth in the Twentieth Century', International Monetary Fund Working Paper, 00/44 (March 2000). See also Richard E. Baldwin and Philippe Martin, 'Two Waves of Globalization: Superficial Similarities, Fundamental Differences', NBER Working Paper 6904 (January 1999).

11. Barry R. Chiswick and Timothy J. Hatton, 'International Migration and the Integration of Labor Markets', in Michael D. Bordo, Alan M. Taylor and Jeffrey G. Williamson (eds.), *Globalization in Historical Perspective* (Chicago, 2003), pp. 65–120.

12. Maurice Obstfeld and Alan M. Taylor, 'Globalization and Capital Markets', in Michael D. Bordo, Alan M. Taylor and Jeffrey G. Williamson (eds.), *Globalization in Historical Perspective* (Chicago, 2003), pp. 173f.

13. Clark, *Farewell*, chs. 13, 14.

14. David M. Rowe, 'The Tragedy of Liberalism: How Globalization Caused the First World War', *Security Studies*, 14, 3 (Spring 2005), pp. 1–41.

15. See for example Fareed Zakaria, *The Post-American World* (New York, 2008) and Parag Khanna, *The Second World: Empires and Influence in the New Global Order* (London, 2008).

16. Jim Rogers, *A Bull in China: Investing Profitably in the World's Greatest Market* (New York, 2007).

17. Robert Blake, *Jardine Matheson: Traders of the Far East* (London,

1999), p. 91. See also Alain Le Pichon, *China Trade and Empire: Jardine, Matheson & Co. and the Origins of British Rule in Hong Kong, 1827–1843* (Oxford / New York, 2006).

18. Rothschild Archive London, RFamFD/13A/1; 13B/1; 13C/1; 13D/1; 13D/2; 13/E.

19. Henry Lowenfeld, *Investment: An Exact Science* (London, 1909), p. 61.

20. John Maynard Keynes, *The Economic Consequences of the Peace* (London, 1919), ch. 1.

21. Maddison, *World Economy*, table 2-26a.

22. Lance E. Davis and R. A. Huttenback, *Mammon and the Pursuit of Empire: The Political Economy of British Imperialism, 1860–1912* (Cambridge, 1988), p. 46.

23. Ranald Michie, 'Reversal or Change? The Global Securities Market in the 20th Century', *New Global Studies* (forthcoming).

24. Obstfeld and Taylor, 'Globalization'; Niall Ferguson and Moritz Schularick, 'The Empire Effect: The Determinants of Country Risk in the First Age of Globalization, 1880–1913', *Journal of Economic History*, 66, 2 (June 2006). But see also Michael A. Clemens and Jeffrey Williamson, 'Wealth Bias in the First Global Capital Market Boom, 1870–1913', *Economic Journal*, 114, 2 (2004), pp. 304–37.

25. The definitive study is Michael Edelstein, *Overseas Investment in the Age of High Imperialism: The United Kingdom, 1850–1914* (New York, 1982).

26. Michael Edelstein, 'Imperialism: Cost and Benefit', in Roderick Floud and Donald McCloskey (eds.), *The Economic History of Britain since 1700*, vol. II (2nd edn., Cambridge, 1994), pp. 173–216.

27. John Maynard Keynes, 'Foreign Investment and National Advantage', in Donald Moggridge (ed.), *The Collected Writings of John Maynard Keynes*, vol. XIX (London, 1981), pp. 275–84.

28. *Idem*, 'Advice to Trustee Investors', in ibid., pp. 202–6.

29. Calculated from the data in Irving Stone, *The Global Export of Capital from Great Britain, 1865–1914* (London, 1999).

30. See the very useful stock market index for Shanghai Stock Exchange between 1870 and 1940 at *http://icf.som.yale.edu/sse/*.

31. Michael Bordo and Hugh Rockoff, 'The Gold Standard as a "Good

Housekeeping Seal of Approval"', *Journal of Economic History*, 56, 2 (June 1996), pp. 389–428.

32. Marc Flandreau and Frédéric Zumer, *The Making of Global Finance, 1880–1913* (Paris, 2004).
33. Ferguson and Schularick, 'Empire Effect'. , pp. 283–312.
34. For a full discussion of this point, see Niall Ferguson, 'Political Risk and the International Bond Market between the 1848 Revolution and the Outbreak of the First World War', *Economic History Review*, 59, 1 (February 2006), pp. 70–112.
35. Jean de [Ivan] Bloch, *Is War Now Impossible?*, trans. R. C. Long (London, 1899), p. xvii.
36. Norman Angell, *The Great Illusion: A Study of the Relation of Military Power in Nations to their Economic and Social Advantage* (London, 1910), p. 31.
37. Quoted in James J. Sheehan, *Where Have all the Soldiers Gone?* (New York: Houghton Mifflin Co., 2007), p. 56.
38. O. M. W. Sprague, 'The Crisis of 1914 in the United States', *American Economic Review*, 5, 3 (1915), pp. 505ff.
39. Brendan Brown, *Monetary Chaos in Europe: The End of an Era* (London / New York, 1988), pp. 1–34.
40. John Maynard Keynes, 'War and the Financial System', *Economic Journal*, 24, 95 (1914), pp. 460–86.
41. E. Victor Morgan, *Studies in British Financial Policy, 1914–1925* (London, 1952), pp. 3–11.
42. Ibid., p. 27. See also Teresa Seabourne, 'The Summer of 1914', in Forrest Capie and Geoffrey E. Wood (eds.), *Financial Crises and the World Banking System* (London, 1986), pp. 78, 88f.
43. Sprague, 'Crisis of 1914', p. 532.
44. Morgan, *Studies*, p. 19.
45. Seabourne, 'Summer of 1914', pp. 80ff.
46. See most recently William L. Silber, *When Washington Shut Down Wall Street: The Great Financial Crisis of 1914 and the Origins of America's Monetary Supremacy* (Princeton, 2007).
47. Morgan, *Studies*, pp. 12–23.
48. David Kynaston, *The City of London*, vol. III: *Illusions of Gold, 1914–1945* (London, 1999), p. 5.

49. Calculated from isolated prices quoted in *The Times* between August and December 1914.

50. Kynaston, *City of London,* p. 5.

51. For details see Niall Ferguson, 'Earning from History: Financial Markets and the Approach of World Wars', *Brookings Papers in Economic Activity* (forthcoming).

52. See Lyndon Moore and Jakub Kaluzny, 'Regime Change and Debt Default: The Case of Russia, Austro-Hungary, and the Ottoman Empire following World War One', *Explorations in Economic History*, 42 (2005), pp. 237–58.

53. Maurice Obstfeld and Alan M. Taylor, 'The Great Depression as a Watershed: International Capital Mobility over the Long Run', in Michael D. Bordo, Claudia Goldin and Eugene N. White (eds.), *The Defining Moment: The Great Depression and the American Economy in the Twentieth Century* (Chicago, 1998), pp. 353–402.

54. Rawi Abdelal, *Capital Rules: The Construction of Global Finance* (Cambridge, MA / London, 2007), p. 45.

55. Ibid., p. 46.

56. Greg Behrman, *The Most Noble Adventure: The Marshall Plan and the Time when America Helped Save Europe* (New York, 2007).

57. Obstfeld and Taylor, 'Globalization and Capital Markets', p. 129.

58. See William Easterly, *The Elusive Quest for Growth: Economists' Adventures and Misadventures in the Tropics* (Cambridge, MA., 2002).

59. Michael Bordo, 'The Bretton Woods International Monetary System: A Historical Overview', in *idem* and Barry Eichengreen (eds.), *A Retrospective on the Bretton Woods System: Lessons for International Monetary Reform* (Chicago / London, 1993), pp. 3–98.

60. Christopher S. Chivvis, 'Charles de Gaulle, Jacques Rueff and French International Monetary Policy under Bretton Woods', *Journal of Contemporary History*, 41, 4 (2006), pp. 701–20.

61. Interview with Amy Goodman: *http://www.democracynow.org/article.pl?sid=04/11/09/1526251.*

62. John Perkins, *Confessions of an Economic Hit Man* (New York, 2004), p. xi.

63. Joseph E. Stiglitz, *Globalization and Its Discontents* (New York, 2002), pp. 12, 14, 15, 17.

64. Abdelal, *Capital Rules*, pp. 50f., 57–75.
65. Paul Krugman, *The Return of Depression Economics* (London, 1999).
66. 'The Fund Bites Back', *The Economist*, 4 July 2002.
67. Kenneth Rogoff, 'The Sisters at 60', *The Economist*, 22 July 2004. Cf. 'Not Even a Cat to Rescue', *The Economist*, 20 April 2006.
68. See the classic study by Fritz Stern, *Gold and Iron: Bismarck, Bleichröder and the Building of the German Empire* (Harmondsworth, 1987).
69. George Soros, *The Alchemy of Finance: Reading the Mind of the Market* (New York, 1987), pp. 27–30.
70. Robert Slater, *Soros: The Life, Times and Trading Secrets of the World's Greatest Investor* (New York, 1996), pp. 48f.
71. George Soros, *The New Paradigm for Financial Markets: The Credit Crash of 2008 and What It Means* (New York, 2008), p. x.
72. Slater, *Soros*, p. 78.
73. Ibid., pp. 105, 107ff.
74. Ibid., p. 172.
75. Ibid., pp. 177, 182, 188.
76. Ibid., p. 10.
77. Ibid., p. 159.
78. Nicholas Dunbar, *Inventing Money: The Story of Long-Term Capital Management and the Legends Behind It* (New York, 2000), p. 92.
79. Dunbar, *Inventing Money*, pp. 168–73.
80. André F. Perold, 'Long-Term Capital Management, L.P. (A)', Harvard Business School Case 9-200-007 (5 November 1999), p. 2.
81. Perold, 'Long-Term Capital Management, L.P. (A)', p. 13.
82. Ibid., p. 16.
83. For a history of the efficient markets school of finance theory, see Peter Bernstein, *Capital Ideas: The Improbable Origins of Modern Wall Street* (New York, 1993).
84. Dunbar, *Inventing Money*, p. 178.
85. Roger Lowenstein, *When Genius Failed: The Rise and Fall of Long-Term Capital Management* (New York, 2000), p. 126.
86. Perold, 'Long-Term Capital Management, L.P. (A)', pp. 11f., 17.
87. Lowenstein, *When Genius Failed*, p. 127.
88. André F. Perold, 'Long-Term Capital Management, L.P. (B)', Harvard Business School Case 9-200-08 (27 October 1999), p. 1.

89. Lowenstein, *When Genius Failed*, pp. 133–8.

90. Ibid., p. 144.

91. I owe this point to André Stern, who was an investor in LTCM.

92. Lowenstein, *When Genius Failed*, p. 147.

93. André F. Perold, 'Long-Term Capital Management, L.P. (C)', Harvard Business School Case 9-200-09 (5 November 1999), pp. 1, 3.

94. *Idem*, 'Long-Term Capital Management, L.P. (D)', Harvard Business School Case 9-200-10 (4 October 2004), p. 1. Perold's cases are by far the best account.

95. Lowenstein, *When Genius Failed*, p. 149.

96. 'All Bets Are Off: How the Salesmanship and Brainpower Failed at Long-Term Capital', *Wall Street Journal*, 16 November 1998.

97. See on this point Peter Bernstein, *Capital Ideas Evolving* (New York, 2007).

98. Donald MacKenzie, 'Long-Term Capital Management and the Sociology of Arbitrage', *Economy and Society*, 32, 3 (August 2003), p. 374.

99. Ibid., *passim*.

100. Ibid., p. 365.

101. Franklin R. Edwards, 'Hedge Funds and the Collapse of Long-Term Capital Management', *Journal of Economic Perspectives*, 13, 2 (Spring 1999), pp. 192f. See also Stephen J. Brown, William N. Goetzmann and Roger G. Ibbotson, 'Offshore Hedge Funds: Survival and Performance, 1989–95', *Journal of Business*, 72, 1 (January 1999), 91–117.

102. Harry Markowitz, 'New Frontiers of Risk: The 360 Degree Risk Manager for Pensions and Nonprofits', *The Bank of New York Thought Leadership White Paper* (October 2005), p. 6.

103. 'Hedge Podge', *The Economist*, 16 February 2008.

104. 'Rolling In It', *The Economist*, 16 November 2006.

105. John Kay, 'Just Think, the Fees You Could Charge Buffett', *Financial Times*, 11 March 2008.

106. Stephanie Baum, 'Top 100 Hedge Funds have 75% of Industry Assets', *Financial News*, 21 May 2008.

107. Dean P. Foster and H. Peyton Young, 'Hedge Fund Wizards', *Economists' Voice* (February 2008), p. 2.

108. Niall Ferguson and Moritz Schularick, ' "Chimerica" and Global Asset Markets', *International Finance* 10, 3 (2007), pp. 215–39.
109. Michael Dooley, David Folkerts-Landau and Peter Garber, 'An Essay on the Revived Bretton-Woods System', NBER Working Paper 9971 (September 2003).
110. Ben Bernanke, 'The Global Saving Glut and the U.S. Current Account Deficit', Homer Jones Lecture, St Louis, Missouri (15 April 2005).
111. 'From Mao to the Mall', *The Economist*, 16 February 2008.
112. For a critique of recent Federal Reserve policy, see Paul A. Volcker, 'Remarks at a Luncheon of the Economic Club of New York' (8 April 2008). In Volcker's view, the Fed has taken 'actions that extend to the very edge of its lawful and implied powers'.
113. See e.g. Jamil Anderlini, 'Beijing Looks at Foreign Fields in Plan to Guarantee Food Supplies', *Financial Times*, 9 May 2008.
114. In the absence of the First World War, it may be conjectured, Germany would have overtaken Britain in terms of world export market share in 1926: Hugh Neuburger and Houston H. Stokes, 'The Anglo-German Trade Rivalry, 1887–1913: A Counterfactual Outcome and Its Implications', *Social Science History*, 3, 2 (Winter 1979), pp. 187–201.
115. Aaron L. Friedberg, 'The Future of U.S.–China Relations: Is Conflict Inevitable?', *International Security*, 30, 2 (Fall 2005), pp. 7–45.
116. The average length of the financial careers of the current chief executive officers of Citigroup, Goldman Sachs, Merrill Lynch, Morgan Stanley and JP Morgan is just under twenty-five and a half years.

Afterword: The Descent of Money

1. For some fascinating insights into the limits of globalization, see Pankaj Ghemawat, *Redefining Global Strategy: Crossing Borders in a World Where Differences Still Matter* (Boston, 2007).
2. Frederic Mishkin, Weissman Center Distinguished Lecture, Baruch College, New York (12 October 2006).
3. Larry Neal, 'A Shocking View of Economic History', *Journal of Economic History*, 60, 2 (2000), pp. 317–34.

4. Robert J. Barro and José F. Ursúa, 'Macroeconomic Crises since 1870', *Brookings Papers on Economic Activity* (forthcoming). See also Robert J. Barro, 'Rare Disasters and Asset Markets in the Twentieth Century', Harvard University Working Paper (4 December 2005).

5. Nassim Nicholas Taleb, *Fooled by Randomness: The Hidden Role of Chance in Life and in the Markets* (2nd edn., New York, 2005)

6. Idem, *The Black Swan: The Impact of the Highly Improbable* (London, 2007).

7. Georges Soros, *The New Paradigm for Financial Markets: The Credit Crash of 2008 and What It Means*, (New York, 2008), pp. 91 ff.

8. See Frank H. Knight, *Risk, Uncertainty and Profit* (Boston, 1921).

9. John Maynard Keynes, 'The General Theory of Employment', *Economic Journal*, 51, 2 (1937), p. 214.

10. Daniel Kahneman and Amos Tversky, 'Prospect Theory: An Analysis of Decision under Risk', *Econometrica*, 47, 2 (March 1979), p. 273.

11. Eliezer Yudkowsky, 'Cognitive Biases Potentially Affecting Judgment of Global Risks', in Nick Bostrom and Milan Cirkovic (eds.), *Global Catastrophic Risks* (Oxford University Press, 2008), pp. 91–119. See also Michael J. Mauboussin, *More Than You Know: Finding Financial Wisdom in Unconventional Places* (New York / Chichester, 2006).

12. Mark Buchanan, *The Social Atom: Why the Rich Get Richer, Cheaters Get Caught, and Your Neighbor Usually Looks Like You* (New York, 2007), p. 54.

13. For an introduction, see Andrei Shleifer, *Inefficient Markets: An Introduction to Behavioral Finance* (Oxford, 2000). For some practical applications see Richard H. Thaler and Cass R. Sunstein, *Nudge: Improving Decisions About Health, Wealth, and Happiness* (New Haven, 2008).

14. See Peter Bernstein, *Capital Ideas Evolving* (New York, 2007).

15. See for example James Surowiecki, *The Wisdom of Crowds* (New York, 2005); Ian Ayres, *Supercrunchers: How Anything Can Be Predicted* (London, 2007).

16. Daniel Gross, 'The Forecast for Forecasters is Dismal', *New York Times*, 4 March 2007.

17. The classic work, first published in 1841, is Charles MacKay, *Extra-*

ordinary Popular Delusions and the Madness of Crowds (New York, 2003 [1841]).

18. Yudkowsky, 'Cognitive Biases', pp. 110f.
19. For an introduction to Lo's work, see Bernstein, *Capital Ideas Evolving*, ch. 4. See also John Authers, 'Quants Adapting to a Darwinian Analysis', *Financial Times*, 19 May 2008.
20. The following is partly derived from Niall Ferguson and Oliver Wyman, *The Evolution of Financial Services: Making Sense of the Past, Preparing for the Future* (London / New York, 2007).
21. *The Journal of Evolutionary Economics*. Seminal works in the field are A. A. Alchian, 'Uncertainty, Evolution and Economic Theory', *Journal of Political Economy*, 58 (1950), pp. 211–22, and R. R. Nelson and S. G. Winter, *An Evolutionary Theory of Economic Change* (Cambridge, MA, 1982).
22. Thorstein Veblen, 'Why is Economics Not an Evolutionary Science?' *Quarterly Journal of Economics*, 12 (1898), pp. 373–97.
23. Joseph A. Schumpeter, *Capitalism, Socialism and Democracy* (London, 1987 [1943]), pp. 80–4.
24. Paul Ormerod, *Why Most Things Fail: Evolution, Extinction and Economics* (London, 2005), pp. 180ff.
25. Jonathan Guthrie, 'How the Old Corporate Tortoise Wins the Race', *Financial Times*, 15 February 2007.
26. Leslie Hannah, 'Marshall's "Trees" and the Global "Forest": Were "Giant Redwoods" Different?', in N. R. Lamoreaux, D. M. G. Raff and P. Temin (eds.), *Learning by Doing in Markets, Firms and Countries* (Cambridge, MA, 1999), pp. 253–94.
27. The allusion is of course to Richard Dawkins, *The Selfish Gene* (2nd edn., Oxford, 1989).
28. Rudolf Hilferding, *Finance Capital: A Study of the Latest Phase of Capitalist Development* (London, 2006 [1919]).
29. 'Fear and Loathing, and a Hint of Hope', *The Economist*, 16 February 2008.
30. Joseph Schumpeter, *The Theory of Economic Development* (Cambridge, MA, 1934), p. 253.
31. Bertrand Benoit and James Wilson, 'German President Complains of Financial Markets "Monster"', *Financial Times*, 15 May 2008.

List of Illustrations

Photographic acknowledgements are given in parentheses. Every effort has been made to contact all copyright holders. The publishers will be happy to make good in future editions any errors or omissions brought to their attention.

PLATES

1. Page from Fibonacci's *Liber Abaci*, published 1202 (reproduced by kind permission of the Ministero per i Beni e le Attivita Culturali, Italy, Biblioteca Nazionale Centrale Firenze)
2. Botticelli's *Adoration of the Magi* (Alinari)
3. Nathan Mayer Rothschild (N.M. Rothschild & Sons)
4. Cartoon from *Le Rire* (Mary Evans Picture Library)
5. Union gunships on the Mississippi (Museum of the Confederacy)
6. The Dutch Empire (Dutch National Archives)
7. Emanuel de Witte, *Beurs van Amsterdam*, 1653 (Rijksmuseum Amsterdam)
8. Portrait of John Law (Louisiana State Museum)
9. Map of Louisiana (Louisiana State Museum)
10. Louisiana (Louisiana State Museum)
11. Tokyo earthquake
12. Richard 'Dickie' Scruggs (*New York Times*)
13. Ken Griffin, founder and CEO of Citadel (Citadel)
14. Grenville diptych
15. Diego Rivera's Garden Court Mural, North wall (Detroit Institute of Arts)
16. Diego Rivera's Garden Court Mural, South wall (detail) (Detroit Institute of Arts)
17. Details from Charles Darrow's original Atlantic City *Monopoly*
18. The original Mr Monopoly
19. Old Chongqing (photograph by G. H. Thomas, author of *An American in China: 1936–1939*)
20. Modern Chongqing

Index

Pages with illustrations are shown in *italic*.

stability 58, 164, 296
and First World War 299
see also European Exchange
Rate Mechanism
excise *see* taxes
extraterritoriality 291

Falkland Islands 111
famines 183, 184
Fannie Mae (Federal National
Mortgage Association) 249,
251, 260, 264, 267, 273
fascist and totalitarian
governments 232, 246
Fastow, Andrew 172–3
fat tails 165, 225
Faulkner, Danny 256–8
f.c.s. ('free of capture and seizure')
203
Federal Emergency Management
Agency (FEMA) 178
Federal Home Loan Bank Board
250, 258
Federal Home Loan Mortgage
Corporation *see* Freddie Mac
Federal Housing Administration
(FHA) 248–50
Federal National Mortgage
Association *see* Fannie Mae
Federal Open Market Committee
166–7
Federal Reserve Bank of New
York 161
Federal Reserve System:
and 1990s euphoria 167–8, 174
and Black Monday (1987)
165–6

criticisms of 161–3, 395
founding of 57
increases in short-term rates
116
and Long Term Capital bail-out
327
and mortgages 266
Rothschilds' alleged influence
on 86
target rate 9, 166–7
and Wall Street Crash/Great
Depression 161–4, 212
Federal Savings and Loan
Insurance Corporation
(FSLIC) 258
Fermat, Pierre de 188
Fermat Capital 227
feudalism 341
FHA *see* Federal Housing
Administration
Fibonacci (Leonardo of Pisa)
32–3, 35
fiction 195, 304
fiduciary note issues 55
financial crises 2, 3, 64, 158, 164,
342, 354
'American crisis'/credit crunch
8, 225, 272, 283, 331n., 338,
347, 348, 354–5
Asian *see* Asia
'Black Monday' (1987) 159,
165–6, 324
escaping investors' memory-
span 332, 340
and fiscal deficits 313
frequency and unpredictability
of 2, 14, 332, 340, 342, 347

financial crises – *cont.*
  international effects of 283,
    339–40
  Keynes on 328
  first Latin American debt crisis
    (1826–9) 88, 98, 196n., 288
  second Latin American debt
    crisis (1980s) 288, 308
  likely locations for 283
  liquidity crises 55, 300, 347
  Savings & Loan 253–60, 322,
    349, 352, 354, 356
  in First World War 299–304
  see also bubbles; Great
    Depression; inflation
financial history 10–15, 343n.
financial innovations *see* financial
  system
financial services *see* financial
  system
financial system:
  absolutist theories 140
  benefits of 2–3, 342
  evolutionary extinctions and
    destruction in 14–15, 53–4,
    59–61, 272, 348–9, 351–3,
    354, 355, 357–8
  financial services 353, 356–7
  'great dying' scenario 14–15
  ignorance of 10–12, 316,
    328
  innovations 3, 6, 53, 297,
    304, 341, 350, 352, 353
  instability of 316, 342–58
  integration of financial markets
    14
  'intelligent design' in 54, 356

'monster' or mirror of mankind
  358
see also regulation
financiers:
  gender imbalance 5
  graduates and 5
  hostile views of 2, 13
fire 186–7
firms *see* companies
Fisher, Irving 157, 160
Flanders 74
Florence 33, 35, 41, 69–72, 187
  and bonds 69–72
  under the Medici 41–7
  taxes and financial records 45,
    71, 72
Flores, Betty 278–9
flotations 156
food prices 26, 235, 284, 338. *see
  also* grain
Ford, Edsel 242–3
Ford, Henry 61, 242
Ford Motor Company 242–3
forecasting *see* economists
foreclosures *see* mortgages
foreign exchange dealers and
  markets 4
  early 42, 47, 48
  and First World War 300
forgery 97
forward contracts 226
401(k) plans 11
fractional reserve banking 49, 50,
  51
France 232, 304
  banks 56, 142
  bonds 86, 101–2, 297, 302

currency 142, 154
financial difficulties in C18 3,
  75–6, 126–7, 138–56
government bankruptcies 138
under Napoleon 80–85; *see also*
  Napoleonic Wars
overseas possessions and trade
  140, 147; *see also* Louisiana
property price boom 233
rentes 73–4, 99, 302
Revolution 126, 154
royal funding 3, 74, 75, 138–9,
  153–5
stock market 154
taxes 76, 142, 146
and US 307–8
and First World War 101,
  103–4, 302, 304
franchise, widening of *see*
  electoral reform
fraud and misconduct:
  bubbles and 168–74
  causing hostility 2
  hedge funds 330–31
  Savings and Loan 255–9
  stock market 122, 159
  see also Enron
Freddie Mac (Federal Home Loan
  Mortgage Corporation) 251,
  260, 267, 273
free trade 306, 339. *see also*
  protectionism
French Revolution *see* France
Friedman, Milton *211–14*
  and Chile 213–14, 217
  and China 214n.
  on Great Depression 161, 163–4

on inflation 100, 104, 211
and welfare state 212, 213
FSLIC *see* Federal Savings and
  Loan Insurance Corporation
FTSE All Share index 261
fuel *see* energy industry
Fujimori, Alberto 276
fungibility of money 24
fur trade 147
futures contracts 225, 226, 341
  as derivatives 227
  pension funds and 123
  'to arrive' contracts 226

Garwin, Richard 223
gas industry 119, 169–71
Gates, Bill and Melinda 280n.
Gates, Henry Louis ('Skip') Jr.
  267–8, 277
GDP *see* gross domestic product
gearing (assets vs. capital) 323
General Motors 160
'genes' in financial system 350, 351
Geneva 43
Genoa 44, 72, 74, 87, 137
geology, compared with financial
  history 343n.
George, Henry 230
Germany 88, 144, 209, 232, 292
  banks 56
  bonds and securities 297, 302,
    303
  and British financial system
    187, 339
  exports 103, 395
  hyperinflation and slump
    101–7, 113, 158, 302

ageing population and pensions
208–10, 221–2
economy 66, 168, 209, 222,
357
government bonds 66–8, 292,
323
insurance 205–11
property prices 263
wars with China 205, 207, 295
welfare state 205–10, 221–2
in Second World War 205–6,
296
Jardine, Matheson 289–92
Jardine, William 289–92
Jews 87n., 99
moneylenders 33–5, 36
Rothschilds see Rothschild
family
in Venice 33–8
see also anti-Semitism
Jivaro people 18
jobbers 299
joint-stock banks/companies 49,
56, 120, 127–31, 174, 297,
299
Jones, Alfred Winslow 314n.

Kaffir (gold mine) bubble 297
Kahn, Herman 209
Kahnemann, Daniel 344–5
Kast, Miguel 214
Katrina (Hurricane) 176–83, 219,
224
Kay, John 330
Kazakhstan 219, 276
Keating, Charles 258n.
Kenya 280

Keynes, John Maynard/
Keynesianism 58, 106, 159,
293, 295, 305, 328
on inflation 106, 115
Keynesian policies 112, 312
on uncertainty 343–4
Klein, Naomi 182
Knight, Frank 343
Kondo, Bunji 206
Krugman, Paul 312
Kuwait Investment Authority
337n.
Kyoto 206

labour:
in Asia 287
forced 19, 21–2
mobility 14, 274, 288
money as chains of 1
organized see trade unions
rural 288
as unit of value 18–19
unskilled and semi-skilled 14
Labour party 251–2
Lackey, Judge 181–2n.
Lamarckian evolution 351
Lamont, Norman 318
Landlord's Game 230–31
landlords, negative views of 230,
247–8, 252
Lasswell, Harold D. 207
Latin America:
aid to 307
British investment in 293
debt crises and currency
depreciations 88, 98, 196n.,
288, 308

425

Peruzzi family 41
petrodollars 308
Philadelphia 195
Philippines 275, 276
Phillips, Elizabeth ('Lizzie') 230
Phoenix 264
Picart, Bernard *154–5*
pieces of eight 25
PIMCO (Pacific Investment Management Company) 68, 107
Piñera, José 215–16, 219
Pingala 32n.
Pinochet, Augusto 213, 215–18
Pisa 32–3, 43, 69, 70
Pius II, Pope 45–6
Pizarro, Francisco 19–21
plagues 182, 184
Poland 107
political reform *see* electoral reform
politicians 12, 221, 222, 357
Pope, Alexander 156
Popper, Karl 316
population issues 192n., 342. *see also* pensions, ageing populations
Portinari, Tommaso 46–7
Portugal 81
    exploration and East Indies trade 127–8, 130, 134
    and Jews 36
'post-American' era 3, 288
Potosí 22–3, 25, 27, 51, 63
pound sterling 55, 317–18. *see also* gold standard

poverty and poor countries:
    causes of 2, 13, 64
    incomes 2
    and international investment 286–7, 293–4, 307
    lack of financial institutions and credit 13, 64, 280
    loan sharks and 13, 38–41
    and microfinance 280–81
    and property ownership 267–8, 274–7
    real estate occupied by 274
    see also aid; emerging markets; incomes; workhouses
pre-modern societies 184
Preobrazhensky, Yevgeni 107
prestanze and *prestiti* 71–2
price controls 338
price-earnings ratios 123–4, 160
'price revolution' 26, 63
price rises 26, 100, 235, 284, 308, 338
Princip, Gavrilo 298, 300
private equity partnerships/firms 5, 9, 336, 337, 353
privatization 116, 171, 213–14, 352
probability 188–90, 198, 343–6
Proctor & Gamble 160
productivity 210, 211
promissory notes 27, 49. *see also* paper money
Pro Mujer 278–80
property-owning democracies 233, 241–51, 266, 274, 276, 341